Spurlock

EXAM CRAM™

D1712836

SAT

Mike Gunderloy

Susan Sales Harkins

CERTIFICATION

SAT Exam Cram

Copyright © 2006 by Que Publishing

International Standard Book Number: 0-7897-3545-8

Library of Congress Catalog Card Number: 2004118020

Printed in the United States of America

First Printing: October 2005
08   07   06   05   4   3   2   1

Trademarks

Warning and Disclaimer

Bulk Sales

Que Publishing offers excellent discounts on this book when ordered in quantity for bulk purchases or special sales. For more information, please contact

U.S. Corporate and Government Sales

1-800-382-3419

corpsales@pearsontechgroup.com

For sales outside the U.S., please contact

International Sales

international@pearsoned.com

Publisher
Paul Boger

Executive Editor
Jeff Riley

Acquisitions Editor
Jeff Riley

Development Editor
Steve Rowe

Managing Editor
Charlotte Clapp

Project Editor
Tonya Simpson

Copy Editor
Rhonda Tinch-Mize

Indexer
Erika Millen

Proofreader
Juli Cook

Technical Editor
Teresa Stephens

Publishing Coordinator
Pamalee Nelson

Graphics
Laura Robbins

For Mrs. Swenson. See, I didn't waste that potential after all.

—Mike Gunderloy

To Joey Ansback—the only teacher who suggested I might want to consider writing as a profession.

—Susan Harkins

About the Authors

Mike Gunderloy aced his own SATs and has gone on to two college degrees and a successful career in computer consulting. As lead developer for Lark Group, Inc., Mike has worked with small businesses, nonprofit organizations, and Fortune 500 corporations alike, as well as trained many other developers in the use of Microsoft products. Mike lives on a farm in eastern Washington state, along with his wife and children and an ever-changing array of horses, sheep, llamas, geese, turkeys, chickens, ducks, peacocks, cats, dogs, and guinea fowl. When he's not busy testing and writing about software, Mike can usually be found in his garden or greenhouse, trying to persuade recalcitrant vegetables to grow, or out on the land, trying to persuade noxious weeds to stop growing.

You can reach Mike at MikeG1@larkfarm.com or http://www.larkware.com/.

Susan Sales Harkins has been writing about computer applications since 1992. Before that, she taught general computing classes at a local business college. Her favorite application is Microsoft Access. Her favorite pursuit is a grandbaby. Susan lives in Kentucky, but unlike Mike, with only a few animals, including a few of the two-legged kind. You can reach Susan at ssharkins@bellsouth.net.

About the Technical Reviewer

Teresa Stephens holds a bachelor of science degree in engineering and a masters degree in teaching mathematics and natural sciences. She has been helping students sharpen their math, writing, and test-taking skills for more than 15 years as a teacher, tutor, and test-taking class instructor. She enjoys teaching high school math and physics and has delivered test-taking training classes for many exams, including the ACT, SAT, GRE, and GMAT in Louisville, Kentucky. Currently, she offers individualized instruction for the SAT and ACT, teaches high school mathematics, and offers summer short courses to help students improve mathematics and writing skills in Indianapolis, Indiana.

Acknowledgments

For starters, thanks to Jeff Riley for dragging us into this project. It's nice to have an editor who keeps knocking on the door for more books, especially when they're fun to write. Of course, the rest of Que's editorial staff, including Steve Rowe, Tonya Simpson, Rhonda Tinch-Mize, Juli Cook, and Erika Millen also deserve—and get—our deepest thanks for moving the project along from the initial email to the finished book.

We'd also like to thank the production staff for actually getting this stuff ready to print. So thanks for somehow turning the final manuscript from a mass of Word documents and TIF images into a real printed book, even with all the kooky typesetting requirements that this one had.

Mike would also like to thank "Iron Chef" Adam for providing enthusiasm, Kayla for providing hugs, and Thomas for providing breaks from the computer screen (in the form of wet diapers that needed changing) during the writing of this book. And finally, Dana gets his thanks for being eternally supportive of this crazy book-writing stuff, even though it leaves her holding the bag on chores and childcare on those all-too-frequent nights when he's racing to meet a deadline. Couldn't do it without you, hon.

Susan moved during the writing of this book—more than once when her new place wasn't ready on schedule. She wrote most of this book while living with relatives—need we say more? (No relatives were harmed in the writing of this book.) She'd like to thank Mike and the Que staff for their patience and flexibility through all the confusion of interrupted Internet service and reassessed deadlines.

Our thanks to the textbook authors who generously agreed to let us quote material in the reading comprehension chapters and on the sample exams.

We're grateful for passages from *Environmental Science*, by Denis DuBay, Andrew H. Lapinski, Robert M. Schoch, and Anne Tweed; *Physical Science*, by David Frank, Wysession, and Sophia Yancopoulos; *A History of the United States*, by Daniel J. Boorstin and Brooks Mather Kelley; *Economics: Principles in Action*, by Arthur O'Sullivan and Steven M. Sheffrin; and *Earth Science*, by Edward J. Tarbuck and Fredrick K. Lutgens.

Contents at a Glance

Table of Contents

We Want to Hear from You!

. . . .

As the reader of this book, *you* are our most important critic and commentator. We value your opinion and want to know what we're doing right, what we could do better, what areas you'd like to see us publish in, and any other words of wisdom you're willing to pass our way.

As an executive editor for Que Publishing, I welcome your comments. You can email or write me directly to let me know what you did or didn't like about this book—as well as what we can do to make our books better.

Please note that I cannot help you with technical problems related to the topic of this book. We do have a User Services group, however, where I will forward specific technical questions related to the book.

When you write, please be sure to include this book's title and author as well as your name, email address, and phone number. I will carefully review your comments and share them with the author and editors who worked on the book.

Email: feedback@quepublishing.com

Mail: Jeff Riley
            Executive Editor
            Que Publishing
            800 East 96th Street
            Indianapolis, IN 46240 USA

For more information about this book or another Que Certification title, visit our Web site at www.examcram.com. Type the ISBN (excluding hyphens) or the title of a book in the Search field to find the page you're looking for.

Introduction

Welcome to the *SAT Exam Cram!* Whether this is your first or your fifteenth *Exam Cram* series book, you'll find information here that will help ensure your success as you pursue knowledge, experience, and acceptance to the college of your choice. This introduction explains the SAT in general and talks about how the *Exam Cram* series can help you prepare for the SAT exam. Chapters 1 through 8 are designed to remind you of everything you'll need to know in order to take—and do well on—the SAT exam. Chapter 9 includes a wide-ranging discussion of test-taking strategies for the SAT. The two sample tests at the end of the book should give you a reasonably accurate assessment of your knowledge—and, yes, we've provided the answers and their explanations to the tests. Read the book and understand the material, and you'll stand a very good chance of doing well on the test.

Exam Cram books help you understand and appreciate the subjects and materials you need to pass many types of exams. *Exam Cram* books are aimed strictly at test preparation and review. They do not teach you everything you need to know about a topic. Instead, we'll present and dissect the questions and problems we've found that you're likely to encounter on a test. We've worked to bring together as much information as possible about the SAT exam.

Nevertheless, to completely prepare yourself for this exam, we recommend that you begin by taking the Self-Assessment that is included in this book, immediately following this introduction. The Self-Assessment will help you evaluate your knowledge base against the skills that the SAT tests, and will help you determine the areas where you might need some additional study and practice.

Based on what you learn from the Self-Assessment, you might decide to begin your studies with some classroom training, some practice exams, or some background reading. On the other hand, you might decide to start working immediately with the material in this book.

Taking the SAT Exam

The very first step in taking the SAT is to register for a test session. There are four ways to register for the SAT:

➤ Online registration (go to http://www.collegeboard.com/student/testing/sat/reg.html) is probably the easiest way for most students to register these days. You'll select a test date, pay with a credit card, and complete the transaction entirely online.

➤ Phone registration is available, but only if you've registered by another means at least once before. Call (800) 728-7267 or (609) 771-7600 to use the automated system, or (609) 771-7600 to speak to a customer service representative.

➤ Mail registration lets you do everything with paper rather than online. You'll need a copy of the *Registration Bulletin*, which you should be able to get from your high school guidance counselor.

➤ Standby registration is for the chronic procrastinator. You fill in the same forms that you would to register by mail, but you bring them, along with an extra $35 fee, to the test center on testing day. Then you hope there will be room to cram you in.

Deadlines and prices change from year to year. (though the prices never seem to go down). You can get the details from your guidance counselor or from the College Board website.

However you register, you need to get some information together to navigate through the process. Here's what you'll need:

➤ Your grade point average and class rank.

➤ Your intended college major.

➤ Information about the colleges you're considering, such as whether they're public or private, 4-year or 2-year, and so on. You can just check "undecided" if you want to breeze through this section of the registration.

➤ Information about the high school courses you've taken or plan to take: how many years of math, of English, and so on.

➤ Information about your high school extracurricular activities.

➤ Which exam you want to take (for the regular SAT, select "SAT Reasoning Test").

➤ Your six-digit high school code. You can get this from your guidance counselor. If you're registering online, you can also select your high school from a list.

➤ The date that you intend to take the exam.

➤ Whether you want to sign up for the Student Answer Service. This service will give you a report on whether you answered each question correctly, and helps you find areas where you should study harder. It costs $9 in 2005, and we recommend signing up if you're planning to take the SAT more than once.

➤ The code for the test center where you want to take the test. You can find this in the printed *Registration Bulletin*, or select it from a list if you're registering online. If you're fortunate enough to live in an urban area where several test centers are close to you, talk to students who have already taken the SAT to find out which test centers offer comfortable testing conditions.

➤ The colleges you want to get a copy of your scores. You can select up to four free when you're registering; if you wait until later, you'll need to pay for each score report. If you have any idea which colleges you're going to apply to, you might as well get the scores sent free.

The College Board also offers some special services, including special accommodations for students with disabilities, fee waivers for low-income students, and alternative testing dates for religious reasons. You should discuss these services with your guidance counselor if you feel you qualify.

After you've registered, you've got at least a month (hopefully more, because there's no point in waiting until the last minute to register) to study for the SAT. Of course, we think you can spend that time profitably with this book! This is also a good time to take practice exams so that you become familiar with the format of the SAT.

On test day, you need to be at the testing center a few minutes before 8 a.m. You also need to bring the test day essentials:

➤ Your admission ticket. You'll need this to get in, so don't forget it. If you lose your admission ticket before the test, you can print a fresh one by visiting the College Board website.

➤ A photo ID (usually your driver's license or passport, or a school ID with your photograph).

► Your calculator. You're allowed to use a calculator on the math sections. Make sure that it has fresh batteries.

► At least three No. 2 pencils. If you're hard on pencils, or want to be able to break a few to get over frustrating sections, bring more.

► A travel clock, watch, or stopwatch to keep track of the time even if you can see a clock in the testing center.

For more tips on preparing for the SAT, see Chapter 9, "Strategies for Raising Your Score."

The Format of the SAT

The format of the SAT is fixed. That is, although the questions vary from test date to test date, there will always be the same number of questions. Here's how it breaks down:

► A writing section consisting of 18 questions on identifying sentence errors, 25 questions on improving sentences, 6 questions on improving paragraphs, and 1 essay. You'll have 25 minutes for the essay, and the other questions will be broken up into two 25-minute sections and one 10-minute section. We'll cover the writing section in Chapters 1 and 2.

► A critical reading section consisting of 19 sentence completion questions and 48 passage-based reading questions. This will be broken up into two 25-minute sections and one 20-minute section. We'll cover the critical reading section in Chapters 3, 4, and 5.

► A math section consisting of 44 multiple-choice questions and 10 student-produced response questions. This will be broken up into two 25-minute sections and one 20-minute section. We'll cover the math section in Chapters 6, 7, and 8.

If you add it all up, it comes to 170 questions and an essay, for which you have a total of 3 hours and 45 minutes. That's a long day indeed. One of the 25-minute sections is what the College Board calls a "variable section": This section doesn't count toward your score, but is used to make sure that the different forms of the SAT are comparable. According to the College Board, the set of scored questions is the same, but the order of questions and the content and location of the Experimental section may differ from student to student. The ungraded variable section is used as a way for the College Board to check the difficulty of a particular form of the SAT. But because there's no way for you to know which of the sections is the variable section, you might as well not worry about it.

Understanding SAT Scores

SAT scoring is relatively simple. Your score takes into account three different types of questions:

➤ Most of the SAT questions are multiple-choice questions with five possible answers. Each correct answer adds one point to your raw score, and each incorrect answer subtracts one fourth of a point. If you don't answer a question, it doesn't count one way or the other. But don't guess randomly—it could have a negative impact on your score.

➤ There will be one math section containing *student-produced response* questions. On these questions, you fill in a grid to indicate the digits in your answer, rather than selecting answers from a list. On these questions, each correct answer adds one point to your raw score, but there is no penalty for a wrong answer. So, if you have the slightest idea what the answer is on these questions, go ahead and guess.

➤ Finally, there's the essay. Your essay will be graded by two separate readers, each of whom can assign a score from zero (the lowest) to six (the highest). A score of zero is reserved for essays that are blank, that have nothing to do with the topic assigned, or that are completely illegible.

The raw scores are then converted into a scale that runs from 200 (the lowest) to 800 (the highest) in each of the three areas of the exam (critical reading, writing, and math). Your essay counts for about 30% of the writing score. The conversion process is designed to even out the differences between different forms of the SAT, so that a score of 700 on one date is meant to be exactly equivalent to a score of 700 on another date—even a score of 700 on an SAT taken in a different year. The idea is that no matter which set of SAT questions you saw, you did as well as anyone else who got the same score.

What This Book Will Not Do

This book will *not* teach you everything you need to know about reading, writing, and math, or even about a given topic within those fields. Nor is this book an introduction to the subjects covered on the SAT. For learning the material from start to finish, there's no substitute for your high school textbooks and coursework. This book will review what you need to know before you take the test, with the fundamental purpose dedicated to reviewing the information needed on the SAT exam.

This book uses a variety of teaching and memorization techniques to analyze the exam-related topics and to provide you with ways to input, index, and retrieve everything you'll need to know in order to pass the test. Once again, it is *not* an introduction to the skills covered by the SAT.

What This Book Is Designed To Do

This book is designed to be read as a pointer to the areas of knowledge you will be tested on. In other words, you may want to read the book one time, just to get an insight into how comprehensive your knowledge of the SAT is. The book is also designed to be read shortly before you go for the actual test and to give you a distillation of the entire range of subjects that the SAT covers in as few pages as possible. We think you can use this book to get a sense of the underlying context of any topic in the chapters—or to skim for Exam Alerts, bulleted points, summaries, and topic headings.

We've drawn on material from the College Board's own listing of knowledge requirements, from other preparation guides, and from the exams themselves. We've also drawn from our own experience with writing, critical reading, and mathematics. Our aim is to walk you through the knowledge you will need—looking over your shoulder, so to speak—and point out those things that are important for the exam (using Exam Alerts, practice questions, and so on).

The SAT makes a basic assumption that you already have a strong background of experience with reading, writing, and mathematics on a high school senior level. On the other hand, because the scope of the SAT is so broad, no one can be a complete expert. We've tried to demystify the jargon, acronyms, terms, and concepts. Also, wherever we think you're likely to blur past an important concept, we've defined the assumptions and premises behind that concept.

About This Book

If you're preparing for the SAT for the first time, we've structured the topics in this book to build upon one another. Therefore, the topics covered in later chapters might refer to previous discussions in earlier chapters. However, the writing, reading, and mathematics sections of the book are all independent from one another.

We suggest you read this book from front to back. You won't be wasting your time because nothing we've written is a guess about an unknown exam. We've had to explain certain underlying information on such a regular basis that we've included those explanations here.

Once you've read the book, you can brush up on a certain area by using the Index or the Table of Contents to go straight to the topics and questions you want to reexamine. We've tried to use the headings and subheadings to provide outline information about each given topic. After you've taken the SAT, we think you'll find this book useful as a tightly focused reference that you can use in your future studies as well.

Chapter Formats

Each *Exam Cram* chapter follows a regular structure, along with graphical cues about especially important or useful material. The structure of a typical chapter is as follows:

➤ **Opening Hotlists**—Each chapter begins with lists of the terms you'll need to understand and the concepts you'll need to master before you can be fully conversant with the chapter's subject matter. We follow the hotlists with a few introductory paragraphs, setting the stage for the rest of the chapter.

➤ **Topical Coverage**—After the opening hotlists, each chapter covers the topics related to the chapter's subject.

➤ **Exam Alerts**—Throughout the topical coverage section, we highlight material most likely to appear on the exam by using a special Exam Alert layout that looks like this:

 This is what an Exam Alert looks like. An Exam Alert stresses concepts, terms, or activities that will most likely appear in one or more exam questions. For that reason, we think any information found offset in Exam Alert format is worthy of unusual attentiveness on your part.

Even if material isn't flagged as an Exam Alert, *all* the content in this book is associated in some way with test-related material. What appears in the chapter content is critical knowledge.

➤ **Notes**—This book is an overall examination of the topics covered on the SAT. As such, we'll dip into many aspects of critical reading, writing, and mathematics. Where a body of knowledge is deeper than the scope of the book, we use notes to indicate areas of concern or specialty training. The following is an example of a note.

Cramming for an exam will get you through a test, but it won't make you a competent student. Although you can try to memorize just the facts you need in order to pass the SAT, you'll be much better off to spend time understanding the underlying concepts.

➤ **Tips**—We provide tips that will help you to build a better foundation of knowledge or to focus your attention on an important concept that will reappear later in the book. Tips provide a helpful way to remind you of the context surrounding a particular area of a topic under discussion. The following shows you what a tip looks like.

 You should also read Chapter 9, "Strategies for Raising Your Score," for helpful strategies used in taking the SAT. The introduction to the sample tests at the end of the book contains additional tips on how to figure out the correct response to a question and what to do if you draw a complete blank.

➤ **Exam Prep Questions**—This section presents a short list of test questions related to the specific chapter topic. Following the questions are explanations of both correct and incorrect answers. The practice questions highlight the areas we found to be most important on the exam.

The bulk of the book follows this chapter structure, but there are a few other elements that we would like to point out:

➤ **Practice Exams**—The practice exams, which appear in Chapters 10 and 12 (with answer keys in Chapters 11 and 13), are very close approximations of the types of questions you are likely to see on the current SAT.

➤ **Answer Keys**—These provide the answers to the practice exams, complete with explanations of both the correct and incorrect responses.

➤ **Glossary**—This is an extensive glossary of important terms used in this book.

➤ **Cram Sheet**—This appears as a tear-away sheet, inside the front cover of this *Exam Cram* book. It is a valuable tool that represents a collection of the most difficult-to-remember facts and formulas we think you should memorize before taking the test. Remember, you can dump this information out of your head onto the margins of your test booklet as soon as you enter the testing room. These are usually facts that we've found require brute-force memorization. You only need to remember this information long enough to write it down when you walk into the test room.

You might want to look at the Cram Sheet in your car or in the lobby of the testing center just before you walk into the testing center. The Cram Sheet is divided under headings, so you can review the appropriate parts just before each test.

Contacting the Authors

We've tried to create a real-world tool that you can use to prepare for and pass the SAT. We're interested in any feedback you would care to share about the book, especially if you have ideas about how we can improve it for future test takers. We'll consider everything you say carefully and will respond to all reasonable suggestions and comments. You can reach us via email at MikeG1@larkfarm.com or ssharkins@bellsouth.net.

Let us know if you found this book to be helpful in your preparation efforts. We'd also like to know how you felt about your chances of passing the exam *before* you read the book and then *after* you read the book. Of course, we'd love to hear that you aced the SAT—and even if you just want to share your triumph, we'd be happy to hear from you.

Thanks for choosing us as your personal trainers, and enjoy the book. We would wish you luck on the exam, but we know that if you read through all the chapters and work with the sample exams, you won't need luck—you'll do well on the strength of real knowledge!

Self-Assessment

. . . .

We include a Self-Assessment in this *Exam Cram* book to help you evaluate your readiness to tackle the SAT. It should also help you understand what you need to know to master the topics found in this book, as well as show you the format of the questions that you'll face on the SAT. By completing the Self-Assessment, you'll help pinpoint the areas where you need additional review. That way, you can create a plan of attack to give you the most value out of the study time that you invest.

Put Yourself to the Test

The following series of questions and observations is designed to help you figure out how much work you must do to do well on the SAT and what kinds of resources you should consult on your quest. They are also designed to show you the range of question types that you will see on the SAT. Be absolutely honest in your answers; otherwise, you'll end up wasting time and money on an exam you're not yet ready to take.

Educational Background

1. Are you in your junior or senior year of high school? [Yes or No]

2. Have you taken junior or senior level classes on an accelerated schedule? [Yes or No]

   If the answer to both of these questions is no, you're probably not ready to take the SAT yet. You should look into taking the PSAT instead. The PSAT (Preliminary SAT) is designed to be taken in your sophomore or junior year, and does not include some of the more advanced areas that are covered on the SAT. It does, however, give you valuable experience in the SAT format (as well as serving as a qualifier for National Merit scholarships). You can learn more about the PSAT by visiting http://www.collegeboard.com/student/testing/psat/about.html.

The Writing Section

The following sentence tests your ability to recognize grammar and usage errors. The sentence contains either a single error or no error at all. The error, if there is one, is underlined and lettered. If the sentence contains an error, select the one underlined part that must be changed to make the sentence correct. If the sentence is correct, select choice E. In choosing your answer, follow the requirements of standard written English.

3. The populace <u>are</u> worried <u>that</u> an invading force

                       A   B

<u>could be</u> <u>on the way to</u> our fair shores. <u>No error</u>

    C   D   E

The following sentence tests correctness and effectiveness of expression. Part of the sentence is underlined; beneath the sentence are five ways of phrasing the underlined material. Choice A repeats the original phrasing; the other four choices are different. If you think the original phrasing produces a better sentence than any of the alternatives, select choice A; if not, select one of the other choices.

In making your selection, follow the requirements of standard written English; that is, pay attention to grammar, choice of words, sentence construction, and pronunciation. Your selection should result in the most effective sentence—clear and precise, without awkwardness or ambiguity.

4. The runners in the marathon needed to pay careful attention to increasing their fluid intake, measuring their pace, <u>and watch their closest competitors</u>.
- (A) and watch their closest competitors
- (B) and watch their close competitors
- (C) and watching their closest competitors
- (D) and watching their competitors closely
- (E) and watch their close competition

> The following paragraph is an early draft of an essay. Some parts of the passage need to be rewritten.
>
> Read the passage and select the best answer for the question that follows. The question may be about particular sentences or parts of sentences and ask you to improve sentence structure or word choice. Or the question may ask you to consider organization and development. In choosing answers, follow the requirements of standard written English.

(1) Did you ever consider the steps involved in manufacturing even a simple pencil? **(2)** First, a lumberjack must cut down a tall tree. **(3)** Then the sawmill has to cut the tree into lumber and ultimately into pencil-sized pieces. **(4)** At the factory, these pieces are shaped and a channel scooped out to hold the pencil lead. **(5)** Meanwhile, someone somewhere is mining the graphite to make the lead. **(6)** The graphite needs to be purified, refined, ground, and formed. **(7)** Afterwards, the graphite leads are pressed into the wooden pencil blanks, two of them on each side form a pencil. **(8)** A bit of glue holds each blanks together. **(9)** Tropical plants and chemical labs yield rubber. **(10)** A metal cylinder holds a bit of rubber eraser to the end of the pencil. **(11)** Coated with fresh paint and stamped with the manufacturer's name, each pencil is ready for us to use!

5. In context, which of the following is the best way to phrase sentence 7 (reproduced below)?

Afterwards, the graphite leads are pressed into the wooden pencil blanks, two of them on each side form a pencil.

(A) (As it is now)

(B) Two pencil blanks form a pencil, with graphite leads pressed between them.

(C) Next the graphite leads are pressed into wooden pencil blanks. Each pencil requires two of these blanks.

(D) Next the graphite leads are pressed into the wooden pencil blanks, two of them on each side form a pencil.

(E) After this, the pencil blanks are pressed together, with the graphite leads between them.

6. Think carefully about the issue presented in the following quotation and the assignment below.

> Essential truth, the truth of the intellectualists, the truth with no one thinking it, is like the coat that fits tho no one has ever tried it on, like the music that no ear has listened to. It is less real, not more real, than the verified article; and to attribute a superior degree of glory to it seems little more than a piece of perverse abstraction-worship.
>
> From William James, "The Pragmatist Account of Truth and Its Misunderstanders"

Assignment: Is there a difference between essential truth and verified truth? Plan and write an essay in which you develop your point of view on this issue. Support your position with reasoning and examples taken from your reading, studies, experience, or observations.

Questions 3 through 6 are typical of the questions that you'll find on the writing portion of the SAT. For question 3, the best answer is A: The problem with the sentence is that the subject of the sentence is "populace," which takes a singular verb rather than a plural one. For question 4, the best answer is C. At issue in this question is the need to make all the clauses of the sentence parallel, so "watching" is needed to match "increasing" and "measuring." Answer C is preferable to answer D because C doesn't change the meaning of the sentence, whereas D does. For question 5, the best answer is C, which preserves the information in the passage while eliminating the run-on sentence.

We can't tell you what the absolute answer to question 6 is, but your own reaction to the question should tell you how ready you are for the essay question that will be a part of your SAT experience. You should be able to sit down to any assignment of this complexity and start writing a four or five paragraph essay with only enough delay to organize your thoughts.

You'll find more help for the multiple choice writing questions in Chapter 1. Chapter 2 is all about the essay question on the SAT.

The Critical Reading Section

> The sentence below has two blanks, each blank indicating that something has been omitted. Beneath the sentence are five sets of words labeled A through E. Choose the set of words that, when inserted in the sentence, <u>best</u> fits the meaning of the sentence as a whole.

7. Although the judiciary was _____ independent of the legislature, in _____ this was not always the case.

(A) legally . . effect
(B) never . . retrospect
(C) morally . . fact
(D) sometimes . . essence
(E) theoretically . . practice

The passage below is followed by a question based on its content. Answer the question on the basis of what is <u>stated</u> or <u>implied</u> in the passage.

Gutenberg and his successors built on earlier advances. Methods of making paper had reached Europe from China about 1300. The Chinese and Koreans had been using movable metal type for centuries, although
Line Europeans may have developed their technology independently. The
5 printing revolution brought immense changes. Printed books were cheaper and easier to produce than hand-copied works. With books more readily available, more people learned to read. Readers gained access to a broad range of knowledge, from medicine and law to astrology and mining. Printed books exposed educated Europeans to new
10 ideas, greatly expanding their horizons.

8. Why does the author refer to printing as a "revolution"?

(A) Printing made it possible for more people to read and exposed them to more ideas.
(B) Printing transmitted revolutionary ideas from China and Korea to Europe.
(C) Printing was carried out underground by small groups.
(D) Printing in Europe was completely different from anything that had happened in the world before.
(E) The character of printed books was vastly different from those that had gone before.

Questions 7 and 8 are typical of those that you'll find on the critical reading section of the SAT. For question 7, the best answer is E; only that substitution produces a sentence that makes sense. For question 8, the answer is A. Note in particular that answer E might be a true statement, but it isn't supported by the facts set out in the passage.

You'll find more help for the critical reading section in Chapters 3, 4, and 5. Chapter 3 covers the sentence completions skills, whereas Chapters 4 and 5 are both devoted to the passage-based reading skills that you'll need to do well on the SAT.

The Mathematics Section

For this section, solve each problem and decide which is the best of the choices given. Select the corresponding answer.

9. A train's speed is increasing by 10% per minute as it leaves the station. Currently, its speed is 50 miles per hour. What was its speed 3 minutes ago?

(A) 30 miles per hour
(B) 35 miles per hour
(C) 37.57 miles per hour
(D) 40 miles per hour
(E) 47 miles per hour

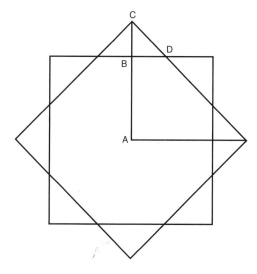

10. The preceding figure shows 2 squares, each with a side of 2 units. The squares share a common center at point A, with one square being rotated 45° from the other. What is the area of the regular octagon formed by the overlap of the 2 squares?

(A) 1
(B) $8\sqrt{2}-8$
(C) 2
(D) $4\sqrt{2}$
(E) $4-\sqrt{2}$

11. A jar contains 18 white beans and 32 black beans. What is the probability that 2 beans drawn from the jar at random will be the same
color?

(A) $\dfrac{18}{32}$

(B) $\dfrac{18}{50}$

(C) $\dfrac{18}{576}$

(D) $\dfrac{50}{576}$

(E) $\dfrac{649}{1225}$

The correct answer to question 9 is C. If the speed is increasing by 10% per
minute, you need to divide by 1.1 three times to get the original speed. This
is a question where it definitely helps to have a calculator with you on the day
of the exam. Alternatively, you can use the strategy of working backward
from the answers to the question here. Pick the answer that looks likely to
you (or the one in the middle, if you have no idea) and increase it by 10%
three times. If you wind up with the stated speed of 50 miles per hour, you've
chosen the right answer.

For question 10, the correct answer is B. To see this, note that AB is half the
side of one of the squares, so it is 1 unit. AC is the distance from the center
to a corner of the other square, making it $\sqrt{2}$ by the Pythagorean Theorem.
Thus BC = $\sqrt{2}$ – 1. $\triangle$BCD is a 45°–45°–90° triangle (because it contains both
a 45° angle and a 90° angle), so BD is also $\sqrt{2}$–1. Now you can calculate the
area of $\triangle$BCD:

$$A = \frac{1}{2} bh$$
$$A = \frac{1}{2} (\sqrt{2} - 1)(\sqrt{2} - 1)$$
$$A = \frac{1}{2} (2 - 2\sqrt{2} + 1)$$
$$A = \frac{3}{2} - \sqrt{2}$$

From inspection, you can see that the area of the octagon is the area of one
of the squares minus the area of eight of these little triangles:

$$A = 4 - 8\left(\frac{3}{2} - \sqrt{2}\right)$$
$$A = 4 - 12 + 8\sqrt{2}$$
$$A = 8\sqrt{2} - 8$$

The correct answer to question 11 is E. You can analyze the situation this way: First, there is an $\frac{18}{50}$ chance of pulling out a white bean. After that, there is a $\frac{17}{49}$ chance of pulling out another white bean. This means that there is an $\frac{18}{50} \times \frac{17}{49} = \frac{306}{2450}$ chance of pulling out 2 white beans. Now, think about pulling out a black bean first. There is a $\frac{32}{50}$ chance of doing this, followed by a 31/49 chance of pulling out a second black bean. That makes a $\frac{992}{2450}$ chance of pulling out 2 black beans. The probability of pulling out 2 beans of the same color is the sum of these probabilities, or $\frac{1298}{2450}$. Reduced to the lowest common denominator, that's $\frac{649}{1225}$.

Student-Produced Responses

Some of the mathematics questions will be what the College Board calls *student-produced response* or *grid-in* questions. For these questions, you aren't given a set of answers to choose from. Instead, you need to calculate an answer and then fill in bubbles to indicate the answer. The instructions for the grid-in questions are reproduced below. Remember, there's no penalty for getting a grid-in answer wrong, so it's always to your advantage to guess.

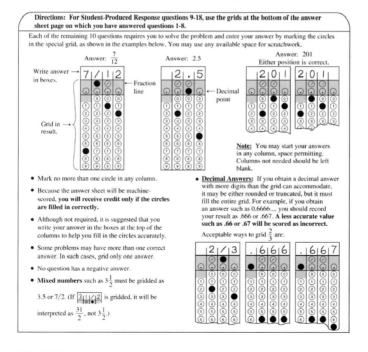

What's Next?

After you've taken your courses, assessed your readiness, and reviewed this book, you'll be ready to take a round of practice tests. When your scores come back positive enough to get you through the exam, you're ready to go after the real thing. If you follow our assessment regime, you'll not only know what you need to study but also when you're ready to make a test date with the College Board. Good luck!

The Writing Section:
Multiple-Choice Questions

Terms you'll need to understand:

✓ Verb phrase
✓ Verb tense
✓ Verb mood
✓ Participle
✓ Participial phrase
✓ Dangling participle
✓ Gerund
✓ Pronoun
✓ Antecedent

✓ Preposition
✓ Prepositional phrase
✓ Idiom
✓ Comparative adverb
✓ Comparative adjective
✓ Parallelism
✓ Infinitive
✓ Split infinitive

Techniques you'll need to master:

✓ Match verb and subject number and tense
✓ Use verb tense and mood correctly
✓ Use participles and participial phrases correctly
✓ Identify and use pronouns correctly
✓ Use prepositions correctly—omitting when necessary

✓ Recognize and use idioms correctly
✓ Use comparative adjectives and adverbs
✓ Balance phrases and clauses using parallelism
✓ Improve sentences and paragraphs

Grammar is the foundation of good writing. If you don't know the underlying rules, you'll find writing and reading difficult. The exam tests your grammar skills in three sections:

➤ You'll be asked to identify errors in a sentence.

➤ You'll be expected to improve poorly written sentences.

➤ You'll be expected to improve paragraph structure.

This section of the exam will consist of 49 multiple-choice questions on grammar and usage. The exam won't ask you to repeat grammatical terms or rules.

Each sentence will have only one error. Correcting a single underlined component should produce a grammatically correct sentence. Deleting an underlined phrase is never an option. Not all sentences will have an error.

Guidelines for Identifying Sentence Errors

You'll begin the exam by identifying errors in single sentences. The exam presents a sentence with four underlined sections. It's up to you to determine which of the underlined phrases is incorrect. A fifth response will be "No error," and you should choose that when the sentence is correct.

Before you start reminiscing through all those grammar school grammar rules, let's discuss a few pointers that you can use to help identify sentence errors:

➤ Always begin by reading the sentence as if it were correct. During this first reading, don't assume there's a problem. Read it, and listen to how it sounds. If something sounds bad to you, it probably is (but that's not a guarantee).

➤ Once you identify a phrase as not sounding quite right to you, try to identify the appropriate—and seemingly broken—grammatical rule. Don't worry if you can't recite the rule perfectly; a general understanding of the rule is enough. You don't have to explain the rule on the exam. You'll only be expected to apply it.

➤ At this point, if you still haven't found an error, begin eliminating the phrases that you know are correct and see what's left. Choose a response from the phrases you can't eliminate as correct. Remember, you will be penalized for incorrect answers. If you simply can't identify a best-guess response, skip the question.

During practice sessions, read the sentences aloud if possible. Often, the sound of the sentence points directly to the error. Unfortunately, you won't be able to read questions aloud during the actual exam, but practicing this way might make spotting errors easier in general.

During the exam, you'll only have to identify the error. While practicing, we recommend that you actually correct the error. Correcting the errors will help solidify the rules in your mind, making them that much easier to identify the next time.

Identifying Errors in Sentences

In this next section, you'll review common grammatical rules. You'll need to have a good understanding of the rules and how to apply the rule to correct errors in order to score well on the grammar portion of the SAT exam.

Identifying Verb Errors

When checking verb phrases, look for the following problems:

➤ The verb must agree with the subject in person and number.

➤ The verb must be the proper tense.

➤ The verb must be in the proper form (subjective mood).

➤ When a verb is a participle, it must be in the correct form.

Verb Agreement

A verb must agree in number with the subject. That means if the subject is singular, the verb must be singular. Likewise, both the subject and verb must be plural. Fortunately, there's a simple way to find subject-verb disagreement. Say the subject and the verb together—omitting everything else. You'll need to understand the following rule well enough to apply them correctly:

➤ Combining two subjects with the word *and* produces a plural subject.

Plural Example: *Susan and Bill* <u>are</u> celebrating their anniversary in Hawaii.

➤ Use the phrases *in addition to*, *together with*, *along with*, and *as well as* to keep the subject singular. Remember, the object of the phrase is *not* the subject of the sentence. For instance, in the following sentence, Susan is the subject, not Susan and Bill.

Singular Example: *Susan*, in addition to Bill, <u>is</u> in Hawaii.

➤ The following words always identify a singular subject: *each, anyone, anybody, anything, another, neither, either, every, everyone, someone, no one, somebody*, and *everything*. Try replacing the subject with the word *it* for clarification. If the sentence works, the subject is singular. If the word *they* is a better fit than *it*, you have a plural subject.

Singular Example: *Everyone* <u>walks</u> to the park on nice days.

Singular Example: *It* <u>walks</u> to the park on nice days.

Plural Example: *They* <u>walk</u> to the park on nice days.

➤ The following words can identify a singular or plural subject: *none, any, some, most, more*, and *all*. You'll need to refer to the actual subject (noun) to determine the number.

Plural Example: None of those *birds* <u>are</u> eating the seed.

Singular Example: None of the *seed* <u>is</u> left.

➤ Verbs combined with a noun phrase using either/or and neither/nor must agree with the item that's closest to the verb. More often than not, the item will be the last item in the comparison, but not always.

Singular Example: Neither Bill nor *Susan* <u>spends</u> enough time considering the consequences of their actions.

Plural Example: Neither Bill nor the *kids* <u>spend</u> enough time considering the consequences of their actions.

Singular Example: Either doughnuts or a *chili dog* <u>entices</u> me enough to thwart my new diet.

Plural Example: Either a chili dog or *doughnuts* <u>entice</u> me enough to thwart my new diet.

When the subject follows the verb, as in sentences that begin with *here* and *there*, remember that the subject is always the word about which something is said. Inverting the sentence can simplify determining the subject, which makes it easier to check subject/verb agreement.

➤ Inverted Example: There <u>are</u> lots of *rumors* clouding the real issue.

➤ Uninverted Example: Lots of *rumors* <u>are</u> clouding the real issue.

Verb Tense

A verb's tense identifies place (or perspective) and time. There are three verb tenses: *present, past*, and *future*. It would be great if that short list was the gist of verb tense, but it's just the beginning. Each of the tenses comes in three forms:

➤ *Simple Form*—Use the *simple* form with the present form of a verb: walks, talks, sits, cries, and so on.

➤ *Perfect Form*—The *perfect* form uses a verb that indicates a completed action: walked, talked, sat, cried, and so on.

➤ *Progressive Form*—The *progressive* form uses a verb that indicates an ongoing action: *am*, *is*, *are*, and *so on*.

In all, there are nine verb tenses you should be able to use correctly. Table 1.1 lists all nine.

Table 1.1 Verb Tense			
Form	**Tense**	**Explanation**	**Example**
Simple	Present	Indicates the current state.	Susan *walks* the dog around the lake.
	Past	Indicates the past state.	Susan *walked* the dog around the lake.
	Future	Indicates the future state.	Susan *will walk* the dog around the lake.
Perfect	Present	Implies an event that began in the past but that extends to the present. Sometimes this tense indicates an unspecified time.	Susan *has walked* the dog around the lake.
	Past	Implies that an event has been completed in the past. This tense is seldom necessary and can usually be rewritten without changing the timing.	Susan *had already walked* the dog around the lake.
	Future	Implies that something will be completed in the future.	Susan *will have walked* the dog around the lake by the time we return from shopping.
Progressing	Present	Indicates an ongoing state.	Susan *is walking* the dog around the lake.
	Past	Indicates an ongoing state in the past.	Susan *was walking* the dog around the lake.
	Future	Indicates an ongoing state in the future.	Susan *will be walking* the dog around the lake.

Most of us can use *simple* and *progressive* correctly with no trouble. The *perfect form* is the trouble spot. Unfortunately, there's no easy trick to using the perfect tenses correctly. We recommend that you spend some time working on the perfect tenses to prepare for the exam. Regardless of tense, you must keep tense consistent.

You can expect to encounter perfect tense errors in the grammar section of the exam. In addition, although you don't have to write in any particular tense in your essay, you will be expected to use tense correctly and consistently throughout your essay.

Not all verbs indicate a time, as some phrases are timeless. When this is the case, use *present tense*. In the following example, the correct tense shows that gold is a timeless entity—gold was and still is priceless. The forty-niners are our history, but the value of gold is timeless.

Wrong Example: The forty-niners knew that gold *was* a priceless gem.

Right Example: The forty-niners knew that gold *is* a priceless gem.

Verb Mood

Verbs have three moods:

➤ *Indicative* mood indicates something real or factual.

Indicative Example: Susan *left* Bill just before the holidays.

➤ *Subjunctive* mood indicates something hypothetical, conditional, wishful, suggestive, or counter to the fact.

Subjunctive Example: Bill hoped Susan *would never* leave him.

Subjunctive Example: Bill thought he *might keep* the house if Susan left first.

Subjunctive Example: We thought Susan *should leave* Bill, but he left first.

➤ *Imperative* indicates a direct command.

Imperative Example: *Get* out!

Verb Participles

Participles take on three roles:

➤ They act as part of a verb.

➤ They act as an adjective.

➤ They act as a noun in the form of a gerund (more about the gerund later).

Like nouns, verbs often come in the form of a phrase. When that's the case, you have a verb and a helping verb, known as a *participial phrase*.

There are two types of participles: *present* and *past*. Present participles end with the suffix "ing." Past participles end with the suffix "ed," "en," or "t."

Present Example: They played in the *falling* <u>leaves</u>.

Past Example: She liked to walk through the *fallen* <u>leaves</u>.

A *participial phrase* is simply a modifying phrase that begins with a participle. Similarly to the participle, the participial phrase acts as an adjective to modify a noun. Usually, a participial phrase is separated from the main clause by one or two commas. A properly placed participial phrase clarifies who or what is acting. The following five sentences are examples.

Bad Example: The mud-covered <u>players</u> scrambled for the ball, *running quickly*.

Better Example: *Running quickly*, the mud-covered <u>players</u> scrambled for the ball.

Best Example: The mud-covered <u>players</u>, running quickly, scrambled for the ball.

Bad Example: The excited <u>children</u> tried to burst the piñata, *laughing and squealing*.

Better Example: *Laughing and squealing*, the excited <u>children</u> tried to burst the piñata.

Best Example: The excited <u>children</u>, *laughing and squealing*, tried to burst the piñata.

Most problems occur when you position the participial phrase improperly. This can happen easily enough when the sentence assumes a subject. The following examples demonstrate this:

Bad Example: *Laughing and squealing*, the <u>piñata</u> burst open.

Surely the piñata was not laughing and squealing just before it burst.

Better Example: *Laughing and squealing*, the excited <u>children</u> rushed forward to collect the piñata's treasures.

The following are a few rules and guidelines to help you identify and use participial phrases correctly:

➤ When using a participial phrase to begin a sentence, you must follow the phrase with a comma and then the word it modifies. Note the following examples.

Bad Example: *Standing in the rain* for the bus, <u>she</u> waited.

Better Example: *Standing in the rain*, <u>she</u> waited for the bus.

➤ When correcting a dangling participle, place the subject or noun next to the participial phrase.

Bad Example: <u>She</u> waited for the bus *standing in the rain*.

She was not waiting for the bus that was standing in the rain.

Better Example: *Standing in the rain*, <u>she</u> waited for the bus.

➤ If the subject is assumed, adding a subject might help you identify a dangling or misplaced participle.

Bad Example: *Standing in the rain*, the bus left.

The bus did not leave standing in the rain.

Better Example: The bus left <u>her</u> *standing in the rain*.

Better Example: *Standing in the rain*, <u>she</u> watched the bus leave.

 It's easy to confuse a present participle with a gerund because they seem so similar in syntax. A present participle acts as an adjective; a gerund acts as a noun. Note the following examples:

Present Participle Example: *Smiling*, the young <u>girl</u> opened her present.

Gerund Example: *Smiling* <u>is</u> infectious.

 On the grammar section of the exam, watch for participial phrases that have no subject.

Identifying Pronoun Errors

Pronouns identify proper nouns in a generic way. At some point, the actual noun (using concrete language, as defined in Chapter 2, "The Writing Section: Student-Written Essay") must be known. The pronoun is just another way to refer to the subject.

There are two types of pronouns:

➤ *Definite*: Refers to a specific person, place, or thing. These pronouns include *it, you, she, he, him, her, who, I*, and so on.

➤ *Indefinite*: Does not refer to a specific person, place, or thing. These pronouns include *anyone, neither, those*, and so on.

The SAT exam probably won't contain any questions that confuse the use of *who* and *whom*. We seem to be slowly dropping the pronoun whom from common speech. For instance, the question, "For whom did you baby-sit?" is grammatically correct, but it is too formal. The question, "Who did you baby-sit for?" is common and acceptable.

If you face a who/whom question, don't despair. There's an easy trick for determining the grammatically correct example. Replace the who/whom pronoun with he/him. If him works, then use whom. Just remember that both whom and him end with the letter "m." For instance, you would say, "I baby-sat for him." You would not say, "I baby-sat for he." After running this quick check, you know that "For whom did you baby-sit?" is the most grammatically correct option.

Pronoun Agreement

The noun that a definite pronoun refers to is called the *antecedent*. These two components—the noun and the antecedent—must agree both in number and kind. By *number*, we mean the number of entities (singular or plural). The term *kind* refers to a personal or impersonal entity. The following examples demonstrate incorrect and correct pronoun/antecedent number agreement:

Incorrect Number: *Everyone* should be in <u>their</u> seats by the time the bell rings.

Correct Number: *Everyone* should be in <u>his or her</u> seat by the time the bell rings.

Correct Number: *They* should be in <u>their</u> seats by the time the bell rings.

Incorrect Person: *Mark* was the one <u>that</u> started the whole thing.

Correct Person: *Mark* was the one <u>who</u> started the whole thing.

Pronoun Clarity

Another pronoun/antecedent problem is *clarity*. The antecedent should always be clear. This problem crops up when a pronoun could refer to more than one noun, as seen in the following examples.

Ambiguous Antecedent Example: *Bill* passed the mashed potatoes to *Mark*, but <u>he</u> didn't want any.

Who didn't want mashed potatoes?

Clear Antecedent Example: <u>Bill</u> passed the mashed potatoes to <u>Mark</u>, but <u>Mark</u> didn't want any.

Interrogative Pronouns

Interrogative pronouns, such as *who, what, when, where*, and *why*, ask a question. When an interrogative pronoun refers to a definite pronoun, make sure that the antecedent matches the question as follows:

➤ Use *what* to refer to a <u>thing</u>.

➤ Use *where* to refer to a <u>place</u>.

➤ Use *when* to refer to a <u>time</u>.

➤ Use *why* to refer to a <u>reason</u>.

➤ Use *who* to refer to a <u>person</u>.

➤ Use *how* to refer to an <u>explanation</u>.

Note the use of the interrogative pronoun "when" in the following sentences:

> Wrong Example: An *allergic reaction* is <u>when</u> you suffer a sensitivity to a specific thing.

An allergic reaction isn't a time; in this context, it is a thing.

> Better Example: You suffer an *allergic reaction* <u>when</u> you come into contact with something to which you are sensitive.

One way to catch these pronoun errors is to watch for commas following an interrogative pronoun. When you follow an interrogative pronoun with a comma, the preceding noun must be the antecedent. Note the following examples:

> Wrong: The *children* wrote their own lines, <u>who</u> are in the play.

This syntax requires that who defines lines, and that's incorrect. By repositioning the pronoun (and often removing the comma), you can rewrite the sentence correctly:

> Right: The *children* <u>who</u> are in the play wrote their own lines.

Identifying Preposition Errors

Prepositions show position or direction. Prepositional phrases are phrases that consist of a preposition and an object that modifies the preposition in some way.

There are two common prepositional errors:

➤ Including unnecessary prepositions

➤ Using the wrong preposition

Unnecessary prepositions are hard to find, mostly because we're just so used to hearing them. Identifying unnecessary prepositions might take a little practice.

We watched the squirrel climb ~~up~~ the tree.

Please close ~~down~~ that office—it's losing money.

While cleaning, she found lots of dirt ~~in~~ between the stove and the refrigerator.

Each of the previous examples uses an unnecessary preposition. None of the sentences suffer when you omit the prepositions. In fact, eliminating the preposition makes each sentence smoother.

Often, the preposition is necessary, but you use the wrong one. You might just have to memorize the appropriate prepositions because there's no concrete rule you can apply. The following is a list of prepositional mistakes you might encounter:

➤ Concerned ~~with~~/about

➤ Different ~~than/to~~/from

➤ Plan to/~~on~~

➤ Prefer ~~more than~~/to/~~over~~

➤ Agree on/~~with/about~~/to

This list is by no means comprehensive. Awareness is the key to identifying these mismatches.

You may see prepositional errors referred to as *idiom errors* on the exam. An *idiom* is a common phrase that doesn't translate literally. For instance, come on strong, get your feet wet, all ears, got your goat, get on board, and so on are all idioms. Notice that most come with a preposition. It can be difficult to distinguish between an idiom and a cliché. (You can read about clichés in Chapter 2.) A cliché is a phrase that's overused. An idiom does not express the literal meaning of the words.

In addition, authorities no longer enforce the old rule that you can't end a sentence with a preposition. The exam will not use a preposition at the end of a sentence as a grammatical error. There's no reason to avoid the sentence-ending preposition in your essay either.

Identifying Adjective and Adverb Errors

Adjectives and adverbs are both modifiers, but they modify different things. An *adjective* modifies a *noun* or a *pronoun*; an *adverb* modifies a *verb*, an *adjective*, or another *adverb*. Adjectives and adverbs aren't interchangeable.

You probably learned to identify adverbs by looking for the "ly" suffix on the end of an adjective.

> Adjective: Get that *gross* <u>sushi</u> out of my sight.

> Adverb: Sushi <u>is</u> *<u>grossly</u>* <u>overrated</u>.

Although this clue can help, it isn't an absolute rule. Not all adverbs end in "ly," as seen in the following example.

> Adverb: She <u>talks</u> so *fast* I can't understand her.

In addition, not all adjectives can be used as an adverb by adding the "ly" suffix.

> Adjective: The *brown* <u>fence</u> obstructed our view of the lake.

Note in the preceding example that there's no way to turn brown into an adverb by adding "ly"—the result would be totally illogical.

Furthermore, some adjectives can serve as an adverb without adding the "ly" suffix, as seen here:

> Adjective: <u>I</u> am *well* today.

> Adverb: She <u>embroiders</u> *well* for a beginner.

The correct use of bad/badly and good/well probably won't show up in the grammar portion of the essay. The following sentences are all correct as far as the SAT exam is concerned:

> ➤ She feels good today.

> ➤ She feels well today.

> ➤ She feels bad today.

As long as you use the word feel/feels as a linking verb, it's fine to use good, well, and bad as an adjective. If you truly mean to use one of these words to modify the verb, you might find a different way to express that particular thought. The following sentence actually means that she is not very good at feeling: She feels badly. Such a sentence would be confusing, even if grammatically correct.

Comparative adjectives and adverbs create another problem. First, a comparative adjective or adverb is exactly what it sounds like: It's an adjective or adverb that expresses a difference.

Comparative adjectives and adverbs come in two forms:

➤ Add the suffix "er" to the adjective, as in cold and colder.

➤ Precede the adjective or adverb with the word "more," as in more likely. (You would not use the word likelier.)

Note the following examples:

Comparative adjective: <u>This morning</u> is *colder* than I expected.

Comparative adjective: <u>She</u> is *more precious* than gold.

Comparative adverb: Please <u>talk</u> *quieter*.

Comparative adverb: My car <u>runs</u> *more efficiently* on the high octane gas.

Not all adjectives and adverbs can take the comparative form. Watch for illogical comparisons that seem redundant. This type of error occurs when you try to use the comparative form with an absolute. By definition, there is no comparison to an absolute. For instance, terms such as *impossible*, *final*, and *unique* are absolutes. Don't use them in the comparative form.

Wrong: The lack of an airbag made the crash more fatal.

Right: The lack of an airbag made the crash fatal.

Fatal is fatal enough by itself; more fatal is illogical.

Guidelines for Improving Sentences

The previous section was a succinct review of the most common grammatical errors. This next section, although similar to the last, deals with the sentence as a whole. The exam will present a complete sentence. A portion of the sentence or the entire sentence will be underlined. Five responses will give you the opportunity to change the underlined portion or leave the underlined component as is.

This section reviews concepts rather than actual rules. You will apply rules you learned in the last section to make the whole sentence better (or not, as the case may be). In the previous section, the emphasis was on finding errors. In the second portion of the exam's writing section, you'll be expected to fix errors. In this section, you'll find few grammar rules, but we do want to share a few guidelines for this part of the exam:

➤ Read the sentence completely first.

➤ Read each of the five possible responses along with the sentence. Don't try to choose a response on its own. You must read each response within the context of the sentence.

➤ Check the noun/verb agreement.

➤ Check modifiers.

➤ Check for parallelism.

➤ Make sure that pronouns are clear and necessary.

➤ Compare the underlined clause's tense to the rest of the sentence.

Applying Parallelism

Good writing isn't an exact science. Sometimes there's no absolute rule to apply. Parallelism falls into this category. There's no hard and fast grammar rule other than this: Items should have the same grammatical form. In other words, you should balance phrases and clauses on both sides of a sentence.

Fortunately, there's one simple rule to cover the subject: When combining two nouns in a series, you must balance both. If the first item in a list is an infinitive, gerund, adjective, or preposition, the other items should also be infinitives, gerunds, adjectives, or prepositions, respectively, as evidenced in the following examples.

Not balanced: Buffalo once roamed *gentle hills* and *valleys* on the prairie.

Balanced: Buffalo once roamed *gentle hills* and *rolling valleys* on the prairie.

Balanced: Buffalo once roamed *hills* and *valleys* on the prairie.

Not balanced: Buffalo once roamed *over gentle hills* and *rolling valleys* on the prairie.

Balanced: Buffalo once roamed *over gentle hills* and *through rolling valleys* on the prairie.

You already know about prepositions and adjectives, so let's review the infinitive and gerund in relation to parallelism. An *infinitive* is a verb-like phrase, such as to walk, to run, to weep, and so on, that usually acts as a noun. In addition, an *infinitive* may also act as an adjective or verb. It's a very versatile part of speech.

Not balanced: She couldn't decide whether *to walk* or *ride* her bike.

Balanced: She couldn't decide whether *to walk* or *to ride* her bike.

Gerunds are also verb-like words that act as nouns. Words, such as walking, running, weeping, and so on are gerunds.

Not balanced: She couldn't decide between *walking* or to *ride* her bike.

Balanced: She couldn't decide between *walking* or *riding* her bike.

Both the infinitive and the gerund can be a prepositional phrase or a single word. For the exam, you'll be asked to identify and correct parallelism errors. You won't have to know the definition of an infinitive or gerund to do so.

In addition, don't worry about split infinitives on the exam. A split infinitive is an infinitive that includes a modifier between the infinitive and the verb. For instance, to walk is an infinitive. The phrase to quickly walk is a split infinitive, which you might want to rewrite as to walk quickly. Although you should avoid splitting infinitives in your essay, the exam itself will not include any split infinitives.

Because infinitives are modifiers, we tend to misplace them. In this way, infinitives are similar to participial phrases. Just remember that the infinitive should be as close as possible to the noun it modifies.

Eliminating the Problems

In this section of the exam, only one part of the sentence (or the entire sentence) is underlined. You must identify what's wrong with the underlined section and then find the most correct response for correcting the error. One response will always be to leave the section just as it is, meaning there's nothing wrong with the underlined section.

Sometimes the error is obvious. That's great. Mark the correct response and move on. When the error isn't so obvious, eliminate the responses that you know are wrong. Consider the following example:

Multiculturalism is the convergence of many cultures or a <u>culture different than your own</u>.

(A) culture different to your own.

(B) culture which isn't your own.

(C) culture besides your own.

(D) culture different from your own.

(E) culture different than your own.

In the preceding question, read the sentence, and then read all five responses within the context of the sentence. Sometimes the responses themselves will give you clues. After reading all five responses, you realize that the problem is probably the prepositional phrase. Specifically, does the preposition "than" match the phrase different? You know "different to" is incorrect; scratch response A. Response B is a possibility, but it's awkward. Wait!

There's no comma between culture and which; that can't be right either. Response C is a possibility, but, like B, it's awkward. You don't have to eliminate it yet, but continue in hopes of finding something better. But at this point, it seriously looks like D or E will be the appropriate response. You've already decided that the phrase is incorrect, so that leaves D (because E just repeats the phrase that's already there). D is the correct response. Before choosing your answer, read the sentence one last time, inserting the response you've chosen—just to check one last time. If you're curious about C, consider that the prepositional phrase besides your own really isn't the best fit for the subject. The sentence is comparing your culture to someone else's. The word different is a better choice than besides within the context of this particular sentence.

In this section, you may find two responses that correct errors in the sentence. Be careful—the exam wants only the response that corrects the underlined segment. Even though a response might correct an error, unless it corrects the underlined segment, the response is the wrong answer. In addition, a response may correct the error yet introduce a new one. When this is the case, keep shopping for a better response.

Brevity Matters

Not all errors are grammatical in nature. Remember, clarity and succinctness count—only poets and great writers have the luxury of using more words than are truly necessary. You may find a sentence that doesn't seem to have any obvious grammatical errors. When this happens, check all the responses. Do any of the responses say the same thing but use fewer words to do so? If this is the case, the shorter response is the correct answer. Let's look at an example.

> <u>The result of the situation is that</u> I am often expected to carry a heavier workload than the other employees.
>
> (A) The results is that
> (B) Consequently,
> (C) The results are that
> (D) The result of the situation is
> (E) The result of the situation is that

The only thing really wrong with the underlined phrase is that it's wordy. Depending on the context of the sentence within the paragraph, the phrase may not be necessary at all, but we don't know this to be true. Given just the one sentence, we should assume that the transition is necessary. In that case, response B is the best choice. It uses just one word to say the same thing as the underlined phrase of seven words.

Guidelines for Improving Paragraphs

Improving an essay, sentence by sentence, is definitely part and parcel of good writing. You'll also need to understand how those sentences fit together to support the essay's thesis.

This part of the exam will provide an essay that needs work. Each sentence is prefaced by a number, and questions will refer to those numbers. In this part of the exam, you'll combine sentences and alter the general structure of the paragraph in one of three ways:

➤ You'll improve single sentences; these questions are similar to the questions in the last section. For that reason, we won't review single sentences in this section.

➤ You'll improve single sentences within the context of the entire paragraph.

➤ You'll organize the paragraph's structure.

Context Counts

We suggest that you begin each question by actually reading the passage or essay. Context questions will ask for improvements based on the entire passage. Sometimes this will take the guise of adding transitions or improving comparative phrases. Just remember that the point of the exercise is to consider how the sentence in question fits within the entire essay. If you don't read the actual essay, you could easily respond incorrectly to these questions. Let's work through an example to demonstrate this.

(**1**) Snowshoe Thompson negotiated a deal to deliver mail over the treacherous Sierra Nevada Pass during the harsh winters when mail service was impossible. (**2**)Using an early form of skis, he succeeded where all others had failed—he delivered mail during the winter. (**3**)He never received compensation for his efforts.

In context, which of the following improves sentence 3 the most?

He never received compensation for his efforts.

    (A) As is, make no changes.

    (B) He never received any

    (C) He received no

    (D) Despite negotiations and his accomplishments, he never received

    (E) Thompson never received

Keeping in mind that the question is a context question, D is the best response. It works as a subtle transition, but it also changes the character of the paragraph.

In this section of the exam, you will be expected to choose the best or most appropriate response. More than one answer may improve the sentence. Be sure to read all of the responses and to choose the best.

Organization Counts

Each sentence should be grammatically correct, and each sentence should be appropriate within the context of the paragraph's purpose. Sometimes that means you must reorganize the existing passage in some way:

➤ You may need to move a sentence.

➤ You may need to add a new sentence.

➤ You may need to completely delete a sentence.

Consider the following example, which demonstrates this idea.

(**1**)Snowshoe Thompson negotiated a deal to deliver mail over the treacherous Sierra Nevada Pass during the harsh winters when mail service was impossible. (**2**)Using an early form of skis, he succeeded where all others had failed—he delivered mail during the winter. (**3**)Thompson learned to ski as a youngster in his native Norway. (**4**)Despite negotiations and his accomplishments, he never received compensation for his efforts.

In context, which of the following improves the paragraph the most?

Thompson learned to ski as a youngster in his native Norway.

  (A) As is, make no changes.
  (B) Thompson learned to ski as a youngster in Norway.
  (C) Thompson learned to ski in Norway.
  (D) Thompson learned to ski as a child.
  (E) Delete sentence 3.

There's nothing grammatically wrong with sentence 3. The problem is it doesn't add to the paragraph's purpose. Answer E is the best response.

Exam Prep Questions

Read each question carefully and choose the response that corrects the underlined portion. Remember, response A repeats the underlined section as is—the underlined segment may be correct as is.

1. Chuck Yeager, a famous <u>aviator, he</u> was the first to travel faster than the speed of sound.

(A) aviator, he

(B) aviator that

(C) aviator who

(D) aviator, who

(E) aviator,

2. She <u>seeks regularly, guidance</u> from her guardian angel.

(A) seeks regularly, guidance

(B) regularly seeks guidance

(C) seeks regular guidance

(D) seeks guidance regularly

(E) seeks guidance

3. She returned to the motel room one last time and found <u>an angel ornament, a comb, and shampoo</u> in the shower.

(A) an angel ornament, a comb, and shampoo

(B) an ornament, comb, and shampoo

(C) an angel ornament, a comb, and a bottle of shampoo

(D) an ornament, a comb, and a bottle of shampoo

(E) an angel ornament, a blue comb, and a small bottle of shampoo

4. Neither the <u>hens nor the cow type</u> mysterious notes to the farmer as the story suggests.

(A) hens nor the cow type

(B) hen nor the cows type

(C) hens nor the cow types

(D) hens or the cow type

(E) hen or the cows type

5. The owner <u>has already accepted</u> our offer when we arrived to plead our case.

(A) has already accepted

(B) accepted

(C) has accepted

(D) had already accepted

(E) refused

6. (1)Chuck Yeager, a famous aviator, was the first to travel faster than the speed of sound. (2)Years later, Chuck commanded the first school for astronauts. (3)He never realized his dream of flying into space.

In context, which of the following improves sentence 3 the most?

He never realized his dream of flying into space.

(A) As is, make no changes.

(B) However, he never realized his dream of flying into space.

(C) Despite his pioneering contributions to the aviation industry, he never realized his dream of flying into space.

(D) He never flew into space as an astronaut.

(E) Chuck Yeager never flew into space as an astronaut.

7. (1)Mental health experts agree that individuals who don't dream are psychopaths and unable to function in society. (2)If you don't remember your dreams and you're currently locked in a mental ward or you're carrying around an ax for no better reason than you like to, you might be a psychopath. (3)On the other hand, many seemingly normal people insist that they don't dream. (4)The truth is, these people are perfectly normal—they dream, they just don't remember their dreams.

In context, which of the following improves sentence 4 the most?

The truth is, these people are perfectly normal—they dream, they just don't remember their dreams.

(A) As is, make no changes.

(B) They dream; they just don't remember their dreams.

(C) The truth is, these people are perfectly normal—they just don't remember their dreams.

(D) The truth is, they dream; they just don't remember their dreams.

(E) They just don't remember dreaming.

8. (1)On the last day of every month, children across Great Britain end their day by saying "rabbits" three times before falling asleep. (2)Upon waking on the morning of the first day of the new month, they say "hares" three times. (3)According to the old superstition, the accommodating child will soon receive a present.

In context, which of the following improves sentence 2 the most?

Upon waking on the morning of the first day of the new month, they say "hares" three times.

(A) As is, make no changes.

(B) Upon waking the next morning, they say "hares" three times.

(C) Upon waking on the morning of the first day of the new month, these same children say "hares" three times.

(D) Upon waking, they say "hares" three times.

(E) Upon waking, these same children say "hares" three times.

9. (**1**)Susan sat on the cold, hard bench in the light winter rain. (**2**)After awhile, she spoke aloud to her dead father. (**3**)The past week had shattered her life—or at least the illusions she thought were her life. (**4**)There was no running from the truth. Her mother was certifiably insane, and no one but Susan knew the truth. (**5**)"Daddy, I need help," she said meekly.

   In context, which of the following improvements would strengthen the paragraph the most?

   (A) As is; make no changes.
   (B) Omit 4.
   (C) Position 5 between 2 and 3.
   (D) Omit 3.
   (E) Position 2 between 4 and 5.

10. (**1**)Rocky, a beatnik from the late '60s, took his young sons to a peaceful demonstration. (**2**)A few days before the event, he and the boys discussed the event's purpose. (**3**)Rocky also shared personal stories from his youth of protesting the Vietnam war. (**4**)Unfortunately, the event had little impact on the boys. (**5**)Being children of the new century, the boys were more interested in eating hot dogs than carrying protest signs.

    In context, which of the following improvements would strengthen the paragraph the most?

    (A) As is; make no changes.
    (B) Rewrite 5: The boys were more interested in eating hot dogs than carrying protest signs.
    (C) Omit 3.
    (D) Rewrite 2: He and the boys discussed the event's purpose.
    (E) Combine 4 and 5: Unfortunately, the event had little impact on the boys who were more interested in eating hot dogs than carrying protest signs.

Answers to Exam Prep Questions

1. Response E is the most correct response. As is, the pronoun *he* is redundant. Answer A is incorrect because the sentence is not correct as is. Response B is incorrect because *that* is the wrong pronoun; we know aviator refers to Chuck Yeager, a proper noun. Who would be the appropriate pronoun. Response C is incorrect because that would create a sentence fragment, not a complete sentence. Response D is incorrect; adding a comma doesn't help to complete the sentence.

2. Answer B is correct because regularly is a misplaced modifier. Regularly modifies the verb seek. Answer A is incorrect because the underlined section is incorrect. The adverb regularly is misplaced. Answer C is incorrect because it changes the meaning of regularly from an adverb to an adjective that modifies guidance. Answer D is incorrect because the adverb should be as close as possible to the verb it modifies. Response E is incorrect; omitting the adverb isn't the best solution because it changes the sentence's meaning.

3. Answer E is correct because it applies the rule of parallelism to the sentence. Each item should be treated the same, by adding (or deleting as the case may be) any modifiers. All items need a modifier in the form *a/an adjective*. Answer A is incorrect because shampoo is not pre-ceded with *a*. Answer B is incorrect because neither comb nor shampoo is preceded with *a*. Answer C is incorrect because neither comb nor bottle of shampoo is modified by an adjective. Answer D is correct, but because you've deleted the adjective *angel*, the sentence isn't as strong. The noun ornament isn't as specific without the adjective.

4. Answer C is correct because the verb and noun must match in number. When using neither/nor, the verb must match the closest noun. Cow is singular, so you must use the singular form of the verb, which in this case is types. Answer A is incorrect because the underlined section isn't correct as is. When combining two subjects using nor, the verb must match the number of the nearest subject. In this case, that's cow and cow is singular. Answer B is incorrect; it is grammatically correct, but you can't arbitrarily change the noun's number without more informa-tion. Answers D and E are incorrect because or is incorrect with nei-ther.

5. Answer D is correct because the past perfect tense of has (had) matches the verb tense (accepted). Answer A is incorrect because the underlined section is incorrect as is—the verb tense of doesn't match the second verb phrase. Answer B is incorrect because it changes the tense. Answer C is incorrect because the tense of has still doesn't match the verb tense (accepted). Answer E is incorrect because it changes the sen-tence's purpose.

6. Answer C is correct because the transitioning clause *Despite his pioneer-ing contributions to the aviation industry*, pulls the sentences together to better clarify the paragraph's point. Answer A is incorrect because the sentence can be improved. Answer B is incorrect because the transi-tion, *however*, isn't as strong as the one used in Answer C. Answer D is incorrect because the sentence isn't any better than the original.

Answer E is incorrect because there's no need to replace the pronoun *he* with a proper noun. In this case, the pronoun is clear.

7. Answer D is correct. Although there's nothing grammatically wrong with the sentence, it's wordy and the phrase *these people are perfectly normal* is unnecessary. Answer A is incorrect because the sentence can be improved. Answer B is incorrect because omitting the transition *the truth is*, weakens the paragraph. Answer C is incorrect because the very phrase *they dream* is important to the contrast drawn between the truly dreamless and those who don't remember dreaming. Answer E is incorrect because it weakens the paragraph.

8. Answer B is correct. The original sentence is wordy; the phrase *on the morning of the first day of the new month* is redundant. Within the context of the sentence, the reader can assume the child is waking on the first day of the new month, since the reader knows the child is going to sleep on the last day of the month. Answer A is incorrect because the sentence can be improved. Answers C and E are incorrect because nothing is wrong with the pronoun *they* as used. Answers D and E are incorrect because the phrase *the next morning* is relevant—the child could wake first in the middle of the night.

9. Answer E is correct because the new organization provides the best flow of thoughts from beginning to ending. Answer A is incorrect because the paragraph can be improved. Answer B is incorrect because 4 tells us the actual problem. Answer C is incorrect. Although sentence 5 does need to follow 2, putting the two sentences in the middle of the paragraph disrupts the sequence. Answer D is incorrect; that sentence establishes the severity of the problem.

10. Answer A is correct. There's really nothing wrong with this paragraph. The flow is logical, and it transitions easily. Although you might be able to improve the paragraph, none of the other responses actually strengthens the paragraph, so A is the best response. Answer B is incorrect; removing the transition *being children of the new century* weakens the paragraph. Answer C is incorrect; the sentence helps support Rocky's hopes. Answer D is incorrect; the phrase *a few days before the event* helps establish the flow of events. Answer E is incorrect. You could combine the two sentences, but the impact isn't as strong as the two separate thoughts.

The Writing Section: Student-Written Essay

Terms you'll need to understand:

- ✓ Thesis
- ✓ Introduction
- ✓ Conclusion
- ✓ Abstract and concrete language
- ✓ Passive and active voice
- ✓ Personal nouns
- ✓ Active verbs
- ✓ Prepositions and prepositional phrases
- ✓ Transition
- ✓ Jargon
- ✓ Cliché

Techniques you'll need to master:

- ✓ Develop a position from the exam's writing challenge
- ✓ Quickly formulate a four or five paragraph outline to support your position
- ✓ Use abstract language to communicate broader thoughts and ideas
- ✓ Use concrete language and terms to describe and support abstract thoughts
- ✓ Recognize and omit jargon, clichés, and redundant phrases
- ✓ Use transitions to smooth the way from sentence to sentence and paragraph to paragraph
- ✓ Recognize and omit wordy passages
- ✓ How to use the right word in the right spot at the right time
- ✓ Use prepositional phrases wisely and infrequently

As far as the SAT exam is concerned, being expressive isn't as simple as a coy smile or a raised eyebrow at just the right moment. You must be able to relay your ideas, beliefs, and perhaps even feelings in writing. You'll be given 25 minutes and a writing challenge. Don't shrug off this part of the exam—your ability to express yourself in writing is important. Don't show off, don't be flashy, but do put your best foot forward. All things being equal, the essay portion of this test could be your edge over other students. If you don't consider yourself a strong writer, don't worry, practice can make a difference.

The essay portion doesn't measure your knowledge. Rather, this section tests your ability to analyze a thought and express your support for or against that thought. You don't have to be an expert in a subject to write a compelling essay.

What They're Looking For

Two experts will read and appraise your essay. Yes, it's subjective, but the process is still sound. The readers will grade your essay based on the following:

➤ The readers are looking for a well developed, insightful, and focused point of view.

➤ Your essay should illustrate your ability to think critically. You'll want to use clear and appropriate examples, anecdotes, and reasons to support your position.

➤ Organize your thoughts logically to pull your reader from the introduction to the end. The reader expects a smooth ride.

➤ A good essay uses a variety of writing techniques, such as varied sentence structure and length.

➤ Your choice of words needs to be appropriate and to the point. The readers won't penalize you for not including big words; they will penalize you for using words incorrectly.

➤ Your essay should be free of grammatical and spelling errors.

In short, your essay needs to convince the readers that you have mastered the English language. You'll do this by writing about what you know using the writing techniques and vocabulary that you're comfortable using.

The best essay will receive a low score if the readers can't read it. Spend some time practicing your handwriting, both cursive and printing. Ask a few people you trust to read your samples. Did they have any problems reading what you wrote? If they did have trouble, work on correcting those problems. You may need to practice a little every day.

The SAT exam will present you with a question. Answer the question directly and answer only the question asked. Don't be wishy-washy and don't go off on some wild tangent. Stick to the subject, focus on the answer, and don't be distracted by extraneous thoughts and ideas that don't necessarily support your position. Stick with what you know and fully develop each thought by using strong examples or meaningful anecdotes.

 When writing your essay, stick to the subject, focus on the answer, and don't be distracted by extraneous thoughts and ideas that don't necessarily support your position.

Someone once said that chaos was just organization without order. When you've established your position, or thesis, you must develop it. Write a thoughtful and succinct introduction that expresses your thesis in general terms. Use appropriate transitions to lead the reader from one paragraph to the next, developing that position in an orderly manner. Finally, conclude by restating your thesis in a conciliatory manner.

There's no room for beating around the bush—say what you mean and own it. Present the readers with something they haven't already read a hundred times over, but don't make them suffer for it by forcing them to wade through flowery or otherwise extraneous nonsense. If a word doesn't fully support the statement, don't use it. If another, perhaps shorter, more common word is more to the point, use it. You won't impress anyone with your huge vocabulary if you're wielding it incorrectly.

Remember that boring, monotone teacher who you dreaded every day? That teacher seldom showed any excitement or enthusiasm for the subject, and after a few minutes, you were snoring alongside the rest of your classmates. Your essay might put people to sleep too. The most accurate examples can also be very boring. The best way to keep your reader's attention is to show a little creativity. Don't go overboard. You're not writing a literary masterpiece, so show some restraint, but a little character can go a long way. If you truly lack the creative edge, vary the sentence length and structure just to keep things interesting.

The term *position*, within the context of this chapter, refers to the component of the essay known technically as a *thesis*. You should be able to state a position or thesis in one or two sentences.

Keep your audience in mind at all times. You want to produce an accurate, well-developed essay that the readers will enjoy. If the readers learn something new from your essay, so much the better. If the readers are actually inspired, great. But the readers only require that you inform them of your position in an essay that's clear and concise.

 The perfect essay is worth a total of 12 points. Two readers will each give your essay up to 6 points. Most 12-point essays have only four paragraphs, so plan to write four paragraphs. Add a fifth paragraph only if you can fully develop the additional example or thought. Likewise, no matter how succinct and direct you are, you probably won't get a perfect score with a three-paragraph essay.

Before you start compiling your thoughts, take the time to read and reread the writing challenge. Be absolutely sure that your response answers the question the way the readers expect it to. For instance, the challenge may ask you if you agree or disagree with a particular statement, and then you must support your position. If the challenge asks for two or more examples, don't stop with one. If asked to provide just one example, don't give them two or three. Read the instructions carefully and give them what they request—no more, no less.

Be precise in your answer. If the question asks you to comment on a quote, do so deliberately and thoughtfully. It's alright to develop the subject a bit in general terms, but be sure to give them what they ask for—your response to the quote. Be specific, be thorough, and be personal. Why personal? Because sharing personal experiences and ideas is the best (and perhaps easiest) way to develop your thesis. Otherwise, you might miss the mark.

Getting Started

Writing your essay will comprise several short intervals of thought, inspiration, writing, and rewriting. Don't spend all your time writing; take time to think. In this next section, we'll review the techniques you need to master to receive a high score on your essay.

Now let's imagine that you're sitting for the exam. You've read and reread your writing challenge. You're ready to attack your essay, right? Wrong. Slow down just a bit and let the creative juices flow. You're not wasting precious time; you're organizing your thoughts.

First, try to state your position in one or two sentences. For instance, let's suppose that you're given the following writing challenge:

> An old farmer warns you that "… you can't kick manure without getting some on your shoes." What, do you suppose, is the farmer trying to tell you? Use historical events or personal anecdotes to support your position.

After a few minutes of thought, you might write down one of the following positions:

> Watch where you're going and don't walk into a fight.

> Even if provoked, revenge almost always comes with unintended repercussions.

Which thesis do you think is the strongest? The first one is too general; the second is more specific. Once you have a thesis, concentrate on your position for a few minutes, jotting down any inspirations. You're looking for examples that support your position. Organize your inspirational bits into a loose outline. You'll use this outline to develop your essay.

Your outline doesn't have to be complex or follow any strict structural rules. The readers won't grade your outline. All you need is one succinct sentence that accurately depicts each paragraph's purpose:

1. Paragraph 1 should state the thesis and summarize your story or examples.

2. Paragraph 2 tackles the first example or supporting story.

3. Paragraph 3 tackles the second example or supporting story.

4. Paragraph 4 concludes the essay and ties up any loose strings.

You don't have to state the thesis first. As an alternative to this more traditional structure, consider stating the thesis at the end using the following structure:

1. Paragraph 1 is a short story or example that introduces the topic in a meaningful way.

2. Paragraph 2 states the story's meaning or purpose—in other words, it provides an analytical review from your perspective.

3. In paragraph 3, you finally get to state your thesis.

4. Paragraph 4 should connect your thesis to a broader theme or draw the mood to a close.

This latter format is difficult to pull off; only experienced and artful writers should attempt this arrangement. Used correctly, it can be very effective because it's different and allows the writer a little more creative license.

If you need five paragraphs, go ahead and insert an additional paragraph between three and four. Just remember to maintain the logical flow from one paragraph to another. However, we recommend that you keep the essay to four paragraphs because most essays that receive perfect scores (of 6 points from two readers = 12 total points) have four paragraphs (not five, not three).

Before you start writing, make sure that you have the appropriate amount and the specific types of examples to support your position. If the challenge asks for two examples, give them two examples—not one, not three. If the challenge requests that your example be historical, don't use a childhood anecdote.

If you can't come up with a reasonable example, you're probably taking the wrong side. Rethink your position if you can't come up with an appropriate example or anecdote. Furthermore, you should take the position that you can write about, not necessarily the position that you personally support.

Only once you have an outline and the appropriate number of examples should you start writing. You may think you can skip this brainstorming period and still do a good job, but most of us can't. Those who think they can usually score poorly on the essay.

Suck Them Right In with a Strong Introduction

Used correctly, words are magical. You can persuade, teach, or elicit emotions. You won't have to produce joy or tears from your reader to get a good score on your essay, but a good introduction will go a long way toward gaining your reader's confidence. You're only tricking the reader if the remaining essay is weak. If you're smart enough to come up with a good strong introduction, you're smart enough to complete a good, strong essay.

The Essence of Your Essay

Each paragraph tells its own little story. Because you're limited in time and subject matter, the more specific you are, the stronger your paragraphs will be. The following are a few guidelines you should apply while writing your essay.

Use Concrete Language to Describe the Abstract

One of the most confusing issues writers struggle with is the difference between using concrete and abstract language. Abstract deals with the ideas, feelings, and beliefs about which you write, but you'll use concrete language to convey those mental images. There's a difference, and knowing the difference will help you score well on the essay portion of the SAT.

First, let's start with a few simple definitions. *Abstract language* conveys the essence of a thought, idea, or belief in a nonspecific manner. You may recognize and agree with the essence of the statement, but expounding on the writer's exact intentions might be difficult as the writer's intentions aren't really clear. *Concrete language* is specific. A concrete reference or statement states a clear noun and verb. There's no doubt what the writer intended to say.

  Abstract: Wendy watched the happy child.

  Concrete: The baby laughed and squealed as she reached for her mother.

The first sentence tells us almost nothing about what Wendy sees, as happy is an abstract term. The reader's interpretation will greatly influence how the reader reacts to the statement; the author's intent is mostly lost.

The second sentence fills in a lot of holes:

1. The child is actually a baby girl. In this case, the word "baby" is more important than the child's sex, but sex might become relevant later. The word "child" could include any child from birth to adolescence. The word "baby" is much more specific.

2. How do we know the baby is happy? The baby is laughing and squealing.

3. Why is the baby laughing? The baby is laughing and squealing because she sees her mother.

See how much more the second sentence tells us? That's concrete language. The abstract sentence tries to share a child's happiness with us, but without the details, the actual scene is lost. We know that the child is happy, that's all. In fact, if we didn't have a good idea of what the word happy meant, the sentence would mean almost nothing. The second sentence conveys the essence of happiness, an abstract term, without actually using the word at all.

Finding the Abstract

Finding abstract language is a skill that just takes some time and experience. There are a few tricks we can pass along.

Abstract words aren't bad, but you do need to use concrete terms to fully clarify their purpose in your essay. Synonyms do not clarify; synonyms repeat. Sometimes a word's suffix will identify a word as abstract. Look for nouns that end with the following suffixes:

➤ *-age*: courage, advantage, encourage

➤ *-ance*: arrogance, endurance, elegance

➤ *-ity*: complicity, equity, accountability

➤ *-ment*: judgment, mistreatment, refinement

➤ *-ness*: happiness, sadness, candidness

➤ *-ty*: beauty, ability, authority, capacity

> *Abstract:* Clearly, Mark had an advantage on the basketball floor.
>
> *Concrete:* Mark was the tallest on the basketball team, and his arms seem to be everywhere at once.
>
> *Abstract:* It's easy to love a beauty, until you get to know her.
>
> *Concrete:* From afar, people admired Betsy's silken hair and lush lips, but few people were able to get past her haughty disposition. Consequently, Betsy had few friends.

 So how do you get around the abstract problem? Don't think of abstract language as a problem because it isn't. Used correctly, it works well. You'll often begin a paragraph with an abstract thought, and then use the remaining paragraph to develop that thought with concrete examples.

Use Informal Language

You're not writing a legal brief or a Constitutional amendment. Although your essay shouldn't be as informal as conversation, your essay should be conversation-like. You want your essay to be palatable to a wide audience. Relax, and apply grammar rules, but do so in a natural manner. Stiff, formal language can confuse the reader and often makes the reader uncomfortable.

Don't Use Jargon

Unless you're using technical terms that are necessary within the context of the subject, avoid jargon. Jargon comes in two forms:

➤ Hybrid language or dialect

➤ Specialized or technical language used in a trade, professional, or group.

For the most part, we're talking about the first type, which includes slang and colloquialisms. Both are fine in a short story, poetry, or novel if they truly belong within the context of the subject. However, don't include these types of terms in your essay, unless specifically asked to. We don't think that you'll run into such a request on your SAT exam.

Technical terms, although sometimes considered jargon or even slang, can be used, if used appropriately. The following example uses both slang and technical jargon.

Bad: Owen, the computer geek, carries a briefcase from class to class, which makes him look like a nerd.

Okay: Kids see Owen carrying his briefcase from class to class and automatically assume he's a computer geek or nerd.

The second sentence is acceptable because you've placed the terms in the appropriate context—what the other kids think. However, we recommend that you resist using slang or technical jargon in your SAT essay. This is one of those areas in which unless you're an expert and you really know how to manipulate the words, you might get into trouble.

Avoid Redundancy

This guideline can be difficult to put into action because no one would purposely include redundant phrases. Unfortunately, they seem to just roll off our tongues and worm their way right into our passages. We're just so used to using and hearing them that we don't recognize them when we encounter them.

Redundant: We watched the werewolf *revert back* to his former self.

Better: We watched the werewolf *revert* to human form.

Redundant: Please find *each and every* redundant phrase in your essay before passing it in.

Better: Please find *all* redundant phrasing in your essay before passing it in.

Along the same lines, don't repeat yourself just to make the essay longer. The judges won't appreciate the deception. If two sentences seem to repeat the same thought, cut one of them, no matter how fond you are of both sentences. Combine the best of both if you must, but by all means, reduce both sentences to just one.

Don't Include Clichés

There's almost no place for clichés in your essay. They may make good punch lines or greeting card sentiments, but there's no room for them in a good essay. A cliché is a trite or overused expression.

> I always suspected Lily was a *fair-weather friend*.
>
> Like most of the folks on Elm Street, the Joneses *lived from paycheck to paycheck*.
>
> You never see one without the other; they're just *two peas in a pod*.
>
> "It's the *end of the world, as we know it*," warned the speaker.

Unless the cliché is the subject, don't use it, and if a cliché is the subject of your essay, consider another subject. If you're smart enough to apply a cliché correctly, you're smart enough to recognize it, avoid it, and express your thoughts using your own words. Don't let clichés hijack your essay—rely on your own words.

Movement Is Key

If a sentence doesn't move your essay along, rewrite, or better yet, remove it. By itself, the sentence may be artful or even poignant, but if it doesn't support your position, delete it. Consider the following example:

> The leash law exists for a good reason. Too many dogs are running around loose in the neighborhood. Almost every day, I see a stray dog in the neighborhood. Some days, I see two or three. I run into them at the grocery store. Just last week, I had to dodge one coming out of the doctor's office.

Now, this writer might be a great writer, but none of the statements support the point, which is why leash laws are good for the community. The number of stray dogs is important, but it isn't the issue. Instead, the writer needs to discuss the problems perpetrated by stray dogs. Frankly, you just don't have the time to waste on anything that doesn't support your position.

You can cross out a word or sentence if necessary. You don't have to erase unnecessary words or sentences that on second thought you'd like to omit. The readers will grade on the essay's content, without considering marked out content. We don't recommend crossing out every other word, but a few strikethroughs are acceptable. You're also allowed to insert words or even an entire sentence. Use the caret character (^) to point to phrases or words above the line.

Use transitions to help your reader move from thought to thought, which in this case, will probably be paragraph to paragraph. There are lots of transitional words:

➤ However

➤ Therefore

➤ Nevertheless

➤ Furthermore

➤ Although

➤ For instance and for example

➤ In addition, in contrast, and in comparison

➤ First, second, and third (to transition through a sequence of ordered ideas or events)

➤ Now, next, and then

➤ Similarly and likewise

➤ Fortunately and unfortunately

➤ By no means and in no way

➤ Subsequently, consequently, and as a result

➤ On the other hand, in other words, and otherwise

This list is by no means comprehensive, but rather it should spark your imagination. You're simply lighting a candle to help your readers find their way from one thought to another.

Keep in mind that there needs to be a logical choice to your use of transitions, and they aren't always necessary. Don't overuse them and make sure that they match the current thought.

The transitions in the following example aren't necessary, but they do make the paragraph more comfortable. You know that both points are working together to draw you to a conclusion.

Every payday, the IRS and the state of Kentucky slice themselves a big piece of my pie. *Likewise*, once a year, my local government taxes my collection of pie plates. *Consequently*, I have decided to start eating cake.

Transitions help pull together statements that might otherwise stand alone. Not every sentence needs a transition. Use them sparingly and effectively.

Make Every Word Count

Just as each sentence should move your reader to discovering your position, each word should be as specific as possible. Remove words that aren't necessary. In addition, don't use big words just because you can. This doesn't mean that a large word can never be the best choice. Use the best word, not the biggest word—make every word count.

> *Bad*: The *gargantuan* elephant towered over the *insignificant* mouse.
>
> *Better*: The *huge* elephant towered over the *tiny* mouse.
>
> *Bad*: The elephant *compacted* the trainer's head with its *formidable stance*.
>
> *Better*: The elephant *crushed* the trainer's head with its *enormous foot*.

Use only words you actually know well enough to use and spell correctly. The readers will probably forgive a misspelled word, but spelling does count. Avoid using a word if you're not sure of its spelling.

It's fine to introduce terms and concepts that might not be conversational, but do so only to strengthen your position. When you use these terms or concepts, be sure to thoroughly define them within the context of your thesis. Don't leave your readers hanging—they won't be impressed with your knowledge. Most likely, the readers will deem your diminutive treatise obtuse and insipid. In other words, you'll be up the estuarial without the proper means of propulsion.

Variety Enhances Style

For the sake of variety and style, vary the sentence length and structure. Long sentences are fine, and often necessary, especially when sharing complicated ideas or circumstances. However, long sentences can be confusing and unnecessarily convoluted. A short sentence isn't the sign of a dull writer. "Oh!" in the right context is a very effective sentence.

Bad: The government took over the distribution of many essential food items and allotted specific amounts to each individual or family. As a result, I seldom had the pleasure of chewing bubble gum when I was a child.

Better: Sugar was rationed during the war. We often went for weeks without a sweet treat, but word spread quickly when the corner store had a new box of bubble gum.

We can just about guarantee you that no reader is interested in government allotted distribution of food items. But any reader with a heart the right size will have no problem understanding both the sacrifice and the occasional excitement of forced rationing.

Don't get too caught up in the subject, verb structure. Life isn't predictable, so don't hesitate to throw your reader a little turn now and then. For instance, the improved sentence in the previous example varies both sentence length and structure.

 Be careful that you don't vary sentence length and structure to cover up bad grammar or underdeveloped examples. The readers will see right through that gimmick. Vary sentence length and structure to enhance your writing style, not to cover up your incompetence.

Use Personal Nouns

The best essay will create a relationship between the author and the reader. In other words, strive to keep the reader close. One way to do so is to use personal and very specific nouns. Think of the five human senses: sight, smell, hearing, taste, and touch. When possible, use nouns that refer to something the reader can see, smell, hear, taste, or touch (or be touched by).

Personal nouns are far superior to the more abstract nouns that leave the reader free to wander a bit—and yes, we meant wander, not wonder. If the reader has to think too hard about what you mean, you'll lose his or her interest, and that's bad. Keep the reader close and engaged.

Bad: We don't believe all the facts have been completely uncovered.

Better: You haven't told us the whole truth.

The first sentence doesn't make the circumstances clear. This sentence could be part of a scientific discovery process or part of a courtroom drama. The second sentence clarifies things quite a bit, just by using personal nouns:

➤ "You" have the facts—now we know who the writer is talking about.

➤ The facts are "the whole truth"—now we know what the writer is looking for. The whole truth is much more specific than facts.

Omit Most Prepositional Phrases

It might come as a shock, but most prepositional phrases can be omitted. Almost anytime a prepositional phrase describes a noun, you can omit the phrase and use the phrase's object as an adjective.

Prepositional phrases are fine and often necessary, but keep them to a minimum. Whereas, a long sentence can handle two or maybe three if pressed and truly necessary. More than that, and you probably need to rewrite the sentence.

Avoid using any prepositional phrases in a short sentence. You have perhaps five to eight words to make your point—a prepositional phrase probably isn't the best way to do that in a short sentence.

By definition, a prepositional phrase is a phrase that consists of a preposition, as well as a noun or pronoun that acts as the object of the preposition. Clear as mud, right? Simply put, prepositional phrases usually answer the question when or where. Mostly, they are unnecessary.

> *Bad*: The girl played outside the station in the sun while her parents sat at a table in the shade and waited, out of the sun.
>
> *Better*: The girl played outside the station in the sun while her parents sat at a shaded table and waited.
>
> *Better*: The girl played in the sun while her parents sat at a shaded table and waited.

Not every prepositional phrase is bad. Used correctly, they supply answers. The girl played outside the station, and she played in the sun. Her parents sat at a table, and they sat in the shade. Because the phrase "in the shade" actually defines where the parents sat, you can use the word "shade" as an adjective to describe where the parents sat. On the other hand, "the sun" doesn't describe the station, so you can't use the word "sun" as an adjective for station in the same way.

The third sentence isn't better than the second; it's just different. If you can assume that the reader will know that the girl and her parents are all outside the station, you can remove that reference altogether. In some cases, omitting the phrase would be preferable—you don't want to waste words repeating information the reader already has.

Use Active Voice

We could write a whole manual on the subject of active and passive voice, and we need to reduce the subject to just a few paragraphs. Here's the easiest way to discern the difference between the two. Active voice has an apparent subject; passive voice has an assumed subject. Now, that won't always be the case, but it's a good way to watch for those sneaky passive fragments. Remember, you won't have a spell-check that identifies passive passages during the exam.

The best way to catch passive voice is to catch weak verbs. Weak verbs aren't really verbs, they just play them on TV. Seriously, weak verbs are phrases used as verbs and easily replaced with active verbs. Watch for the following verb phrases:

➤ Replace *to be* when possible (that includes *be, am, are, is, was, were, begin,* and *been*).

➤ Be careful with past tense verbs such as *was* and *were*. When combined with another verb to create a verb phrase, it's probably passive voice.

➤ Omit *have* whenever possible. The word *have* is necessary, used correctly, but it often points to passive voice.

Passive: The eel was caught while Joe fished for trout.

Active: Joe caught an eel while fishing for trout.

If the subject of your sentence isn't performing the action, the sentence is passive. Rewrite the sentence so that the subject actually performs the action.

Passive: The performance of the small theatre company's rendition of *The Death of a Salesman* was applauded meekly by the audience.

Active: The audience applauded meekly at the end of the small company's performance of *The Death of a Salesman*.

Even if you didn't know the preceding example was passive, you'd still know it was bad. Not all of its problems are passive voice, but changing it to active voice certainly helps.

For Heavens Sake, Don't Apologize

If you say it, own it. You don't think, believe, or feel an essay. Let the thoughts and examples roll into your conclusion, and don't apologize or cushion your readers. Don't be embarrassed by what you have to share. It's unnecessary and distracting, and an apology weakens your position, and hence your essay. Avoid phrases such as

➤ In my opinion

➤ I, some, or many think

➤ I, some, or many believe

In fact, avoid using the personal pronoun I altogether. Anytime you feel compelled to say, "I..." stop, rethink, revise, and state your thought without using I. Your essay will be better for it. The reader isn't really all that interested in "you." The reader wants to know how your thoughts affect him or her. Don't grab the attention; be courteous to your reader and allow him or her the luxury of applying your thoughts to his or her own world.

> *Bad*: Many believe the issue of tort reform may become prominent in the next election.
>
> *Better*: Because of the rising cost of malpractice insurance, tort reform is sure to become an important issue in the next election.

Remember, this essay doesn't belong to some or many—it belongs to you. Don't drag anyone else into it. It's your position, support it with facts, events, and anecdotes. Save your opinions for the editorial pages, unless of course the essay question asks for your opinion.

Give Them a Powerful Ending

Ever left a movie thinking, "I didn't see that coming!" We don't expect you to work in a twist your reader doesn't see coming. In fact, by the time your reader reaches your final, and concluding paragraph, he or she should pretty much be able to surmise your position without even reading the conclusion.

This doesn't mean that the conclusion isn't important. In some cases, the conclusion is as simple as restating the thesis, without the expectations of development. You're closing the thought, not initiating it. After reading the conclusion, the reader should think, "Oh... yes, I see that." If the reader thinks, "But what about...," your conclusion is weak. You don't have to deal with all those buts in the actual essay, but you should at least deal with them in the conclusion.

Although what we're about to say is true for the SAT exam, it's also true for most any essay. Never, never, never use the phrase "in conclusion." You don't need to tell the readers you're through, they'll figure it out for themselves when they stop reading. Don't insult your reader.

Resist the urge to summarize your essay. Although this usage might be appropriate in some mediums, it isn't appropriate for your essay. This is your last chance to express your position to the readers. Don't waste it by summarizing what you've already told them.

Avoid using overused words that don't *really* support your position or add anything—such as the word "really" in this sentence's main clause. These words slip in easily, so be on the watch for them: very, great, really, and so on.

Find a Mentor

It's very difficult to edit your own writing. Your mind knows what it meant to say, and you believe that you've accomplished your task. That's why it's so difficult to find your own errors or improve your own work. For this portion of your preparation, we suggest that you find a mentor—a teacher or perhaps even a professional editor—who's willing to read and critique your writing examples.

When an essay is returned with corrections or suggestions, rewrite it, incorporating the editor's ideas, where appropriate. Only in this way can you retrain your brain to recognize and eventually avoid your weaknesses.

There's simply no substitution for practice where writing is concerned. Writing is like playing a musical instrument—the more you practice, the more proficient you will become. You may never write poetry or novels, but you should be able to express yourself succinctly and effectively through the written word.

When practicing, watch for words and phrases that you tend to repeat (overuse). Train yourself to omit them unless they're truly appropriate.

Exam Prep Questions

One road to good writing is knowing how to recognize bad writing. This section presents bad writing examples. Your job is to recognize what's wrong and fix it by choosing the best response or responses. (Some questions will have more than one problem.) When taking the actual SAT exam, each question will have only one response—the best response. Our practice exams in Chapters 10 and 12 reflect this format. For now, we just want to get the most action out of each question.

These are not actual SAT-like questions, but they will help you improve your writing skills!

1. Unhappily, Susan confronted the truth that her mother was insane.

   The sentence above demonstrates which of the following?
   (A) passive voice
   (B) concrete language
   (C) active voice
   (D) parallelism
   (E) abstract language

2. Imitation is the sincerest form of flattery.

   Which of the following statements is the strongest thesis for this statement?
   (A) Flattery is a good way to get what you want.
   (B) People often ridicule what they secretly admire.
   (C) People tend to dislike in others what they see in themselves.
   (D) Don't make fun of people; they'll think you like them.
   (E) Acting like someone is a way of showing your approval of their actions.

3. She strung together several beads of shades of pink and green and hung them across the branches of the tree.

   To make this sentence clearer and stronger, which of the phrases could be omitted or rewritten?
   (A) strung together
   (B) of shades
   (C) of pink and green
   (D) across the branches
   (E) of the tree
   (F) All of the above

4. Every cloud has a silver lining, and being dumped by a cad is probably a blessing in disguise.

   How would you make this sentence stronger?

   (A) Rewrite the cliché every cloud has a silver lining.
   (B) Substitute the slang dumped.
   (C) Substitute the slang cad.
   (D) Rewrite the cliché a blessing in disguise.
   (E) All of the above.

5. (1) Everything I ever really need to know about life, I learned on my granddad's farm. (2) Perhaps most importantly was that everything eliminates. (3) Manure is a fact of life. (4) No matter how far we run, no matter what direction we take, we will come face to face with manure on a regular basis. (5) It goes without saying that because of the nature of manure, we should avoid coming into contact with manure whenever possible. (6) As my granddad would say, if you kick it, you're going to wear it all day. (7) Avoid kicking manure whenever possible unless you want to smell of manure.

   Suppose the above paragraph is the introduction to an essay. It contains many examples of weak writing. Can you spot them and improve the paragraph?

   (A) It's great, I wouldn't change a thing.
   (B) It's wordy; I would make it shorter.
   (C) A few transitions wouldn't hurt.
   (D) It stinks, I'd start over.

6. The frivolous lawsuit was thrown out of court.

   How would you improve this sentence?

   (A) Substitute frivolous because it's used incorrectly.
   (B) Substitute frivolous because a smaller word would be better.
   (C) Do nothing; it's fine as is.
   (D) Change passive voice to active voice.

7. The deity is ubiquitous.

   What's wrong with this sentence?

   (A) Everything. I have no idea what it means. I'll have to use a dictionary to decipher it.
   (B) Nothing. it's a great sentence.
   (C) Deity should be proper case.
   (D) Ubiquitous is misspelled, and spelling counts.
   (E) None of the above.

8. I believe that the facts will show that it is better to give than to receive.

What's wrong with this sentence?

(A) It's apologetic and abstract.

(B) Nothing, I'd use it.

(C) It's too formal.

(D) None of the above.

9. To many, the works of great writers, such as Hemingway and Joyce, are lost because they lay unchosen and thus unread on the library shelves.

Is this sentence a good sentence? Would you improve it? If so, how?

(A) Use personal nouns.

(B) It's too abstract; I'd make it more concrete.

(C) It's a bit too formal.

(D) All of the above.

10. The best tasks for teleworking are those jobs that require little or no interaction with fellow co-workers.

Can you find a problem with this sentence?

(A) What's teleworking?

(B) It's okay as is.

(C) It's a little wordy.

(D) It's a little formal.

Essay

Think carefully about the issue presented in the excerpt and the assignment that follows.

> Statistics show that millions around the globe die each year from starvation. On the other hand, agriculture of the world's grasslands feeds billions.

Assignment: Do you think more land should be developed strictly for agricultural purposes? Write an essay that develops your point of view on this issue. Support your position with reasoning and examples taken from reading, studies, personal experience, or observation.

Answers to Exam Prep Questions

1. Answer E is correct. The entire sentence is subjective and fails to develop the abstract terms: unhappily and truth.

   A better version of this sentence might be—The orderlies held down Susan's mother so the nurse could inject the raving woman with a sedative. Susan sobbed quietly nearby as she watched her mother relax and then slip into a quiet sleep.

2. Either answer B or E is correct within the context of your essay. Whichever answer you choose, be sure to back it up with examples and argument. Answer D is weak. Answers A and C don't really deal with the actual topic.

3. Answer F is the most correct. Answer A is a redundant phrase. Answer B isn't completely necessary, but could be retained if critical to the thought. Answer C is a prepositional phrase that describes beads, so you can use the phrase as an adjective rather than a prepositional phrase. Answer D is unnecessary. If you hang the strands on the tree, across the branches is assumed. Answer E remains a prepositional phrase, but we did change the preposition from "of" to "on." There's more than one way to rewrite this sentence. It's okay to get a different answer. The aim is to produce a clear, thoughtful sentence.

   A better version of this sentence might be—After stringing the pink and green crystal beads, she hung the strands on the tree.

4. Answer E is the most correct. You should consider rewriting both cliché phrases and substituting the jargon. The word "cad" might not be considered jargon in some circles, so depending on your audience, cad might be an acceptable term. We would recommend you skip it for your SAT exam, unless you have a very specific reason for using it.

   A better version of this sentence might be—An unexpected breakup, although painful, is preferable to shabby treatment.

5. Answers B and C are correct. It is wordy and a little choppy. Answer A is incorrect because it could be better. Answer D is incorrect because although the subject matter may stink; the paragraph doesn't. The thoughts are sound; they just need work. We've made some improvements below. The following changes organize the thoughts and help hone in on the actual topic. Compare your improved version to ours:

➤ **Sentence 2**—<u>Perhaps</u> is an apologetic word; omit it.

Rewrite <u>was that</u>. Use a personal noun or pronoun to correct the passive/abstract statement. The existing syntax isn't exactly wrong; it's just awkward.

Substitute <u>eliminates</u> with poops. Eliminates is way too stuffy for the discussion. In this case, poop is a much better word, even if it seems a bit off color. It will get your reader's attention and even add a bit of humor.

➤ **Sentence 3**—Delete the whole sentence; it repeats the prior thought.

➤ **Sentence 4**—Change the words <u>run</u> and <u>take</u> to go and roam; both terms are more appropriate to the topic and work better together.

<u>Face to face</u> is a bit of a cliché; it isn't horrible, but you should try to make your point without using it.

Omit <u>on a regular basis</u>; in this case, it is assumed.

➤ **Sentence 5**—Add <u>however</u> to transition between the idea that you can't avoid manure, but you should at least be careful.

Completely delete this sentence. It's wordy, and the previous thought flows well into the granddad's statement without the interruption.

➤ **Sentence 6**—Replace <u>would say</u> with "used to say" or some other more active verb phrase; "would say" is weak.

➤ **Sentence 7**—Insert appropriate quotation marks to make it clear that the grandfather is speaking.

Add the transition <u>in other words</u> to make it clear that the subsequent statement clarifies the previous thought.

Last sentence is too wordy.

A better version of this paragraph might be—Everything I ever really need to know about life, I learned on my granddad's farm. Most importantly, I learned that everything poops. No matter how far we go, no matter what direction we roam, we will encounter manure. However, as my granddad used to say, "If you kick it, you're going to wear it all day." In other words, don't kick manure unless you want to stink of it.

6. Answer D is correct. The statement is in passive voice, which you should avoid. To rewrite, use a personal noun or an active verb.

Remember, the verb "was" often points to passive voice. Answers A and B are incorrect because, as used, the term "frivolous" is correct and the best word for the job. Answer C is incorrect because you can improve the sentence.

A better version of this sentence might be—The judge threw out the frivolous lawsuit.

7. Answer A is the most correct, although you may not really need a dictionary. However, it is unnecessarily obtuse. Answer B is wrong because the sentence is bad. Answer C is incorrect because "deity" should not be proper case. Answer D is incorrect because "ubiquitous" is spelled correctly. The readers will forgive you one misspelled word as long as you use the word correctly and it's the best word for the job. Answer E is incorrect because A is the correct answer.

A better version of this sentence might be—God is everywhere.

8. Answers A and C are correct. Don't use "I believe"—it's redundant (it's your essay), and it's apologetic. Believe is also an abstract term, as is the second phrase about giving and receiving. Answer B is incorrect; we hope you wouldn't use it. Answer D is incorrect as A and C are both correct answers.

The following uses concrete terms to develop the notion that it's better to give than to receive: The old woman closed her eyes and rocked to the rhythm of the caretaker's rhythmic voice. Her voice often cracked as she read aloud the old woman's poems. The old woman was sharing the most precious and tragic moments of her life. Sometimes, the caretaker had to stop to smother the emotion that swept over her as she read. When the old woman was finally asleep, the caretaker continued to read alone.

Granted, our improved example has little to do with the original sentence, but that's because the original sentence is so horribly abstract. It means absolutely nothing. In the above passage, is there really any doubt that by giving of her time, the caretaker received a far greater gift in return? There's no need to tell us that it's greater to give than receive. You could rewrite this sentence any number of ways, and that's the heart of the problem.

9. Answer D is correct. The sentence is awkward and although the thought is clearer than many abstract sentences, it could be improved on that account. Who does "many" refer to? What does the writer

mean by "lost"? Is the library reference really necessary to make the writer's point?

A better version of this sentence might be—Students often avoid the works of great writers such as Hemingway and Joyce.

10. Answers A, C, and D are all correct. Teleworking is a technical term that needs an additional definition—either directly or indirectly. The sentence is also a little wordy and formal. Answer B is incorrect because you can improve it.

A better version of this sentence might be—Teleworking is a growing trend that allows employees to work from home. Tasks that require little or no input from other employees are well suited for teleworking.

The Critical Reading Section: Sentence Completions

Terms you'll need to understand:

✓ Context clues
✓ Synonym
✓ Antonym
✓ Transitional phrases
✓ Root word
✓ Prefix
✓ Suffix

Techniques you'll need to master:

✓ How to determine a word's meaning by breaking it down into individual elements.
✓ How to determine a word's meaning using clues, such as synonyms and antonyms.
✓ Using the most appropriate and logical word.

The Critical Reading portion of the SAT exam will contain 19 sentence completion questions. These questions test your ability to deduce a word's meaning from its usage. You don't have to have a huge vocabulary to do well on this section, but it helps.

When you encounter a word you don't know, read the sentence carefully first to determine the sentence's purpose. Understanding the sentence will help you choose the most appropriate word or words to complete the sentence. That's the single best piece of advice you'll get in this chapter—read the complete sentence carefully before you do anything else.

The astute reader might notice that we seem to repeat ourselves throughout this chapter. That's partially true, but there's a reason for doing so. On the surface, this entire chapter is about vocabulary, but taking command of new words isn't as simple as memorizing thousands of words. The true strength to acing this section of the exam lies in your ability to use context and reason to determine the meaning of words that may be unfamiliar to you.

Everyone interprets data and learns differently. This section isn't as cut and dry as the others—we can't provide one rule or method that will work for everyone. Therefore, you'll find a few different systems. Each one is unique but similar to the others.

In the end, this is what you'll find. Sometimes it takes the entire sentence to determine the missing word's meaning. Sometimes, the sentence uses specific words to give clues. You'll use both methods on the exam.

Improving your vocabulary won't just benefit this section of the exam. A substantial vocabulary, used correctly, will improve your essay score. Just one word of warning—if you don't have full command of a word, don't use it in your essay. The readers will not be impressed by inappropriate usage.

Sentence Completion

The sentence completion section of the exam is about vocabulary. This part of the exam tests your ability to understand complex sentences. The test will present a sentence that's missing one or two words. You'll be expected to choose the appropriate word or words.

There are two types of sentence completion questions:

➤ *Vocabulary-in-context*—You'll discern the missing words by recognizing how the missing words relate to what's there. By considering the context of their use, you'll determine the appropriate words.

➤ *Logic*—You must know the meaning of the missing word, how it's used within context, and understand the sentence's purpose.

The two types of questions seem very similar, but there's a subtle difference. The words in the logic questions are generally simpler words that you probably know well. The question tests your ability to use those words correctly. These questions can be a tad tricky. You must read them carefully to make sure that you respond correctly. The logic questions will help you determine the right word even if you might be unfamiliar with it using methods we'll discuss later in this chapter.

 Lots of words have more than one meaning, and some of those meanings can be rather obscure. This part of the exam will stick with the standard definitions. You won't be expected to know little known uses for a word.

The General Process

Gleaning the best response isn't guesswork. As a general rule, we recommend the following process:

1. Read the entire sentence and actually say "blank" for the missing words. This process helps you integrate the missing word with the rest of the sentence.

2. If you encounter any unfamiliar words in the actual sentence, try to discern their meanings before attempting to discern the missing word or words.

3. Before reading the answers, try to fill in the blank using your own words.

4. After choosing a word of your own, review the answers for a word that's similar to yours. If you don't find an exact match, choose the word that's the closest to your word.

5. If you don't find a good match, repeat the sentence and fill in the blank with each response. Be sure to review each response—don't stop with the first one that seems right.

Let's look at an example:

Alexis' artwork was _____ by those who admired it.

   (A) feared
   (B) lauded
   (C) criticized
   (D) purchased
   (E) misunderstood

How should you break down this question? The following items will help you:

1. Say the sentence as follows: "Alexis' artwork was blank by those who admired it."

2. More than likely, you probably know all the existing words. If not, take the time right now to look up any unfamiliar words.

3. Before reading the possible responses, can you think of any words that might fill the blank appropriately? The word "admired" is one clue—you can quickly discern that the missing word is most likely a positive word such as complimented.

4. Search the list and see if you can find any word that's close to one of your own. Lauded is a synonym for complimented, so at first guess, that would seem the best choice.

5. If you're still stuck, repeat the sentence using each response. In this case, step 5 isn't necessary.

Answer B is the correct response. Someone who admires artwork might praise or speak well of it. Answers A, C, D, and E are all incorrect because none of them convey the positive tone required by the word admired.

In this case, you must know the meaning of the word "lauded." However, you could, by process of elimination, come to the conclusion that lauded is the correct response. This can be a bit tricky with logic questions. In this example, "purchased" might seem like the right response if you didn't know the meaning of the word lauded. Just remember that you are always looking for the best response, not just any response that fits. You can't assume that every purchaser will admire the artwork. Some might purchase it as an investment or even as a gift—purchased is not the best response.

Using Keywords

Introductory and transitional words are important. They can completely change the sentence's meaning. They can also help you understand the sentence. For instance, the following words indicate a conflict, contradiction, or contrast between the two main thoughts:

➤ Although

➤ But

➤ Even though/so

➤ However

➤ Yet

Let's cover some examples to solidify this:

> <u>Although</u> Alexis sold all of her work, she remained relatively unknown in the art community.

> Alexis never received raving reviews in the art periodicals, <u>but</u> she sold all of her work.

> <u>Even though</u> Alexis wasn't well known by her peers, she was popular with art collectors.

> The art gallery turned down Alexis' request for a showing. <u>However</u>, she sold all of her work through word of mouth.

> Alexis hasn't made a name for herself among the elite in the art community, <u>yet</u> she continues to sell every piece almost as soon as the paint dries.

All of these sentences have a similar purpose—to express Alexis' success even though she is not a big name in the art community. The conflict is her seeming monetary success despite the fact that she is not yet a well-known artist. Now, let's take the first sentence and format it as a question.

> Although Alexis sold all of her work, she remained relatively _____ in the art community.
> (A) unhappy
> (B) anonymous
> (C) unknown
> (D) popular
> (E) strange

You already know that C is the correct answer, but let's work through the other possible responses. A is incorrect because it isn't the best choice. Yes, Alexis may be unhappy with her position, or lack of position, in the art community, but that sentiment doesn't match the fact that she's selling all her work. Besides, logically it just isn't a good fit. Answer B is incorrect, although it might fit. It's incorrect because nothing in the first part of the sentence suggests that she's working anonymously. Remember, the clues are in the sentence. Answer D is incorrect because the word "although" suggests a conflict between the two ideas. Hence, the word "popular" simply doesn't make sense. Answer E is like Answer B; it just doesn't fit logically. Answer C is the best choice because it's the best extension of the conflict suggested by the word "although." You know that she's selling her work, despite something.

The following transitional words and phrases indicate the result of the first clause, which will help you determine the most appropriate response:

➤ As a result

➤ Consequently

➤ Resulting in

➤ Subsequently

➤ Subsequent to

➤ Therefore

The following sentences help demonstrate this:

<u>As a result</u> of talent and hard work, Alexis was becoming a successful artist.

Alexis put in long hours at the easel. <u>Consequently</u>, she was quite successful.

Alexis' hard work and talent were <u>resulting in</u> a measured success as an artist.

Alexis put in long hours at the easel. <u>Therefore</u>, she was quite successful.

Like the last example, all of these sentences have a similar purpose—to express Alexis' success. This time instead of conflict, the sentences express the result of her hard work and talent—the result being success. Now, let's turn one of these sentences into an example question.

<u>As a result</u> of talent and hard work, Alexis was becoming a(n) _____ artist.

(A) triumphant
(B) anonymous
(C) successful
(D) profitable
(E) strange

Again, C is the correct answer because it completes the sentence best. Answers A and B are incorrect. Nothing in the sentence logically leads us to the words "triumphant" or "anonymous." Triumphant suggests some kind of battle or fight. Anonymous suggests she remains unknown, which is probably a negative to an aspiring artist, and we know that the sentence's tone is positive. Answer D is incorrect, although it might fit. She may be profitable, but you're assuming that she's selling her work. Success doesn't necessarily mean wealth. Answer E is incorrect because it doesn't logically complete the sentence's purpose.

Most likely, you won't encounter a question in which two answers could fulfill the sentence's purpose so well. In this example, both "successful" and "profitable" could fill the bill, although "successful" does have the edge. Nothing in the sentence implies that she's making money. You'd need more information before you could assume that she's making a profit from her hard work and talent.

Watch for sentences in which one clause negates another. Most negative words are well known to you already: *no, not, none, nothing,* and so on. However, their use can completely change the meaning of a sentence. Consider the following examples:

<u>Nothing</u> meant as much to Alexis as <u>not</u> having to explain her work.

It can be easy to misconstrue the meaning of such a sentence. Remove the word "not" and the sentence has a completely different meaning—Alexis enjoys talking and explaining her work. When you encounter such a sentence, try removing one of the negative words. Doing so will help you determine the sentence's purpose. In this case, you learn that Alexis doesn't want to explain her work.

Not making a decision is not the same as being _____.
(A) adamant
(B) confused
(C) decisive
(D) indecisive
(E) inconclusive

Answer D is the best response. In a roundabout way, the sentence is defining the word "indecisive." Specifically, the sentence explains that not making a decision isn't a definition of indecisive. Remove the second "not" to read the opposite of what the sentence really means: Not making a decision is the same as being indecisive. Reading the opposite statement will help you find the most appropriate response. Answers A, B, C, and E are incorrect. It doesn't make much sense to use any of these words within the context of "not making a decision."

Such a sentence can be confusing, and truthfully, there are better ways to make this statement. Regardless, you'll probably encounter one on the sentence completion section of the exam. Read carefully.

Employing Elimination

When the sentence requires you to fill in two blanks, you can usually complete the sentence after determining just one of the words. Once you know one of the words, you can determine the other by eliminating the answers that don't correspond appropriately.

Even if you think you've found the right answer, be sure to read all the answers. The exam expects you to choose the best answer, not the first one that you think fits.

Once you settle on an answer, reread the sentence, filling in the blanks accordingly. Sometimes reading the completed sentence will expose mistakes in your logic. Take a look at an example:

> The celebrities were accustomed to being chauffeured about at the festival and were understandably _____ when the service was _____.
>
> (A) content . . eradicated
> (B) disconcerted . . sporadic
> (C) displeased . . unrequited
> (D) irritated . . terminated
> (E) concerned . . unresolved

Now, let's use the process of elimination to determine the right response. A is out—they wouldn't be content if the service was eliminated. Even if the first word had made sense, eradicated is a rather strong word for this particular sentence. Answer B is a possibility—the celebrities might be confused if the service isn't predictable, but let's continue. There might be a better response. Remember, you are expected to choose the best response, not the first one that might do. Frankly, there are better ways to express that particular sentiment, so that's a clue that there might be a better response. Answer C is incorrect because the word "unrequited" doesn't make sense within the context of the second phrase. Answer D is good—the celebrities would definitely be irritated if the service were terminated. This could be the right answer, but there's one more. Answer E is incorrect. The word "unresolved" doesn't make sense within the context of the second phrase. So far, you've eliminated three responses: A, C, and E. When comparing B and D, you can see that D is definitely the stronger of the two, so D is the correct answer.

Occasionally, you may find yourself doubting your first answer. Change your first answer only if you're positive that you've made a mistake. If there's any doubt in your mind and you're waffling between two answers, trust your first instincts. Chances are, it's the correct one.

If you can't find the right answer, compare the sentence's tone with that of the answers. Remember to consider the logical relationship used between the clauses. If that doesn't work, restate the sentence using your own words. Paraphrasing the sentence will force you to concentrate on the logical relationships and hopefully highlight clues.

Using Logic

By logically dissecting each sentence, you should be able to fill in the blanks. It will help if you can remember that there are four logical relationships in a complex sentence (a sentence with two clauses):

➤ Contrast

➤ Support

➤ Cause and effect

➤ Definition

All four relationships are fairly self-explanatory, but recognizing them can help you discern the best answer. Careful reading is imperative.

Some sentences will employ more than one logical relationship. Distinguishing each relationship is critical to picking the right answer. Specific words and phrases can clue you in to the type of relationship in use, such as those found in the following list:

➤ *Supporting keywords*—additionally, also, besides, furthermore, in addition, likewise, moreover, similarly, and so on

➤ *Contrasting keywords*—although, but, conversely, despite, even though, however, in contrast, in spite of, instead of, nevertheless, nonetheless, on the contrary, on the other hand, rather, yet, and so on

➤ *Definition keywords*—am, are, as, especially, for example, for instance, including, to be, is, means, refers to, that is, and so on

➤ *Cause and effect keywords*—as a result, because, consequently, due to, if…then, in order to, since, so, subsequently, therefore, and so on

A subcategory of both the supporting and definition relationships is restatement. Sometimes an author will clue you in by restating the word's meaning. More often than not, this type of relationship is supportive, but it can fall into the definition category. Look for the following keywords: that is, or, in other words, in a nutshell, and so on.

Semicolons and colons always indicate a supporting relationship, but they aren't interchangeable. Semicolons are used when the second clause develops the first. Colons are used when the second clause explains the first.

Once you've defined the relationship, a little reasoning can usually determine the meaning of any unfamiliar words. Look for the context clues. A *synonym* is a word that means roughly the same thing and indicates a supportive relationship. Note this in the following example:

> The _____ award was a *fortunate* offering just as the author was looking for a new publisher.
>
> (A) unexpected
> (B) prestigious
> (C) elite
> (D) monumental
> (E) auspicious

Answer E is the best answer—it fits without adding any additional nuances to the context. The word "fortunate" is a synonym for auspicious. If you didn't know the meaning of "auspicious," the word "fortunate" would at least point you in the right direction. Answers A, B, and D work, but none is as good a fit as E when considering the relationship between the missing word and the synonym fortunate that further defines it. Answers B and D both imply subtleties that are supported by the sentence. Answer C is incorrect because it just doesn't make sense.

This sentence doesn't use a supportive keyword, but there is a supportive relationship between the missing word and the synonym "fortunate."

An *antonym* is a word that conveys the opposite meaning and indicates a contrasting relationship.

> Despite the child's angelic appearance, she was quite _____.
>
> (A) impish
> (B) naughty
> (C) wicked
> (D) harmless
> (E) playful

Answer B is the best response. In this example, angelic is an antonym for naughty. The word "despite" indicates a contrasting relationship, so you know that you're looking for an antonym for "angelic." Answers A and C are incorrect. Either might fit, but answer B is a better fit than both. Answer A implies a playfulness that the sentence doesn't support. Answer C is far too strong. Answers D and E are incorrect because you're looking for an antonym, and both "harmless" and "playful" could be considered synonyms for angelic within the context of the sentence.

A definition relationship offers clues in the form of a literal translation or alternative for the missing word and indicates a defining or a supportive relationship.

_____ is the expensive process of separating the salt from sea water.
(A) Desalinization
(B) Evaporation
(C) Mining
(D) Ionization
(E) Fusion

There are no tricks here. Answer A is the correct response. The word "is" clues you in right away that you're looking at a definition relationship. There are no other clues other than the word's definition. Answers B, C, D, and E are all incorrect because they do not fit the definition.

The cause and effect relationship is usually easy to spot. There's an action and a reaction. You might think of this relationship as a before and after sequence, although you can't take the notion of time literally when doing so. Often, the cause and effect comes in more than one sentence, which is fine in your essay, but you won't run across any two-sentence examples on the exam. When trying to determine the missing word in a cause and effect sentence, think of the natural flow of the sentence's purpose. (Keep in mind that a cause and effect sentence doesn't have to include one of the keywords or phrases listed earlier.)

Poor planning and a lack of resources were at the root of the company's _____.
(A) success
(B) origin
(C) demise
(D) termination
(E) confinement

Answer C is the correct answer. You know right away that something bad happened to the business because "poor planning and a lack of resources" are negative attributes. Something bad happened (effect) to the business *as a result* of these things (cause). Answer A is incorrect because you know that the missing word should have a negative connotation. Answers B and E are incorrect because they're illogical. Answer D is incorrect even though it might tempt you. Termination carries a strong sense of maliciousness or purpose; the word is simply too strong for this sentence.

When using this method to determine the missing word, read the sentence carefully. Then, use the words around the missing word to help determine the missing word's meaning.

Building an SAT Vocabulary

Easily, the best way to ace this portion of the test is to take as much guess-work out of the process as possible. You can arm yourself by building your vocabulary. This next section contains words that you might encounter on the SAT exam. This list is not comprehensive and should not be your only resource. Instead, we offer the list as a means of introducing you to the process of building a large and flexible vocabulary.

 NOTE Pearson Education publishes a number of excellent vocabulary workbooks, such as *Building College Vocabulary Strategies*, and *Basic College Vocabulary Strategies* by Darlene Pabis and Arden Hamer.

We suggest that you commit a few new words to memory every day. Then, do yourself a big favor—use the words in your daily life. That's really the only way you can take command of these new words—you must use them!

Along with each new word, we include its pronunciation, a definition, any synonyms (when applicable), and an example sentence. To use the guide, begin by saying the word out loud. If you don't already know the word, break it down and try to determine its meaning by reviewing its root word, prefix, and suffix. Next, review the actual definition and finally, use the word as much as you can during the next few days.

Word Elements

You can't possibly memorize every word that might appear on the exam. The next best thing is to be familiar with elements. By elements, we mean the pieces that make up each word, such as the prefix, suffix, and root word. Knowing these elements can help you determine an unfamiliar word's mean-ing just by breaking it down into these components. Table 3.1 is a list of the most common elements.

Table 3.1 Common Word Elements	
a	without or not
ad	toward; near
al	relating or pertaining to
ambi	both; around
an	without or not

(continued)

Table 3.1	Common Word Elements *(continued)*
ance	state of being full of
ante	before
arch	ruler
archy	one who rules
ate	make or pertaining to
bi	two
cata	down
co	together
col	together
con	together
contr	against or opposite
corp	body
counter	against or opposite
cracy	government
crat	leader
de	down, away, or apart
dec	ten
di	two; away from
dic	speak or say
e	out
ec	out
em	out; into or in
en	into or in; to put in
ence	state of being full of
ex	out
fac	make
fer	one that bears
her	to stick
hyper	over or beyond
hypo	under or below
ian	person who
ic	relating or pertaining to
ify	make
il	not; in or into

(continued)

Table 3.1	Common Word Elements *(continued)*
im	not
in	not or in
ir	not
ion	act of or state of
intra	within or into
inter	between
ist	person who
ium	relating or pertaining to
ive	relating, belonging, or tending to; of
lat	side
min	small
mit	to send
mono	one
mor	manners or behavior
mort	death
non	not
nov	new; nine
ology	the study of
omni	all
pan	all; also
pathy	feelings
ped	foot; child
penta	five
philo	love of
pod	foot
port	carry
pre	before; preceding
quad	four
re	back or again
sion	act of or state of
sive	relating, belonging, or tending to; of
soph	wise, wisdom
spec	see
temp	time

(continued)

Table 3.1	Common Word Elements *(continued)*
term	end
tion	act of or state of
tive	taking part
trans	across or change
tri	three
un	not
uni	one
vi	life
viv	life

Learning Cues

It's hard to associate a word element with anything meaningful, so using them as clues to discerning the meaning of an unfamiliar word can be difficult. There are a few ways to help commit these elements to memory.

Write each element and then list as many words as you can think of that use this element. You might be surprised how easy this technique is once you get started. Often, what seems unfamiliar really isn't—it's just temporarily out of context. In other words, you already use these elements all the time within words. You're just not used to seeing them by themselves. Once you begin to evaluate these elements individually, you'll find it easier to dismantle unfamiliar words and determine their meanings by reviewing their individual elements. For example, the element "bi" has some familiar words associated with it.

bi- two
bicycle
biped
bicep
bicentennial
biannually
bimonthly
biweekly

You probably already know all of these words, but if you didn't, just knowing that the element "bi" means two would help. For instance, if you know that "bi" means two and "ped" means foot, it's easy to determine that the elemental definition of the word biped is "two feet."

Use index cards or a dedicated notebook for these lists. Regardless of how you store them, don't throw these lists away. Once a week, or so, review your lists and add new words as you think of them. Doing so will help further commit these elements to memory.

Some elements can work as a prefix, a suffix, or even a root word. When this is the case, a simple list isn't always adequate. Write the word in the middle of the index card or notebook page. Then, list the words around the element. The order doesn't really matter. Visually, what matters is that you see the element surrounded by words.

Vocabulary Words to Learn

To help you in your quest for SAT language mastery, we've supplied some sample words to learn. It's important to realize that this list isn't comprehensive; you'll probably encounter other words on the reading portion of the SAT and use other words in your essay. But we think these words are indicative of the difficulty that the SAT authors will expect you to know. Rather than spend time trying to memorize a list of thousands of vocabulary words, we suggest that you learn a shorter list well and use them where they're appropriate. We italicized sections of some example sentences to help illustrate the word's definition.

aberrant (ăb´-ər-ənt)—*adjective*—irregular, unusual; deviating from what's normally expected or accepted.

Your daughter's **aberrant** behavior has *ostracized her from the entire group*.

abridge (ə-brij´)—*verb*—shorten, edit, condense; to condense or reduce the length of.

She realized that reading the **abridged** version of the Dickens classic was a mistake—there were questions on the test she couldn't answer.

accelerate (ăk-sĕl´-ə-rāt)—*verb*—hasten; to increase speed.

The engines **accelerate** briefly to change the craft's trajectory.

acute (ə-kyo͞ot´)—*adjective*—keen, discriminating, severe; impossible to ignore.

The stomach pain was so **acute** she ended up in the *emergency room*.

adage (ăd´-ĭj)—*noun*—saying, proverb, axiom; well-known or recognized saying with a moral connotation.

The teacher preferred to spout old **adages** to make the kids think instead of preaching literal lessons that the kids often found boring.

adversary (ăd´-vər-sĕr´-ē)—*noun*—enemy, opponent; someone who opposes you; an enemy.

They are often friendly **adversaries** in their quest for the perfect *chess match*.

adversity (ăd-vur´-sĭ-tē)—*noun*—difficulty, hard times; a state of hardship or misfortune.

Adversity can build character and integrity—if you survive it.

advocate (ăd´-və-kāt)—*noun, verb*—supporter, believer, activist; a person who takes up another's cause or lends support to another. The action of taking up another's cause or lending support to.

Family courts have **advocates** who *represent just the children* in each case.

The principal **advocates** free lunches for all school children.

aesthetic (ĕs-thĕt´-ĭk)—*adjective*—visual, artistic; concerning the appreciation of beauty or good taste.

Her designs were always an **aesthetic** blend of the client's preferences.

albatross (ăl´-bə-trôs)—*noun*—millstone, burden, impediment; an obstacle.

Once the prospective employer saw her resume, he rescinded his previous offer, calling her an **albatross** because so *many companies she had worked for had gone out of business.*

ambiguous (ăm-bĭg´-yoo-əs)—*adjective*—vague, uncertain; doubtful or uncertain; unclear.

Her feelings were a bit **ambiguous** and neither fellow was quite sure where he stood.

ambivalent (ăm-bĭv´-ə-lənt)—*adjective*—undecided, unsure; indecisive; not sure.

Her **ambivalent** attitude toward the company made her a bad candidate for the management position.

ameliorate (ə-mēl´-yə-rāt´)—*verb*—improve, remodel; to improve or make better.

> Management **ameliorated** some of the plant's infrastructure after gaining a new and rather large client.

amoral (ā-môr´-əl)—*adjective*—neutral; the state of being neither moral nor immoral.

> Many New Age philosophers are **amoral** and *deny* the *existence of good and evil* as opposing energies that rule the universe.

analogy (ə-năl´-ă-jē)—*noun*—equivalence, parallel, comparison; a statement or story that expresses similar attributes.

> He explained how an airplane flies by using an **analogy** to show how air escaping from a toy balloon propels the balloon through the air.

anarchy (ăn´-ər-kē)—*noun*—disorder, chaos, lawlessness; the absence of authority.

> **Anarchy** followed on the heels of the *retreating soldiers*.

annotate (ăn´-ō-tāt´)—*verb*—gloss, explain; to add a short explanation or to paraphrase a passage.

> I decided to purchase the book after reading the **annotations** at the *beginning* of the first few chapters.

apathy (ăp´-ə-thē)—*noun*—indifference; lack of interest or concern.

> Her **apathy** toward her fellow students eventually made her an outcast.

archetype (är´-ki-tīp)—*noun*—prototype, model, epitome; the original model for an accepted or widely used pattern or thought.

> Psychologists use symbolic character **archetypes** to explain dream characters and their actions.

articulate (är-tĭk´-yə-lāt)—*verb* or *adjective*—eloquent, clear, fluent; the ability to speak clearly, coherently, and enunciate properly; the act of speaking clearly and coherently.

> She was an **articulate** speaker, making her the *perfect candidate for the debate team*.

bevy (bĕv´-ē)—*noun*—crowd, horde, multitude; a group.

The **bevy** of shoppers pressed against the door waiting for the shop to open.

catalyst (kăt´-l-ĭst)—*noun*—method, means, mechanism; what causes change.

Her mother's caustic remarks were the **catalyst** to their estrangement.

caustic (kô´-stĭk)—*adjective*—cutting, sarcastic, biting; harsh or offensive.

Her **caustic** remarks *hurt* the child more than a spanking.

celestial (cə-lĕs´-chəl)—*adjective*—extraterrestrial, outer space, heavenly; relating to the sky or heavens.

The *astronomers* studied the newly discovered **celestial** body to determine if it was a *planet* or an anomaly.

chronic (krŏn´-ĭk)—*adjective*—continual, persistent; constant or frequent recurrence.

Chronic back pain *kept the old woman in a chair* most of the time.

coerce (kō-ûrs´)—*verb*—bully, intimidate, force; to force thought or action through pressure or intimidation.

The gang members **coerced** the younger neighborhood kids into keeping the members' secrets.

cognitive (kŏg´-ni-tĭv)—*adjective*—thinking, aware; being aware of or knowledge.

Although the patient was **comatose**, the doctors suspected he had cognitive skills.

coherent (kō-hîr´-ənt)—*adjective*—consistent, rational, lucid; parts that stick together in a logical, concise order.

The prosecutor presented a **coherent** story, but the jury still found the defendant innocent.

collaborate (kə-lăb´-ə-rāt)—*verb*—cooperate; to work together; to share information toward a larger goal.

The teams were ordered to **collaborate** until they found a solution to the company's financial difficulties.

compensate (kŏmʹ-pən-sāt)—*verb*—reimburse, pay; to balance; to allow for.

Her attitude more than **compensated** for her lack of ability.

comply (kəm-plīʹ)—*verb*—obey, conform; to follow a suggested or mandated set of instructions or wishes.

It was easy to **comply** with her mother's wishes because they both wanted the same thing.

component (kəm-pōʹ-nənt)—*noun*—part, section, piece; a part of a bigger whole.

All the **components** you need are stored in our warehouse.

connotative (kŏnʹə-tāʹ-tĭv)—*adjective*—meaning; the association of a feeling with a word.

The word mother isn't **connotative** of home, hearth, and apple pie to every one; some of us don't like our mothers.

consolidate (kən-sŏlʹ-ĭ-dāt)—*verb*—To combine or unite into one group, unit, or system.

The two small companies **consolidated** their resources.

contend (kən-tĕndʹ)—*verb*—compete, challenge; argue, assert; assert something to be true.

The lawyer **contended** that his client was innocent.

contingent (kən-tĭnʹ-jənt)—*adjective*—dependent, conditional; dependent on circumstances; conditional.

The outdoor wedding is **contingent** *on fair weather*.

contrary (kŏn-trĕrʹ-ē)—*adjective*—adverse, opposed; opposed to or opposite in position.

She found her new daughter-in-law's behavior very **contrary** but was gracious nonetheless.

controversy (kŏn´-trə-vur´-sē)—*noun*—argument, debate; a serious argument or problem usually in the public domain.

The alderman's stand on polygamy started quite a **controversy** in the usually quiet community.

counterpart (koun´-tər-pärt)—*noun*—corresponding, equal; a person performing or serving in a similar role.

Her **counterpart** at the company received a higher salary and even had an assistant.

covert (kō-v´ərt)—*adjective*—secret, clandestine, stealthy; concealed or secret.

The elite squad was trained in **covert** activities.

crucial (krōō´-shəl)—*adjective*—significant, vital; very important; vital or of value to.

Those reports are **crucial** to the department; *they can't be late.*

curtail (kər-tāl´)—*verb*—limit; to cut short or reduce.

He had to **curtail** his campaigning activities long enough to recover from the flu.

deceptive (dĭ-sĕp´-tĭv)—*adjective*—misleading, dishonest; to hide the truth.

The defense lawyer was able to expose the plantiff's **deceptive** testimony.

decimate (dĕs´-ə-māt)—*verb*—destroy; to destroy, or use up completely.

The tornado **decimated** several towns.

decipher (dĭ-sī´-fər)—*verb*—translate, interpret, decode; interpret illegible script.

Deciphering *ancient script* was the librarian's real expertise.

deem (dēm)—*verb*—believe, judge; believe to be true.

Our forefathers **deemed** that all men were created equal, although they failed to put that *belief* to practice.

deficit (dĕf´-ĭ-sĭt)—*noun*—shortage, arrears; lack of something; having less than required.

The company's third quarter reports showed a **deficit,** and *layoffs* would definitely follow.

deleterious (dĕl´-ĭ-tir´-ē-əs)—*adjective*—harmful, deadly, lethal; having a harmful effect.

Bee stings can have a **deleterious** effect on Neal.

demeanor (dĭ-mē´-nər)—*noun*—behavior, character; one's behavior or attitude.

Her **demeanor** was usually childlike, but stomping her feet was immature.

demise (dĭ-mīz´)—*noun*—end, death; the death or end of something or someone.

His dreams of being a famous writer came to a quick **demise** after reading the editor's insulting remarks on his manuscript.

demure (dĭ-myo͝or´)—*adjective*—modest, shy, reserved; modest in behavior and dress.

The **demure** girl hesitated *to remove her hat and gloves* in public.

denote (dĭ-nōt´)—*verb*—to name, designate, or represent.

John used different colored pushpins to **denote** sales regions on the map.

depletion (dĭ-plē´-shən)—*noun*—reduction, weakening; a reduced amount or size.

Some environmentalists feel we are **depleting** our natural resources too quickly.

deride (dĭ-rīd´)—*verb*—scoff, mock, disparage; to ridicule or laugh at in a menacing manner.

The editor **derided** the young author's work, without consideration of the author's lack of experience.

derive (dĭ-rīv´)—*verb*—get, obtain; to gain or obtain; to determine.

He **derived** pleasure from his paintings.

designate (dĕz´-ĭg-nāt)—*verb*—select, delegate, allocate, assign; to indicate or otherwise specify or point out.

The committee **designated** a student monitor for each hall.

detriment (dĕt´-rə-mənt)—*noun*—disadvantage, damage; personal harm or undoing.

To his own **detriment,** he continued his rant against his boss in front of his colleagues.

disparage (dĭ-spăr´-ĭj)—*verb*—belittle, mock, ridicule; to speak of negatively or disrespectfully.

Disparaging your boss at the weekly meeting is not a good idea, *no matter how badly the boss is running things.*

disperse (dĭ-spûrs´)—*verb*—dissolve, separate, diffuse; to distribute or divide.

The remaining funds will be **dispersed** equally *among* the departments.

emigrate (ĕm´-ĭ-grāt)—*verb*—To leave your country, move abroad.

Many Russian Jews **emigrated** *from the Pale* during the early twentieth century.

Don't confuse emigrate and immigrate. To immigrate means to enter a country legally. Emigrate means to leave a country.

empathy (ĕm´-pə-thē)—*noun*—understanding, sympathy, compassion; sharing feelings through thought or imagination rather than experience.

The nurse was **empathic** to the victims' pain, and it was *difficult for her to maintain her composure* during the worst of the disaster.

empirical (ĕm-pîr´-ĭ-kəl)—*adjective*—experimental; based on observation or experience.

The theory is backed up by **empirical** evidence *gathered in the field.*

endanger (ĕn-dān´-jər)—*verb*—jeopardize, imperil; to put in danger.

Social services felt the mother had **endangered** her children by *leaving them alone.*

endorse (ĕn-dôrs´)—*verb*—support, sanction, approve; to give approval of or support; to recommend.

Our representatives **endorsed** the new bill, but it still didn't pass.

entrench (ĕn-trənch´)—*verb*—establish, embed, ingrain; to take up a strong position.

The EPA protected the **entrenched** bats, even though they were destroying the historic church.

epidemic (ĕp´-ĭ-dĕm´-ĭk)—*noun*—plague, outbreak, scourge; rapid spread or growth.

The flu **epidemic** during the early twentieth century *killed millions* of people around the globe but is seldom remembered in historical discussions.

eradicate (ĭ-răd´-ĭ-kāt)—*verb*—eliminate, exterminate; to destroy completely.

The crabgrass was **eradicated** by the weed *killer*.

excerpt (ĕk´-sûrpt)—*noun*—passage, extract, selection.

Her performance was predicable, having chosen a well-known **excerpt** from Shakespeare.

excursion (ĭk-skur´-zhən)—*noun*—outing, jaunt, expedition; a short pleasure trip.

The class took an **excursion** to the community college.

exonerate (ĭg-zŏn´-ə-rāt)—*verb*—absolve, acquit; to clear of wrong doing.

Susie was **exonerated** when Mikey *confessed* to eating the cookies.

expertise (ĕk´-spur-tēz´)—*noun*—skill, proficiency; a high level of knowledge or specific skill.

Her **expertise** in technical jargon made her a *good candidate* for documenting the new software.

exuberant (ĭg-zoo-bər-ənt)—*adjective*—enthusiastic, excited, lively; very energetic and happy.

Her **exuberance** was catchy, and soon all of her friends were learning the new dance.

facilitate (fə-sĭl´-ĭ-tāt)—*verb*—help, aid, assist; to make easier or to assist.

The U.S. military was on hand to **facilitate** food distribution after the hurricane.

fervent (fûr´-vənt)—*adjective*—passionate, zealous; feeling much passion or enthusiasm for.

The beauty queen said her **fervent** wish was for world peace.

fratricide (frăt´-ri-sīd)—*noun*—killing a sibling.

You might say that Cain invented **fratricide** when he *slew his brother* Abel.

fundamental (fŭn´-də-mĕn´-tl)—*adjective*—basic, essential; relating to the foundation or base; an essential part of something.

Students must learn **fundamentals**, such as *reading and writing*, before they can tackle more complicated subjects.

genesis (jĕn´-ĭ-sĭs)—*noun*—origin, beginning, birth; the time when something comes into being; the origin.

Listening to my mother sing while she washed dishes was probably the **genesis** of my love for my music.

genetics (jə-nĕt´-ĭkz)—*noun*—heredity; the study of how characteristics are passed on from the parents to their offspring.

Many doctors and scientists are studying **genetics** in hopes of someday preventing birth defects.

genocide (jĕn´-ə-sīd)—*noun*—killing an entire group or race.

His entire family was gone—victims of **genocide** during the Civil War.

hierarchy (hī´-rär´-kē)—*noun*—pyramid, ladder; a serial and ordered group.

Peons are at the bottom of the company's **hierarchy**.

hone (hōn)—*verb*—sharpen; to perfect or complete.

She spent hours on the court, **honing** her tennis skills.

hyperbole (hī-pur´-bə-lē)—*noun*—exaggeration; figure of speech that exaggerates something in order to emphasize or make a point.

A good essay has little room for **hyperbole**—always use the most accurate and appropriate terms possible.

hypothesis (hī-pŏth´-ĭ-sĭs)—*noun*—theory, premise, supposition.

Other experts ridiculed his **hypothesis** on kinetic energy.

impending (ĭm-pĕnd´-ing)—*verb*—imminent, looming, awaiting, approaching, coming; going to happen soon.

Folks decorated their houses and yards in *preparation* of the **impending** festival.

incentive (in-sĕn´-tĭv)—*noun*—motivation; expectation that motivates you toward specific action.

Management offered a *bonus* as **incentive** for working so much overtime.

incognito (ĭn´-kŏg-nē-´tō)—*adjective*—disguised, undercover, anonymously, secretly.

She slipped into the boardroom **incognito**; no one suspected a *caterer* of industrial sabotage.

increment (in´-krə-mənt)—*noun*—increase, augment; something added; one of a consecutive series.

Increments of .01 percent will be added to each inoculation until the dosage reaches full potency.

indict (in-dīt´)—*verb*—accuse, charge; to accuse of wrongdoing; bring charges against.

After reviewing the evidence, the prosecutor began to suspect that he had **indicted** the wrong man.

indigenous (ĭn-dĭj´-ə-nəs)—*adjective*—native, aboriginal.

The **indigenous** people still practice most of their spiritual beliefs, despite *centuries of attempts by the conquering government* to convert them from their old ways.

indoctrinate (ĭn-dŏk´-trə-nāt´)—*verb*—brainwash, persuade; to repeat an idea or belief frequently in order to influence or persuade.

The activist used short films and speeches to **indoctrinate** his followers.

infanticide (ĭn-făn´-tĭ-sīd)—*noun*—killing an infant or child.

Some tribes still practice **infanticide** today, especially if the child is a girl.

infer (ĭn-fûr´)—*verb*—conclude, deduce, conjecture.

Mikey **inferred** from his mother's angry glance that he should not have eaten all the cookies.

infiltrate (ĭn´-fĭl-trāt)—*verb*—penetrate; to pass secretly or undiscovered.

Security on the base was so lax that Bill was easily able to **infiltrate** its *deepest sectors.*

ingest (ĭn-jĕst´)—*verb*—eat, swallow, consume; to take food or liquid into the stomach.

You must **ingest** this medication—*you can't take it by injection.*

inherent (ĭn-hîr´-ənt)—*adjective*—natural, intrinsic, innate; a natural and permanent attribute; born with; belonging to from the beginning.

Her **inherent** ability to see the future *had always* spooked her friends and family.

insidious (ĭn-sĭd´-ē-əs)—*adjective*—sinister, dangerous, menacing; spreading harm in a malicious manner.

The cult's **insidious** influence was victorious, and she broke all ties with friends and family.

insomnia (ĭn-sŏm´-nē-ə)—*noun*—sleeplessness; the condition of being unable to fall asleep or stay asleep.

Money worries were giving me **insomnia** at night.

integrate (ĭn´-tĭ-grāt)—*verb*—assimilate, combine; to join or unite.

It was difficult for the drill sergeant to **integrate** himself with nonmilitary society after he retired.

interim (ĭn´-tər-ĭm)—*adjective*—interval; the time between two events.

Before getting a real job after graduation, Joe filled the **interim** by traveling across Europe.

interstate (ĭn´-tər-stāt´)—*adjective*—involving more than one state.

Interstate issues are usually controlled at the *federal* level.

intramural (ĭn´-trə-myŏŏr´-əl)—*adjective*—involving members of one school, college, or university.

She enjoyed **intramural** sports but never tried out for a *conference team*.

intrastate (ĭn´-trə-stāt)—*adjective*—relating to or existing within the boundaries of one state.

Intrastate issues are usually controlled by *state and local governing bodies*.

introspection (ĭn´-trə-spĕkt-shen)—*noun*—contemplation; the act of spending time in private thought.

Choosing between the seminary and a state college took months of **introspection**.

introvert (ĭn´-trə-vûrt)—*noun*—shy, recluse; a person who's shy and keeps to themselves.

We suspected that she was just an **introvert**, but many accused her of being conceited.

intuition (ĭn-too´-ĭsh´-ən)—*noun*—perception, insight; the ability to know without reasoning.

My **intuition** told me that he couldn't be trusted.

irrelevant (ĭ-rĕl´-ə-vənt)—*adjective*—extraneous, unimportant.

Cinderella was **irrelevant** both in her stepmother's household and in her thoughts.

lateral (lăt´-ər-əl)—*adjective*—sideways; situated at or on the side.

The restructuring caused lots of **lateral** personnel changes, but *no promotions or demotions*.

laudable (lô´-də-bəl)—*adjective*—admirable, worthy, commendable; deserving or worthy of praise.

Laudable results were demanded by her talented and successful family.

malice (măl´-ĭs)—*noun*—hatred, malevolence, meanness.

The victim's mother hoped for the death penalty, even though she no longer felt any **malice** toward the convicted killer.

mandatory (măn´-də-tor´-ē)—*adjective*—compulsory, obligatory; required or commanded to comply.

Many thought a **mandatory** gym class was a waste of time.

maritime (măr´-ĭ–tīm)—*adjective*—marine, nautical, naval, sea; relating to the sea.

The **maritime** unit was on call during the hurricane.

minuscule (mĭn´-ĭ-skyool)—*adjective*—tiny, diminutive; very small.

The raise was **miniscule** and made the workers angry.

narcissism (när´-sĭ-sĭz´-əm)—*noun*—vanity, conceit, egotism; excessive love of oneself.

Her **narcissism** made her a *bad candidate for motherhood*.

notorious (nō-tôr´-ē-əs)—*adjective*—well-known in a negative way.

The inspector was **notorious** for taking bribes to look the other way.

nuance (noo´-äns)—*noun*—shade, trace; subtle difference.

The **nuances** of browns and maroons created a sense of lush comfort.

omnipotent (ŏm-nĭp´-ə-tənt)—*adjective*—all-powerful, invincible, supreme; having unlimited power or authority.

The early Egyptians thought the pharaoh was **omnipotent** and consequently granted him a *godlike* status.

omniscient (ŏm-nĭsh´-ənt)—*adjective*—all-knowing; knowing all events and decisions in all times.

Sue's **omniscient** mother *always seemed to know* about Sue's mistakes before Sue could even confess.

opulent (ŏp´-yə-lənt)—*adjective*—luxurious, rich, affluent, wealthy, lavish.

Celebrities often live **opulent** lifestyles that seem obnoxious and *wasteful* to many.

overt (ō-vûrt´)—*adjective*—obviously, explicit; not hidden, in the open; obvious.

His **overt** overtures embarrassed her.

panacea (păn´-ə-sē´-ə)—*noun*—cure-all, cure, solution, answer; a remedy for all diseases or problems.

Good works aren't a **panacea** for all the world's *problems*.

panorama (păn´-ə-răm´-ə)—*noun*—view, landscape; the unbroken view of the surrounding area.

She bought the old place just for the **panorama** of the surrounding valleys.

paraphrase (păr´-ə-frāz)—verb—summarize, rephrase; to restate, usually summarizing a passage of text.

It's a good idea to **paraphrase** a passage when being quizzed on its content.

passive (păs´-ĭv)—*adjective*—submissive, inert; submitting with little or no resistance.

People living under a tyrannical dictatorship are often **passive**—*making no attempt to correct the situation out of fear.*

pedestal (pĕd´-ĭ-stəl)—*noun*—dais, platform, podium; a raised and supported area for standing or display.

Elegant **pedestals** were used to *display* the antique sculptures.

perceive (pər-sēv´)—*verb*—distinguish, recognize, identify, sense; to see or become aware of.

I **perceive** your displeasure, but you brought it on yourself.

perplex (pər-plĕkz´)—*verb*—confuse, bewilder, baffle.

She was **perplexed** to find a sink full of dishes, knowing that she'd just washed them all.

perspective (pər-spĕk´-tĭv)—*noun*—viewpoint, outlook, side; one particular way of thinking or considering.

From her **perspective**, the business trip was coming at a bad time.

pervasive (pər-vā´-sĭv)—*adjective*—invasive, persistent.

Bamboo is quite an **invasive** plant and not recommended for the average backyard.

philosophy (fĭ-lŏs´-ə-fē)—*noun*—beliefs, viewpoint; the science that deals with life principles.

Great **philosophers** shake things up too much and, as a result, are seldom appreciated by their peers.

podium (pō´-dē-əm)—*noun*—platform, dais, pedestal; a platform used for speaking.

Professor Marks always spoke from a **podium,** whereas Professor Tatum preferred to walk about the class

precedent (prĕs´-ĭ-dənt)—*noun*—example, model, guide.

Courts give great weight to **precedent**—using these cases as a *template* for subsequent trials.

precipitous (prĭ-sĭp´-ĭ-təs)—*adjective*—abrupt, steep; to happen suddenly or unexpectedly.

The **precipitous** phone call was just a warning of things yet to come.

predict (prĭ-dĭkt´)—*verb*—forecast, foresee, foretell; to suggest or know what will happen in the future.

You didn't have to be a psychic to **predict** Bill's big win after seeing his supporters at the rally.

prejudice (prĕj-ə-dĭs)—*verb, noun*—bigotry, chauvinism; 1. To unfairly influence an opinion; 2. A presumed opinion, without evidence.

Many college professors **prejudice** their impressionable young students against conservative policies.

Her **prejudice** against the smaller girls on the team was unwarranted as they were great players.

preserve (prĭ-zûrv´)—*verb, noun*—protect, conserve, save; 1. To prevent decay or damage; to keep something in its original state; 2. A place where natural resources are protected.

> She was unable to **preserve** her seat on the school board.
>
> *Hunting* on the **preserve** was prohibited by law.

pristine (prĭs´-tēn)—*adjective*—unspoiled, untouched, immaculate; free from change; remaining in its original state without dirt or decay.

> Many thought the **pristine** wilderness was worth saving and worked diligently to see it *preserved*.

ratify (răt´-ə-fī)—*verb*—sanction, authorize.

> The legislative body **ratified** the new bill despite public resistance.

rationalize (răsh´-ə-nə-līz´)—*verb*—deduce, reason; to explain or reason.

> Bill was unable to **rationalize** his need for more office space, so management turned down his request.

relinquish (rĭ-lĭng´-kwĭsh)—*verb*—surrender, renounce; to give back or surrender.

> After hearing the diagnosis of Alzheimer's, the father sadly **relinquished** control of his business to his sons.

repercussion (rē´-pər-kŭsh´-ən)—*noun*—consequence, effect, outcome, ramification; reaction to or result of.

> Failing to study for his midterms had **repercussions** he hadn't considered.

repudiate (rĭ-pyōō´-dē-āt)—*verb*—disclaim, renounce, deny; reject as untrue.

> The jury **repudiated** the testimony of the eyewitness after the defense attorney exposed him as a *liar*.

rural (rŏŏr´-əl)—*adjective*—country, pastoral, rustic; relating to the country; opposite of urban.

> The **rural** route was a welcome change of scenery after hours on the boring interstate.

sector (sĕk´-tər)—*noun*—segment, area; a group or division.

After the civil unrest, a few **sectors** of the city remained unstable for a while.

secular (sĕk´-yə-lər)—*adjective*—worldly.

The **secular** committee refused to accept the minister's nomination on the grounds that he might be religiously biased.

sedentary (sĕd´-n-tĕr´-ē)—*adjective*—inactive; very little or no physical movement.

The old woman's **sedentary** lifestyle led to several health problems.

suburban (sə-bûr´-bən)—*adjective*—suburbs, uptown; relating to a residential district located on the outskirts of an urban area.

Most people tend to move to **suburban** areas once they gain a little success.

surpass (sər-păs´)—*verb*—exceed, outdo; to go beyond the limit; to exceed.

The class far **surpassed** the teacher's *expectations*.

temporal (tĕm´-pər-əl)—*adjective*—sequential, of time; referring to a specific time period.

Jules Verne's time machine was a **temporal** device that carried its passenger into the *past or future*.

transpire (trăn-spīr´)—*verb*—happen, occur.

The eyewitness told *her account* of what **transpired** on the night in question.

ubiquitous (yōō-bĭk´-wĭ-təs)—*adjective*—omnipresent; seeming to be everywhere at once.

We laughed as the exhausted grandmother shared some of her grandson's **ubiquitous** antics with us.

urban (ûr´-bən)—*adjective*—city, municipal, inner city; related to a city or city life.

The **urban** areas had more to offer the immigrants than the *countryside*.

vehement (vē´-ə-mənt)—*adjective*—fervent, intense, passionate; strong or forceful feelings.

Mel was **vehemently** *opposed* to the new living arrangements.

verbatim (vər-bā´-tĭm)—*adjective, adverb*—precise, word for word; repeating using the exact words.

She was asked to *repeat*, verbatim, the teacher's instructions before beginning the exam.

verbose (vər-bōs´)—*adjective*—wordy, talkative; using more words than necessary—wordy.

She was generally *a succinct writer* and disagreed with the editor's suggestion that she was **verbose**.

vicarious (vī-kar´-ē-əs)—*adjective*—taking part through others' experiences via feelings rather than participation.

Many parents make the mistake of living **vicariously** *through their children* when they fail to fulfill their own dreams.

virulent (vîr´yə-lənt)—*adjective*—contagious, contaminated; capable of causing disease.

Early small pox vaccinations were a **virulent** inoculation of the *live virus*.

wallow (wŏl´-ō)—*verb*—surround; to overindulge in or to completely immerse oneself.

Wallowing in self-pity simply distracts from the task at hand—that of fixing the problem.

Learning Cues

The larger your vocabulary, the less time you'll spend on this section of the exam. There's simply no substitute for actually knowing the words on the exam. That's why we're including the vocabulary list. You can spend a lot of time trying to memorize all these words by rote, but that's not the best way. The best way to truly integrate these words into your vocabulary is to learn them and use them. To do so, try one of the following methods to help speed things up:

➤ Transfer each word to an index card—that'll take a bit of work, but the simple process of writing the words and their definitions will go a long way toward committing them to memory. Then, each day, choose a few cards and carry them with you. Review them often and try to use these words in your conversations. Later in the evening, write the words and their meanings without using the index card or the list in this book. Compare your unassisted definition with the index card or the list in this book. Depending on how many words you tackle each day, write a sentence or paragraph that uses each of the new words.

➤ Make an audio tape or CD of the list. Play the tape while riding in the car, waiting in line or at a doctor's office, or anytime you have a few minutes. Just stop and go as you can. After listening to a new word, try to use it in subsequent conversations. Later in the evening, write the words and their meanings without using the audio aid or the list in this book. Compare your unassisted definition with the audio aid or the list in this book. Depending on how many words you tackle each day, write a sentence or paragraph that uses each of the new words.

➤ As you learn new words, add them to the appropriate elemental lists created in the previous section.

➤ This next cue is for only those students who insist that they learn better if they study while music is playing. When studying your vocabulary words, listen to some of your favorite music. Later, when reviewing the words, listen to the same music. The explanation is more complicated than we have time for here, but it really does work—but only with people who find background music helpful. If you find music or noise distracting, skip this cue.

➤ Don't stop with our list. Anytime you encounter a word that you don't know, take the time to learn it. If it isn't possible to stop right then, jot it down and look it up later. Create an index card for it or add it to your audio aid. Incorporate each new word into your routine using the techniques outlined in this chapter.

➤ Create visual clues to help you remember difficult words. For example, to help you remember the word "abduct," you might visualize a man kidnapping a duck.

You might elicit the help of your friends and family in helping you learn these new vocabulary words. If they're willing, share these words with them and see how often they can use the new words while talking with you. This suggestion may seem lame at first, but you'd be surprised how eager your family probably is to help, and most of your friends are going to be taking this exam themselves. It's worth a shot—the more you hear and use these words, the quicker you'll take command of their usage and the better you'll perform on the vocabulary section of the exam.

Once a week or so, review the words you've already tackled. You may find that you're actually using these words consistently now—they're no longer mystery words. These new words will probably become part of your every-day vocabulary, and that's good. When this happens, you have full command of these words and you should have no difficulties if you encounter them on the exam.

On the other hand, don't worry if you're not using every new word in every-day conversation—that would be a lot to expect and it just wouldn't be nat-ural. However, if none of the new words are making their way into your vocabulary, you may not actually be learning them and you may forget them before exam time.

Exam Prep Questions

Each sentence has one or two blanks, representing an omitted word or words. Choose only one of the responses following the sentence to correctly complete each sentence. Remember, choose the best response, not the first response that seems appropriate.

1. The congressman's _____ responses in regards to the missing funds might cost him votes in the _____ election.
   - (A) exemplary . . sector's
   - (B) considerate . . forthcoming
   - (C) impetuous . . special
   - (D) evasive . . subsequent
   - (E) incriminating . . preceding

2. The jury's hasty decision was cause for a(n) _____.
   - (A) reprimand
   - (B) appeal
   - (C) mistrial
   - (D) retrial
   - (E) dismissal

3. Despite _____ odds, Mother Teresa gave aid and comfort to the poor, the sick, the homeless, and the _____.
   - (A) irreversible . . ugly
   - (B) complex . . itinerant
   - (C) strenuous . . destitute
   - (D) challenging . . indigent
   - (E) insurmountable . . disenfranchised

4. The unexpected _____ of the popular actress has driven many of her fans to _____.
   - (A) incarceration . . celebrate
   - (B) demise . . despair
   - (C) emigration . . digress
   - (D) regrets . . reconsider
   - (E) deterioration . . wane

5. The principal preferred to use the _____ retained instead of failed when a student was forced to repeat a grade.
   - (A) synonym
   - (B) phrase
   - (C) eulogy
   - (D) euphemism
   - (E) antonym

6. Despite his _____ contributions to the aviation industry, Chuck Yeager never _____ his dream of flying into space.

(A) pioneering . . realized
(B) numerous . . accomplished
(C) laudable . . disregarded
(D) various . . deserted
(E) progressive . . tolerated

7. Not admitting your guilt is not the same as being _____.

(A) innocent
(B) guilty
(C) mute
(D) virtuous
(E) dishonest

8. Pedagogy is a _____ to teaching, but nothing can truly prepare you for the classroom but the act of teaching itself.

(A) godsend
(B) precursor
(C) triumph
(D) boon
(E) stage

9. After her initial stint in the classroom, she was ready to _____ her pointer and _____ on a new career—any career that didn't include children.

(A) surrender . . try
(B) renounce . . disembark
(C) relinquish . . embark
(D) break . . think
(E) bronze . . endeavor

10. She thought her cause might be _____, but to the contrary, she found everyone very _____.

(A) controversial . . supportive
(B) misunderstood . . helpful
(C) rejected . . apologetic
(D) distracting . . encouraging
(E) terminated . . contingent

Answers for Exam Prep Questions

1. Answer D is the best response. We know that his responses were somehow negative, and the word *might* indicates that the election is still to come. Answer A is incorrect because "exemplary" would suggest that the congressman answered well, and we know by the tone of the sentence that he did not. We can eliminate that response without even considering the second word, "sector's." Answer B is incorrect for the same reason—"considerate" simply isn't a logical choice. Answer C may trip you up a bit, but remember, you're looking for the best response, not any response that seems to fit. The responses could be rash or hasty—an impetuous response might not be harmful. Answer E is incorrect because "preceding" would imply a past election, and we know the election is still to come.

2. Answer B is correct. An appeal occurs after the verdict and sentencing and usually is a means of rehearing the case when something went wrong with the first one. Answer A is incorrect. You can't reprimand a jury after the fact, and it would be irrelevant even if you could. Answer C is incorrect as a mistrial happens before a jury verdict. The sentence indicates that the jury did hand down a verdict. Answer D is incorrect because there really isn't any such thing. You may see the term retried, or a defendant may get a new trial. Answer E is incorrect for the same reason as C.

3. Answer E is the best response because both words fit well within the context of the sentence. Answers A and B are both incorrect because none of the words really express the logic of the sentence. Answer C is incorrect; although "destitute" would fit, "strenuous" really doesn't. Besides, destitute is redundant to poor. Answer D is incorrect. Although "challenging" might fit, it isn't as good as "insurmountable." In addition, similar to destitute, indigent is redundant to poor.

4. Answer B is the best response. It's logical to assume that fans would find the loss of an admired celebrity hard to accept or overcome for a while. Answers A and C are incorrect because they're totally illogical. Answer D is incorrect. Even though it could be a true statement, nothing really supports it—what were the fans reconsidering? Answer E is incorrect. Although the sentiment might be true, there are certainly better ways to express it. Besides, that statement almost seems incomplete. The statement needs to include just what the fans are waning—their devotion, their support?

5. Answer D is correct. A "euphemism" is a word or phrase that restates another in a pleasant or inoffensive manner. In this case, the principal wants to avoid using the word "failed" to describe a student that needs to repeat a grade. Answers A, B, C, and E are all incorrect because they are the wrong words.

6. Answer A is the best response, given the creative nature of the sentence. It also helps to be familiar with Chuck Yeager and his accomplishments, but the hint is in the sentence. Space travel is still on the cutting edge of our technology, so it should be fairly easy to deduce that Chuck Yeager was a pioneer in that industry. Okay, it is a bit of a trick question, but remember, context is everything in this section of the exam. Answer B is incorrect because "numerous" is not a good way to describe his contributions within the context of this sentence. Numerous really doesn't prepare you for the statement's dream component; the thoughts aren't parallel and fail to support one another. Besides, one doesn't accomplish one's dream; one realizes a dream. Accomplish simply isn't the most appropriate word. Answer C is incorrect. Although "laudable" would fit, "disregarded" doesn't. The two phrases might be correct alone, but they don't fit well together. Like answer B, they don't support one another. Answer D is incorrect because it isn't the best response. Although the words would work logically, they aren't as expressive as answer A. Answer E is incorrect because "tolerant" isn't logical within the context of the sentence. Therefore, even though "progressive" might work, the two phases don't fit together.

7. Answer A is correct. If you find the sentence confusing, remove one of the negatives: Not admitting guilt is the same as being innocent. You know that statement isn't true, but it does help clarify the statement's meaning. In a nutshell, just because you don't admit something, doesn't mean that you're innocent. Answers B, C, and D are all incorrect because they simply don't express the right sentiment. Answer E is incorrect although you might be fooled by this one. Remember the context and keep the thoughts parallel, and you'll see that "dishonest" doesn't fit. The sentence isn't about honesty, it's about guilt and innocence. Dishonest isn't parallel with guilt within the context of this sentence.

8. Answer B is correct. If you know your elemental components, you can figure this one out even if you don't know that pedagogy is the study of teaching. You can't teach until you've studied teaching, so "precursor" is the most appropriate choice. The clue is the word "prepare." Answers A, C, D, and E are all incorrect because they are illogical choices.

9. Answer C is the best response. Both words fit logically within the individual phrases. She wants to quit teaching and do something else. Answer A is incorrect. First, "surrender" has a different connotation than "relinquish"; there's a sense of force in the word "surrender" that isn't in "relinquish." In addition, "try" doesn't fit well grammatically. Although you might say, "try on," the context is wrong for that usage. Answer B is incorrect because "disembark" isn't logical, with the clue being the word "new" to describe the career. Answer D is incorrect. She might want to break her pointer, but you don't "think on" a new career. You might consider or think about a new career, but "think on" is bad grammar. Answer E is incorrect. First, "bronze" isn't logical. You bronze baby shoes—things you treasure. Even if you wanted to use the word humorously or creatively, "endeavor" doesn't work grammatically.

10. Answer A is the best response because it presents the most logical statement. The clue is the phrase "to the contrary." This phrase lets you know that everyone's response is not the one she expected. Answer B is incorrect. People don't have to fully understand the cause to be helpful; they might help and support her just because they like her, regardless of the actual cause. The statement makes sense, but it is *not* the best response. Answer C is incorrect. The phrase "to the contrary" makes the statement illogical. Answer D is incorrect. Although that statement might be true, it isn't the strongest, best response. The fact that her cause is distracting doesn't really support the statement or why people are encouraging despite the distraction. You'd need more information for this statement to make sense. Answer E is incorrect because you don't terminate a cause. You might change your mind; you might drop a cause. In addition, "contingent" is just plain wrong in the context of this sentence.

The Critical Reading Section: Reading Comprehension

Terms you'll need to understand:

✓ Analysis
✓ Anecdote
✓ Argument
✓ Counterexample
✓ Extended reasoning
✓ Hyperbole
✓ Irony
✓ Literal comprehension
✓ Metaphor
✓ Narrative
✓ Simile
✓ Vocabulary-in-context

Techniques you'll need to master:

✓ Identify and compare facts
✓ Draw conclusions based on facts, opinion, or anecdote
✓ Use context to define unfamiliar or subjective terms

You can't learn if you can't read. The SAT exam tests your ability to comprehend and to retain what you read in two ways: *sentence completion*, which you reviewed in Chapter 3, and *passage-based readings*. The exam will have 48 passage-based reading questions. These questions will test your ability to understand what you've read. Don't let this part of the exam throw you. These questions aren't testing what you know, but rather what you discern while reading. Everything you need to answer each question will be in the passage.

The SAT exam will consist of two critical reading sections, short and long passages. This chapter tackles the short passages. Chapter 5, "The Critical Reading Section: Longer Passages and Paired Passages," covers long and paired passages.

Reading Skills

For the purposes of the SAT exam, there are three things about each passage you should know after reading:

➤ The passage's *purpose*

➤ The passage's *main idea*

➤ The passage's *structure*

The place to start is with the passage itself—always begin by reading the passage. Don't try to skip this section in an effort to save time. You need the context of the passage to answer most of the questions. If you have trouble with the passage, you can stop and read a few questions. Doing so may help you discern the passage's meaning. When you think you've finally got a handle on the passage, finish reading it before you actually try to answer any questions.

Some students may benefit from reading the questions before the passage. Doing so may help you hone in on the facts within the passage while reading. However, reading the questions before reading the passage does require more time because you'll need to reread the questions again when you're ready to answer them. There's no right or wrong to your choice, but keep in mind that you will have limited time to get through all the questions.

If you're in doubt as to which method suits you best, practice both. Time yourself both ways, and then compare your results.

Everything you need to answer each question is in the passage. Most of the questions will be very literal, and you're expected to respond with a concrete answer. The questions will not ask you for your opinion or your personal experience. There will be no questions regarding the passage's symbolism, nor will you be expected to glean some deep but hidden meaning. You won't be asked to draw on extraneous information but you might need to make inferences or extrapolations. All answers will be supported by the passage, and that's the key to getting through this section of the exam—remember that all the answers are in the passage.

Make Brief Notes While Reading

While reading the passage through, consider making brief notes in the margins. Don't get carried away, and keep these notes specific to the three questions you'll be expected to answer: the *purpose*, *central idea*, and *structure*. Also consider paraphrasing each paragraph in the margin. That'll help you find the right facts later when answering questions.

An alternative to paraphrasing each paragraph is to read so that you're looking for the topic sentence of each paragraph. Once you've found it, underline it. This method highlights main ideas and makes it easier to go back and find specific topics in the passage.

Read Questions Efficiently for Time Management

Efficiency matters, and one way to whiz through this section is to visualize what you read. Ever notice when you're reading a great book that you can see the action and characters as you read? It might be effective to also use that trick on these critical reading passages. Relax and allow your mind to commit what you read to pictures. You'll find the information much easier to access when answering questions.

However, don't read too fast. Reading too quickly actually slows you down because you miss too much. Consequently, you find yourself referring back to the passage too often when trying to answer questions. You may actually have to reread large sections. If you're prone to reading too fast, practice reading aloud. Doing so will force you to slow down.

It's possible for students with some specific learning or physical disabilities to get extra time for this portion of the test. If you believe you might qualify, see your guidance counselor for more information.

Many of you may be dreading this part of the exam, and you shouldn't. This section may be the easiest section of the exam if you approach it enthusiastically. Read each passage with the attitude that you're simply learning something new. Don't sweat the questions that are coming. If you can relax, you'll recall more about the passage.

Keep Your Focus on the Passage's Content

When reading each passage, be careful to keep your own opinions separate from the author's. It's fine to form an opinion, but you must be careful not to confuse your thoughts with the passage's point. The questions will concern the passage's literal content, not any opinions you may form while reading.

 There's simply no substitute for reading the passages and all answers carefully. You can expect some answers in this particular section to add additional pieces of information with the correct information in an effort to trick you. Do *not* be fooled. Choose the answer that includes only information from the essay.

Answering Reading Passage Questions

If you don't understand the question, or if more than one answer seems to be correct, rephrase the question as an open-ended question and then answer that question as fully as possible. While you're answering the rephrased question, the passage's purpose will become clearer and one of the answers will stand out. The following items are examples of a question and then that same question rephrased in an open-ended manner.

> **Actual question**—The author's attitude toward feminism is....
>
> **Open-ended**—How does the author feel about feminism?

If you can't choose between two similar answers, go with the less absolute of the two. Statements with words such as *never*, *always*, *only*, and *so on* are less likely to be true. In addition, extreme statements are less likely to be true. For instance, *hate*, and *vehemently abhorred* might mean roughly the same thing, but it's your job to decide which is the most appropriate—more often than not, the less extreme response would be the right answer.

Passage Readings

The 48 questions in this section of the exam are based on passage readings from 100–850 words. Subjects are similar to those you can expect to encounter in your college texts. Passages will vary both in style and content.

 The passages cover a lot of material, but don't worry about being an expert in these subjects. In fact, you don't need to have any prior knowledge of a subject to answer all the questions correctly. This part of the exam tests your ability to comprehend and remember what you read. Everything you need to answer the questions will be in the passage.

When a question refers to a specific sentence, reread the sentence before trying to answer the question. Some questions are based on a single passage. Others work with a pair of passages, which share a subject. The paired passages will complement or oppose one another.

Finding a Passage's Form and Purpose

Although the passages will cover a wide range of topics, each will have a specific purpose:

➤ To tell the reader a story

➤ To persuade the reader

➤ To inform the reader

Technically, these three purposes come in the following forms:

➤ *Narrative*—A *narrative* is a story. These passages will describe a main character's ordeal or conflict. Biographies and memoirs are narratives.

➤ *Argument*—An *argument* attempts to persuade the reader to a specific point of view. Although these types of passages often include facts, they are subjective in content, not factual. The author is merely using facts to persuade you over to his or her side.

➤ *Analysis*—An *analysis* informs the reader by providing facts in an objective format. Just the opposite of the *argument*, an analysis presents facts and offers no attempt to persuade.

Identifying which of the previous forms the passage follows can help you discern the three questions we discussed earlier: the passage's purpose, main idea, and structure. Using the information in Table 4.1, you can quickly determine a passage's purpose and main idea just from identifying its structure.

Table 4.1	Determining a Passage's Purpose/Main Idea from Its Structure	
Passage Form	**Purpose**	**Main Idea**
Narrative	To tell a story	Conflict
Argument	To persuade	A thesis or point of view
Analysis	To inform the reader	Objective facts

It isn't critical that you remember these three prose forms, but being able to identify a passage's structure can help you more quickly discern its purpose. As you read through this chapter, try to identify each example passage as narrative, argumentative, or analysis.

Understanding the Questions

Understanding the question is just as important as understanding the passage. In this section of the exam, you'll encounter three types of questions:

➤ *Extended Reasoning Questions*—These questions will expect you to evaluate information and draw a conclusion. These questions do not have a literal or direct answer within the actual passage content; you will have to infer the answers from the reading. In other words, you will have to reason through the question.

➤ *Vocabulary-in-Context Questions*—These questions will test your understanding of word usage within the context of the passage. It's important to keep context in mind when answering these questions. Words often have more than one meaning, and reading just the sentence in which the word is used won't always be enough.

The vocabulary-building exercises in Chapter 3 will help you on this part of the exam.

➤ *Literal Comprehension Questions*—These questions ask about the facts presented in the passage.

Remember that an answer can be true, but still be the wrong answer for the question. Always search for the *best answer*, don't mark the first true response you come to.

Chances are you won't answer every question. Since it takes a while to read each passage, we suggest that you answer the questions that you can answer easily. Then, instead of going on to the next passage, return to the skipped questions and try again while the passage is still fresh in your mind. If you wait to answer these unanswered questions later, you may have to completely reread the passage, or at the very least reread large sections of it, which will be time-consuming. Besides, subsequent questions may actually trigger inspiration and help you answer those skipped questions.

The questions in this portion of the SAT exam may use the following words in the questions to qualify the appropriate response:

➤ *Anecdote*—An anecdote is a personal accounting that usually illustrates a point (but doesn't have to).

Anecdote Example:

As a youngster, I didn't understand how witches made it into the Pledge of Allegiance—"…and to the republic for witches stands…".

➤ *Counterexample*—A counterexample contradicts a point that has already been made.

Counterexample Example:

All prime numbers are odd. How can that be since the number *two* is a prime number?

➤ *Hyperbole*—Hyperbole exaggerates a point.

Hyperbole Example:

That woman can talk a mile a minute.

➤ *Irony*—Irony produces results you didn't expect, but that are understood once all the facts are known.

Irony Example:

"Who would have guessed that our sweet and outgoing little niece would be the murderer? She was always so happy and well-adjusted," stated our mother. "That seems true, but now that we know her mother's life was regularly threatened it isn't a stretch to see why she acted like that," father interjected.

➤ *Metaphor*—A metaphor describes something by comparing it to something else.

Metaphor Example:

My life has more ups and downs than a yo-yo.

➤ *Simile*—A simile compares two things using words such as *like* or *as*.

Simile Example:

My life has been like a yo-yo lately—up and down, up and down.

Extended Reasoning Questions

Extended reasoning questions are just what the title suggests. There's no literal fact in the passage to turn to—you must reason through what you've read to discern the most likely response. You can identify most extended reasoning questions just by their wording, but watch for the following words and phrases:

➤ According to the author/passage

➤ Apparently

➤ Implies

➤ Inferred

➤ Probably

➤ Seems

➤ Suggests

 Don't be confused by imply and infer. They are both verbs; the main difference is in perception. The author implies something; the reader infers the author's intent.

Another thing to watch for is the use of personal pronouns such as *I*, *me*, *my*, and *mine*. These are clues that the author is speaking from personal experience or expressing a personal opinion.

The key to answering extended reasoning questions correctly is the ability to know what's a fact and what isn't. Both a narrative and an argumentative passage may imply or suggest certain points, and you must know the difference between a universally accepted fact and what the author thinks. Sometimes the difference is subtle and hard to spot. Consider the following example:

> Martha screamed at the first firefighters to arrive on the scene, "Where have you been? I called nearly 20 minutes ago! My house is completely gone! Save my 10 cats!"

Which of the following is the most factual?

   (A) Seventeen minutes lapsed between the first call to 911 and the fire truck's arrival.

   (B) Something surely went wrong if it took nearly 20 minutes for the first fire truck to arrive.

   (C) Nearly 20 minutes lapsed between the first call to 911 and the fire truck's arrival.

   (D) Kids call Martha "that crazy cat lady."

   (E) Nearly 20 minutes lapsed between Martha's first call and the fire truck's arrival.

Answer E is correct. This statement is the only statement that repeats only facts we know from the statement, and nothing more. Answer A is incorrect because it says 17 minutes lapsed. The exact time might have been 17 minutes, but we only know that it was nearly 20 minutes. Answer A misstates the fact we know. Answers A and C are incorrect because we don't know who Martha called. She might have called the police or the fire department. These two answers assume she called 911. Answer B is incorrect. Although nearly 20 minutes might seem like a long time, there's no way to discern from the timing of events that something went wrong. Seventeen minutes might actually be normal. The author is assuming a problem that's not supported by fact. Answer D is incorrect. The children may indeed call Martha the crazy cat lady, but there's nothing in the statement to suggest that's true.

Vocabulary-in-Context Questions

Your vocabulary skills get a real workout in the SAT exam. We've discussed vocabulary in Chapters 2 and 3. In Chapter 2, you learned not to use big words just to impress readers and that words used incorrectly will cost you points on your essay. You must be able to discern the author's intent by keeping context in mind. It's not as simple as memorizing the definitions of hundreds of words. This doesn't mean that the word in question is subjective and open to opinion. Rather, it means that you should be able to get the gist of the word, even if you don't know the word formally.

The word in question will most likely have many meanings. You can expect the answers to utilize all those meanings. It's up to you to find the appropriate answer—the most correct answer, within the context of the passage. You may have to reread the sentence before and after again, and we suggest that you do so if you're unsure.

Knowing the definition of the words in question is always a bonus. That's where building your vocabulary (as discussed in Chapter 3) will help. But you don't have to know the exact definition—that's what reading comprehension is all about. Often, you can discern the word's meaning because of the context in which the word is used. Consider the following example that requires you to find the definition to the word sage.

The old woman's *sage* advice saved the day.

The word sage, as used in the above sentence most nearly means

>   (A) A plant that grows in the desert
>   (B) Wise
>   (C) Bad
>   (D) Uneducated
>   (E) Worldly

Answer B is the best answer. You know from the phrase "saved the day" that the advice worked.

Literal Comprehension Questions

Literal comprehension questions are fact-based questions. It's as simple as that. The question will ask you to find the answer to a question that is answered, quite literally, within the passage. These types of questions sometimes use qualifying terms such as *except, only, not, other than,* and so on.

Answers will seldom be repeated in the same form using the same exact words. In addition, you may have to review the passage to get the most specific and correct answer. Don't depend on your memory or prior knowledge on the subject if there's any doubt. Take the time to reread the appropriate section of the passage if necessary. Let's look at an example.

Except for the Wolfhawk, which hunts in packs, hawks are solitary hunters.

Which statement about hawks is the most accurate?

>   (A) Hawks are solitary hunters.
>   (B) Wolfhawks are solitary hunters.
>   (C) Wolfhawks hunt in packs.
>   (D) All hawks hunt in packs.
>   (E) Wolfhawks are the only hawks that hunt in packs.

Answer E is correct. Watch for the use of the words except and only—both are absolute terms. You might be tempted to choose C because it is a true statement. However, within the context of the original statement, it is not the most correct statement. Watch for these types of responses on the exam. Always answer with the most appropriate, the most accurate response and not the first response that seems true. You should always read all the responses before making a choice.

You'll encounter at least one pair of related passages on the exam. Questions will ask you to compare the passages in some way. Be careful to read the question carefully. Questions may ask for choices that both passages share, or not. You'll learn more about these questions in Chapter 5.

Exam Prep Questions

Note that the following questions are in chronological order in regards to the referencing lines in the passage. For instance, if questions 1 and 3 refer to lines 1 and 7, respectively, you know that question 2 will refer to any line or lines from line 2 to 6.

Questions 1–4 are based on the following passage from a history text.

The Espionage Act of 1917 gave the President powers of censorship. It enacted heavy penalties against anyone who handed out information about any place connected with the national defense. To urge
Line resistance to the laws of the United States, to refuse to do military
5   duty, or to hinder the draft now became crimes punishable by prison terms. The Trading with the enemy Act of 1917 obliged any newspaper printed here in a foreign language to furnish the Postmaster General with English translations of everything it published about the war.

10   The Sedition Act of 1918 went even further than the infamous Sedition Act of 1798 against which Jefferson and Madison had protested. For the 1918 law imposed penalties on anyone who used "disloyal, profane, scurrilous, or abusive" language about the United States government, flag, or uniform. It empowered the Postmaster General to
15   refuse to deliver mail to anyone who, in his opinion, was using the postal service in violation of the act.

With this barrage of propaganda and new laws, Americans who disagreed in any way with the activities of the government were hounded and harried. In 1917, more than 1100 striking copper miners who were
20   members of the radical Industrial Workers of the World were taken forcibly from Arizona to New Mexico, where they were interned. IWW leaders were thrown into jail. Eugene V. Debs, the many-time Socialist candidate for President, was sentenced to jail for ten years for denouncing the war in 1918. While still in jail he ran for President in
25   1920. His sentence was finally commuted in 1921.

This was a strange way to fight a war for freedom and democracy. How could the nation improve its war effort if citizens were not allowed to criticize the government or the armed forces? In fact, opposition to the war was slight and scarcely hampered the war effort. But
30   the mania of these times would last even after the war. The virus of witch-hunting and super-patriotism was not easy to cure.

1. The primary purpose of this passage is to

(A) describe laws used to encourage patriotism during World War I

(B) discuss how well-meaning laws are often abused

(C) describe the attack on civil liberties during World War I

(D) describe the socialist threat during the early twentieth century

(E) discuss the danger of laws that curtail civil liberties

2. Persons guilty of this/these were in violation of the Espionage Act of 1917 and could be sent to prison.

(A) Disloyal, profane, scurrilous, or abusive language

(B) Speaking against the war

(C) Striking against an employer

(D) Refusing military duty, hindering the draft, or urging resistance to the laws of the United States

(E) Criticizing the government or the armed forces

3. In lines 7–19, the author suggests that these laws were what?

(A) Abused to silence anyone who opposed the war

(B) Effective in putting draft dodgers in jail

(C) A balance against the Socialist party

(D) A means of fighting for freedom and democracy

(E) Necessary to protect freedom and democracy

4. In lines 30–31, the author uses the word virus to suggest that

(A) witch-hunting and super-patriotism are hard to cure

(B) witch-hunting and super-patriotism should be avoided

(C) witch-hunting and super-patriotism can kill

(D) civil liberties must be protected

(E) witch-hunting and super-patriotism are as dangerous to our civil liberties as the plague is to our population

Questions 5–7 are based on the passage from a science text:

During the 1800s, many people moved westward to farm the fertile land of the Great Plains. This vast grassland was believed to be large enough to support many farms and ranches.

Line   Farmers plowed under the tough, drought-resistant native grasses
5   and planted corn and wheat. Ranchers turned out herds of cattle and sheep to graze on the grassland. Over time, more and more acres of prairie were converted to farms and ranches.

The change in vegetation had unforeseen results. The native prairie grasses have extensive root systems, which hold the soil in place. As
10   these plants were weakened by overgrazing or replaced by crops, the soil was poorly protected against the winds that blew across the land.

Settlement in the southern part of the Great Plains was especially active during the 30 years before 1915. In 1931, a drought began and lasted for several years. The corn, wheat, and other crops were not
15 resistant to drought, so they died. The native vegetation, which was already weakened, died too. When the wind blew, there was nothing left to hold the soil in place, and it began to blow away.

Dust filled the air. It was like a dust blizzard, and people began to call the region the "dust bowl." Prevailing winds blew lighter particles
20 as far as the Atlantic Ocean. Heavier particles were carried shorter distances, piling up on farm equipment, fences, and buildings. In many places, more than 8 cm of topsoil were lost.

Farms failed, and many families from Colorado, New Mexico, Kansas, and Oklahoma had no choice but to move away in search of
25 work. Many people moved to California. Without money to buy new farms, they became migrant farm workers.

In 1935, the government began a program of soil conservation in the dust bowl region. Measures such as crop rotation, contour plowing, and terracing have helped to rehabilitate the region. In areas where
30 there is enough rainfall to support the growth of trees, trees have been planted as windbreaks. Although many farmers are practicing soil conservation techniques, erosion and loss of nutrients continue to be problems, both in the United States and around the world. Wherever there is deforestation or overgrazing, there is the risk of soil loss.

5. According to line 13, what event hastened the erosion of the Great Plains?

(A) A drought
(B) The overpopulation of the plains
(C) Abuse of the land
(D) A drought that began in 1931
(E) Erosion, grazing, and a drought

6. Reading lines 14–17, you might draw what conclusion?

(A) The prairie, left in its original state probably would have survived the drought of 1931.
(B) Supplanting the native grasses caused the soil to erode.
(C) Supplanting the native grasses weakened the soil and made it ripe for erosion once the drought started.
(D) Wind and drought helped create the dust bowl.
(E) Food crops weren't a good choice for the prairie.

7. According to the last paragraph, how can farmers prevent soil erosion?

(A) Crop rotation, contour plowing, and terracing

(B) Crop rotation, contour plowing, terracing, and trees used as windbreaks

(C) Crop rotation, contour plowing, terracing, trees used as windbreaks, and controlled grazing

(D) Crop rotation, contour plowing, terracing, trees used as windbreaks, and controlled grazing and planting

(E) Growing only native plants

Questions 8–10 are based on the following passages from a science text:

Passage 1

    People can continue to use the known supply of fossil fuels at current rates for many years. New technology makes finding and extracting oil, coal, and natural gas easier. For example, in 1978, scientists

Line thought there was about 648 billion barrels of oil remaining world-

    5 wide. However, with new discoveries and improved technology, optimists now think there may be as much as 3 trillion barrels remaining. Even if the use of oil increased, scientists would still have several hundred years to develop alternative fuels and new refining processes. In addition, technologies are reducing the amount of sulfur dioxide and

  10 nitrogen oxides released when fossil fuels are burned.

Passage 2

    Advances in technology will serve only to speed up the rate at which oil is extracted from oil reserves. The amount of oil available for consumers will rise, and people will feel no need to conserve. At some

Line point, production will decrease as supplies dwindle. The emissions pro-

    5 duced when fossil fuels burn put society as a whole at risk. Despite more efficient methods of combustion, more than 6 billion tons of carbon dioxide was released into the atmosphere in 1997. Developing alternative sources of energy now will reduce pollution in the future. These alternatives also free fossil fuels for use in the production of

  10 plastics, paints, medicines, and other essential materials.

8. Both passages are primarily concerned with the subject of

(A) how to reduce the use of fossil fuels

(B) the need to reduce the use of fossil fuels

(C) modern techniques for drilling and refining fossil fuels

(D) the availability of fossil fuels

(E) developing alternate fuel sources

9. After reading both passages, what is the main issue that needs to be resolved regarding the use of fossil fuels?
   (A) Finding safer ways to burn fossil fuels
   (B) Determining whether the conservation of fossil fuels is necessary
   (C) Agreeing upon a way to reduce our dependency on fossil fuels
   (D) Determining how much of the remaining fuel deposits should be used
   (E) Without alternative energy sources, we will use up all the fossil fuel

10. Both passages discuss the following subjects, within the context of the position the passage supports.
    (A) Advances in technology and pollution
    (B) The amount of remaining oil, advances in technology and pollution
    (C) The amount of remaining oil, advances in technology and pollution, and alternate energy sources
    (D) Advances in drilling and refining technologies, and fossil fuel as a pollutant
    (E) Advances in technology, other uses for oil besides energy, and cleaner ways to burn fossil fuels

Answers to Exam Prep Questions

1. Answer C is the correct response. This passage reviews some of the ways the government trounced civil liberties in an effort to silence opposition to the war. Answer A is incorrect because the passage doesn't discuss patriotism. Answer B is incorrect because it's too general; the passage draws the conclusion that civil liberties were attacked. Answer D is incorrect because the laws didn't attack socialism but rather opposition to the government and war effort. Answer E is incorrect even though the passage does use a few examples to support the claim that civil liberties were under attack; the main point isn't the effects of the attacks but rather that the attack occurred.

2. Answer D is correct because it's the most comprehensive of all the responses. Answer A is incorrect because it's part of a description from The Sedition Act of 1918. Answer B is incorrect because speaking against the war isn't specifically used in the act (as far as we know from the facts given). Answer C is incorrect. Although striking workers were jailed in 1917, they weren't violating The Espionage Act by striking. Answer E is incorrect because it's too general a statement.

3. Answer A is correct, even though you had to reason a bit to get from the actual sentence to the response. Answers B and C are incorrect, even though they might be true. They're not discussed in this

sentence. Answers D and E are incorrect because they aren't discussed in this sentence, nor is the idea expressed by either answer properly developed in the passage.

4. Answer E is correct. This statement is a metaphor that compares witch-hunting and super-patriotism to a virus. This is a vocabulary-in-context question. Answers A, B, and C are all incorrect because they are too vague. Answer D is incorrect even though the statement is true; the comparison is to the damage of witch-hunting and super-patriotism.

5. Answer D is correct. The question specifically points you to line 13, and the discussion in that line is about the drought of 1931. Although some of the responses are true in that they occurred before the destruction of the plains, the question specifically requests the item mentioned in line 13. You must read the question carefully and respond to it exactly as asked. Answer A is incorrect because it isn't as complete as answer D. Remember, don't choose the first true answer; there might be another answer that's more complete. Answers B, C, and E are all true, but not correct because they refer to items not discussed in line 13.

6. Answer A is correct. The settlers, albeit unknowingly, changed the ecosystem to the point where it could no longer survive the climate. Answers B, C, D, and E are all true statements, but they aren't a conclusion; they're facts.

7. Answer B is correct, according to the last paragraph, even though we are left to draw this conclusion. The article tells us that the government put these measures into action. Answer A is incorrect because it's incomplete. Answers C, D, and E are incorrect because they include measures not discussed in the last paragraph, within the context of solving the problem. Overgrazing is mentioned in the last sentence as part of the problem. However, controlled grazing isn't discussed in the last paragraph within the context of solutions.

8. Answer D is correct; the passages are a counterpoint discussion on the availability of fossil fuels. Answers A, B, and D, and E are all incorrect. These subjects are part of the discussion, but they are not the main point of the discussion.

9. Answer B is correct. One passage concludes that there's plenty of oil and conservation isn't necessary. The second passage supports reducing the amount of fossil fuel we use. Answers A, C, D, and E are all incorrect. Although these points are all made in at least one passage, they aren't the main disagreement between the two passages.

10. Answer D is correct. The answer is essentially the same as Answer A, but it's more specific. Answer A is incorrect because it's incomplete. Answers B and C are incorrect because passage 2 doesn't discuss the amount of fossil fuel remaining. Rather, passage 2 makes the point that conservation is necessary regardless of the amount left. Answer E is incorrect because passage 1 doesn't discuss alternate uses for fossil fuels.

The Critical Reading Section: Longer Passages and Paired Passages

Terms you'll need to understand:

✓ Passage theme
✓ Paragraph purpose
✓ Transitions between paragraphs
✓ Paired passages

Techniques you'll need to master:

✓ Analyze the structure of a long passage
✓ Recognize what is being asked of you in each question
✓ Manage your time efficiently with long critical reading passages
✓ Compare two passages on the same topic

In Chapter 4, "The Critical Reading Section: Reading Comprehension," you reviewed the short passages on the critical reading section of the SAT. This section of the SAT includes two other types of passages. First, there are longer passages, up to 850 words or so. Second, there are paired passages (which can be either short or long) in which you must work with two reading selections on the same topic. Although these SAT questions require some of the same skills as the shorter reading passages, there are also some specific skills and strategies that will help you get through this portion of the test.

Working with Longer Passages

The SAT critical reading passages that we've discussed so far are short: perhaps 100–200 words in length. But the SAT also includes longer passages ranging from 400–850 words long. You'll still need to answer the same types of questions about each passage; but with the longer passages, your skill at identifying the overall structure of the passage and finding relevant information for each question will become crucial. You simply won't have enough time to reread the entire passage for each question.

Determining the Structure of a Passage

You should keep in mind three things when reading a longer passage:

➤ What is the overall theme of the passage?

➤ What is the purpose of each paragraph within the passage?

➤ What are the important transitions between paragraphs?

Answering these three questions will help you understand the structure of the passage, which in turn will help you answer the questions. The goal is to transform reading from a passive practice to an active one. When you make notes, highlight sentences, and otherwise work with the text, you'll find that it's easier to recall the information in the passage. Here's an example to show what we mean:

The following passage is an excerpt from a modern earth sciences textbook.

During most of the late Paleozoic, organisms diversified dramatically. Some 400 million years ago, plants that had adapted to survive at the water's edge began to move inland, becoming land plants. These earliest
Line land plants were leafless vertical spikes about the size of your index finger.
5 However, by the end of the Devonian, 40 million years later, the fossil record indicates the existence of forests with trees tens of meters high.

In the oceans, armor-plated fishes that had evolved during the Ordovician continued to adapt. Their armor plates thinned to lightweight scales that increased the organisms' speed and mobility. Other fishes evolved during
10 the Devonian, including primitive sharks that had a skeleton made of cartilage and bony fishes—the groups to which virtually all modern fishes belong. Because of this, the Devonian period is often called the "age of fishes."

By late Devonian time, several fish became adapted to land environments.
15 The fishes had primitive lungs that supplemented their breathing through gills. Lobe-finned fish likely occupied tidal flats and small ponds. Through time, the lobe-finned fish began to use their lungs more than their gills. By the end of the Devonian period, they had developed lungs and eventually evolved into true air-breathing amphibians with fishlike
20 heads and tails.

Modern amphibians, like frogs, toads, and salamanders, are small and occupy limited biological niches. However, conditions during the remainder of the Paleozoic were ideal for these newcomers to the land. Plants and insects, which were their main diet, already were very abundant and
25 large. The amphibians rapidly diversified because they had minimal competition from other land dwellers. Some groups took on roles and forms that were more similar to modern reptiles, such as crocodiles, than to modern amphibians.

By the Pennsylvanian period, large tropical swamps extended across
30 North America, Europe, and Siberia. Trees approached 30 meters, with trunks over a meter across. The coal deposits that we use today for fuel originated in these swamps. These lush swamps allowed the amphibians to evolve quickly into a variety of species.

The Paleozoic ended with the Permian period, a time when Earth's major
35 landmasses joined to form the supercontinent Pangaea. This redistribution of land and water and changes in the elevation of landmasses brought pronounced changes in world climate. Broad areas of the northern continents became elevated above sea level, and the climate became drier. These climate changes are believed to have triggered extinctions of many
40 species on land and sea.

By the close of the Permian, 75 percent of the amphibian families had disappeared, and plants had declined in number and variety. Although many amphibian groups became extinct, their descendants, the reptiles, would become the most successful and advanced animals on Earth. Much of the
45 marine life did not adapt and survive. At least 80 percent, and perhaps as much as 95 percent, of marine life disappeared. Many marine invertebrates that had been dominant during the Paleozoic, including all the

remaining trilobites as well as some types of coral and brachiopods, could not adapt to the widespread environmental changes.

Here's how you might go about summarizing this particular passage. First, make note of the introductory sentence in italics. This isn't part of the passage, but the way that the SAT introduces the passage. There will always be at least one of these sentences, and perhaps as many as three or four, before a longer reading section. In this case, because you're told that the excerpt is from a textbook, you can make the assumption that it is likely an analysis (refer to Chapter 3, "The Critical Reading Section: Sentence Completions," for the distinction between narrative, argument, and analysis in critical reading).

Next, try to identify the purpose of each paragraph. You can do this by underlining or circling words or sentences, or by writing notes in the margin (if your handwriting is reasonably small and neat). With this selection, you might underline these sentences and fragments:

Plants that had adapted to survive at the water's edge began to move inland, becoming land plants.

The Devonian period is often called the "age of fishes."

By late Devonian time, several fish became adapted to land environments.

The amphibians rapidly diversified because they had minimal competition from other land dwellers.

Lush swamps allowed the amphibians to evolve quickly into a variety of species.

This redistribution of land and water and changes in the elevation of landmasses brought pronounced changes in world climate.

By the close of the Permian, 75 percent of the amphibian families had disappeared,

We'd also write the word "extinctions" next to the final paragraph because it talks about how many different types of organisms died out. The net effect of this underlining and note taking is to provide a sort of roadmap of the passage. Just as a highway map shows all the roads but makes the interstate highways bigger and more obvious, underlining key sentences helps the structure of the passage stand out.

While you're identifying the main idea of each paragraph, be aware of the transitions between paragraphs. In this case, the transitions are fairly obvious: The narrator is moving forward through time, describing what happened in each successive period.

Remember, transitions are those words and phrases that help you move through the passage by indicating the relationship between each paragraph or idea.

Finally, look back over the sentences and words that you've noted and come up with an overall theme for the entire passage. In this case, we'd suggest "how life changed in the late Paleozoic." The writer is concerned with surveying the subject and telling you something about plants, fishes, and amphibians, as well as how each group of organisms evolved.

Remember, you shouldn't be put off by the unfamiliar terms in the reading passages. You won't need to know when the Paleozoic was, or what a trilobite looks like, to answer the questions from this passage. The SAT always asks questions that you can answer purely from the material you've just read.

Using the Questions for Information

Some people recommend reading the questions before the critical reading passages, particularly with the longer passages. Although we won't recommend this strategy for everyone, some students find it very effective. Let's look at an example of a long passage together with its questions as a way to consider this strategy. If you want to "play along," you might skip down and read the questions first, and then come back to read the passage.

The following passage comes from the popular history The Story of Mankind, by the Dutch-American author and journalist Hendrik Willem van Loon. Here van Loon discusses the ideals of ancient Greece.

Indeed, ancient Athens resembled a modern club. All the freeborn citizens were hereditary members and all the slaves were hereditary servants, and waited upon the needs of their masters, and it was very pleasant to be

Line a member of the organisation.

5 ...

The Greeks accepted slavery as a necessary institution, without which no city could possibly become the home of a truly civilised people.

The slaves also took care of those tasks which nowadays are performed by the business men and the professional men. As for those household

10 duties which take up so much of the time of your mother and which worry your father when he comes home from his office, the Greeks, who understood the value of leisure, had reduced such duties to the smallest possible minimum by living amidst surroundings of extreme simplicity.

To begin with, their homes were very plain. Even the rich nobles spent
their lives in a sort of adobe barn, which lacked all the comforts which a
modern workman expects as his natural right. A Greek home consisted of
four walls and a roof. There was a door which led into the street but there
were no windows. The kitchen, the living rooms and the sleeping quarters
were built around an open courtyard in which there was a small fountain,
or a statue and a few plants to make it look bright. Within this courtyard
the family lived when it did not rain or when it was not too cold. In one
corner of the yard the cook (who was a slave) prepared the meal and in
another corner, the teacher (who was also a slave) taught the children the
alpha beta gamma and the tables of multiplication and in still another corner the lady of the house, who rarely left her domain (since it was not considered good form for a married woman to be seen on the street too often)
was repairing her husband's coat with her seamstresses (who were slaves,)
and in the little office, right off the door, the master was inspecting the
accounts which the overseer of his farm (who was a slave) had just brought
to him.

When dinner was ready the family came together but the meal was a
very simple one and did not take much time. The Greeks seem to have
regarded eating as an unavoidable evil and not a pastime, which kills many
dreary hours and eventually kills many dreary people. They lived on bread
and on wine, with a little meat and some green vegetables. They drank
water only when nothing else was available because they did not think it
very healthy. They loved to call on each other for dinner, but our idea of
a festive meal, where everybody is supposed to eat much more than is
good for him, would have disgusted them. They came together at the
table for the purpose of a good talk and a good glass of wine and water,
but as they were moderate people they despised those who drank too
much.

The same simplicity which prevailed in the dining room also dominated their choice of clothes. They liked to be clean and well groomed, to
have their hair and beards neatly cut, to feel their bodies strong with the
exercise and the swimming of the gymnasium, but they never followed the
Asiatic fashion which prescribed loud colours and strange patterns. They
wore a long white coat and they managed to look as smart as a modern
Italian officer in his long blue cape.

They loved to see their wives wear ornaments but they thought it very
vulgar to display their wealth (or their wives) in public and whenever the
women left their home they were as inconspicuous as possible.

In short, the story of Greek life is a story not only of moderation but
also of simplicity. "Things," chairs and tables and books and houses and

55 carriages, are apt to take up a great deal of their owner's time. In the end they invariably make him their slave and his hours are spent looking after their wants, keeping them polished and brushed and painted. The Greeks, before everything else, wanted to be "free," both in mind and in body. That they might maintain their liberty, and be truly free in spirit, they
60 reduced their daily needs to the lowest possible point.

1. The phrase "household duties" in lines 9–10 describes
   (A) work brought home from the office
   (B) household chores such as cooking and ironing
   (C) anything requiring effort at home
   (D) taxes paid by a freeman for the privilege of living in a house
   (E) teaching and cooking

2. According to the author, the Greeks regarded dinner as a time for
   (A) eating simply and good conversation
   (B) killing time that would otherwise pass too slowly
   (C) feasting and heavy drinking
   (D) enjoying meals cooked with their own hands
   (E) making appointments for later discussions

3. The word "vulgar" in line 52 is used to mean
   (A) crudely indecent
   (B) deficient in taste, delicacy, or refinement
   (C) associated with the common people
   (D) off-color
   (E) used in everyday language

4. The main theme of the passage is that
   (A) the few freemen in ancient Greece rested on the backs of many slaves
   (B) only men could be truly free in Greek society
   (C) eating is a dreary thing that is best avoided
   (D) the Greek ideal of freedom required living a moderate and simple life
   (E) in a free civilization, the family unit is the core of society

 In the real SAT, you should expect the long passages to be followed by anywhere up to a dozen questions.

 The long passage questions are always given in the order that you'll encounter the answers in the passage.

If you decide to read the questions first, here's what you might come up with:

➤ Question 1 tells you exactly which words in which line you need to understand. At this point, you could underline the words "household duties" on lines 9–10 meaning in context. Put the number 1 in the margin of the passage to note that this is where you'll find the information for question 1.

➤ Question 2 doesn't include a line number. But it does include the word "dinner." That should tip you off to keep an eye out for portions of the passage that deal with dinner.

➤ Question 3 again points you at a particular line and word. Underline "vulgar" on line 52 and put the number 3 in the margin. Now you know the answer to question 2 should be somewhere between the two numbers you've marked in the margin.

➤ Question 4 asks about the overall theme of the passage. As soon as you realize this is an "overall" question, move on. This question is going to require you to understand the whole passage, not to focus in on one particular section.

The issue is whether the effort of reading the questions first is worth it. If there are a dozen questions, and it takes you twenty seconds to skim each one, underline words, and write numbers in the margin, you've just spent four minutes on the questions without reading the passage at all. Four minutes might not sound like much time when you're reading this Exam Cram, but in a 25-minute critical reading section of the real thing, you might feel a lot of pressure over spending that much time. But if you're good at skimming questions, you'll find that you make up the time spent reading them by being able to concentrate on the important parts of the passage. Also note that you don't have to read the questions in detail. You only need to identify the themes and line numbers to watch out for.

The best advice we can give is that you need to practice both ways (reading the questions first or reading the passage first) and decide which way works best for you. Given that the real SAT tends to focus at least as much on large ideas and themes as on individual words and phrases, our own preference is for reading the passage first. But we're not taking the SAT: You are. You need to do what works best for you, and you can figure out what works best by trying both strategies on a few sample exams.

If you do decide to read the questions and mark lines first, keep one point in mind: The answer to a question is not necessarily found in the line number that the question refers to. The meaning of a phrase, for example, might not be clear until you've read the next half-dozen lines after the point where it is introduced.

As long as we're talking about this selection, let's go over the answers to these four questions. For the first question, the best answer is C. Remember, the critical reading questions only depend on information contained directly in the passage. You can eliminate answers A, B, and D because the passage doesn't mention offices, ironing, or taxes. Teaching and cooking (answer E) are mentioned in the passage—but they are mentioned as activities of slaves, whereas it's clear that "household duties" refers to the activities of the freemen.

The second question requires you to understand the meaning of the paragraph about dinner. If you followed our advice to identify the purpose of each paragraph, this should be easy: The purpose of this paragraph is to explain that the Greeks viewed dinner as a time for a simple meal and a good talk. That makes it clear that answer A is correct.

Question 3 asks you to choose the proper meaning of "vulgar" in context. All of the definitions given are possible meanings of the word, so knowing the dictionary definition won't help you here. The question is which of these meanings is something that the ancient Greeks would think about displaying their wealth or wives in public. Answers A and D are too strong for the passage. Answer E, referring to language, doesn't make sense in context. Answer C can be eliminated by the rule about the passage containing the answers: You're not told anything about the common people. This leaves answer B, which fits well.

Finally, you need to identify the main theme of the passage to answer question 4. Answers A and B are tempting because they are "politically correct"—but they're not supported by the actual passage. Answer C is a minor point from the passage, hardly its main theme. Answers D and E are both plausible, but of the two, D is a much better answer: Answer E requires making the jump from ancient Greece to civilization in general, whereas the passage only discusses Greece.

Budgeting Your Reading Time

The long passages are one of the sections of the SAT (the other being the essay) where you are most likely to get into time trouble. It's easy to get involved with a long passage, spending more time than you planned looking for answers to the questions. This can be a big problem because if you spend too much time on any one passage, you won't have time to even try the other questions in the section—which would be bad news for your score.

Typically, the critical reading sections of the SAT allow about one minute per question—and that has to include the time it takes you to read the passages!

So if there are a dozen questions after one of the long passages, you need to get them all done in about 12 minutes. You can allow a bit of extra time for the long passages because it's easier to refer back to text for the shorter critical reading selections. As a rough rule of thumb, you should be able to allocate about 15 minutes for a long passage.

When you're tackling a long passage, don't rush, but make sure that you stick with the passage and its questions until you're satisfied that you can't reasonably answer any more of the questions. Rushing is likely to work to your disadvantage because you'll miss details and need to reread to find them. On the other hand, it's usually not a good strategy to answer a few of the questions, and then move to another portion of the test and come back later. Doing that is likely to force you to reread the passage to refresh your memory.

If you're running out of time and you have only a few minutes left for a long passage, take a look at the first few questions before you start reading. Remember, the questions will be in order, so you're most likely to find the answer to those questions in the part of the passage that you have time to read. It's better for your score to answer a few questions correctly than to guess blindly on all of the questions.

Key Types of Questions to Watch For

As you work through SAT practice exams, you'll realize that the SAT uses some types of questions over and over again. By recognizing the patterns in these questions, you'll be better prepared to read the passages with an eye for important information. Here are some of the question types that you should be prepared for:

➤ Some questions will ask you what a particular word or phrase refers to. Most often, these questions will not be looking for a dictionary definition. Rather, they want you to understand the term in the context of the particular passage. If you have trouble with one of these questions, try substituting each of the possible answers in the sentence containing the phrase to see whether the sense of the sentence remains the same.

➤ Some questions will ask why a particular sentence or image occurs in the passage. To answer these questions, you'll need to understand the argument that the author is making. Identifying the theme of each paragraph and of the passage as a whole are your best tools for answering these questions.

➤ Some questions will ask you what a particular word or phrase emphasizes or highlights. Watch out for these questions! Remember, your job is to pick the best answer, not the first true answer that you run across. Make sure that you read all of the answers to these questions so that you can pick the best one.

➤ For analytical passages, questions will often ask you to identify a fact from the passage: Why did something happen, or what was the result of an action? On these questions, pay close attention to what's in the passage, rather than to any knowledge of the field you might already have. You need to answer these questions (and any others) based only on what's in the passage that you read.

Keep in mind that the SAT scoring subtracts one fourth of a point for each wrong answer on multiple-choice questions. In practice, this means that there's no point to random guessing: The subtracted points should balance out the correct answers you get from guessing. If you can eliminate one or two answers as obviously wrong, it's definitely to your benefit to guess from the remaining answers because your chance of adding a point is even higher. So even if a question looks hard to you, read the answers to see if you can increase your odds.

For more on general strategies, see Chapter 9, "Strategies for Raising Your Score."

Working with Paired Passages

The critical reading section of the SAT also contains paired passages. The College Board says that there will be at least one long pair and at least one paragraph-sized pair on the exam. For each of these pairs, one passage will support, oppose, or complement the point of view of the other passage. Here's an example:

The following passages represent two views on the state of mind of the French people in the years leading up to the French revolution. Passage 1 is from a French historian, originally published in 1880. Passage 2 is from a history written in 1892 by an American historian.

Passage 1

To comprehend their actions we ought now to look into the condition of their minds, to know the current train of their ideas, their mode of thinking. But is it really essential to draw this portrait, and are not the
Line details of their mental condition we have just presented sufficient? We
5 shall obtain a knowledge of them later, and through their actions, when, in Touraine, they knock a mayor and his assistant, chosen by themselves, senseless with kicks from their wooden shoes, because, in obeying the national Assembly, these two unfortunate men prepared a table of taxes;

or when at Troyes, they drag through the streets and tear to pieces the
10 venerable magistrate who was nourishing them at that very moment, and
who had just dictated his testament in their favor. Take the still rude brain
of a contemporary peasant and deprive it of the ideas which, for eighty
years past, have entered it by so many channels, through the primary
school of each village, through the return home of the conscript after
15 seven years' service, through the prodigious multiplication of books,
newspapers, roads, railroads, foreign travel and every other species of
communication. Try to imagine the peasant of the eighteenth century,
penned and shut up from father to son in his hamlet, without parish highways, deprived of news, with no instruction but the Sunday sermon, con-
20 tinuously worrying about his daily bread and the taxes, "with his
wretched, dried-up aspect," not daring to repair his house, always perse-
cuted, distrustful, his mind contracted and stinted, so to say, by misery.
His condition is almost that of his ox or his ass, while his ideas are those
of his condition. He has been a long time stolid; "he lacks even instinct,"
25 mechanically and fixedly regarding the ground on which he drags along
his hereditary plow. In 1751, d'Argenson wrote in his journal: "nothing in
the news from the court affects them; the reign is indifferent to
them....the distance between the capital and the province daily widens.
...Here they are ignorant of the striking occurrences that most impressed
30 us at Paris....The inhabitants of the country side are merely poverty-
stricken slaves, draft cattle under a yoke, moving on as they are goaded,
caring for nothing and embarrassed by nothing, provided they can eat and
sleep at regular hours." They make no complaints, "they do not even
dream of complaining;" their wretchedness seems to them natural like
35 winter or hail. Their minds, like their agriculture, still belong to the middle ages.

Passage 2

There are two ways in which the French Revolution may be considered. We may look at the great events which astonished and horrified
Europe and America: the storming of the Bastille, the march on Versailles,
40 the massacres of September, the Terror, and the restoration of order by
Napoleon. The study of these events must always be both interesting and
profitable, and we cannot wonder that historians, scenting the approaching battle, have sometimes hurried over the comparatively peaceful country that separated them from it. They have accepted easy and ready-made
45 solutions for the cause of the trouble. Old France has been lurid in their
eyes, in the light of her burning country-houses. The Frenchmen of the
eighteenth century, they think, must have been wretches, or they could
not so have suffered. The social fabric, they are sure, was rotten indeed,
or it would never have gone to pieces so suddenly.

50   There is, however, another way of looking at that great revolution of which we habitually set the beginning in 1789. That date is, indeed, momentous; more so than any other in modern history. It marks the outbreak in legislation and politics of ideas which had already been working for a century, and which have changed the face of the civilized world.
55 These ideas are not all true nor all noble. They have in them a large admixture of speculative error and of spiritual baseness. They require today to be modified and readjusted. But they represent sides of truth which in 1789, and still more in 1689, were too much overlooked and neglected. They suited the stage of civilization which the world had reached,
60 and men needed to emphasize them. Their very exaggeration was perhaps necessary to enable them to fight, and in a measure to supplant, the older doctrines which were in possession of the human mind. Induction, as the sole method of reasoning, sensation as the sole origin of ideas, may not be the final and only truth; but they were very much needed in the world in
65 the seventeenth and eighteenth centuries, and they found philosophers to elaborate them, and enthusiasts to preach them. They made their way chiefly on French soil in the decades preceding 1789.

1. In line 2 of passage 1, the word "train" most closely means

    (A) a long line of moving people or animals

    (B) a set of linked mechanical parts

    (C) a part of a formal gown that trails behind the wearer

    (D) a string of gunpowder used as a fuse to explode a charge

    (E) an orderly succession of related items

2. The author of passage 1 lists means of communication (lines 16–18) in order to

    (A) emphasize the rate of progress in the modern world

    (B) help the reader understand why peasants in pre-revolutionary France might not have advanced ideas

    (C) show how revolutionary ideas propagated from Paris to the French provinces

    (D) hint that things were really not so bad for French peasants

    (E) demonstrate that the French revolution was a good thing for the peasantry

3. In passage 2, the phrase "comparatively peaceful country" (lines 43–44) means

    (A) the years leading up to the French revolution

    (B) the Netherlands, where no revolution occurred

    (C) the French agricultural provinces

    (D) areas of France that Napoleon's armies did not ravage

    (E) an area behind the battlefront where no troops are active

4. In speaking of "another way of looking at that great revolution," (line 50) the author of passage 2

(A) sees the French revolution as part of a long process rather than as a singular event

(B) suggests that ideas of reason rather than popular discontent drove the French revolution

(C) introduces a conspiracy theory to explain the French revolution

(D) claims to have the final and only truth about the origins of the French revolution

(E) proves that he is more interested in the causes of the French revolution than its effects

5. The author of passage 2 would most likely view passage 1's view of the failings of the pre-revolutionary peasantry as what sort of an explanation of the revolution?

(A) Important

(B) Sufficient

(C) Glib

(D) Incorrect

(E) Insightful

As you can see, the paired passages give rise to three types of questions:

➤ Questions about the first passage

➤ Questions about the second passage

➤ Questions about both passages together

Thus, to answer all of the questions, you need to understand not just the two passages in isolation, but the way in which they relate to one another. Here's how you can reason your way through the five sample questions that you just saw:

The first question asks you to find the appropriate definition of "train" in the sentence, "To comprehend their actions we ought now to look into the condition of their minds, to know the current train of their ideas, their mode of thinking." You can answer this question by substituting each proposed definition in turn back into the original sentence. This makes it clear that answer E, "an orderly succession of related items," is the best fit. Note that both answers A and D contain imagery that might make you think of the mass of people preparing for a revolution, but they're not supported by the context.

The second question checks your ability to reason through a complex passage. You might find it helpful to reduce the author's argument to simple terms: Contemporary peasants have all these means of communication, but eighteenth century peasants didn't. This points to answer B. If you've studied the French revolution, you might be tempted by any of the other answers—but remember, what you've studied is irrelevant. Only what the author says in the passage counts.

Question 3 is designed to trap you into a wrong answer if you're reading quickly. Although answers B, C, D, and E all refer to land, which is the usual definition of "country," they're all wrong. That's because the author of the passage is using "comparatively peaceful country" in a figurative sense to mean the time before the revolution.

The fourth question checks that you understand the main point that the author of the second passage is trying to make. Again, depending on what you know, you might read too much into the answers. If you summarize the two paragraphs, though, you'll see that the first one is about a traditional understanding of the causes of the revolution, whereas the second paragraph suggests another theory. Answer B is the only one that mentions two theories, and it's the correct answer.

The final question asks you to compare the two passages. It should be evident from your reading that the two authors disagree: The first sees the mass of discontented peasants as the cause of the revolution, whereas the second points to new ideas. This lets you dismiss answers A, B, and E because the second author is unlikely to use positive words about the first one. Of the remaining terms, "glib" (answer C) is a better choice than "incorrect" (answer D). The second author makes it clear that he thinks other authors make the easy choice in blaming wretched social conditions for the definition without thinking—a perfect definition of "glib."

When you have to choose between answers that both seem correct but are subtly different, it can be helpful to ask, "How does the author want me to feel about this subject?" This question can help you clarify the author's tone, which may make the most correct answer stand out.

Developing a Strategy for Paired Passages

Consider the three ways that the paired passages might be related in a bit more detail:

➤ The second passage may support the first passage.

➤ The second passage may oppose the first passage.

➤ The second passage may complement the first passage.

If you can identify which of these situations applies to a particular pair of passages, you'll have a good idea of what to look for:

➤ If the second passage supports the first passage, expect questions about what evidence each passage brings to bear on the question at hand. But beware of attempts to trick you by assuming that both passages say exactly the same thing. For example, one passage might condemn large cars for wasting gasoline, whereas the second condemns large cars for causing accidents. This doesn't mean that the second author thinks large cars waste gas, even though he's supporting the first author's contention that large cars are bad.

➤ If the second passage opposes the first passage, be prepared for questions about how the author of one passage would view a word, phrase, or idea from the other passage. You might also be asked to determine how the two passages are opposed: Does the second depend on more recent research, different underlying assumptions, or just different experience on the part of the authors?

➤ If the second passage complements the first passage, you should expect them to be about the same general subject, but to each contain their own information and point of view. Such pairs are ripe for questions about aspects of the subject that the two authors give different emphasis to. You might also be asked to pick out statements on which the two authors agree. Here you'll have to read carefully to determine what's actually said in each passage to find the overlaps.

Reading the italicized text that introduces a pair of passages may help you determine which of these three situations you're in. There won't always be such introductory text, but if there is, watch for telltale words like "both" (indicating agreement) or "but" (indicating disagreement). Don't just skip this in your haste to get to the actual passages!

Working with Paired Passage Questions

You can apply the same basic strategy to questions on paired passages that we already suggested for long passages: Read the questions first and mark the lines in the text that they refer to before you read the passages. But even if you don't choose to do this, you'll probably find that it's worth your while to switch back and forth between the passages and the questions. That's because paired passage questions will almost always occur in this order:

➤ Questions about the first passage

➤ Questions about the second passage

➤ Questions about both passages together

So, the first few questions will be exclusively about the first passage. Particularly if you're in time trouble, there's no point to reading the second passage before you tackle questions about the first passage—and you might do better on them if the first passage is still fresh in your mind. We suggest the following order for dealing with paired passages and their questions:

1. Read the introductory text (if any).

2. If you've decided to read the questions first, read them and mark the passages accordingly.

3. Read the first passage.

4. Skip to the questions and answer questions that are about the first passage.

5. Read the second passage.

6. Answer the rest of the questions.

Remember, split up the reading and questions on paired passages to make the most efficient use of your time.

Exam Prep Questions

Questions 1–10 are based on the following passage.

The following passage is taken from an essay by the English journalist and social critic G.K. Chesterton.

The fairy tales we were all taught did not, like the history we were all taught, consist entirely of lies. Parts of the tale of "Puss in Boots" or "Jack and the Beanstalk" may strike the realistic eye as a little unlikely and out

Line of the common way, so to speak; but they contain some very solid and very

5 practical truths. For instance, it may be noted that both in "Puss in Boots" and "Jack and the Beanstalk" if I remember aright, the ogre was not only an ogre but also a magician. And it will generally be found that in all such popular narratives, the king, if he is a wicked king, is generally also a wizard. Now there is a very vital human truth enshrined in this. Bad govern-

10 ment, like good government, is a spiritual thing. Even the tyrant never rules by force alone; but mostly by fairy tales. And so it is with the modern tyrant, the great employer. The sight of a millionaire is seldom, in the ordinary sense, an enchanting sight: nevertheless, he is in his way an enchanter. As they say in the gushing articles about him in the magazines,

15 he is a fascinating personality. So is a snake. At least he is fascinating to rabbits; and so is the millionaire to the rabbit-witted sort of people that ladies and gentlemen have allowed themselves to become. He does, in a manner, cast a spell, such as that which imprisoned princes and princesses under the shapes of falcons or stags. He has truly turned men into

20 sheep, as Circe turned them into swine.

Now, the chief of the fairy tales, by which he gains this glory and glamour, is a certain hazy association he has managed to create between the idea of bigness and the idea of practicality. Numbers of the rabbit-witted ladies and gentlemen do really think, in spite of themselves and their

25 experience, that so long as a shop has hundreds of different doors and a great many hot and unhealthy underground departments (they must be hot; this is very important), and more people than would be needed for a man-of-war, or crowded cathedral, to say: "This way, madam," and "The next article, sir," it follows that the goods are good. In short, they hold

30 that the big businesses are businesslike. They are not. Any housekeeper in a truthful mood, that is to say, any housekeeper in a bad temper, will tell you that they are not. But housekeepers, too, are human, and therefore inconsistent and complex; and they do not always stick to truth and bad temper. They are also affected by this queer idolatry of the enormous and

35 elaborate; and cannot help feeling that anything so complicated must go like clockwork. But complexity is no guarantee of accuracy—in clockwork

or in anything else. A clock can be as wrong as the human head; and a clock can stop, as suddenly as the human heart.

40 But this strange poetry of plutocracy prevails over people against their very senses. You write to one of the great London stores or emporia, asking, let us say, for an umbrella. A month or two afterwards you receive a very elaborately constructed parcel, containing a broken parasol. You are very pleased. You are gratified to reflect on what a vast number of assistants and employees had combined to break that parasol. You luxuriate in
45 the memory of all those long rooms and departments and wonder in which of them the parasol that you never ordered was broken. Or you want a toy elephant for your child on Christmas Day; as children, like all nice and healthy people, are very ritualistic. Some week or so after Twelfth Night, let us say, you have the pleasure of removing three layers of paste-
50 boards, five layers of brown paper, and fifteen layers of tissue paper and discovering the fragments of an artificial crocodile. You smile in an expansive spirit. You feel that your soul has been broadened by the vision of incompetence conducted on so large a scale. You admire all the more the colossal and Omnipresent Brain of the Organiser of Industry, who amid
55 all his multitudinous cares did not disdain to remember his duty of smashing even the smallest toy of the smallest child. Or, supposing you have asked him to send you some two rolls of cocoa-nut matting: and supposing (after a due interval for reflection) he duly delivers to you the five rolls of wire netting. You take pleasure in the consideration of a mystery: which
60 coarse minds might have called a mistake. It consoles you to know how big the business is: and what an enormous number of people were needed to make such a mistake.

1. By contrasting fairy tales and history in line 1, the author immediately suggests that
   (A) the main subject of his essay will be fairy tales
   (B) he is concerned with debunking some common theories of history
   (C) he will employ irony to make his point
   (D) fairy tales are as important to study as history
   (E) you need a good grasp of history to understand the essay

2. In lines 1–12 the author refers to the great employer as "the modern tyrant." What does he mean by this?
   (A) Great employers act arbitrarily when it suits them
   (B) Great employers have taken over the functions of government
   (C) Employees are now slaves to their employers
   (D) Great employers have a magical hold over the populace
   (E) Being a tyrant has become a good thing

3. In line 15, the word "fascinating" in the phrase "At least he is fascinating to rabbits" most nearly means

(A) interesting
(B) bewitching
(C) terrifying
(D) unusual
(E) absorbing

4. How does the author feel about the association between "the idea of bigness and the idea of practicality" (line 23)?

(A) It bears further scrutiny
(B) It makes a lot of sense
(C) It is an inevitable fact of life
(D) It acts to make life better
(E) It is nonsensical

5. What is the purpose of the discussion of clocks and clockwork in lines 34–38?

(A) To emphasize that an intricate mechanism is not necessarily a working mechanism
(B) To serve as an example of the sort of shoddy goods that are sold
(C) To provide a metaphorical way of speaking about people
(D) To relate big business to a familiar saying
(E) To inform the reader that timekeeping is dehumanizing

6. The author uses the example of the parasol (lines 40–46) to

(A) describe his own personal experience
(B) elicit sympathy from the reader
(C) demonstrate the inefficiency of business
(D) emphasize a psychological fact
(E) surprise the reader

7. In referring to "three layers of pasteboards, five layers of brown paper, and fifteen layers of tissue paper" (lines 49–50), the author is

(A) warning about the waste of natural resources
(B) describing an actual parcel that he received
(C) instructing the reader how to wrap things
(D) exaggerating for humorous effect
(E) constructing an elaborate metaphor

8. The sentence, "You take pleasure in the consideration of a mystery: which coarse minds might have called a mistake" (lines 59–60) implies that

(A) some people might call shipping the wrong item a mistake, but the reader is smart enough to know otherwise
(B) the operations of big business firms are a mystery to the average person

    (C) the human mind can find pleasure in any activity if only you maintain a positive attitude

    (D) the examples given are obviously mistakes, but somehow people are tricked into believing that they are something more

    (E) nothing happens in business without a careful plan

9. The author of the passage apparently believes that

    (A) it's worth putting up with some inefficiency to gain the benefits of large businesses

    (B) the average person never thinks honestly about his or her interactions with large firms

    (C) large businesses exercise a tyrannical influence on our lives

    (D) christmas gifts should be ordered well in advance

    (E) fairy tales are our best guide to finding truth

10. Why does the author present three examples of broken or wrong shipments in the third paragraph?

    (A) To add humor to an otherwise dry essay

    (B) To illustrate his contention that big business is impractical business

    (C) To show the sort of goods that you ought not order by mail

    (D) To complain about the poor quality of the post office in his area

    (E) To draw on the reader's personal experiences

Answers to Exam Prep Questions

1. Answer C is correct. You should know that irony is the use of words to express something different from (and often opposite to) their literal meaning. By stating that history consists entirely of lies, the author of the passage is being ironic, and sets the tone of his entire essay. The other answers are incorrect because (as you can confirm by reading the rest of the passage) he's not writing about either fairy tales or history as his main subject. Remember, even though a question may refer to a particular line, the answer does not necessarily lie in that line.

2. Answer D is correct. To properly answer this question, you must carefully follow the thread of the author's argument. He states that in fairy tales, wicked kings are also wizards. He goes on to say that these tyrants rule by fairy tales. Finally he switches the word "tyrant" to refer to employers rather than kings, implying that the employers too rule by fairy tales. The other answers could be correct if you read only the sentence in question, but they don't make sense in the context of the entire essay.

3. Answer B is correct. There is a slight trick here because the author uses "fascinating" in two different senses in successive sentences; if you read too quickly, you'll choose answer A. But in the second sentence, where he talks of a snake being fascinating to rabbits, the word is used in the sense of bewitching prey. Even if you don't recognize this, you can increase your chances of guessing right on the question if you realize that neither "terrifying" nor "unusual" (answers C and D) are synonyms for "fascinating."

4. Answer E is correct. The rest of the passage after the indicated line is concerned with demonstrating, by giving examples, just how incorrect this association is. The author is obviously convinced that the association is incorrect, so answer A can't be right. He also doesn't see the association as a positive thing, which eliminates answers B and D. Answer C might be correct, but answer E is more strongly supported by the passage given.

5. Answer A is correct. Once again it helps to understand the author's argument to this point. He says that we feel a complex organization "must go like clockwork," and then goes on to indicate ways in which clockwork can fail. By extension, this tells us that the complex organization can fail as well. Answer B may be tempting, but in fact the examples come in the next paragraph. Answer C is meant to trap you because the end of the section refers to human heads and human hearts, but the author is not writing about people, merely using them as a poetic illustration. Answer D is part of the truth, but does not explain things as well as answer A, and answer E is a point that's not contained in the passage.

6. Answer C is correct. You should see this as part of your work in summarizing each paragraph of the passage to determine its point. The third paragraph is generally about showing by example just how inefficient big business really is in the author's view. The author presents the example as hypothetical rather than real, which eliminates answer A. Also, there's no reason why the reader should be sympathetic to an imagined hurt, which rules out answer B. Answer D is too abstract for the concrete example, and answer E is incorrect because the reader ought not be surprised by examples that illustrate a point which the author has already made.

7. Answer D is correct. You can eliminate answers B and C because the author is describing another hypothetical example. Answer E is incorrect because there's no hint of a metaphor in the text of the passage; the SAT might throw in a term such as "metaphor" to try to trick you.

Nothing is said or implied about natural resources in the passage. That leaves answer D as the correct one.

8. Answer D is correct. As you're reading the essay, it seems obvious that the examples are all mistakes on the part of the business involved, but the author continues to say that the reader enjoys these mistakes. Answer A is too literal a reading of the irony in these statements. Answers B and E are not supported by the passage, which doesn't discuss the inner workings of business in any detail, and answer C is not related to the topic of the passage at all.

9. Answer C is correct. Summing up the overall theme of the essay, you should come up with something like "large businesses claim to be practical but really they cause trouble for their customers." This points to answer C as correct. Answer A is incorrect because the author doesn't hint that there's anything positive about this state of affairs. Answer B is almost but not quite correct: The absolute word "never" rules it out because the example of the housekeeper shows that people do think honestly about their interactions with large firms. Answer D inflates a minor example beyond its actual importance. Answer E may be tempting to the time-pressed reader because fairy tales are mentioned early in the passage—but they are just used as a literary device to give the passage an interesting beginning.

10. Answer B is correct. The examples serve as illustrations of the passage's overall thesis. The author uses three examples because he seems to be convinced that most people would not believe him without evidence. Answer A is incorrect because the entire passage is light and humorous. Answers C and D are incorrect because the passage is about business in general, not the perils of shipping goods. Answer E is incorrect because there's little chance that the reader has personally experienced any of the examples.

The Mathematics Section: Numbers and Algebra

Terms you'll need to understand:

- ✓ Absolute value
- ✓ Associative Law
- ✓ Base
- ✓ Commutative Law
- ✓ Composition
- ✓ Denominator
- ✓ Directly proportional
- ✓ Distributive Law
- ✓ Divisibility
- ✓ Domain
- ✓ Element
- ✓ Exponent
- ✓ Factor
- ✓ Function
- ✓ Greatest common factor (GCF)
- ✓ Inequality
- ✓ Integer
- ✓ Intersection
- ✓ Inversely proportional
- ✓ Least common multiple (LCM)
- ✓ Numerator
- ✓ Percent
- ✓ Prime
- ✓ Proportion
- ✓ Quadratic formula
- ✓ Range
- ✓ Ratio
- ✓ Rational number
- ✓ Reciprocal
- ✓ Scientific notation
- ✓ Sequence
- ✓ Set
- ✓ System of equations
- ✓ Union
- ✓ Zeroes

Techniques you'll need to master:

- ✓ Perform basic operations on real numbers including integers and fractions, as well as equations
- ✓ Apply the laws of arithmetic
- ✓ Work with sets and sequences
- ✓ Determine the range and domain of functions
- ✓ Graph and transform functions
- ✓ Solve equations for a variable
- ✓ Factor polynomial equations
- ✓ Solve inequalities
- ✓ Solve systems of equations
- ✓ Translate word problems to equations

The SAT tests several types of mathematical knowledge: numbers and algebra, geometry, and probability and analysis. In this chapter, we'll cover the first set of mathematical techniques that you'll find on the exam—those that are taught in Algebra I and Algebra II courses. But just as you can't go straight into Algebra I when you enroll in elementary school, the SAT doesn't start with Algebra I material; you need to know the basic concepts of arithmetic that serve as the underpinnings for algebra. So in this chapter, we'll start with the basic concept of different number types and work up through the more complex problems that the SAT will ask you to solve.

Types of Numbers

Numbers come in many varieties. The SAT generally limits its questions to two types of numbers:

➤ Integers

➤ Rational numbers

Integers are the "counting numbers": They are numbers such as 12, –82, and 0. Integers can be positive (greater than zero) or negative (less than zero). The integer zero is neither positive nor negative. There are an infinite number of integers, both positive and negative. Sometimes you'll see zero and the positive integers referred to as the *whole numbers*.

The SAT also uses the *rational numbers*. Rational numbers can be expressed as the ratio of two integers. Like integers, rational numbers can be either positive or negative. Every integer is a rational number, but not every rational number is an integer. Examples of rational numbers that are not integers are –12.75, 837.668, and $\frac{2}{3}$. The latter may be indicated by 0.666... (where the ellipsis indicates that the sixes repeat forever) or $0.\overline{6}$.

You may also see numbers on the exam expressed using *scientific notation*. For example, 23,000 can be expressed as 2.3×10^4—that is, 2.3 times the fourth power of 10.

You may also recall the real numbers, which are a larger set that includes rational and irrational numbers (those that can't be expressed as a fraction). The only irrational numbers that you'll need to be familiar with for the SAT are π, the ration of the circumference of a circle to its diameter, and such roots as $\sqrt{2}$, which cannot be expressed as a fraction.

The absolute value of a number is the "size" of the number: how far the number is from zero. It's denoted by the notation $|x|$. So

$|3| = 3$

$|-3| = 3$

$-|-3| = -3$

 There are other types of numbers, such as imaginary numbers (numbers that result from taking the square root of a negative number). You won't find these other number types on the SAT.

Using Arithmetical Operators

You can expect to find six fundamental arithmetic operations on the exam:

➤ Addition, indicated by +

➤ Subtraction, indicated by –

➤ Multiplication, indicated by × or ·

➤ Division, indicated by ÷ or /

➤ Power, indicated by a superscript

➤ Root, indicated by $\sqrt{}$

 Addition and subtraction of negative numbers can be converted to operations with positive numbers by interchanging the operation as well. Thus, $4-(-3) = 4+3 = 7$. If you're having trouble with this, mentally insert addition signs in front of each number and then work out which way the signs go. For example, $-(-4) - (-5) + 3 + -6$ becomes $(-(-4)) + (-(-5)) + (+3) + +(-6)$, which gives $4 + 5 + 3 + (-6)$, and the answer is 6.

Power and Root Operations

Of these operations, the only two that you might find tricky are power and root. You're allowed to use a calculator on the math sections, but you should understand what you're calculating anyhow. Knowing how these operations work will sometimes let you answer a question without even picking up the calculator.

Remember, you *can* use a calculator on the math sections of the SAT—but you're not *required* to do so. Don't use a calculator just because you can: Doing so may rob you of precious time that could be better used working on another question.

To calculate a power of a number, you multiply the number by itself that many times. For example, four raised to the third power (also called the third power of four), expressed as 4^3, works out this way:

$4^3 = 4 \times 4 \times 4 = 64$

Here, 4 is the *base* and 3 is the *exponent*. The exponent tells how many times to use the base as a factor.

The second power has the special name of *square*, and the third power has the special name of *cube*.

To calculate a negative power of a number, divide one by the base raised to the equivalent positive power. Thus,

$4^{-2} = \dfrac{1}{4^2} = \dfrac{1}{16}$

Watch out for the order of operations when working with exponents. For example, $-3^2 = 9$, but $-(3)^2 = -9$ because the parentheses tell you to do the power operation first.

A special case of the power operator is the zeroth power. The zeroth power of any number is defined as one, so, for example,

$17^0 = 1$

The square root of a number is the number that you must multiply by itself (square) to get the original number. Similarly, the cube root is the number that you must cube to get the original number, the fourth root is the number that you must raise to the fourth power to get the original number, and so on. Thus,

$\sqrt{16} = 4$

and

$$\sqrt[3]{27} = 3$$

Fractional powers are the equivalent of roots. The $\frac{1}{3}$ power of a number is the same as its cube root, the $\frac{1}{4}$ power is the same as its fourth root, and so on. For example,

$$25^{\frac{1}{2}} = \sqrt{25} = 5$$

The general formula for converting a fractional power to a root is

$$x^{\frac{a}{b}} = \sqrt[b]{x^a} = \left(\sqrt[b]{x}\right)^a$$
$$9^{\frac{3}{2}} = \sqrt[2]{9^3} = \left(\sqrt[2]{9}\right)^3 = 3^3 = 27$$

You need to remember three rules when working with exponents. First, when multiplying expressions with the same base, add the exponents:

$$3^3 \times 3^5 = 3^8$$

Second, when dividing expressions with the same base, subtract the exponents:

$$\frac{4^7}{4^3} = 4^4$$

Third, when raising an exponent to a second exponent, multiply the exponents:

$$\left(2^2\right)^5 = 2^{10}$$

The Order of Operations

When you're faced with a complex mathematical expression to simplify, you must perform the operations in a particular order to get the right answer:

1. Perform any operations inside of parentheses or brackets. If there are multiple sets of parentheses or brackets, start from the innermost set and work your way out.

2. Perform power and root operations in order from left to right.

3. Perform multiplication and division operations in order from left to right.

4. Perform addition and subtraction operations in order from left to right.

Here's an example showing how to calculate the value of an expression one step at a time using these rules:

$$22 + (5 \times 3) \times 2^2 + \sqrt{9} - 4 \div 2$$

$$22 + 15 \times 2^2 + \sqrt{9} - 4 \div 2$$

$$22 + 15 \times 4 + 3 - 4 \div 2$$

$$22 + 60 + 3 - 2$$

$$83$$

If an expression is in the form of a fraction, simplify both the numerator and denominator separately. Then as a final step, either perform the division or leave the answer in the form of a fraction.

Working with Divisibility, Primes, and Factors

You're likely to find some questions that check your grasp of *divisibility* and related topics. An integer is said to be divisible by another integer if the result of dividing the first integer by the second integer is an integer. So, 4 is divisible by 2 (because 4 divided by 2 is 2), but 7 is not divisible by 4 (because 7 divided by 4 is 1.75). If an integer is not divisible by another integer, the *remainder* is the amount "left over" after subtracting the largest possible multiple of the second integer from the first. So, the remainder of 7 divided by 4 is 3, and the remainder of 15 divided by 5 is zero. If an integer a is divisible by another integer b, the remainder of a divided by b is zero.

An even number is an integer that is divisible by two; an odd number is an integer that is not divisible by two. This applies to both positive and negative integers. So, the even numbers include

... −6, −4, −2, 0, 2, 4, 6 ...

whereas the odd numbers include

... −5, −3, −1, 1, 3, 5 ...

 Zero is an even number.

A *prime number* is an integer that is only divisible by itself and by 1. The first few prime numbers are 2, 3, 5, 7, 11, 13, 17, 19, 23, and 29.

The *factors* of an integer are those integers that can be multiplied together to return the original integer. So, 4 and 3 are factors of 12 because $4 \times 3 = 12$. The prime factors of an integer are those prime numbers that can be multiplied together to return the original integer. So, 2, 2, and 3 are the prime factors of 12 because $2 \times 2 \times 3 = 12$.

 Every non-prime integer has only one set of prime factors.

To discover the prime factors of an integer, follow this recipe:

1. Make a list of the first several primes. For most problems involving prime factors on the SAT, the first five primes (2, 3, 5, 7, and 11) should be sufficient.

2. Examine the first prime remaining in the list. If the integer is divisible by this number, the prime is a factor of the integer. Divide the integer by this prime number, and repeat step 2 with the smaller integer that results.

3. If the integer is not divisible by the prime, cross the prime off the list. Repeat step 2 with the next largest integer.

4. Continue until the integer remaining after performing step 2 is itself a prime.

As an example, we'll apply this technique to find the prime factors of the integer 60.

1. The integer is 60, and the lowest remaining prime is 2. 60 is divisible by 2, so 2 is a prime factor of 60. Divide 60 by 2 to get the remaining integer 30.

2. The integer is 30, and the lowest remaining prime is 2. 30 is divisible by 2, so 2 is a prime factor of 60 (the original integer). Divide 30 by 2 to get the remaining integer 15.

3. The integer is 15, and the lowest remaining prime is 2. 15 is not divisible by 2. Cross 2 off the list of primes.

4. The integer is 15, and the lowest remaining prime is 3. 15 is divisible by 3, so 3 is a prime factor of 60. Divide 15 by 3 to get the remaining integer 5.

5. The remaining integer 5 is itself a prime number, so 5 is a prime factor of 60 and the process stops here.

Thus, the prime factors of 60 are 2, 2, 3, and 5 (the numbers that were used in the successful steps 1, 2, 4, and 5 above). To check,

$$2 \times 2 \times 3 \times 5 = 60$$

Two concepts closely related to prime factors are the *greatest common factor (GCF)* and *least common multiple (LCM)*.

The greatest common factor of two integers is the largest factor (prime or otherwise) that the two numbers have in common. To reduce a fraction, you find the GCF of the numerator and denominator, and divide both by the GCF. The easiest way to identify the GCF of two integers is to multiply the prime factors that the two integers have in common. For example, to determine the GCF of 28 and 40, you begin by finding their prime factors:

$$28 = 2 \times 2 \times 7$$
$$40 = 2 \times 2 \times 2 \times 5$$

Keeping only the prime factors that are the same between the two numbers, the GCF of 28 and 40 is 4. That's the largest number that is a factor of both 28 and 40. Thus, if you were given the fraction $\frac{28}{40}$, you could use the GCF to convert to the simplified form $\frac{7}{10}$.

The least common multiple of two integers is the smallest number that has both integers as factors. The LCM is useful when you want to find the common denominator of two fractions. To find the least common multiple, you multiply all the unique prime factors of the two integers. For 28 and 40, you calculate the LCM this way:

$$28 = 2 \times 2 \times \times 7$$
$$40 = 2 \times 2 \times 2 \times 5$$
$$280 = 2 \times 2 \times 2 \times 5 \times 7$$

Thus, 280 is the LCM of 28 and 40.

 If a is divisible by b, the GCF of a and b is b, and the LCM of a and b is a.

Using the Laws of Arithmetic

Three fundamental ways to rearrange arithmetical expressions are sometimes called laws of arithmetic:

➤ The Commutative Law

➤ The Associative Law

➤ The Distributive Law

You can sometimes make it easier to calculate results by applying these laws.

The Commutative and Associative Laws

The Commutative Law applies to addition and multiplication, and says that you can rearrange terms as you like. That is,

$$a + b = b + a$$
$$a \times b = b \times a$$

The Associative Law also applies to addition and multiplication, and says that you can regroup terms as you like. That is,

(a + b) + c = a + (b + c)

(a × b) × c = a × (b × c)

 Note that the Associative Law only applies when you have the same operator in two places. Otherwise, you need to take the order of operations into account. For example, (2 × 2) + 3 = 7, but 2 × (2 + 3) = 10: clearly not equal!

By repeatedly applying these laws, you can rearrange and regroup any number of additive or multiplicative terms. Sometimes you can use this knowledge to simplify an expression. For example,

2 × 3 × 5 × 2 × 3 × 5

(2 × 5) × (2 × 5) × (3 × 3)

10 × 10 × 9

900

The Distributive Law

The Distributive Law says that multiplication and division *distribute* over addition and subtraction. That is, when you multiply or divide a grouped sum or difference, you can do the multiplication first (instead of the parenthetical operation first) as long as you do it to each piece of the parenthetical expression. Schematically, distribution looks like this:

a × (b + c) = (a × b) + (a × c)

$$\frac{(a - b)}{c} = \frac{a}{c} - \frac{b}{c}$$

As with the Commutative and Associative Laws, you're not required to apply the Distributive Law; you should do so when it makes your work easier. For example,

7 × (100 − 3)

(7 × 100) − (7 × 3)

700 − 21

679

You'd get the same answer by doing the subtraction first and multiplying 7 times 97 (try it and see), but using the Distributive Law makes this a problem that you can easily do in your head without reaching for the calculator.

Understanding Fractions and Percentages

The SAT will require you to have a good knowledge of fractions and related topics such as ratios, proportions, and percentages. It may have been quite a few years since you learned the fundamental operations on fractions, so it's a good idea to brush up while you can.

Performing Arithmetic with Fractions

A *fraction* is a way of representing a real number by the quotient of two integers: the *numerator* divided by the *denominator*. For example, the real number 1.5 can be represented by the fraction $\frac{3}{2}$, where 3 is the numerator and 2 is the denominator.

To convert a fraction to a decimal number, you perform the division. You can do this by hand using long division, but because you're allowed to use a calculator on the math sections of the SAT, you probably won't choose to do it by hand. But it's worth knowing the most common ones so that you don't need to even pick up the calculator. You may find problems in which the answer is difficult to calculate using one form, but easy using the other:

$$\frac{1}{10} = .1$$

$$\frac{1}{8} = .125$$

$$\frac{1}{5} = .2$$

$$\frac{1}{4} = .25$$

$$\frac{1}{3} = .\overline{3}$$

$$\frac{2}{5} = .4$$

$$\frac{1}{2} = .5$$

$$\frac{3}{5} = .6$$

$$\frac{2}{3} = .\overline{6}$$

$$\frac{3}{4} = .75$$

$$\frac{4}{5} = .8$$

The decimal equivalent of a fraction doesn't change if you multiply or divide both the numerator and denominator by the same value. For example,

$$\frac{1}{3} = \frac{(3 \times 1)}{(3 \times 3)} = \frac{3}{9}$$

Note that in the case of $\frac{3}{9}$, the numerator and denominator have a common factor of 3. A reduced fraction is one whose numerator and denominator have no common factor. To reduce a fraction, find the greatest common factor of the numerator and denominator and divide both the numerator and denominator by that value.

A proper fraction is one whose decimal equivalent is less than one (such as $\frac{4}{5}$). An improper fraction is one whose decimal equivalent is greater than or equal to one (such as $\frac{5}{4}$). You can write an improper fraction as the combination of an integer and a proper fraction (this is also known as a *mixed number*):

$$\frac{5}{4} = \frac{4}{4} + \frac{1}{4} = \frac{5}{4}$$

To add or subtract fractions, you must perform two steps:

1. Make sure that the two fractions have the same denominator. (This is referred to as a *common denominator*.)

2. Add or subtract the numerators and keep the denominator.

$$\frac{17}{34} - \frac{8}{34} = \frac{(17-8)}{34} = \frac{9}{34}$$

If the two fractions already have the same denominator, this process is easy:

If the two fractions do not already have the same denominator, the common denominator is the least common multiple of the two denominators. Convert both fractions to the same denominator by multiplying each by the remaining factors. For example, to add $\frac{1}{2}$ and $\frac{1}{3}$, note that the least common multiple of 2 and 3 is 6. Thus,

$$\frac{1}{2} + \frac{1}{3} = \frac{(3 \times 1)}{(3 \times 2)} + \frac{(2 \times 1)}{(2 \times 3)} = \frac{3}{6} + \frac{2}{6} = \frac{5}{6}$$

To multiply fractions, multiply both the numerator and denominator:

$$\frac{1}{2} \times \frac{3}{5} = \frac{(1 \times 3)}{(2 \times 5)} = \frac{3}{10}$$

If you want to make sure that the answer of multiplying fractions is a reduced fraction, eliminate common factors from the numerator and denominator before finishing the multiplication. For example,

$$\frac{4}{9} \times \frac{3}{2} = \frac{(4 \times 3)}{(9 \times 2)} = \frac{(2 \times 2 \times 3)}{(3 \times 3 \times 2)} = \frac{(\cancel{2} \times 2 \times \cancel{3})}{(\cancel{3} \times 3 \times \cancel{2})} = \frac{2}{3}$$

To divide fractions, remember the rule "invert and multiply":

$$\frac{\frac{2}{3}}{\frac{1}{2}} = \frac{2}{3} \times \frac{2}{1} = \frac{4}{3}$$

 To multiply or divide mixed numbers, first convert them to improper fractions.

You'll also need to know how to find the *reciprocal* of a number. The reciprocal of a number is the result of dividing one by the number. Of course, you can use the invert and multiply rule to perform this operation as well. For instance, to get the reciprocal of $\frac{9}{16}$,

$$\frac{1}{\frac{9}{16}} = 1 \times \frac{16}{9} = \frac{16}{9}$$

Or simply note that the reciprocal of a fraction can be calculated by switching the numerator and denominator of the fraction. To find the reciprocal of a number such as $4\frac{2}{9}$, first convert it to an improper fraction:

$$4\frac{2}{9} = \frac{36}{9} + \frac{2}{9} = \frac{38}{9}$$

So the reciprocal of $4\frac{2}{9}$ is $\frac{9}{38}$.

Using Ratios and Proportions

A *ratio* is the quotient of two quantities. For example, suppose you're told in a question that the Pennsylvania Railroad has nine miles of track for every five miles of track that belong to the Erie Railroad. This sets up a ratio between the amount of track that belongs to the two railroads. There are quite a few ways that you can express this ratio (or that the SAT might express it in a question):

➤ The ratio of Pennsylvania Railroad track to Erie Railroad track is nine to five.

➤ 9/5

➤ 9:5

➤ 9 to 5

A *proportion* is an equation in which two ratios are set equal to one another. You'll typically run across proportions in word problems on the SAT. For example, the previous ratio could be turned into a proportion question this way:

> The Pennsylvania Railroad has nine miles of track for every five miles of track that belongs to the Erie Railroad. The Erie Railroad has 125 miles of track. How many miles of track does the Pennsylvania Railroad have?

To solve this question, set up two ratios: the one that you're given for the relative amounts of track between the two railroads, and another that represents the actual ratio of track. Make sure that both ratios are in the same order! The second ratio includes an unknown quantity, the actual miles of Pennsylvania Railroad track, which we'll call p:

$$\frac{9}{5} = \frac{p}{125}$$

To solve a proportion such as this, you can begin by *cross-multiplying*: Multiply the numerator of the first ratio by the denominator of the second, and vice versa, to get two quantities that are equal to one another:

$$5p = 125 \times 9$$

Now you can take advantage of the fact that you can always divide two sides of an equation by the same number without changing the equation:

$$p = \frac{(125 \times 9)}{5}$$

$$p = 25 \times 9$$

$$p = 225$$

So the Pennsylvania Railroad has 225 miles of track.

For more information on solving equations, see the section "Solving Equations" later in this chapter.

You should expect to find ratio questions combined with other mathematical concepts. For example, you may be asked to find the proportion of two angles or two line segments or the areas of two rectangles. There's no difference between solving such equations and solving those involving railroad tracks.

Working with Percentage and Change

A *percent* is a ratio in which the denominator is 100. For example, $80\% = \frac{80}{100}$. Percents typically turn up on the SAT in problems involving proportion or change. For example, here's a proportion problem that uses percent:

> Thirty-five percent of the students in Advanced Placement biology are studying fish. There are 20 students in the class. How many are studying fish?

To solve using a proportion and cross-multiplication,

$$\frac{35}{100} = f/20$$

$$100f = 35 \times 20$$

$$f = \frac{(35 \times 20)}{100}$$

$$f = 7$$

This is a good place to remember that there's usually more than one way to solve a mathematical problem. If you recognize that $35\% = .35$, you can also solve this problem by a simple multiplication:

$$f = .35 \times 20 = 7$$

You'll also find change problems that involve percent. For example,

> The pressure in a steam boiler is 250psi. If the pressure increases by 20%, what is the new pressure?

To solve this problem, first calculate the increase in pressure. The problem specifies that the increase is 20% of the original pressure, which you can calculate as follows:

20% of 250

$$\frac{20}{100} \times 250$$

$$\frac{(20 \times 250)}{100}$$

50

So the increase in pressure is 50psi. But the problem doesn't ask for the increase in pressure; it asks for the new pressure, which is the original pressure plus the increase. So the answer is 300psi.

 On a problem such as this, you're almost certain to see the intermediate calculation as one of the wrong answers. Make sure that your answer is actually what the question asked for!

Another type of percentage question you may see on the exam asks you to calculate one number as a percent of another. As an example, suppose that you're asked this question:

> A class that started with 30 students now has 27 students. What percent decrease is this?

To solve these percent change problems, you can use the following formula:

Percent change =   ×100%

In this case, the final number is 27, and the starting number is 30. So to calculate the answer

Percent change = $\dfrac{(27 - 30)}{30}$ ×100%

$$\text{Percent change} = -\frac{3}{30} \times 100\%$$
$$\text{Percent change} = -10\%$$

So the number of students in the class has decreased by 10 percent.

Working with Sequences

A *sequence* is an ordered set of numbers. The SAT can include questions on two specific types of sequences. An *arithmetic sequence* is one in which adjacent terms differ by a constant value:

2, 4, 6, 8 ...

To get each term of this arithmetic sequence, you add 2 to the preceding term.

A *geometric sequence* is one in which adjacent terms have a constant ratio. For example,

1, 4, 16, 64 ...

To get each term of this geometric sequence, you multiply the preceding term by 4.

The SAT might ask three different things about sequences:

➤ What is the sum of certain terms of a sequence?

➤ What is the average of certain terms of a sequence?

➤ What is the value of a specific term in a sequence?

If you're dealing with terms near the start of a sequence, these questions are easy. For example,

What is the average of the first five terms of the sequence 1, 3, 5 ... ?

In this case, it's easy to just write out the five terms and average them:

$$\frac{(1 + 3 + 5 + 7 + 9)}{5} = 5$$

For more information on averages, see Chapter 8, "The Mathematics Section: Statistics, Probability, and Data Analysis."

But what do you do if you need to calculate something about the fiftieth term of a sequence? Rather than take out your calculator and start multiplying, it's better to take a few moments to derive the formula for the sequence. For an arithmetic sequence, the general formula for the nth term is

$$a + ((n-1) \times b)$$

Here *a* is the value of the first term, *n* is the number of the term you're looking for, and *b* is a constant.

For a geometrical sequence, the general formula for the nth term is

$$a \times (b^{n-1})$$

Here again, *a* is the value of the first term, *n* is the number of the term you're looking for, and *b* is a constant.

Of course, it's up to you to determine the values of *a* and *b* to make the appropriate equation work. Here's how we'd work through the answer for a specific problem:

A biologist inoculates a culture dish with bacteria. After one hour, there are 300 bacteria on the dish; after two hours 900, after three hours 2700, and so on. How many bacteria are on the dish after 10 hours?

To solve this question, first extract the basic sequence:

300, 900, 2700 ...

Because the terms have a constant ratio, this is a geometrical sequence. The constant *a* is the greatest common factor of these three numbers; this is apparently 300. So you can rewrite the sequence:

$$300 \times (1, 3, 9 \dots)$$

And the nth term is then

$300 \times (3^{n-1})$

Recall that any number to the power of zero is 1, so the first term is 300×3^0, or 300, which checks. Now you can calculate the tenth term, which is what the question calls for:

$300 \times 3^{10-1} = 300 \times 3^9 = 300 \times 19{,}683 = 5{,}904{,}900$

Performing Basic Operations on Sets

A *set* is a collection of things that are called the elements or members of the set. Questions on the SAT might ask about the *union* or *intersection* of two sets.

The union of two sets is another set that contains all the elements from the first two sets, without counting any common elements twice. Sets are normally indicated by curly braces containing members separated by commas. So, for example, here are two sets:

{1, 17, 49, 82, 100}
{3, 22, 49, 82, 99}

The union of these two sets is

{1, 3, 17, 22, 49, 82, 99, 100}

Note that the elements 49 and 82 only show up once in the union, even though they occur in each of its constituent sets. The intersection of two sets is the set consisting of elements that are in both sets. So starting with the same two sets, their intersection is

{49, 82}

Functions

A mathematical *function* is a rule for associating elements of one set with elements of another set. To indicate a function, you use a special notation, as shown in this example:

$$f(x) = x^2$$

That particular function can be read as "f of x is equal to x squared."

 Functions can also be indicated using $g(x)$, $h(x)$, or any other letter. Don't get confused if the SAT uses a letter other than f to indicate a function.

Two important properties of a function are its *domain* and its *range*. The domain of a function is the set of all input values for which the function is defined, and the range of a function is the set of all values that can be produced by applying the function to values in its domain.

For example, consider the function

$$g(x) = \frac{1}{x}$$

The domain of the function g is all the real numbers except zero (because division by zero is undefined). What about the range of the function? You can get any arbitrarily small value as the result of the function by choosing a large value for x, and any arbitrarily large value by choosing a small value for x. But you can never get exactly zero for the output; one divided by anything is always larger than zero. Hence the range is also the entire set of real numbers except zero.

If you're given a function and asked to determine the value of the function for a particular input, just plug the input in to the function and find the answer. For example, if $f(x) = 3x^2 - 7$, the notation $f(3)$ indicates the value of the function for the input 3, referred to as "f of three." You'd calculate it this way:

$$f(x) = 3x^2 - 7$$
$$f(3) = 3 \cdot 3^2 - 7$$
$$f(3) = 20$$

Functions can also have more than one input variable. For instance, you might have $f(x,y) = 2x + y$. In this case, $f(3,5) = 2 \cdot 3 + 5 = 11$.

Composition of Functions

Given two functions, you may be asked to work with the *composition* of the functions. The composition of two functions is a function produced by performing first one function and then the other. For example, consider these two functions:

$f(x) = x^2$

$g(x) = x + 2$

Then the composition $f(g(x))$ can be simplified this way:

$f(g(x)) = (x + 2)^2$

$f(g(x)) = (x + 2)(x + 2)$

$f(g(x)) = x^2 + 2x + 4$

Note that composition is not commutative. That is, $f(g(x))$ is not necessarily the same as $g(f(x))$.

Solving Special Symbol Problems

The SAT won't necessarily use standard $f(x)$ notation when working with functions. In fact, you're nearly certain to run into at least one "special symbol" problem, where some bit of typography is used to indicate a function. For example,

Define x§y to be equal to $x^2 - xy$. Is 3§4 larger or smaller than 4§3?

To solve such a problem, substitute the numbers as indicated. You may find it useful to translate back to standard functional notation to do so. In this case, you could write the original special symbol equation as

$f(x,y) = x^2 - xy$

Then

$$f(3,4) = 3^2 - 3 \cdot 4 = -3$$
$$f(4,3) = 4^2 - 4 \cdot 3 = 4$$

So 3§4 is smaller than 4§3. Just be careful to substitute numbers in the right order.

Graphing and Transforming Functions

You won't need to draw any graphs to pass the SAT, but you will need to answer questions involving graphs of functions. Three areas that you should understand are

➤ Graphs of linear functions

➤ Graphs of quadratic functions

➤ Transforming graphs

Graphing Linear Functions

A *linear function* is one of the general form y = mx + b, where *m* and *b* are constants. Such functions are represented by a straight line on the graph. Figure 6.1 shows the graph of y = 3x + 4.

In the case of a linear equation, there are two important numbers to be aware of. The slope is the constant m in the equation, and the *y-intercept* is the constant b. You can see from Figure 6.1 that this particular line intersects the y axis at the coordinate (0, 4)—four units up on the y axis at x = 0. You can remember the slope by the mnemonic "rise over run." This particular line, with a slope of 3, rises 3 units for every 1 unit that you move out on the x axis.

You might also need to go the other way on the SAT. For example, if you're given a graph with the y-intercept of a line at –4 and are told that the slope of the line is $\frac{1}{2}$, what is the value of y at the position x = 30? To solve this, take the information given to calculate the equation of the line:

$$y = \frac{1}{2}x - 4$$

And plug in the value for x:

$$y = \frac{1}{2} \times 30 - 4$$

$$y = 11$$

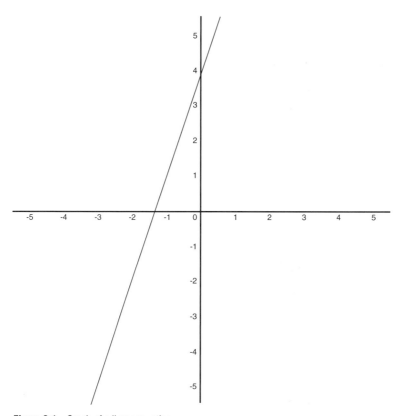

Figure 6.1   Graph of a linear equation.

Graphing Quadratic Functions

A *quadratic function* is one that contains an x^2 term (in general, $ax^2 + bx + c$). In the general case, the graph of a quadratic function is a parabola. For example, Figure 6.2 shows the graph of the function $y = x^2 - 2x - 3$.

For a quadratic function, you may be expected to find the highest or lowest point, identify whether the graph extends up or down infinitely, and find the *zeroes* of the equation. The zeroes (sometimes called the *roots*) are the points at which the function crosses the x axis.

Start with determining whether the function extends up or down. You know that the square of any number, positive or negative, is always positive. So if the coefficient of the x^2 term is positive, the ends of the graph extend upward (and the graph has a minimum y value). If the coefficient is negative, the ends extend downward (and the graph has a maximum y value).

Next, find the zeroes of the equation. Sometimes you can do this just by inspecting the graph (if you're given a graph to work from, of course). For example, in Figure 6.2, the roots are clearly −1 and 3, the two points where the graph crosses the x axis. To check, plug those values in to the formula for the graph:

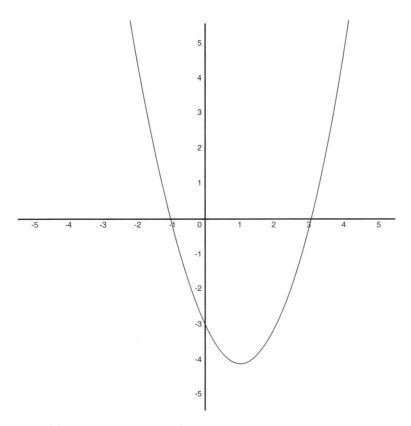

Figure 6.2 Graph of a quadratic equation.

$y = x^2 - 2x - 3$

$y = -1^2 - 2 \cdot -1 - 3$

$y = 1 + 2 - 3$

$y = 0$

$y = x^2 - 2x - 3$

$y = 3^2 - 2 \cdot 3 - 3$

$y = 9 - 6 - 3$

$y = 0$

To solve a quadratic equation in the general case, you may need to use the *quadratic formula*. You won't be required to use the quadratic formula to solve any problem on the SAT, but it may still come in handy. The quadratic formula will give you the roots of any quadratic equation. The two solutions to the equation $ax^2 + bx + c = 0$ are given by the formula

$$x = \frac{-b \pm \sqrt{b^2 - 4ac}}{2a}$$

So, if you're told a particular parabola has the formula $y = 4x^2 + 6x + 2$, you can find its zeroes this way:

$$x = \frac{-b \pm \sqrt{b^2 - 4ac}}{2a}$$

$$x = \frac{-6 \pm \sqrt{6^2 - 4 \times 4 \times 2}}{2 \times 4}$$

$$x = \frac{-6 \pm \sqrt{36 - 32}}{8}$$

$$\frac{x = (-6 \pm 2))}{8}$$

$$x = -1 \text{ or } \frac{-1}{2}$$

Finally, to find the maximum or minimum value of a quadratic formula, calculate the value of the formula for the point halfway between the two zeroes. Going back to Figure 6.2, we know that the zeroes are at –1 and 3, and the formula of the graph is y = x² – 2x – 3. So the lowest point is found by calculating y for x = 1 (halfway between –1 and 3):

$$y = x^2 - 2x - 3$$
$$y = 1^2 - 2 \cdot 1 - 3$$
$$y = 1 - 2 - 3$$
$$y = -4$$

Transforming Graphs

You should also understand what happens to the graph of a function as you change the function in various ways. Suppose you have an arbitrary function y = f(x). Then,

➤ y = f(x + k) is the same graph shifted k units to the left.

➤ y = f(x – k) is the same graph shifted k units to the right.

➤ y = f(x) + k is the same graph shifted k units up.

➤ y = f(x) – k is the same graph shifted k units down.

➤ y = kf(x) is narrower than the original graph if |k|>1 and wider than the original graph if |k|<1.

You can use this knowledge even if you have no idea what the actual function is. For example, if Figure 6.3 shows a graph of y = f(x) and you're asked to select the picture from various choices of y = f(x) + 3, you know you're looking for a graph shifted three units up, and Figure 6.4 is the correct answer.

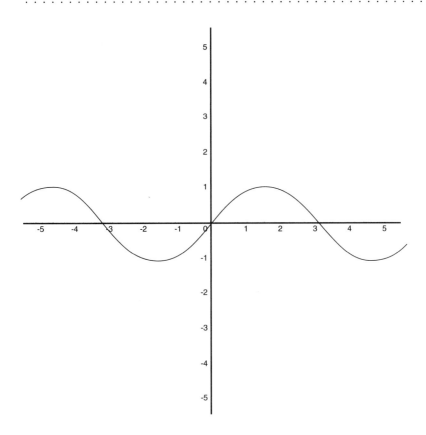

Figure 6.3   Graph of y = f(x).

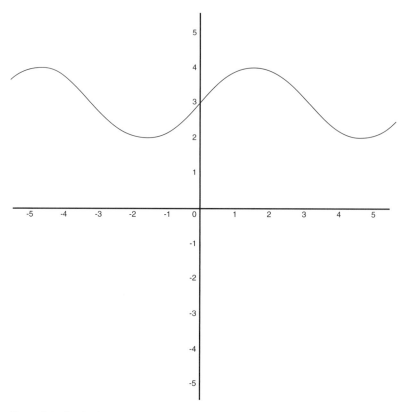

Figure 6.4   Graph of y = f(x) + 3.

Solving Equations

Solving an equation means evaluating the equation to determine the value of the unknown value in the equation. You'll need some skills in this area to ace the SAT:

➤ Performing operations on equations

➤ Factoring equations

➤ Finding solutions

Performing Operations on Equations

The basic rule of performing operations on equations is simple: If you do something to one side of an equation, you must do the same thing to the other side of the equation. This applies to addition, subtraction, multiplication, division, and operations involving exponents and roots. For example, if the original equation is $4x = 42$, all these equations are valid:

$4x + 1 = 43$ (add 1 to each side)

$4x - 10 = 32$ (subtract 10 from each side)

$8x = 84$ (multiply each side by 2)

$x = 10.5$ (divide each side by 4)

$16x^2 = 1764$ (square each side)

Factoring Polynomials

A polynomial equation is one that consists of a series of terms of the form ax^n. For example,

$3x^4 + 2x^3 + 5x^2 + 6 = 0$

Like numbers, equations can have factors—quantities that you can multiply to return the original equation. You may need to recognize three types of factors for equations on the SAT. The first of these is the difference of two squares equation:

$a^2 - b^2 = (a + b)(a - b)$

The second type of factoring you need to recognize is pulling out common factors to simplify an equation:

$x^3 + x^2 + x = x(x^2 + x + 1)$

$10x^2 + 5x - 15 = 5(2x^2 + x - 3)$

Finally, some quadratic equations can be factored into two linear terms:

$x^2 - x - 12 = (x + 3)(x - 4)$

The key to factoring the quadratic equation $a^2 + bx + c$ is to find two numbers that add up to b and that multiply together to give c. In the previous example, $3 - 4 = -1$ and $3 \times -4 = -12$. As another example,

$x^2 + 5x + 6 = (x + 3)(x + 2)$

Not every polynomial can be factored this way. For example, there are no factors of $x^2 + 8x - 6$ because there aren't any numbers that add up to 8 but multiply to –6. This is a prime polynomial.

 If you can factor a polynomial, it's easy to find its zeroes (also called the roots if the polynomial is in the form of an equation): They're the values that make one or the other term go to zero. For example, because $x^2 - x - 12 = (x + 3)(x - 4)$, you know the zeroes of $x^2 - x - 12$ are –3 and 4.

Solving an Equation

To solve an equation containing a single variable, you need to isolate that variable on one side of the equation. You can do this by "unwinding" the equation, applying operations to both sides of the equation to remove, one by one, any terms that appear with the variable. For example,

$4x^2 - 5 = 31$

$4x^2 = 36$ (Add 5 to each side.)

$x^2 = 9$ (Divide each side by 4.)

$x = 3$ or -3 (Take the square root of each side—remember, there are two square roots of 9.)

When you've calculated a solution, you should always check by substituting it back into the original equation:

$4x^2 - 5 = 31$

$4 \cdot 3^2 - 5 = 31$

$36 - 5 = 31$

$31 = 31$

 You also might be asked to solve multiple equations together. See the section "Systems of Equations" later in this chapter to deal with those problems.

Another type of equation you may be asked to solve is the rational equation—that is, one that is the ratio of two quantities. For example, find the value of x that makes this equation true:

$$6 = \frac{(x-1)}{(x+2)}$$

To solve this equation, first multiply both sides by the term $(x + 2)$ to eliminate the ratio, and proceed to solve as usual:

$$6 = \frac{(x-1)}{(x+2)}$$

$$6(x + 2) = x - 1$$

$$6x + 12 = x - 1$$

$$6x - x = -1 - 12$$

$$5x = -13$$

$$x = -\frac{13}{5}$$

Solving Inequalities

An inequality is a statement similar to an equation, except that it specifies one quantity as larger or smaller than another, rather than equal. You might run across four types of inequalities on the SAT:

➤ >, read as "greater than"

➤ <, read as "less than"

➤ ≥, read as "greater than or equal to"

➤ ≤, read as "less than or equal to"

Solving an equality means to isolate the variable on one side of the operator, just as it does with an equation. For example,

$$6x + 2 > 14$$

$$6x > 14 - 2$$

$$6x > 12$$

$$x > 2$$

This means that any value of x greater than 2 will make the original inequality a true statement. There's one rule that you need to remember when solving inequalities, though: When you multiply or divide by a negative number, you must switch the direction of the inequality:

$$-3x + 4 < 13$$

$$-3x < 9$$

$$x > -3$$

In the last step, where you divide both sides of the equation by –3, you must also change the less than to a greater than.

Systems of Equations

A *system of equations* is a set of equations, all of which must be true simultaneously. Generally, with a system of two linear equations, you can solve for two variables; with a system of three equations, three variables, and so on. Consider these two equations:

$$x + 2y = 5$$
$$x - y = -1$$

That's enough information to find both x and y. To proceed, you must first eliminate one variable. You can do this by changing equations until their sum gets rid of a variable. For instance, in this case, multiply the second equation by –1 on both sides to give

$$-x + y = 1$$

Now add this back to the first equation:

$$x + 2y - x + y = 5 + 1$$

The two x terms cancel out and you're left with

$$3y = 6$$
$$y = 2$$

Now that you know what y is, substitute it back into either of the original equations to get x:

$$x + 2 \cdot 2 = 5$$
$$x + 4 = 5$$
$$x = 5 - 4$$
$$x = 1$$

To check, plug the values of x and y in to the other equation:

$$x - y = -1$$
$$1 - 2 = -1$$
$$-1 = -1$$

Dealing with Word Problems

If the SAT just gave you mathematical formulas to work with, the math section would be pretty easy. But you're more likely to be asked to apply your mathematical and reasoning skills to problems laid out in words rather than equations. You need to know how to convert word problems to equations so that you can solve them.

Solving Counting, Permutation, and Combination Problems

The SAT might ask you to count some things, but it won't be as simple as tapping your pencil on a series of pictures! For counting problems, you should know the Fundamental Counting Principle: If an event can happen m ways and a second, independent event can happen n ways, the total number of ways in which the two events can happen is m times n. That's pretty abstract, so we'll put it in the form of a word problem:

> John has 7 dress shirts, 5 ties, and 6 pairs of dress slacks. How many different ways can he make up an outfit consisting of one shirt, one tie, and one pair of slacks?

To solve this problem, you can apply the fundamental counting principle. Each of the three events (choosing a shirt, choosing a tie, and choosing slacks) is independent, so the answer is $7 \times 5 \times 6 = 210$.

In permutation problems, you're selecting from a pool of items that is not replenished, so each selection reduces the pool. To solve these problems requires some reasoning and multiplication. Here's an example:

A bingo cage contains 75 different numbered balls. The game is played by a caller removing one ball at a time, calling out its number, and discarding the ball. How many ways can the caller call the first 5 numbers?

To solve this problem, note that the first ball comes from a pool of 75 choices, and is then thrown away, reducing the pool. The second ball therefore comes from a pool of 74 choices, and so on. The answer is

$75 \times 74 \times 73 \times 72 \times 71 = 2{,}071{,}126{,}800$

Combination problems are like permutation problems, except that the order of results doesn't matter. An example will make this clear:

A pond contains 15 ducks. You pick 3 ducks from the pond at random. How many different groups of 3 ducks could you form this way?

To start solving this problem, treat it as a permutation problem: For the first duck, there are 15 choices, and then 14, and then 13. So there are $15 \times 14 \times 13 = 2730$ ways to choose the 3 ducks. But not all of those ways are distinct. Suppose that the ducks are all assigned letters. If you pull out duck A, and then duck B, and then duck C, you get the same group as if you'd pulled out C, and then B, and then A. In fact, there are 6 different ways to arrange a group of 3 ducks:

A B C

A C B

B A C

B C A

C A B

C B A

So the final answer is $\dfrac{2730}{6} = 455$

Converting Word Problems to Equations

One of the keys to solving word problems is to convert them to equations as you're reading them. There are a few key words and phrases that you'll see frequently on the SAT. Recognizing these will give you a boost in solving word problems. Table 6.1 lists some of the key phrases and words to watch out for.

Table 6.1 Key Words and Phrases for Word Problems		
Words	**Convert to**	**Example**
is, has, was	=	John is 57 years old J = 57
more than, greater than, farther than, older than, sum of	+	The blue bowl contains ten more balls than the red bowl. B = R + 10
Difference, less than, younger, fewer	−	Betty is two years younger than John B = J − 2
of	× or %	50% of the students take calculus. C = .5S
for, per	÷, ratio	Bill paid $5 for every $3 that Mary paid. $\frac{B}{5} = \frac{M}{3}$

You'll also run into the terms *directly proportional* and *inversely proportional*. Two quantities are directly proportional when they vary with each other—that is, they are related by multiplying by some constant. For example, if you're told that the number of bolts is directly proportional to the number of assemblies, and that 30 assemblies require 270 bolts, you can write the equation

$$30A = 270B$$

This simplifies to A = 9B: For each assembly, there are 9 bolts.

Two quantities are inversely proportional when they are related according to an equation such as

$$A = \frac{k}{B}$$

for some constant k. For example, you may be told that a company's profits are inversely proportional to the current price of wheat. This tells you that

$$P = \frac{k}{W}$$

You'd need more information to determine the constant k, but you already know that as the price of wheat goes up, profits go down, and vice versa.

Working with Rate Problems

When you see the word *per* in a problem, you're working with a rate. For example, consider this problem:

> A train is moving at 75 miles per hour. How many hours must elapse for the train to cover 350 miles?

To solve a rate problem, you can draw a circle to relate three quantities: the rate (in this case the speed of the train) and the two parts that make up the rate. Figure 6.5 shows the rate circle for this problem.

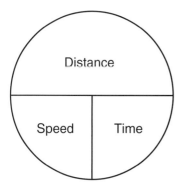

Figure 6.5 A rate circle.

Having drawn the rate circle, remember one simple rule: If you're missing the quantity in the top half of the circle, multiply the other two quantities together to get it. If you're missing one of the other two, divide the top half by the remaining quantity to get the answer.

In this case, you know the distance (350 miles) and the speed (75 miles per hour), so the answer is $\frac{350}{75} = 4\frac{2}{3}$ hours.

Exam Prep Questions

1. The first three terms of a sequence are 12, 24, and 36. Which term in the sequence is equal to 12^2?

(A) The 9th
(B) The 12th
(C) The 13th
(D) The 15th
(E) The 144th

2. John and Arlene both leave their high school at the same time. John walks due west at 4 miles per hour, and Arlene walks due east at $2\frac{1}{2}$ miles per hour. At the end of 3 hours, how far apart are John and Arlene?

(A) 4.5 miles
(B) 6.5 miles
(C) 19.5 miles
(D) 9.5 miles
(E) 14.5 miles

3. Which of the following graphs corresponds to the equation $x^2 + 2x + 1$?

(A)

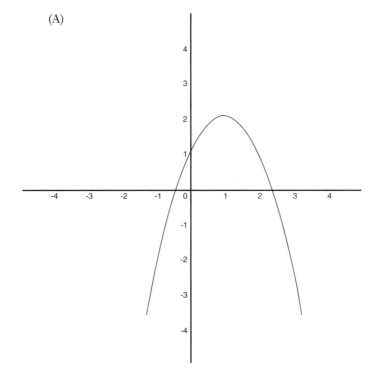

(B)

(C)

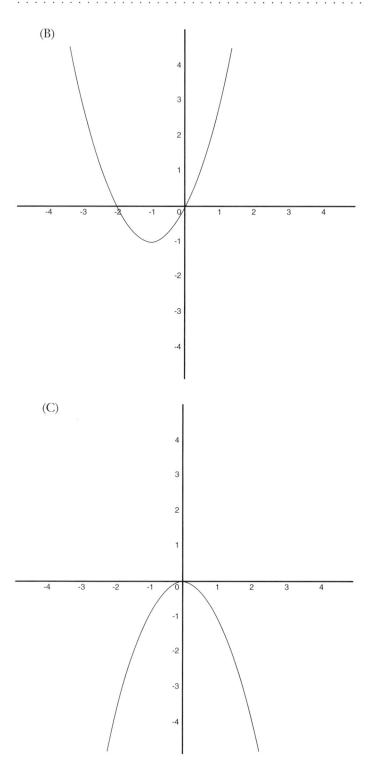

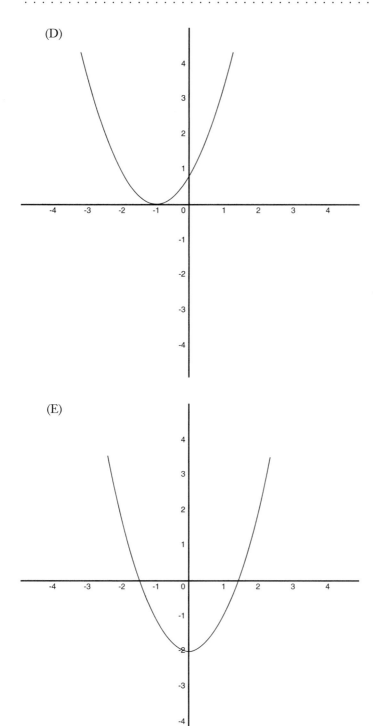

(D)

(E)

4. If x is directly proportional to $\dfrac{y}{5}$, and x has the value 12 when y has the value 10, what is the value of x when y has the value of $\dfrac{27}{4}$?

(A) $\dfrac{10}{81}$

(B) $\dfrac{81}{10}$

(C) $\dfrac{4}{27}$

(D) 15

(E) $9\dfrac{1}{10}$

5. If x + y = 12 and x is a positive integer, what is the value of 4x + 4y?

(A) 4

(B) 12

(C) –12

(D) 48

(E) It cannot be determined from the information given.

6. A teacher is assigning teams of 2 students each for tennis doubles. There are 24 students in the tennis class. How many different choices are there for the first team chosen?

(A) 23

(B) 24

(C) 276

(D) 552

(E) 1,104

7. The cost of belonging to the homeowners' association goes up by 5% each year. This year the cost was $132.30. What was the cost two years ago?

(A) $118.00

(B) $119.40

(C) $120.00

(D) $122.30

(E) $126.00

8. Let the symbol r[[s]]t represent $x^r + sx + t$. What are the zeroes of 2[[6]]8?

(A) 0 and 1

(B) –2 and –4

(C) –1 and –2

(D) 6 and 8

(E) –6 and –8

9. The sum of three consecutive integers is 15. What is the ratio of the largest of these integers to the smallest of these integers?

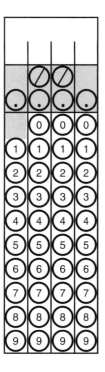

10. The marching band decided to raise money by selling candy bars. They invested $50 in advertising, and sold the candy bars for a profit of $2 per box. If they sold 311 boxes of candy bars, what was their total profit after advertising costs were deducted? (Disregard the dollar sign and any cents when gridding your answer. For example, if the answer is $230.00, grid 230.)

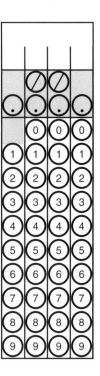

Answers to Exam Prep Questions

1. Answer B is correct. You can see that the sequence is arithmetic, with a constant difference of 12 between the terms. The formula for the nth term of the sequence is 12n. This gives you an equation from the second sentence: The sequence is arithmetic.

$12n = 12^2$

$12n = 144$

$n = 12$

So the 12th term is the one whose value is 12^2, and the other four answers are incorrect.

2. Answer C is correct. You can solve this by turning it into a pair of rate problems. The rate circle has distance on the top, and speed and time on the bottom, so to get distance, you multiply speed by time. John goes $3 \times 4 = 12$ miles in three hours, and Arlene goes $3 \times 2.5 = 7.5$ miles in the same time. Since they're walking directly opposite to each other, you add these two figures to get the correct answer 19.5 hours. As a shortcut, you may notice that each hour they get 6.5 miles further apart (John walks 4 miles west, while Arlene walks 2.5 miles east), so the total distance at the end of 3 hours is $3 \times 6.5 = 19.5$ miles. Answers A, B, D, and E are incorrect.

3. Answer D is correct. Because the x^2 term is positive, you know that the graph goes to positive infinity on each side. This immediately lets you eliminate answers A and C because those two parabolas are upside down for the equation. Answer B has a zero at $x = 0$. Plugging that in to the equation gives $0 = 0^2 + 2 \cdot 0 + 1$, or $0 = 1$, which is not true. This eliminates answer B. Answer D has a zero at $x = -1$. Plugging that in gives $0 = (-1)^2 + 2 \cdot -1 + 1$, which is a true statement, so answer D is correct. To check answer E, note that this graph has the value -2 for $x = 0$. But $0^2 + 2 \cdot 0 + 1 = 1$, so this point is not on the line and answer E is incorrect.

4. Answer B is correct. This question looks complex, but when you reduce it to equations, it's pretty simple. The first part tells you that there is a direct relation between x and $\frac{y}{5}$:

$$x = k\left(\frac{y}{5}\right)$$

$$5x = ky$$

Now plug in the known values of x and y from the second clause to determine k:

$$5 \cdot 12 = k \cdot 10$$

$$60 = 10k$$

$$6 = k$$

Thus the equation for the proportion is

$$x = \frac{6y}{5}$$

Now plug in $\frac{27}{4}$ for y and solve to get x:

$$x = \frac{\left(6 \times \frac{27}{4}\right)}{5}$$

$$5x = \frac{(6 \times 27)}{4}$$

$$5x = \frac{162}{4} = \frac{81}{2}$$

$$x = \frac{81}{10}$$

This is answer B, so B is correct and the other answers are incorrect.

5. Answer D is correct. It's tempting to choose answer E because you know that a system of two equations is required to solve for two variables, and you're only given one equation. But note that the question doesn't require you to solve for x or y; you need the value of the expression 4x + 4y. Because 4x + 4y = 4(x + y), and you know from the original equation that x + y = 12, 4x + 4y = 4 · 12 = 48. So answer D is correct, and the others are incorrect.

6. Answer C is correct. This is a classic combination problem. There are 24 choices for the first student, and then 23 choices for the second student on the team (because the first student can't be assigned to the same team twice). But a team consisting of Bill and Joe is the same as a team consisting of Joe and Bill, so you need to divide the number of potential teams by 2. The final number is given by $(24 \times 23) \div 2 = 276$, which is answer C.

7. Answer C is correct. Call the cost two years ago c. Each year the cost goes up by 5%, which means that it is multiplied by 1.05. So,

$$c \times 1.05 \times 1.05 = 132.30$$

$$c = \frac{132.3}{1.05 \times 1.05}$$

$$c = 120$$

This is answer C, and the other answers are incorrect.

8. Answer B is correct. Tackle this one in two steps. First, convert the special symbol to standard notation. If you substitute, you'll find that 2[[6]]8 is $x^2 + 6x + 8$. Now you could graph the function or use the quadratic formula to find its zeroes, but the simplest way to proceed is to factor the polynomial. To do this, note that you need a pair of integers whose sum is 6 and whose product is 8. Two and 4 fit the bill, so $x^2 + 6x + 8 = (x + 2)(x + 4)$. Now remember that the zeroes of the function are values that eliminate one or the other of those terms: -2 and -4. To check, substitute back in to the formula: $(-2)^2 + 6(-2) + 8 = 4 - 12 + 8 = 0$ and $(-4)^2 + 6(-4) + 8 = 16 - 24 + 8 = 0$. The answer checks, so B is correct and the other answers are wrong.

9. To solve this problem, you first need to find the three integers. Because they're consecutive, you can do this with an equation based on the smallest integer:

$x + (x + 1) + (x + 2) = 15$

$3x + 3 = 15$

$3x = 12$

$x = 4$

This tells you the smallest of the integers is 4, so the largest must be 6. The ratio of the largest to the smallest is 6 to 4. You can grid this as $\frac{6}{4}$, $\frac{3}{2}$, or 1.5 to get credit for your answer.

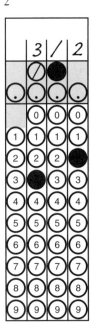

10. This problem asks you to convert words into an equation. Start with the profit per box times the number of boxes:

$P = 311 \times 2$

You then need to reduce this number by the advertising costs:

$P = (311 \times 2) - 50$

$P = 622 - 50$

$P = 572$

Grid 572 in either of the possible positions to receive credit for your answer.

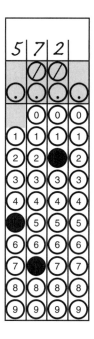

The Mathematics Section:
Geometry

· ·

Terms you'll need to understand:

- ✓ Acute angle
- ✓ Adjacent angle
- ✓ Arc
- ✓ Area
- ✓ Chord
- ✓ Circumference
- ✓ Complementary angle
- ✓ Cone
- ✓ Congruent triangles
- ✓ Coordinate plane
- ✓ Cube
- ✓ Cylinder
- ✓ Diameter
- ✓ Equilateral triangle
- ✓ Hypotenuse
- ✓ Isosceles triangle
- ✓ Leg
- ✓ Line
- ✓ Line segment
- ✓ Midpoint
- ✓ Obtuse angle
- ✓ Parallelogram
- ✓ Perimeter

- ✓ Point
- ✓ Prism
- ✓ Pyramid
- ✓ Pythagorean Theorem
- ✓ Quadrilateral
- ✓ Radius
- ✓ Ray
- ✓ Rectangle
- ✓ Rectangular solid
- ✓ Reflection
- ✓ Right angle
- ✓ Right triangle
- ✓ Rotation
- ✓ Similar triangles
- ✓ Sphere
- ✓ Square
- ✓ Surface area
- ✓ Symmetry
- ✓ Tangent
- ✓ Translation
- ✓ Vertical angle
- ✓ Volume

Techniques you'll need to master:

- ✓ Recognize and use basic geometric notation
- ✓ Apply the Pythagorean Theorem
- ✓ Derive and use facts about special triangles
- ✓ Find the areas and perimeters of squares, rectangles, and other polygons

- ✓ Relate the area, radius, and circumference of a circle
- ✓ Calculate the volume of a solid figure
- ✓ Work with slopes, parallel lines, and perpendicular lines in the coordinate plane
- ✓ Apply transformations to geometric figures

In addition to algebra, the SAT includes a section of problems drawn from high school geometry. These problems require you to have a grasp of basic geometrical facts, to be able to calculate areas and perimeters, and to understand coordinate geometry. You'll also be tested on your ability in *geometric perception*, the art of reasoning about shapes. In this chapter, we'll review the basics of geometrical knowledge that you'll need to do well on this portion of the SAT. You may see the occasional problem where trigonometry could also be used to find the answer—but if you haven't taken trig, don't worry. It's never required to solve any problem on the SAT.

Geometric Notation

Just as you need to understand square root signs and other algebraic notation to solve algebra problems, you must understand basic geometric notation to work with the geometry problems on the SAT. Figure 7.1 shows some basic geometric figures in a plane.

 Unless you're told otherwise, you can assume that all drawings on the SAT geometry section lie in the plane. That is, they're completely "flat" with no third dimension.

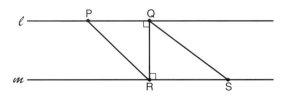

Figure 7.1 Some simple plane geometry.

 By convention, uppercase letters such as P and Q refer to points, and lowercase script letters such as ℓ and m refer to lines.

In writing about this figure, we can use the following notation:

➤ $\overleftrightarrow{PQ}$ indicates the line containing points P and Q. This is the same as line ℓ. A line goes to infinity in both directions.

➤ $\overrightarrow{PQ}$ is the ray starting at P and extending infinitely in the direction of Q. A ray has a single endpoint and goes to infinity in one direction.

➤ $\overleftarrow{PQ}$ is the ray starting at Q and extending infinitely in the direction of P.

➤ $\overline{PQ}$ is the line segment from P to Q. A line segment includes two end-points and all the points between them.

➤ PQ is the length of the line segment from P to Q.

➤ ∠PQR is the angle formed by following the lines from P to Q to R.

➤ m∠PQR is the measure of the angle from P to Q to R. In the case of Figure 7.1, m∠PQR = 90°.

➤ ΔRQS is the triangle with the vertices R, Q, and S.

➤ PQSR is the quadrilateral with the vertices P, Q, S, and R. Note that this is different from PSRQ (whose lines are not all shown on the figure) because you must follow the vertices in the order listed.

➤ $\overleftrightarrow{PQ}$ ‖ $\overleftrightarrow{RS}$ indicates that the two lines are parallel.

➤ $\overline{PQ}$⊥$\overline{QR}$ indicates that the specified line segments are perpendicular. The small square where the lines meet on the diagram also indicates this.

Basic Geometric Facts

The SAT expects you to know the basic facts about a variety of geometric constructs, including

➤ Points

➤ Lines

➤ Angles

➤ Triangles

➤ Other polygons

➤ Circles

You won't need to simply regurgitate any of these facts on the exam. Rather, you'll be expected to apply what you know about geometry to solve problems. For example, rather than being asked the circumference of a circle with a particular diameter, you might be presented with one quarter of a circle and its radius and asked to derive the length of the arc. The more you work with the basic relations of geometry, the more easily you'll be able to solve this sort of problem with little effort.

Points and Lines

A geometrical *point* has no dimension at all: no length, no width, no height. If you're presented with part of a diagram and told that it has a specific size, you know it isn't a point.

Two points define a *line*. This means that

➤ If you're given only a single point, you can come up with infinitely many lines that pass through the point.

➤ If you're given two points, no matter the distance or angle between them, precisely one line can be drawn that includes both of those points.

➤ If you're given three or more points, there may or may not be a line that passes through all of them.

Two other geometric figures are related to lines. A *ray* starts at a fixed point and continues infinitely in one direction. A *line segment* is a portion of a line between two fixed points. A line segment has a length as well as a midpoint— the point halfway between the two endpoints of the line segment.

Multiple line segments can lay along the same line. In this case, you can add and subtract the lengths of the line segments. For example, Figure 7.2 shows a line with several line segments marked.

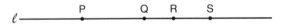

Figure 7.2 A group of line segments.

Suppose you're told that PQ = 4, RS = 3, and PS = 9. You can then calculate QR and PR this way:

QR = PS – PQ – RS

QR = 9 – 4 – 3

QR = 2

PR = PQ + QR

PR = 4 + 2

PR = 6

Angles

Angles are formed where line segments, lines, or rays meet or cross. As Figure 7.3 shows, where two lines cross, there are four angles, identified (in this case) by the letters w, x, y, and z.

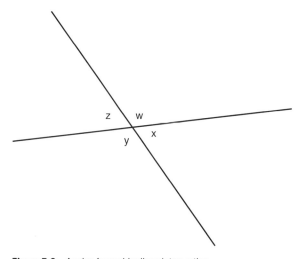

Figure 7.3   Angles formed by lines intersecting.

In this situation, the angles directly opposite each other are referred to as opposite angles or vertical angles. The angles next to each other (that share a common side) are adjacent angles. Thus,

➤ w and y are vertical angles.

➤ x and z are vertical angles.

➤ w and x are adjacent angles.

➤ x and y are adjacent angles.

➤ y and z are adjacent angles.

➤ z and w are adjacent angles.

You'll need to know two special relations involving these angles:

➤ Vertical angles are always equal. Thus, if you're told that w = 120° in Figure 7.3, you know that y = 120°.

➤ Adjacent angles always sum to 180°. So if w = 120° you know that x = 60° and z = 60°.

 You may also be familiar with measuring angles in radians from your geometry class. The basic relationship between degrees and radians is 360° = 2π radians. The SAT doesn't use radians, so you need not worry about remembering this.

A *right angle* is an angle whose measure is precisely 90°. If two lines intersect and one of the angles at their intersection is a right angle, all the other angles are right angles as well. It's easy to see this by following the rules for vertical and adjacent angles. If two angles add up to 90°, they're sometimes called *complementary angles*. An angle of less than 90° is called an *acute angle*, and an angle of more than 90° is called an *obtuse angle*.

You should also recognize the special situation shown in Figure 7.4.

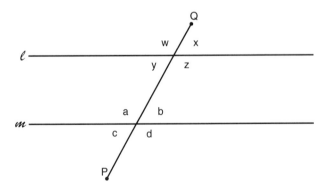

Figure 7.4 Line segment intersecting two parallel lines.

Here the line segment $\overline{PQ}$ cuts the two parallel lines ℓ and m. In this situation, all the acute angles are equal and all the obtuse angles are equal. So in the figure, w = z = a = d and x = y = b = c. If you're given any one of these eight angles, you can always find the other seven.

The rule about all the acute angles being equal holds true only when you know that the two lines are actually parallel. Remember, on the exam, you can assume that two lines are parallel unless it's noted otherwise.

Triangles and the Pythagorean Theorem

There's no trigonometry on the SAT (many of you are now breathing a sigh of relief, we're sure), but that doesn't mean that there are no triangles. In fact, you need to know the basics about a number of special triangles, as well as three overall rules:

➤ The sum of the angles in any triangle is 180°.

➤ The largest side of a triangle is opposite the largest angle, and the smallest side of the triangle is opposite the smallest angle.

➤ The sum of the lengths of any two sides of a triangle is greater than the length of the third side of the triangle. (This fact is called the triangle inequality.)

The SAT may combine these rules with other geometric facts to make you reason to an answer. For example,

Consider a triangle with vertices A, B, and C. $\angle CAB = 50°$ and $\angle BAC + \angle ACB = 140°$. What is $\angle ABC$?

To solve this problem, it helps to realize that it doesn't matter which direction you measure an angle in, so that $\angle CAB$ and $\angle BAC$ are two names for the same angle. So you can rewrite the two facts given as

$\angle CAB = 50°$

$\angle CAB + \angle ACB = 140°$

From this, it is immediately apparent that $\angle ACB = 90°$. Now you know that two of the angles of the triangle are 50° and 90°. Because all three angles must add up to 180°, the third angle (which is the required $\angle ABC$) must be 40°.

You may also see the size of an angle expressed as $m\angle ABC$, where the "m" is read "measure." This means the same as $\angle ABC$, so don't get thrown if you see either notation.

Equilateral Triangles

An *equilateral triangle* is one in which all three sides have the same length. In such a triangle, all three angles are also equal. Because the three angles in a triangle must add up to 180°, you know that each angle in an equilateral triangle is 180° ÷ 3 = 60°.

Isosceles Triangles

An *isosceles triangle* is one in which two sides are of equal length. The angles opposite the equal sides are also equal.

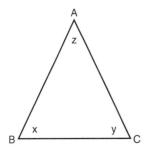

Figure 7.5 If AB = AC, this is an isosceles triangle.

In Figure 7.5, if you're told that $\overline{AB}$ and $\overline{AC}$ are the same length, you know that you have an isosceles triangle; therefore, x and y are equal angles. This does not tell you whether z is larger or smaller than x and y, though, without more information.

Right Triangles and the Pythagorean Theorem

A *right triangle* is one in which one of the angles is a right angle. Note that at most one of the angles in a triangle can be a right angle; if a triangle had two right angles, those two angles would account for 90° each out of the total of 180° for all the angles, leaving nothing for the third angle.

Some special terminology is generally used for right triangles:

➤ The *hypotenuse* is the side of the right triangle opposite the right angle.

➤ The *legs* of the right triangle are the other two sides.

➤ The angles of the right triangle are usually indicated by the letters A, B, and C, with C being the right angle.

➤ The sides of the right triangle are usually indicated by the letters a, b, and c, with c being the hypotenuse.

The SAT isn't *required* to use any of this terminology. If you're told that one angle in a triangle is 90°, you know that it's a right triangle regardless of how the figure is drawn or labeled.

Figure 7.6 shows a typical right triangle using the standard labeling. Note the right-angle indicator inside angle C.

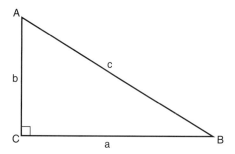

Figure 7.6 A right triangle.

The most important fact to know about right triangles is that every right triangle obeys the Pythagorean Theorem. The theorem may be stated in words as: The sum of the squares of the other two sides is equal to the square of the hypotenuse. Or, using the labeling of Figure 7.6

$a^2 + b^2 = c^2$

If you know the lengths of any two sides of a right triangle, you can use the Pythagorean Theorem to come up with the length of the third side. One special right triangle you should recognize is the 3-4-5 triangle. Any triangle whose sides are in the ratio 3:4:5 (such as one whose sides are 9, 12, and 15) is a right triangle. You can check this with the Pythagorean Theorem:

$a^2 + b^2 = c^2$

$3^2 + 4^2 = 5^2$

$9 + 16 = 25$

$25 = 25$

30°-60°-90° Triangles

Another special triangle is the one whose angles are 30°, 60°, and 90°. This right triangle has sides in the ratio $1:\sqrt{3}:2$ as shown in Figure 7.7.

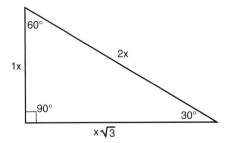

Figure 7.7   A 30°-60°-90° triangle.

 You don't have to memorize this diagram. The math section of the SAT includes a diagram showing the relationships in a 30°-60°-90° triangle.

45°-45°-90° Triangles

Another special right triangle is the one whose angles are 45°, 45°, and 90°. Because the two angles are equal, this means that the two legs of the triangle are also equal; it is an isosceles triangle. You can use this fact together with the Pythagorean Theorem to derive the length of the hypotenuse. Suppose that you have a 45°-45°-90° triangle, and each of the legs has the length 1. Then to calculate the length of the hypotenuse,

$$1^2 + 1^2 = c^2$$

$$1 + 1 = c^2$$

$$2 = c^2$$

$$\sqrt{2} = c$$

So in this case, the length of the hypotenuse is the square root of 2 times the length of either of the legs.

 Remember, when you recognize a special triangle on the SAT, you can use the known ratio of sides rather than the Pythagorean Theorem. This is likely to save you a lot of time.

Congruent and Similar Triangles

Two triangles are said to be *congruent* if they are the same size and shape. Two triangles are said to be *similar* if they have the same shape, but not necessarily the same size.

Two triangles are *similar* if

➤ Their angles are the same. Sometimes you'll see this stated that they have two angles in common, but of course if they have two common angles, the third angle must be the same as well (because the angles of each triangle add up to 180°).

➤ They have one angle in common, and the sides that form those angles have lengths in the same ratio. For example, if one triangle has a 30° angle formed by sides of length 7 and 12, and another triangle has a 30° angle formed by sides of length 14 and 24, the two triangles are similar because $\frac{7}{14} = \frac{12}{24}$.

Two triangles are *congruent* if

➤ Each pair of corresponding sides has the same length.

➤ Two pairs of corresponding sides each have the same length, and the angle that these sides form is the same in each triangle.

➤ One pair of corresponding sides has the same length, and any two corresponding angles are the same.

NOTE Every pair of congruent triangles is also similar, but not all similar triangles are necessarily congruent.

If two triangles are similar, the ratio of the corresponding sides is a constant. You can use this fact to solve problems such as this one:

As shown in Figure 7.8, O is the center of a circle of radius 1, and points A, B, and C all lie on the circumference of the circle. What is CD?

One way to solve this is to realize that ΔAOB and ΔACD are similar triangles because they have two corresponding angles that are the same. ∠AOB and ∠ACD are both shown as right angles in the figure, and ∠OAB is common to both triangles. The fact that the two triangles overlap doesn't prevent them from being similar. Knowing that the two triangles are similar, you know that their sides are in a constant ratio. From the figure, AO = OB = 1 (because both of those line segments are radii of the circle) and AC = 2 (because that line segment is a diameter of the circle). You can now calculate CD:

$$\frac{AO}{AC} = \frac{OB}{CD}$$

$$\frac{1}{2} = \frac{1}{CD}$$

CD = 2

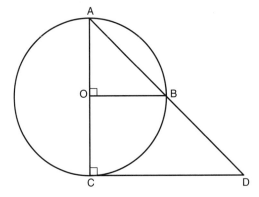

Figure 7.8 A problem of similar triangles.

Quadrilaterals

Just as a triangle is a closed figure with three sides, a quadrilateral is a closed figure with four sides. You should recognize three special types of quadrilateral:

➤ Parallelogram

➤ Rectangle

➤ Square

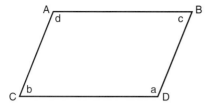

Figure 7.9 A parallelogram.

Figure 7.9 shows a parallelogram, a quadrilateral formed by two sets of parallel sides. In the figure, $\overline{AB} \parallel \overline{CD}$ and $\overline{AC} \parallel \overline{BD}$. In a parallelogram, opposite sides are equal, and opposite angles are equal. In this case,

➤ AB = CD

➤ AC = BD

➤ a = d

➤ b = c

A rectangle is a special case of a parallelogram in which all of the angles are right angles. As with a parallelogram, opposite sides of a rectangle are of equal length. Finally, a square is a special case of a rectangle (and therefore of a parallelogram) in which all of the sides are the same length.

Because the sides of a rectangle or a square always meet at right angles, you can use the Pythagorean Theorem to determine the length of a diagonal in either one. As Figure 7.10 shows, the diagonal forms an embedded triangle within a rectangle.

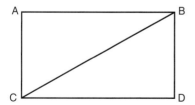

Figure 7.10 A rectangle with its diagonal.

Suppose you're told that the figure is a rectangle with AC = 5 and AB = 12. Then you can use the Pythagorean Theorem to find CB because $\triangle$ABC is a right triangle:

$$AB^2 + AC^2 = CB^2$$
$$\sqrt{AB^2 + AC^2} = CB$$
$$\sqrt{12^2 + 5^2} = CB$$
$$\sqrt{144 + 25} = CB$$
$$\sqrt{169} = CB$$
$$13 = CB$$

Other Polygons

SAT questions may include polygons other than triangles and quadrilaterals. For example, you may run across a five-sided polygon (a *pentagon*) or a six-sided polygon (a *hexagon*). Polygons may be regular or irregular. A *regular polygon* is one in which every side is the same length and every angle has the same measure. An *irregular polygon* is one in which at least one of these conditions is not true.

 CAUTION | Don't assume that a polygon is regular unless it meets both of these criteria. It's perfectly possible for all the sides of a hexagon to be the same, for example, without all the angles also being the same.

Circles

You should also be familiar with the basic geometry and terminology of circles to do well on the SAT. Figure 7.11 shows a circle as well as some additional geometry.

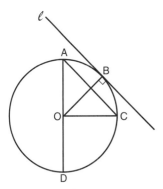

Figure 7.11 The parts of a circle.

Figure 7.11 shows these parts of a circle:

➤ O is the center of the circle. The center is a point that is equidistant from every point on the circle.

➤ $\overline{OA}$, $\overline{OB}$, $\overline{OC}$, and $\overline{OD}$ are all *radii* of the circle. (radii is the plural of *radius*.) A radius is a line segment that extends from the center of the circle to a point on the circle. All radii of a circle have the same length.

➤ $\overline{AD}$ is a *diameter* of the circle. A diameter is a line segment that runs from one point on the circle to another point on the circle, passing through the center of the circle. All diameters of the circle have the same length, which is twice the radius.

➤ $\overline{AC}$ is a *chord* of the circle. A chord is a line segment between any two points on the circle.

➤ The points on the circle from A to B, or from A to C, form an *arc*. Unlike a chord, an arc is measured along the circle. You can measure an arc by the length of the portion of the circle that it contains, or by the angle that it includes. For example, if you're told that ∠AOC is a right angle, the arc from A to C measures 90°.

➤ The line ℓ is *tangent* to the circle. A tangent line touches the circle at precisely one point, and is perpendicular to the radius of the circle at that point. In this case, $\ell\perp\overline{OB}$.

You should also know the two major formulas associated with the circle, both of which involve the irrational number π, which is approximately 3.14159. The circumference of a circle is the distance around the circle. If C is the circumference and d is the diameter of the circle, then

$$C = \pi d$$

The area of a circle also involves π. To determine the area, start with the radius r:

$$A = \pi r^2$$

Solid Geometry

So far, all the geometry we've discussed involves figures that lie in the plane; they are two-dimensional, with no thickness. Solid geometry, on the other hand, is concerned with things that have height or bulk. You will need to know a few basic facts about solid geometry for the SAT.

Prisms, Rectangular Solids, and Cylinders

A *prism* is a solid figure consisting of two identical polygonal faces joined by rectangular faces that are perpendicular to the polygons. The polygons are the *bases* of the prism, and the distance between the faces in a right prism is the prism's *height*.

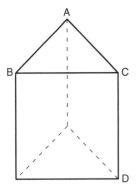

Figure 7.12 A right triangular prism.

If you're presented with Figure 7.12 and told that it is a right triangular prism, ΔABC is one of the two bases and CD is the height of the prism.

The SAT will always tell you if a figure does not lie in the plane. If you're not told so explicitly, do not assume that dashed lines indicate a third dimension. If you weren't told that Figure 7.12 was a triangular prism, it's just a collection of triangles and parallelograms—some of which happen to be drawn with dashed lines.

A *rectangular solid* is a special case of a prism in which the bases of the prism are rectangles. A *cube* is a special case of a rectangular solid in which all the edges have the same length; the height of a cube is the same as one side of the base. (Indeed, in a cube, the base is indistinguishable from any other side.)

A *cylinder* is similar to a prism, except that the bases are circles. In this case, the two bases are joined by a smooth sheet rather than a set of rectangular faces.

Spheres, Cones, and Pyramids

Three other solid figures you may meet on the SAT are the sphere, the cone, and the pyramid. Figure 7.13 shows these three solids.

Sphere   Cone   Pyramid

Figure 7.13   Sphere, cone, and pyramid.

A *sphere* is the three-dimensional version of a circle. It consists of all the points in three dimensions that are equidistant from the center of the sphere. Every radius of the sphere has the same length.

A *cone* has a circular base and a single vertex. A smooth surface joins the points on the circle to the vertex. When the line from the vertex to the center of the circle is perpendicular to the circle, the cone is a *right circular cone*. In this case, the length of that line is the height of the cone.

A *pyramid* has a polygonal base and a single vertex. Triangular faces join the edges of the base to the vertex. If the base is a regular polygon and all the triangles are isosceles triangles, the pyramid is a *regular pyramid*.

Coordinate Geometry

The SAT will also test your knowledge of coordinate geometry. Coordinate geometry uses mathematical equations to manipulate points, lines, and figures in the coordinate plane. Figure 7.14 shows the *coordinate plane*.

The coordinate plane is marked off by two axes, the x axis and the y axis, which meet at a 90° angle. The tick marks on the axes indicate units of length, and the arrows indicate the direction in which the units increase. By convention, positive x is to the right, and positive y is to the top of the

diagram. The point where the axes cross is the origin, labeled O in the figure. This point has an x-value of 0 and a y-value of 0. You can identify any
point in the coordinate plane by giving its x-value and y-value as an ordered
pair, with the x-value first. Thus, the point P in the figure is at the location
(4, 3): four units to the right on the x axis and then three units up in the positive y direction.

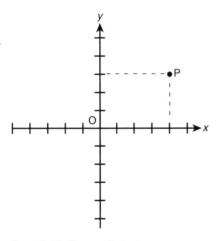

Figure 7.14   The coordinate plane.

Slope and y-Intercept

A line can be characterized in coordinate geometry by an equation of the
form

$$y = mx + b$$

The two numbers m and b are constants, and have a special meaning:

➤ m is the *slope* of the line, which can be positive or negative.

➤ b is the *y-intercept* of the line, the point at which the line crosses the y
axis.

If you're given the equation of a line, you can draw it on the coordinate plane
by finding any two points that fit the equation and then drawing a line that
connects those points. For example, suppose you're given the equation:

$$y = \frac{1}{3}x - 2$$

Figure 7.15 shows how you could graph this line.

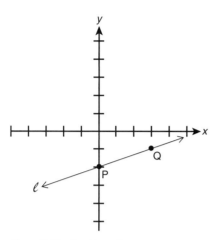

Figure 7.15   Graphing a line.

To graph the line, you need to come up with two points on the line. One easy point to find is the one where x = 0. Plug this value in to the equation to determine the corresponding y value:

$$y = \frac{1}{3}x - 2$$
$$y = \frac{1}{3}(0) - 2$$
$$y = 0 - 2$$
$$y = -2$$

So the point (0, –2) lies on the line. We've added this to the figure as point P. Another easy point to find is the one where x = 3:

$$y = \frac{1}{3}x - 2$$
$$y = \frac{1}{3}(3) - 2$$
$$y = 1 - 2$$
$$y = -1$$

Thus, the point (3, –1) is also on the line. This point is shown on the figure as point Q. Given two points, you can draw the required line ℓ connecting the points.

Look back at the constants in the original equation in light of this figure. You can see that the constant b, –2, is the value of y where the line crosses the y axis. The other constant m, $\frac{1}{3}$, is a measure of the angle that the line makes to the x axis. One way to remember the slope is by the formula "rise over run": The line rises one unit for every three units it runs to the right, and thus has a slope of $\frac{1}{3}$. You can see that understanding the slope and y-intercept allows you to draw a line without the bother of plotting points.

Parallel and Perpendicular Lines

You can also use the equations of lines in the coordinate plane to quickly determine whether two lines are parallel or perpendicular. The rules are simple:

➤ Two lines are parallel if they have the same slope.

➤ Two lines are perpendicular if the product of their slopes is –1.

Sometimes you can use these facts to solve coordinate geometry problems without drawing any figures. For example,

> Lines *l* and *m* are perpendicular and intersect precisely on the y axis. The equation of line *l* is $y = -2x + 4$. What is the equation of line *m*?

To solve this problem, note first that if the two lines intersect on the y axis, they have the same y-intercept. The y-intercept of line *l* is 4, so the y-intercept of line *m* is also 4. Now you can take advantage of the fact that the lines are perpendicular, so the product of their slopes is –1. So the slope of line *m* is a number that, multiplied by –2, is –1. This means that the slope of line *m* is $\frac{1}{2}$. Therefore, the equation of line m is $y = \frac{1}{2}x + 4$.

Midpoints and Distances

You might be called on to calculate the midpoint of a line segment in the coordinate plane, or the distance between two points.

The midpoint is the point precisely between the two endpoints of a line segment. You can think of this as the average of the two points, which makes it easy to find: The x value of the midpoint is halfway between that of the two endpoints, as is the y value. For example, suppose that a line segment has the endpoints (–1, –3) and (5, 3). You'd calculate the midpoint as follows:

$$\left(\frac{-1 + 5}{2}, \frac{-3 + 3}{2}\right)$$

$$\left(\frac{4}{2}, \frac{0}{2}\right)$$

$$(2,0)$$

So the midpoint of the given line segment is the point (2, 0).

To calculate the distance between two points in the coordinate plane, you can use the Pythagorean Theorem. Figure 7.16 shows an example.

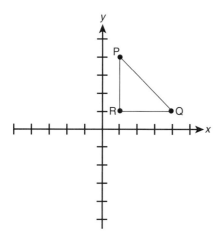

Figure 7.16 Determining the distance between two points.

What is the distance between point P at (1, 4) and point Q at (4, 1)? To solve this problem, we can construct point R that is directly to the left of Q and directly beneath P. R has the coordinates (1, 1). Because of the way that we chose R, ΔPRQ is a right triangle, with $\overline{PR}$ parallel to the y axis and $\overline{RQ}$ parallel to the x axis. The strategy here is to draw a right triangle that has the line segment between the two points as its hypotenuse.

Because they're parallel to the x and y axes, you can read off the lengths of the two sides of the triangle directly: PR = 3 and RQ = 3. Now you can use those values in the Pythagorean Theorem to find $\overline{PQ}$, the desired distance:

$PR^2 + RQ^2 = PQ^2$

$3^2 + 3^2 = PQ^2$

$9 + 9 = PQ^2$

$18 = PQ^2$

$PQ = \sqrt{18}$

$PQ = 3\sqrt{2}$

If you'd like, you can memorize a general formula for the distance between any two points. Given a point with the coordinates (x_1, y_1) and a second point with the coordinates (x_2, y_2), the distance d between them is given by the formula:

$$d = \sqrt{(x_2 - x_1)^2 + (y_2 - y_1)^2}$$

You might find it easier to just draw diagrams and use the Pythagorean Theorem than to memorize this formula, though.

Transformations and Symmetry

Transformations are changes that you can make to a geometric figure. You should be familiar with these key concepts:

➤ Translation

➤ Rotation

➤ Reflection

➤ Reflective symmetry

➤ Rotational symmetry

NOTE For an algebraic approach to transformations, refer to the section "Graphing and Transforming Functions" in Chapter 6, "The Mathematics Section: Numbers and Algebra."

Translation refers to moving a figure without changing its size or shape. In Figure 7.17, the quadrilateral M and the quadrilateral N are congruent. N can be produced by translating M in the positive X direction.

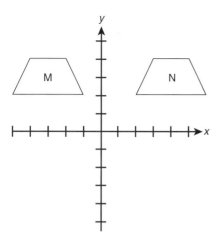

Figure 7.17 Translation in the coordinate plane.

Rotation refers to turning a figure in the plane around a fixed point (called the *center of rotation*). In Figure 7.18, you can produce the square T from the square S by first translating it up and to the right, and then rotating it around the point P.

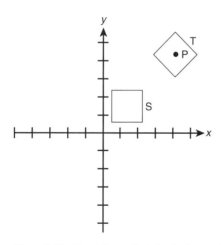

Figure 7.18 Translation and rotation in the coordinate plane.

Reflection refers to drawing a mirror image of a figure on the other side of a line (called the *line of reflection*). In Figure 7.19, the triangle B is a reflection of the triangle A across the line ℓ.

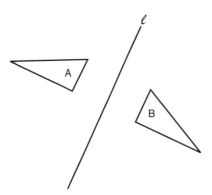

Figure 7.19 A pair of reflected triangles.

If you reflect a figure across a line and then reflect the reflection back across the same line, you get back the original figure.

If you can divide a figure into two parts with a line, and the two parts are reflections of one another, the figure is said to have *reflective symmetry*, or *symmetry across a line*. The line in this case is called a *line of symmetry*. If you can place a point in a figure, and rotate the figure around the point to get back the original figure, the figure is said to have *rotational* symmetry, or *symmetry around a point*. The point in this case is called a *point of symmetry*.

In Figure 7.20, the triangle is an equilateral triangle with its center at P. This triangle has reflective symmetry across the line ℓ because when split by the line, each half of the triangle is a mirror image of the other. The triangle has rotational symmetry around P because any rotation of 60° brings the triangle back to its original position.

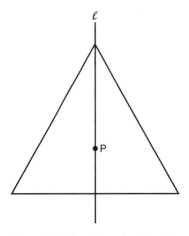

Figure 7.20 Reflective and rotational symmetry.

Any figure can have reflective symmetry, rotational symmetry, both, or neither. If it has reflective symmetry, it might have more than one possible line of reflection.

Special Problem Types

Some problem types are relatively common on the geometry part of the SAT, so it's worth looking at them as special cases:

➤ Area and perimeter problems

➤ Volume and surface area problems

➤ Geometric perception problems

Area and Perimeter

The area of a figure in the plane is the number of unit squares (squares with every side being 1 unit long) that it would take to cover the figure. The perimeter of a figure in the plane is the total length of all the sides of the figure. There are formulas for determining the area and perimeter of common figures, but before you set out to memorize these formulas, you should know that the SAT gives the most common formulas to you. Figure 7.21 shows the reference information that appears at the top of each math section of the SAT.

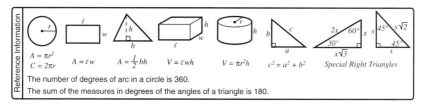

Figure 7.21   SAT math reference information.

The reference information includes the most common formulas that you'll need:

➤ The area of a circle is π times the square of the radius.

➤ The perimeter of a circle (which is called the *circle's circumference*) is π times the diameter of the circle or 2 times π times the radius of the circle.

➤ The area of a rectangle is the length times the width.

➤ The area of a triangle is $\frac{1}{2}$ times the base times the height of the triangle. The base is any side, and the height is a perpendicular line from that side to the opposite vertex. Note that the height must be perpendicular to the base, not just another side of the triangle.

There are some other area and perimeter formulas that you should recognize and be able to apply. The perimeter of any figure is calculated by adding the sides of the figure. Sometimes you can apply special knowledge to make this easier. For example, in a rectangle you know that opposite sides are the same length, so the perimeter is $2l + 2w$, where l is the length of the rectangle and w is the width. For a square, all the sides are the same length, so the perimeter is $4s$, where s is the length of any side.

Figure 7.22 shows how you can calculate the area of a parallelogram.

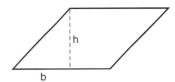

Figure 7.22   Area of a parallelogram.

To calculate the area of a parallelogram, you identify one side as the *base (b)* and then construct a perpendicular line segment from the base to the opposite corner. In the figure, this line segment is marked h, the *height* of the parallelogram. The area of the parallelogram is then given by the product bh. You can remember this by noting that the right triangle to the left of h in the figure would exactly fit under the "overhang" to the right of the figure, turning the parallelogram into a rectangle with sides b and h.

You might also have to work with polygons containing more than four sides. To do this, you'll generally break the polygons up into simpler figures. For example, consider the pentagon shown in Figure 7.23.

The pentagon ABCDE is symmetric about the line ℓ. AB = 2 and EC = 6. The total height of the pentagon, as shown, is 6 units. What is the area of the pentagon?

One way to solve this problem is to add the points and lines shown in Figure 7.24.

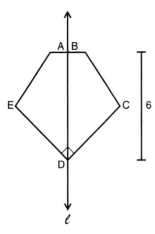

Figure 7.23 Determining the area of a pentagon.

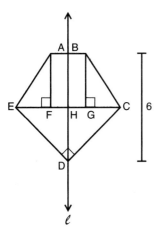

Figure 7.24 Determining the area of a pentagon.

The area of the pentagon is now the sum of the areas of $\triangle ECD$, $\triangle AEF$, $\triangle BGC$, and the rectangle ABGF. Start with $\triangle ECD$. We know from the original problem and the figure that this is a right triangle with the hypotenuse 6 units long. Furthermore, ED = DC because the figure is symmetric. From this we can determine the length of the sides:

$$ED^2 + DC^2 = EC^2$$
$$2(ED^2) = 36$$
$$ED^2 = 18$$
$$ED = \sqrt{18}$$
$$ED = 3\sqrt{2}$$

Now we know the base and height of ΔECD, so we can proceed to calculate its area:

$$A = \frac{1}{2}bh$$
$$A = \frac{1}{2}(3\sqrt{2})(3\sqrt{2})$$
$$A = 9$$

Next, turn to ΔEHD. From symmetry, we know that EH = 3, and we just calculated that ED = $3\sqrt{2}$. $\angle$EHD + $\angle$CHD = 180° because they add up to a straight line. From symmetry, this gives that $\angle$EHD = $\angle$CHD = 90°. This means that ΔEHD is a right triangle with one side of length 3 and the hypotenuse of length $3\sqrt{2}$. This is enough information to calculate the remaining side, HD:

$$EH^2 + HD^2 = ED^2$$
$$3^2 + HD^2 = (3\sqrt{2})^2$$
$$9 + HD^2 = 18$$
$$HD^2 = 9$$
$$HD = 3$$

Now look at the quadrilateral ABGF. From the original problem, AB = 2. The total height of the pentagon is 6, and we just showed that HD = 3, so AF = 3. The area of the quadrilateral is then $2 \times 3 = 6$.

Finally, consider ΔAEF. The height of the triangle, AF, is 3. What about the base EF? Well, FG = 2 and EC = 6, so the total of EF and GC is 4. By symmetry, this means that EF = 2. The area of the triangle is then one-half the base times the height, or 3. Because the pentagon is symmetric, the area of ΔBGC is also 3.

To get the area of the pentagon, just add the area of the four component parts:

$$A = 9 + 6 + 3 + 3$$
$$A = 21$$

Look back at the problem now that you've worked through it: Did you recognize that ΔECD and ΔEHD are both 45°-45°-90° triangles? If you did, you can get the area more quickly by knowing the special relations for those triangles.

Volume and Surface Area

You also might need to calculate the volume or surface area of a solid. The math reference information (refer to Figure 7.21) contains some of the most common formulas:

➤ The volume of a rectangular solid is its length times its width times its height.

➤ The volume of a right circular cylinder is π times the square of the radius times the height.

In general, the volume of a right prism is the height of the prism times the area of the base of the prism.

To calculate the surface area of a solid, you add the areas of its individual faces. For example, consider a rectangular prism with length l, height h, and width w. The faces of this solid are six rectangles:

➤ Two that are *l* by *h*

➤ Two that are *l* by *w*

➤ Two that are *w* by *h*

The surface area for the prism is then *2lh + 2lw + 2wh*.

Geometric Perception

Finally, you should expect to find one or two "geometric perception" problems on the SAT. These problems require you to visualize how plane figures or solids look from different orientations, or how they can be rearranged. Figure 7.25 shows an example.

A and B are squares divided into equal triangles and colored as shown. The squares can be rotated and translated, but not reflected. Which of the figures I, II, and III can be made by combining A and B under these rules?

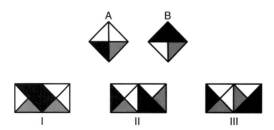

Figure 7.25 A geometric perception problem.

Figure I can be made by placing square B to the left and square A to the right. Figure III can be made by placing square A to the left and a rotated copy of square B to the right. But figure II cannot be made at all under these rules because the copy of square B has been reflected.

Some people find geometric perception problems easy, whereas others find them extremely challenging. Remember, although you can't cut up your test booklet, there's no penalty for rotating the entire booklet to look at it from various angles—no matter how silly that may make you feel! You may also find it useful to sketch in the booklet to solve this type of problem.

Exam Prep Questions

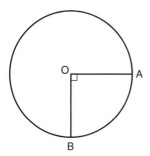

1. In the figure above, O is the center of the circle and the total perime-
   ter of the slice OAB is 4 + π. What is the circumference of the circle?
   (A) 2π
   (B) 4π
   (C) 8 + 2π
   (D) 6 + 4π
   (E) 16 + 8p

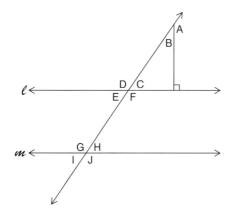

<u>Note:</u> Figure not drawn to scale.

2. In the figure above, lines *ℓ* and *m* are parallel. If angle A is 105°, what
   is angle I?
   (A) 10°
   (B) 15°
   (C) 45°
   (D) 75°
   (E) 105°

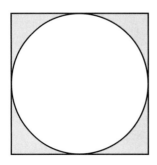

3. The figure above shows a circle embedded in a square, with the sides of the square tangent to the circle. Each side of the square is 2 units long. What is the ratio of the unshaded area to the area of the square?
   (A) 1:2
   (B) 1:π
   (C) 1–π:1
   (D) 1–$\frac{\pi}{4}$:1
   (E) 2:1

4. The coordinates of three points in the xy plane are

   A = (2, 2)

   B = (2, 6)

   C = (5, 2)

   What is the distance BC?
   (A) 3
   (B) 4
   (C) 5
   (D) 6
   (E) 7

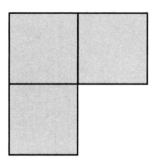

5. The figure above represents a piece of brass constructed of three equal squares. You have an unlimited supply of these pieces. Which of the figures below can be completely filled by these pieces without cutting them or overlapping them?

(A)

(B)

(C)

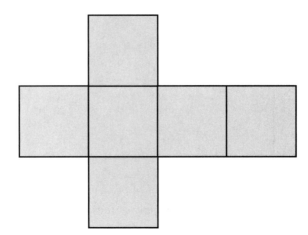

(D)

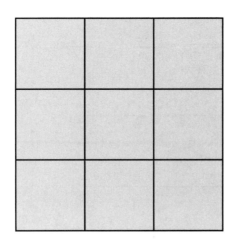

(E)

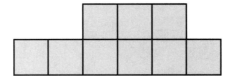

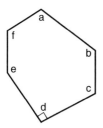

6. In the figure above, what is the sum of the angles a + b + c + d + e + f?

(A) 180°

(B) 360°

(C) 540°

(D) 720°

(E) 900°

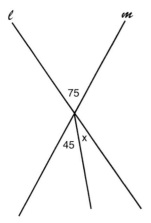

<u>Note:</u> Figure not drawn to scale.

7. In the figure above, *l* and *m* are lines. What is x?

(A) 25°

(B) 30°

(C) 45°

(D) 50°

(E) 75°

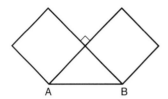

8. The figure shows two squares joined at one corner. Each square has the area 72. What is the distance AB?

   (A) 6

   (B) $6\sqrt{2}$

   (C) 12

   (D) $12\sqrt{2}$

   (E) 36

9. In rectangle ABCD, BC = 12 and BD = 13. What is the perimeter of the rectangle?

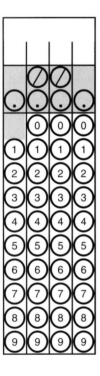

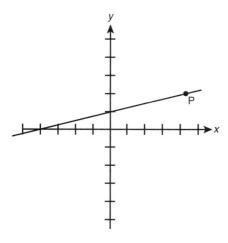

Note: Figure not drawn to scale

10. Point P lies on the line, which has a slope of $\frac{1}{4}$ and which crosses the y axis at y = 1. If the y coordinate of P is 2, what is its x coordinate?

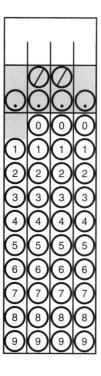

Answers to Exam Prep Questions

1. Answer B is correct. To see this, note that $\overline{OA}$ and $\overline{OB}$ are both radii of the circle, so the diameter of the circle is 2OA. You know that the total circumference of the circle is π times the diameter. Because the slice has a right angle at its center, the length of the curved part is one fourth of the total circumference. Putting all this together, you get an equation you can solve for OA:

$$OA + OB + \frac{2\pi OA}{4} = 4 + \pi$$

$$2\,OA + \frac{2\pi OA}{4} = 4 + \pi$$

$$8\,OA + 2\pi OA = 16 + 4\pi$$

$$OA = \frac{16 + 4\pi}{8 + 2\pi}$$

$$OA = 2$$

If the radius OA = 2, the diameter of the circle is 4 and the circumference is 4π.

2. Answer B is correct. If $\angle A = 105°$, $\angle B = 75$ because they add up to a straight line. Now consider the triangle with B and C as two of its angles. The figure gives you the third angle as a right angle, 90°. Because the sum of the angles in the triangle is 180°, this means that $\angle C = 15°$ (180-90-75). All the acute angles formed by a line cutting a pair of parallel lines are the same, so $\angle I = 15°$ as well.

3. Answer D is correct. Start by calculating the area of the two figures. The area of the square is 4, the product of the sides. The radius of the circle is 1, so the area of the circle is πr^2, or π. So the area of the unshaded region is $4 - \pi$, and the ratio is $4 - \pi$:4, or $\frac{1 - \pi}{4:1}$.

4. Answer C is correct. You can work this out from the general formula for distance in the plane, but there's a faster way. If you plot the three points on a graph, you'll see that they form a right triangle with AB = 4 and AC = 3. You should recognize these as two sides of the 3-4-5 right triangle, so BC = 5.

5. Answer B is correct. This is one of those problems in which you just have to "see" the answer, though it's easy to tell that answer A is incorrect: You can't cover five squares with a multiple of three squares.

6. Answer D is correct. To see this, draw lines between vertices to divide the hexagon into triangles. You'll find that no matter how you do this, you end up with four triangles. Because the sum of the angles in a triangle is 180°, the sum of the angles in the hexagon is $4 \times 180° = 720°$.

7. Answer B is correct. The vertical angles between two lines are equal, so $45° + x = 75°$. This gives $x = 30°$.

$$AB = \sqrt{\left(6\sqrt{2}\right)^2 + \left(6\sqrt{2}\right)^2}$$
$$AB = \sqrt{72 + 72}$$
$$AB = \sqrt{144}$$
$$AB = 12$$

8. Answer C is correct. If the squares have an area of 72, they each have a side of $\sqrt{72} = 6\sqrt{2}$. AB is then the hypotenuse of a right triangle with two sides of $6\sqrt{2}$. This allows you to calculate the length using the Pythagorean Theorem:

9. If you draw the rectangle, you'll realize that BD is a diagonal distance, not one of the sides. You know that the side BC = 12 and need to find the length of the other side. You can calculate this length AB as $\sqrt{13^2 - 12^2}$. Doing the math, you'll find that AB = 5. (You may also remember that 5-12-13 is a right triangle, and save yourself from doing the math at all.) So the perimeter is 2(5 + 12) = 34. Grid 34 in any of the possible positions to get credit for your answer.

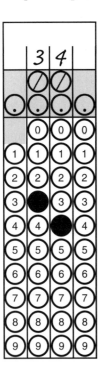

10. From the slope and y-intercept, you can immediately write the equation of the line: $y = \frac{1}{4}x + 1$. Substitute y = 2 and solve for x:

$$y = \frac{1}{4}x + 1$$

$$2 = \frac{1}{4}x + 1$$

$$8 = x + 4$$

$$x = 4$$

So grid 4 in any of the possible positions to receive credit for your answer.

The Mathematics Section: Statistics, Probability, and Data Analysis

Terms you'll need to understand:

✓ Bar graph
✓ Dependent events
✓ Independent events
✓ Line graph
✓ Line of best fit
✓ Mean
✓ Median
✓ Mode
✓ Pictograph
✓ Pie chart
✓ Probability
✓ Scatterplot
✓ Weighted average

Techniques you'll need to master:

✓ Read and understand various types of graphs
✓ Find results in a table of data
✓ Evaluate a line of best fit
✓ Distinguish and use different types of averages
✓ Calculate the probability of independent and dependent events
✓ Determine geometric probability

The most advanced math topics on the SAT concern statistics, probability, and data analysis. These topics don't have to be difficult, but you may find that some of the terms and concepts are new to you because they "fall through the cracks" of the normal high school match curriculum. But if you learn a few skills, you should do fine in this area of the exam.

Interpreting Data

One of the goals of the new SAT is to demonstrate that you know how to apply math to real-world problems, not just how to solve equations. The data interpretation questions are aimed at testing this skill. Given data in a graph, chart, or table, you should be able to use the data in a variety of ways:

➤ Recognize trends

➤ Compare quantities

➤ Extract information

➤ Perform calculations

Understanding Types of Graphs

You might run across five different kinds of graphs on the SAT:

➤ Pie charts (sometimes called circle charts)

➤ Line graphs

➤ Bar graphs

➤ Pictographs

➤ Scatterplots

We'll show examples of each of these in turn and discuss the information that you can extract from each one. No matter what type of graph you see on the test, you should always make sure that you understand three key pieces of information before you try to answer the question:

➤ What are the *axes* of the graph?

➤ What are the *units* of the graph?

➤ What do the *labels* on the graph tell you?

You'll see these three elements in various arrangements in the next few pages.

Reading Pie Charts

A pie chart displays the relative magnitude of several quantities by dividing a circle into wedges. Figure 8.1 shows a typical pie chart.

Christmas Toys Delivered

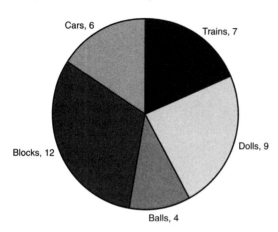

Figure 8.1 A pie chart.

This particular pie chart shows that a number of toys were delivered in five different categories: cars, trains, blocks, dolls, and balls. Each of these categories is represented by a pie slice or wedge, labeled with the category name and the amount. The area of each wedge is proportional to the magnitude of the quantity being represented.

 Even if the wedges on a pie chart aren't labeled with numbers, you can use their relative areas to answer questions about whether one quantity is larger or smaller than another.

A pie chart always represents 100% of something: In the case of Figure 8.1, 100% of the toys are delivered. The total number of toys delivered is 38, the sum of the amounts for each category. Pie charts are thus well-suited to questions involving ratios and percentages.

You can also use your knowledge that the slices add up to 100% to solve problems such as the following:

Figure 8.2 shows the results of a test on experimental animals. Half as many of the animals had a highly positive response as a positive response.

If 17 animals had a highly negative response, how many had a highly positive response?

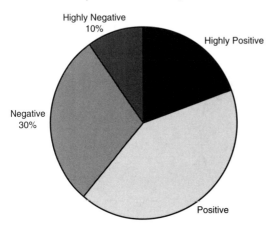

Experimental Response

Figure 8.2 An incomplete pie chart.

To solve this, you need to find out two things: how many animals were in the total experiment, and what percentage were in the highly positive category. The first is easy. From the chart, the highly negative group was 10% of the total. We're told that represents 17 animals, so there were 170 animals total. For the second, note that the two wedges that are labeled account for 40% of the total. Thus, the other two must be 60% of the total because a pie chart always adds up to 100%. Call the number of highly positive animals x; then we know that $x + 2x = 60\%$. This makes it evident that $x = 20\%$, and 20% of 170 is 34, the answer.

Reading Line Graphs

A line graph relates two sets of quantities by plotting related pairs as points on the coordinate plane and connecting the points with a series of line segments. For example, Figure 8.3 shows how a number of measurements of bacterial culture growth relate to one another. In this particular case, the relation shows changes over time.

 Line graphs often show a trend in data over time.

Culture Growth

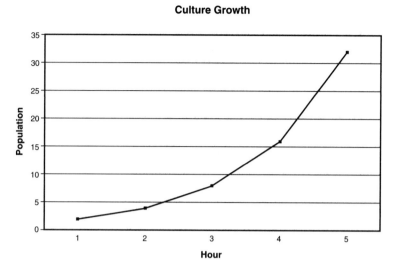

Figure 8.3 A line graph.

Each of the points in Figure 8.3 represents a single measurement at a specific time. For example, at the 3 hour point, the population was roughly 8. The successive measurements are connected by line segments. In this case, the x axis represents a time and the y axis represents an amount. Although this is a common convention for line graphs, it's not the only possibility. For example, Figure 8.4 shows a line graph in which the x axis represents speed and the y axis represents distance. It's evident from this graph that there's a trade-off between speed and distance for the situation depicted by this graph.

Electric Car Range

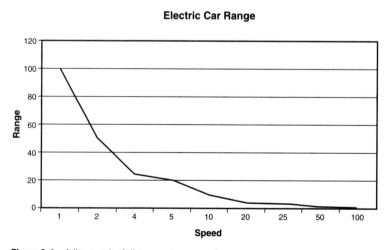

Figure 8.4 A line graph of distance versus speed.

Note that this graph is misleading because the increments on the x axis are not even. Look carefully at graphs on the actual SAT; nothing says that the College Board will draw them to help you to correct conclusions. Sometimes you'll see a break in an axis to indicate that a series is not continuous, but this won't always be the case.

You may also encounter line graphs that show more than one line. Figure 8.5 shows two different lines on the same line graph.

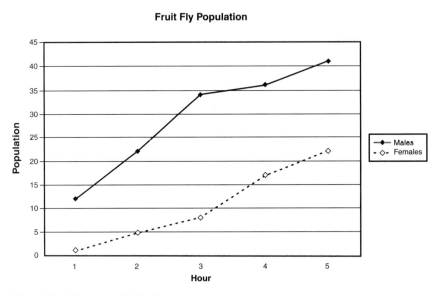

Figure 8.5 A line graph with two lines.

Figure 8.5 lets you see both the population of male fruit flies and the population of female fruit flies on the same graph. In addition to working with the individual populations, this also lets you compare the two. For example, you can tell that the difference between the two populations was highest in hour 3 because the two lines are farthest apart at that point.

Reading Bar Graphs

A bar graph uses a series of bars, either vertical or horizontal, to indicate quantities. Figure 8.6 shows a simple bar graph.

The bar graph in Figure 8.6 shows the distribution of colors in a collection of jelly beans. There are eight red jelly beans, two blue jelly beans, and so on. Bar graphs are well suited to showing comparative quantities across categories, although sometimes you'll see them used for quantity across time as well.

Jelly Beans

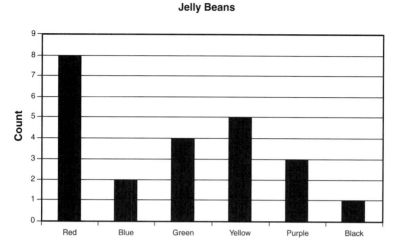

Figure 8.6 A bar graph.

Reading Pictographs

Figure 8.7 shows a pictograph, which is essentially a pictorial version of a bar graph.

Factory Output

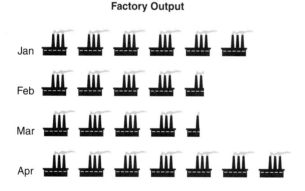

Figure 8.7 A pictograph.

In this case, each horizontal row of factory symbols corresponds to the factory output in a single month. You can see that the output was greatest in April and least in March, and that the January output was about 600 tons. (Refer to the key at the bottom of the graph, which shows that each symbol represents 100 tons.) The output for both February and March was between

400 and 500 tons; the partial symbols indicate some amount less than 100 tons each, though it's difficult to be precise.

 If you see a pictograph on the SAT, be sure that you understand what each symbol represents. Without reading the key, you might be misled into assuming that 5 symbols mean 5 instead of 15 or 100.

Reading Scatterplots

The final type of chart that you may see on the SAT is a scatterplot. You can think of a scatterplot as two bar graphs or pictographs combined; it shows two different series of data and the correlations between them. Figure 8.8 shows an example.

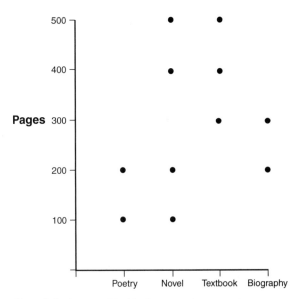

Figure 8.8   A scatterplot of book genre and page counts.

Look first at the rows in Figure 8.8. This provides you with a bar graph of page counts. Two books had 500 pages, two had 400 pages, and so on. Then look at the columns. This gives you a second bar graph, this one of genres: two poetry, four novels, and so on.

But in addition to showing the relative counts of two different categories of data, the scatterplot shows you how those categories are correlated. You can see, for example, that the minimum size for a textbook was 300 pages, whereas poetry topped out at a maximum of 200 pages. You may be asked to calculate things from a scatterplot, such as averages, or to be able to identify simple trends. For example, in Figure 8.8, textbooks clearly average more pages than poetry books: Poetry averages 150 pages, whereas textbooks average 400 pages. (You'll learn more about calculating averages later in this chapter.)

There's another type of scatterplot you might see on the SAT: one that shows two different numerical measurements for the same entity on a single graph.

For example, Figure 8.9 shows a scatterplot of age and weight for a number of animals. Each dot represents a single animal, and you can read its age on the x axis and its weight on the y axis. From a scatterplot such as this, you can look for patterns and draw general conclusions (such as that the older an animal is, the more it weighs).

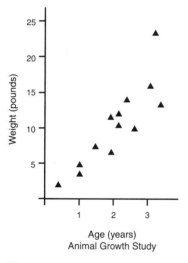

Figure 8.9 A scatterplot of age and weight.

Using Tables of Data

Any graph can also be presented as a table of data. With a table, you can't pick out trends visually, but you can know more precisely the values that you're looking at. Figure 8.10 gives you an example data table.

The caption at the top of the table tells you what information the table is intended to convey. The table in Figure 8.10 shows estimated world population for five different years, with three different authorities providing differing estimates. Because the table shows precise figures, the SAT might ask you to perform calculations based on a table. For example, here's a question about the population table:

Historical Estimates of World Population

Year	Source		
	Durand	McEvedy & Jones	UN
1	270	170	300
1000	275	265	310
1500	440	425	500
1750	735	720	790
1900	1650	1625	1650

All Figures in millions

Figure 8.10 A table of data.

The table above shows population estimates from Durand, McEvoy & Jones, and the UN. Which of these authorities shows the highest rate of population increase between 1750 and 1900?

To solve this problem, you need to look at both the base numbers and the differences. Remember, you can calculate the rate of increase by dividing the difference by the original number. This gives you

Durand: 915/735 = 124%

McEvoy & Jones: 905/720 = 126%

UN: 860/790 = 109%

So, McEvoy & Jones comes up with the highest rate of population increase in this case.

Evaluating Lines of Best Fit

A line of best fit indicates the trend of data on a graph. You can think of it as representing the "average" data points on the graph. Figure 8.11 shows a scatterplot with a line of best fit.

You can use a line of best fit to determine information that's not shown on the graph. Consider this question:

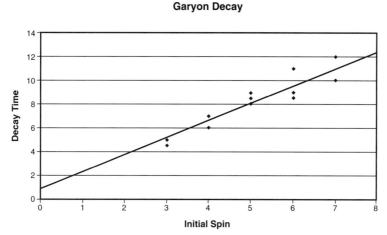

Figure 8.11 A graph with a line of best fit.

The figure above shows a plot of garyon decay times according to the initial spin of the particle across a number of experiments, together with a line of best fit. Which of the following is the most likely decay time for a particle with an initial spin of 8?

(A) 8
(B) 10
(C) 12
(D) 14
(E) 16

First, don't panic just because you don't understand the terms used here! The SAT will throw technical jargon at you to distract you, even though it's not important to solve the problem at hand. Start by looking at the graph. The axes are clearly labeled, so you know that the x-axis shows spin and the y-axis shows decay time. Once you know that, you can convert the question to one that doesn't involve particles at all: What is the most likely y value for an x value of 8? To find the answer, look at the line of best fit, and find the y value that matches this line for the x value of 8. Although you can't calculate that directly from the graph, you can see that 12 is the closest to the line, so C is the correct answer.

Understanding Basic Statistics

You need to know some basic statistics to ace the SAT. Fortunately, the statistics involved are indeed very basic. In fact, if you're comfortable with the four different types of averages, you'll do fine on this part of the SAT:

➤ Mean

➤ Mode

➤ Median

➤ Weighted average

Taking Averages

Given a set of numbers, you should be able to take their average. But which average? Make sure that you read the question carefully, so you know which one you need. In this section, we'll review the four types of averages that you need for the SAT.

Finding the Mean

The *mean* is probably what you think of first when someone asks for an average. To determine the mean of a set of numbers, add them all and divide by the number of values in the set. For example, here's how you'd calculate the mean of 1, 2, 2, 4, 8, 12, and 97:

$$\frac{1 + 2 + 2 + 4 + 8 + 12 + 97}{7}$$

$$= \frac{126}{7}$$

$$= 18$$

Finding the Mode

The *mode* tells you which number in a group is most common. In the set of numbers 1, 2, 2, 4, 8, 12, and 97, the mode is 2 because 2 occurs more often than any other number.

 The mode of a set of numbers is not necessarily unique. In the set 1, 1, 2, 2, both 1 and 2 are the mode because each of these values occurs twice. If there's no repeated value in the set, the set has no mode.

Finding the Median

The *median* of a set of numbers is the number "in the middle" of the set. For 1, 2, 2, 4, 8, 12, and 97, the median is 4. Before you can find the median of a set, you need to put the numbers in order from lowest to highest.

To find the median of an even number of numbers, you need to calculate the mean of the two middle numbers. For example, in the set 1, 2, 3, 4, the median is the mean of 2 and 3 (which equals 2.5).

Finding the Weighted Average

When you're taking the mean of two or more groups with different numbers of members, you need to calculate a *weighted average*. In a weighted average, each group is counted proportionally to the number of members in the group. Try this problem:

Farmer Brown has 12 chickens that lay an average of 6 eggs per week. Farmer Green has 10 chickens that lay an average of 8 eggs per week. Farmer White has 9 chickens that lay an average of 7 eggs per week. What is the average egg production per week for the entire group of chickens?

To get the answer, you need to make sure that each group of chickens is counted according to the number of chickens in the group. You do this by multiplying the number in each group by the average for the group, adding the totals, and then dividing by the total number of chickens, as follows:

$$\frac{(12 \times 6) + (10 \times 8) + (9 \times 7)}{12 + 10 + 9}$$

$$= \frac{215}{31}$$

$$= 6\frac{29}{31}$$

Many weighting problems involve percentages. For example, a course might base its grade by assigning a weight of 40% to the final, 20% to the homework, and 40% to the quizzes. To solve such a problem, just use the percents as the weights.

Working with Statistics and Averages

You might find a couple of types of special average problems on the SAT:

➤ Average of algebraic expressions

➤ Finding missing numbers through averages

It may seem confusing, but you can average algebraic expressions just as you can average numbers. Just make sure that you group like terms together.

This means that you add x^2 terms together separately from x terms, and so on. For example, take an average of these three expressions:

$3x^2 + 5x + 9$
$4x^2 - 3x - 7$
$5x^2 + 4x + 13$

To calculate the average, add them and then divide by three:

$$\frac{3x^2 + 5x + 9 + 4x^2 - 3x - 7 + 5x^2 + 4x + 13}{3}$$

$$= \frac{(3 + 4 + 5)x^2 + (5 - 3 + 4)x + 9 - 7 + 13}{3}$$

$$= \frac{12x^2 + 6x + 15}{3}$$

$$= 4x^2 + 2x + 5$$

Sometimes you might be given an average and need to work back to other information. Be careful with these problems because it might seem like you don't have enough information to get the answer even when you do. Here's an example:

A class of five students has an average height of $5'8"$. Three new students join the class and the new average height is $5'9"$. What is the average height of the three new students?

Don't be in a rush to check an answer that says "not enough information was given" because there's plenty of information here. The key here is that you can figure the total height of the class before and after, which lets you figure the total height of the new students, which lets you get the answer. Remember, each time you figure the average, you use the number of students in the group being averaged. Here's how:

Total height before = 5 x 5'8" = 5 x 68" = 340"
Total height after = 8 x 5'9" = 8 x 69" = 552"
Total height of new students =
552" - 340" = 212"

Average height of new students =
$\frac{212"}{3}$ = 70 2/3" = 5' 10 2/3"

Understanding Basic Probability

Probability problems are new on the SAT beginning in 2005. You won't be quizzed on any advanced probability topics, but you do need to understand the difference between independent and dependent events. You'll also need to be able to calculate probabilities.

Distinguishing Independent and Dependent Events

One of the key concepts that you need to understand is the distinction between *independent* and *dependent events*. Two events are independent if the outcome of one event has no effect on the outcome of the other. But if the outcome of one event can affect the outcome of the other, the two events are dependent events.

For example, consider these two events:

➤ Your car's engine stops working.

➤ You win $1,000 in the lottery.

These are most likely independent events: The state of your car's engine has no effect on whether you win the lottery, and vice versa. Now consider these two events:

➤ Your car's engine stops working.

➤ You drive to the mall for dinner.

These two events are likely dependent events. If your car's engine stops working, that has a direct influence on whether you can drive to the mall for dinner. As you'll see in the next section of the chapter, calculating probabilities follows different rules for dependent events than it does for independent events.

Calculating Probabilities

The *probability* of an event is a number between zero and one (inclusive), indicating how likely an event is to occur. A probability of zero indicates that an event is impossible. A probability of one indicates that an event is certain.

What about events that are neither impossible nor certain? The basic rule for calculating probabilities is to divide the number of ways that the event can occur by the number of possible outcomes. That may sound a bit confusing, but it's easy enough in practice. For instance, what is the probability that a coin will turn up heads if you flip it once? There's one way that this can happen (the coin turns up heads) and two possible outcomes (heads or tails). Thus the probability is $\frac{1}{2}$, or .5.

The total of all the probabilities in an entire set of outcomes will always add up to one. For example, a coin can either come up heads or tails, nothing else. If you know the chance of the coin coming up heads is .5, the chance of the coin coming up tails must also be .5.

What is the probability that a coin will come up once on heads and once on tails if it is tossed twice? To answer this question, start by enumerating the possible outcomes. Using H for heads and T for tails, flipping the coin twice can give you four possible outcomes: HH, HT, TH, and TT. Of these, two have one head and one tail, so the probability is $\frac{2}{4}$, which is again .5.

What is the probability of rolling a total of 4 with two dice? Figure 8.12 can help you answer this question.

Second Die	First Die					
	1	**2**	**3**	**4**	**5**	**6**
1	2	3	4	5	6	7
2	3	4	5	6	7	8
3	4	5	6	7	8	9
4	5	6	7	8	9	10
5	6	7	8	9	10	11
6	7	8	9	10	11	12

Figure 8.12 Probability with a pair of dice.

The chart shows the possible outcomes from rolling two dice. Across the top are the values for the first die; down the left side are the values for the second die. The cells inside the chart show the totals. The three shaded cells are the three ways to roll a total of 4, and there are 36 cells in all. So the probability of rolling a 4 is $\frac{1}{12}$, which is about 0.083.

To find the probability of two or more independent events occurring together, multiply the probabilities of the events. Here's an example:

> You plant five tomato seeds. The seeds are in separate containers and have no effect on one another. Each of the seeds has a 40% chance of germinating. What is the chance that none of the seeds will germinate?

The first thing to note about this question is that it introduces an alternative way to talk about probability. In terms of problem solving, the chance of an event is the same as the probability of the event. Also, it doesn't matter whether you represent the chance as a decimal number, a percentage, or a fraction—.4, 40%, and $\frac{4}{10}$ all mean the same thing.

Now, note the second sentence of the question. This sentence tells you that the probability of each seed sprouting is an independent event. Also, you're told that the chance of a seed germinating is .4, which means that the chance of a seed *not* germinating is .6.

Think about the event that you're interested in: none of the seeds germinating. This is composed of five independent events:

➤ Seed A not germinating

➤ Seed B not germinating

➤ Seed C not germinating

➤ Seed D not germinating

➤ Seed E not germinating

Because these are independent events, you can multiply the individual probabilities together to get the answer: $.6 \times .6 \times .6 \times .6 \times .6 = 0.07776$, or nearly 8%.

Working with Geometric Probability

You may also run across SAT questions dealing with geometric probability. These are just regular probability questions based on geometric figures. Here's one to try:

> Figure 8.13 shows a cube of side 1 with a right cylinder embedded in it. The cylinder has a radius of .5 and the circular face of the cylinder exactly touches the cube at the center of each side as shown. A point is chosen at random from the interior of the cube. What is the probability that this point will lie within the cylinder?

The key to solving this problem is to understand that it's asking for the ratio of the volumes of the two solids. The chance of a point being in the cylinder (the desired outcome) is proportional to the volume of the cylinder; the total number of outcomes is proportional to the volume of the cube. So you can figure the probability this way:

$$\frac{\pi\,(.5)^2 \times 1}{1 \times 1 \times 1}$$
$$= .25\pi$$

Thus the answer is $\pi/4$, or about 79%.

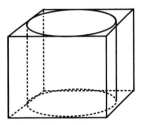

Figure 8.13   A geometric probability problem.

Exam Prep Questions

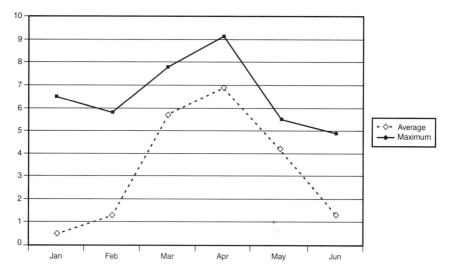

Monthly Rainfall

1. According to the graph above, in which month is the difference between the average rainfall and the maximum rainfall the greatest?

(A) January

(B) February

(C) March

(D) May

(E) June

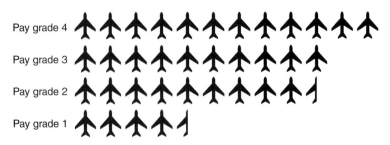

Flights Per Year

Pay grade 4

Pay grade 3

Pay grade 2

Pay grade 1

= 3 flights

2. According to the pictograph above, which of these changes in pay grade would result in $10\frac{1}{2}$ extra flights per year?

(A) A promotion from pay grade 1 to pay grade 2

(B) A promotion from pay grade 1 to pay grade 3

(C) A promotion from pay grade 2 to pay grade 3

(D) A promotion from pay grade 2 to pay grade 4

(E) A promotion from pay grade 3 to pay grade 4

Municipal Waste Pickups	
Year	Tons
1999	142
2000	187
2001	213
2002	234
2003	277
2004	341

3. According to the table above, when was the largest rate of increase in waste pickups?

(A) 1999 to 2000

(B) 2000 to 2001

(C) 2001 to 2002

(D) 2002 to 2003

(E) 2003 to 2004

4. A class with 17 students is averaging 85% on exams. Three students drop out, and the remaining students are averaging 88% on exams. What was the average exam score of the three students who dropped out?

(A) 69
(B) 70
(C) 71
(D) 80
(E) 82

Net Weight, Ounces

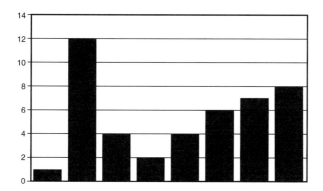

5. What is the median of the observations shown on the graph above?

(A) 3
(B) 4
(C) 5
(D) 5.5
(E) 6

6. In freshman calculus, the three quizzes each count the same toward the final grade, and the final exam counts as much as two quizzes. Mary scored 75, 81, and 93 on the three quizzes. Her final average score in the course was 85. What was her score on the final exam?

(A) 85

(B) 88

(C) 89

(D) 90

(E) 91

7. A drawer contains 4 red socks, 2 blue socks, and 6 green socks. You reach into the drawer and, without looking, take out 2 socks. What is the probability that you have drawn a matching pair?

(A) $\frac{1}{6}$

(B) $\frac{1}{5}$

(C) $\frac{1}{4}$

(D) $\frac{1}{3}$

(E) $\frac{1}{2}$

8. You roll three standard six-sided dice. What is the probability that at least one of the dice will display a 2?

(A) $\frac{1}{216}$

(B) $\frac{3}{216}$

(C) $\frac{91}{216}$

(D) $\frac{125}{216}$

(E) $\frac{215}{216}$

9. A box contains red and blue balls. The probability of drawing a red ball is 24%. There are 190 blue balls in the box. How many red balls are in the box?

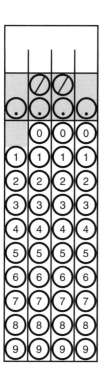

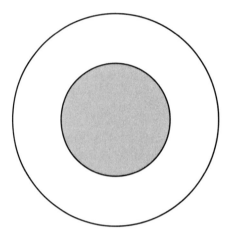

Note: Figure not drawn to scale.

10. The figure above shows two circles, with the smaller circle completely inside the larger one. The larger circle has a radius of 4. A point is chosen at random in the larger circle. There is a 25% chance that the point will also lie in the smaller circle. What is the diameter of the smaller circle?

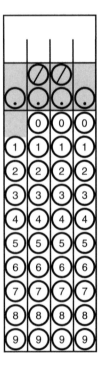

Answers to Exam Prep Questions

1. Answer A is correct. The difference between the average and maximum rainfall for each month is simply the distance between the two graph lines. Just by looking at the graph, you can see that the lines are farthest apart in January.

2. Answer D is correct. Note from the answer key that each plane symbol represents three flights per year. Thus, you want to find a difference of $3\frac{1}{2}$ symbols to account for $10\frac{1}{2}$ flights. The rows for pay grades 2 and 4 differ by this amount, so D is the correct answer.

3. Answer A is correct. Remember that the rate of increase can be calculated by dividing the actual increase by the original amount. To solve this problem, add two more columns to the table, so it looks like this:

Municipal Waste Pickups			
Year	Tons	Difference	Increase
1999	142		
2000	187	45	31.7%
2001	213	26	13.9%
2002	234	21	9.9%
2003	277	43	18.3%
2004	341	64	23.1%

After calculating the values in the last two columns, you can see that A is the correct answer. Don't be fooled by the fact that the absolute increase in tons was largest between 2003 and 2004. Because the starting amount was much higher, this represents a smaller percent increase than that from 1999 to 2000.

4. Answer C is correct. The total score before the three students dropped out was $85 \times 17 = 1445$. The total score after the three students dropped out was $88 \times 14 = 1232$. That leaves a difference of 213 points to be accounted for by the three students, and their average score is $\frac{213}{3}$, or 71.

5. Answer C is correct. The median is the middle of a set of numbers. Because there are an even number of observations on the graph, the median is the mean of the two central observations. But remember:

You have to sort the numbers in order from lowest to highest to find the median! If you do that, you'll find that the set is 1, 2, 4, 4, 6, 7, 8, 12. The two numbers in the middle are 4 and 6, and their average is 5, making answer C correct.

6. Answer B is correct. You can treat this as a weighted average problem, with x representing the score on the final:

$$\frac{75 + 81 + 93 + 2x}{5} = 85$$

$249 + 2x = 5 \times 85$
$249 + 2x = 425$
$2x = 176$
$x = 88$

7. Answer D is correct. Let's think about the red socks first: There are 4 ways to draw a red sock, and then 3 ways to draw another red sock, making 12 ways to get a red pair. For the blue socks, there are 2 ways to do it (first sock 1 and then sock 2, or vice versa). For the green socks, there are 6 ways to draw the first sock and then 5 ways to draw the second sock, for a total of 30 ways to get the desired outcome. So there are a total of 12 + 2 + 30 = 44 ways to get the desired outcome of a matching pair. Overall, there are 12 socks. The total number of possible outcomes is $12 \times 11 = 132$ (12 ways to draw any sock, followed by 11 ways to draw another sock). So the probability of a pair is $\frac{44}{132}$, or $\frac{1}{3}$.

8. Answer C is correct. You could list out all the possibilities, but it's easier to take advantage of the fact that you're dealing with three independent events here. For each die, the probability of *not* displaying a 2 is $\frac{5}{6}$. So the probability of there being no die displaying 2 is

$$\frac{5}{6} \times \frac{5}{6} \times \frac{5}{6} = \frac{125}{216}$$

So, there are 125 chances out of 216 of not seeing a 2. The probability of seeing at least one 2 is given by the remaining 91 chances of 216.

9. Because the probabilities must add up to 1, the probability of drawing a blue ball is 76%. Call the total number of balls in the box x. So then $\frac{190}{x} = .76$. (The probability of drawing a blue ball is the number of blue balls divided by the total number of balls.) Then you know that $.76x = 190$. Solving for x, you get 250 total balls in the box. If 190 of the balls are blue, that leaves 60 red balls. Grid 60 in any of the possible positions to receive credit for your answer.

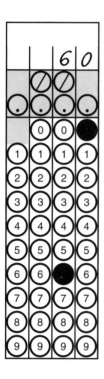

10. To work this geometric probability problem, you must determine the areas of the two circles from the formula $A = \pi r^2$. The area of the larger circle is thus 16π. Now, if there is a 25% chance of a point from the larger circle being in the smaller circle, the smaller circle must have 25% of this area, of 4π. This means that the smaller circle must have a radius of 2. But note that the question asks for the diameter of the smaller circle, not its radius. Multiply the radius by 2 to get 4, the correct answer. Grid 4 in any of the possible positions to receive credit for your answer.

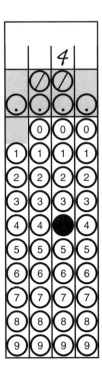

Strategies for Raising Your Score

Now that you've reviewed all the writing, critical reading, and mathematics skills that you'll need to do well on the SAT, it's time to take a step backward. The SAT is supposed to measure your knowledge and reasoning ability, but that doesn't mean that two equally knowledgeable students will always have the same score. In this chapter, we'll explore some of the ways (academic and otherwise) that you can help add points to your SAT score. Remember, every little bit counts.

NOTE Don't forget to review the Tips, Exam Alerts, and Notes in Chapters 1 through 8 for more advice on individual sections of the SAT. The Cram Sheet in the front of the book also provides some handy guidance.

Getting Ready for the SAT

In addition to studying, you can do some other things to make sure that you're prepared on the day of the SAT. The last thing you want is to be feeling your worst when you're trying to sit through nearly four hours of tough questions. A wild party the night before, for example, is probably a bad idea.

Get your regular amount of sleep. Ideally, this means that you go to bed when you usually do and get up when you usually do, so your body isn't trying to cope with any sudden changes. But remember, the SAT starts at 8 a.m. sharp, and you need to get there, so if you usually sleep in until 8:30 a.m., you'll need to make some adjustments. We suggest that you figure out when you need to wake up, and then allow for your normal amount of sleep. For example, suppose you need 45 minutes to get washed, dressed, and have breakfast, and that it takes 30 minutes to get to the test center. You want to be there at 7:45. That means you need to get out of bed (not just hit the snooze button) at 6:30. If your body needs 9 hours of sleep to be fully rested, you'll need to go to bed at 9:30 the night before.

So, if you're used to going to bed at 11 p.m., you need to shift your schedule back by an hour and a half before the SAT test day. Here's a tip: Don't try to do that all at once! If you just go to bed 90 minutes early, you're likely to toss and turn for hours, and get less sleep than ever. That's not going to leave you in top test-taking shape.

Instead, shift your sleep schedule gradually. We recommend moving it by no more than 15 minutes a night. Yes, you might miss a few nights out with friends or favorite TV shows the week before the SAT—but isn't that worth it to up your chances of spending four years at your first-choice college?

And speaking of time: Be on time, or you've wasted your money and your studying. The SAT starts at 8 a.m., and you should plan on being there 15 minutes early to allow for confusion and traffic conditions. If you're late, they won't let you in.

Your SAT-morning breakfast deserves some thought as well. Eat a mix of protein (eggs, bacon, sausage) and carbohydrates (cereal, toast, grits) so that you'll have both quick-energy and slow-energy foods working in your system. Remember, this breakfast has to get you through until lunchtime with no snacks. If you usually have coffee with breakfast, go for it. But if you don't, the day of your SAT is not the day to try coffee for the first time. Three hours and forty-five minutes of concentration doesn't fit well with caffeine-induced jitters. And just like your sleep schedule, don't try to change your eating habits all at once. If you usually skip breakfast, start changing your habits a week or two before the SAT, not the day of the test.

You wouldn't be the first student to smuggle an energy bar or a bag of M&Ms into the testing center, although the SAT rules say you can't do this. If you get caught eating by a particularly tough proctor, you could have your test cancelled. We'll just point out that the proctors can't be everywhere, especially during breaks, and leave your stomach to your conscience.

Double-check the things that you're bringing to the testing center. You might want to put them all into a backpack or purse the night before:

➤ Your admission ticket.

➤ Your photo ID.

➤ As many sharpened No. 2 pencils as you think you'll need, plus a couple of extras.

➤ An eraser. Check to make sure that the eraser really does a good job of removing the pencil marks.

➤ A calculator.

➤ Spare batteries for the calculator.

➤ A watch, stopwatch, or travel alarm with the audible alarm turned off.

When you're choosing a calculator to bring, make sure that you follow the SAT rules. Not everything the size of a calculator is legal. You are not allowed to use a PDA, laptop computer, anything with an alphabetic keyboard, anything with pen input, anything with a printer, anything that makes "unusual noise," or anything that requires an electrical outlet. The intent is to let you check basic math calculations while forbidding anything that you might use to smuggle answers into the SAT, or that might distract other test takers.

Make sure that you put fresh batteries into the calculator (or charge it, if they're rechargeable) and that you understand how to use it. An expensive scientific calculator won't do you much good if you can't figure out how to take a square root with it.

To recap, here's a quick checklist for preparing before the test:

➤ Learn the directions for each section of the test.

➤ Try to get a good night's sleep and eat a good breakfast the morning of the test.

➤ Have everything you need ready to go the night before.

➤ Know the directions to the test site. Better yet, make a practice run a few days before.

➤ Allow enough time to get to the test site. Don't let a traffic jam be your undoing.

➤ Once in the testing center and in your seat, chill out. Take a few deep breaths, and relax. You might even plan what you're going to do afterward to celebrate how well you did!

Tackling the Test

There are some general issues that you should keep in mind across all the sections of the SAT. Some of these tips may seem obvious—but you'd feel pretty silly if you got a lower score because you made an obvious mistake, wouldn't you?

There are only eight different sets of directions for the SAT. There's one set for sentence completions, one for passage comparisons, and so on. These don't change from test to test, and they're the same in the practice tests in this book as they are on the real SAT. Read them on the practice tests, learn them, and understand them. That way, you won't waste any of those precious minutes on test day reading the instructions.

You don't get scratch paper for the SAT, but you can write as much as you like on your test booklet. Don't be afraid to make notes or underline in the reading sections or work out problems in the mathematics section. But keep your answer sheet clean, except for filling in the answer ovals: Extraneous marks might be misread as wrong answers.

While we're talking about the answer sheet, here's a key piece of advice: Keep track of your place. Especially if you're skipping past hard questions, it's easy to fill in an oval on the wrong row, and then to keep going with all of your successive answers in the wrong place. Even if you notice this, you'll waste valuable time with your eraser fixing it up. Any time you're skipping a question, double-check that you end up on the right answer row—and check every few rows even if you're not skipping.

 To save time, mark the questions you skip right in the question booklet. That way, if you've got time to go back and take a second look, you won't waste time looking for the questions you skipped.

Some people will tell you not to guess on the SAT. Remember, you get one point for each right answer and lose one fourth of a point for each wrong answer. If you guess on five questions, you'd expect to get one right (for a point in your favor) and four wrong (for four fourths of a point against you), with no net effect on your score. So random guessing might not hurt you, but be careful. It doesn't help you either. You should avoid guessing unless you can do something to help your chances.

In most cases, you should be able to do better than random guessing. If you can eliminate even one answer as being ridiculously wrong, your chance of gaining a point is better than your chance of losing a point. By all means, start with questions for which you feel you know the answer, but do some strategic guessing if you've got time left at the end of a section.

 When using the process of elimination to answer a question, cross out eliminated choices as you go. Doing so will help you hone your focus in the right direction. Also, if you end up skipping the question and coming back later, you won't waste time rereading answers that you've already determined are wrong.

There's one exception to the rule about being penalized for guessing: The grid-in math answers give you a point if you get them right, and there's no penalty for getting them wrong. So if you have the slightest idea what the answer is, you should always fill in the grids, whether you're confident about that answer or not.

Each section of the SAT tells you right at the top how many questions it contains and how long you get to work on it. Make a note of the time when you start, and keep track of how much time is remaining. From your practice exams, you should have some sense of how much time you want to spend coming up with right answers before resorting to guessing. For example, you might want to reserve the last three minutes of each reading section for guessing on questions that you skipped the first time around.

Every question on the SAT is worth the same number of points, so you should do the easy questions first. On most sections of the SAT, it's simple to find the easy questions because the questions are arranged from easiest to hardest. The exceptions are the passage-based reading and improving paragraph questions: Because these are in order of the passage, they aren't necessarily arranged from easiest to hardest. On these sections, you'll probably want to quickly skim the questions to pick out the ones that seem easiest and answer those questions first

Because the hardest questions come at the end of each section, answers at the end of the section are more likely to be set up to trap you. Take an extra moment on the last few questions of each section to consider whether the obvious answer might actually be wrong.

To recap, here's a quick checklist for your behavior during the actual test:

➤ Answer the easiest questions first—remember, in most sections the questions are arranged from easy to hard.

➤ Pace yourself—give each question a fair chance, but don't belabor a question you simply can't answer.

➤ Eliminate choices when the answer isn't readily apparent.

➤ Make an educated guess.

➤ Mark skipped questions in the booklet and go back later if you have time.

➤ Follow the directions carefully when you use the math grid answer sheet. You cannot enter mixed numbers or negative numbers. You may choose to truncate or round decimals that are longer than the grid space.

➤ Check your answer sheet frequently to make sure that you're answering the right question.

Putting the SAT in Perspective

If you're fortunate enough to be reading this book early in your high school career, there are two things that you can do that will very likely help raise your scores: Take the Preliminary SAT (PSAT), and take the SAT more than once.

The PSAT, offered to high school sophomores and juniors, is a sort of "mini SAT." It has fewer sections than the SAT, has no essay, and takes two hours and ten minutes to get through. But the types of questions are very similar to those on the SAT, and the overall testing experience (in terms of what you can bring, what the testing center is like, and so on) is the same as it is for the SAT. You can think of the PSAT as a preview for the SAT, letting you get familiar with the format of the test before you start taking it "for real." In addition, the PSAT is used as the National Merit Scholarship Qualifying Test: Doing exceptionally well on the PSAT translates directly into money to help pay your college costs.

The official College Board statement on taking the SAT more than once is that "some students do a little better on the SAT if they take the test more than once." An awful lot of students would call that statement hogwash. Whether it's because they learn more, practice more, or just avoid the anxiety of taking the SAT for the first time, many students report substantial gains on their SAT scores the second time they take it.

Whether it helps your scores or not, taking the SAT twice is a relatively risk-free strategy. That's because many college admissions offices take into account your highest score on each section. So if you get 650 reading, 720 writing, and 550 math the first time, and 630 reading, 710 writing, and 700 math the second time, you'll be seen as a 650-720-700 student as far as your overall SAT scores are concerned. All you have to lose is a little more time studying and another long morning taking the exam.

We'll close this section of the book with two final things that you ought to keep in mind. First, your SAT score is not the only thing that college admissions offices will be looking at. Your grades, your transcript, your recommendations, and your extracurricular activities are all part of the decision-making process. It's perfectly possible to get into the college or university of your choice without scoring 2400 on your SAT.

And that leads into the very last piece of advice that we have: don't panic. Yes, taking the SAT is stressful for almost everyone. But it doesn't have to be so stressful that your teeth chatter, your palms sweat, and you feel like throwing up. If you practice, eat sensibly, keep the test in perspective, and know the essential skills we've reviewed in this Exam Cram, you should be able to keep your stress level under control. And that, in turn, will help you get a better score.

It isn't easy to recap this section because everyone has their own strengths and weaknesses. But remember, you didn't get to the SAT in a day—it took years to be ready. You can't prepare for the SAT in one day, so don't set yourself up to fail. Confidence and ability will improve with practice, practice, and more practice. Now, keep the following in mind as you prepare:

➤ Think positively about the test. When that monster inside your head starts screaming "You're a dunce, why even try?" just ignore it and go on. Better yet, talk back to the monster or tell it to shut up. You will do just fine.

➤ Focus on your progress while preparing. Don't be distracted by friends who seem to be further along than you.

➤ Don't sweat the SAT too much. You should take this step very seriously, but the SAT is not the be-all and end-all of your scholastic career.

➤ Don't panic during the test. If you're prone to that sort of thing, plan to visualize a relaxing scene or event during the test if you need to calm down. If you feel a panic attack coming on, spend 30 seconds relaxing, and then proceed refreshed.

➤ Maintain control. You—not your mother who thinks you're brilliant enough without all that studying that wrinkles your forehead, not the nag you have for Research who tells you repeatedly that you're worthless, and not even your best friend who's made straight A's since kindergarten—are in charge.

Practice Exam #1

Do not read Chapters 10–13 until you have learned and practiced all the material presented in the earlier chapters of this book. These chapters serve a special purpose; they are designed to test whether you are ready to take the actual SAT. In these chapters, you will find two self tests. Each self test is followed by an answer key and a brief explanation of correct answers along with explanations as to why the other answers are incorrect. Reading these chapters prior to other chapters is like reading the climax of a story and then going back to find out how the story arrived at that ending. Of course, you don't want to spoil the excitement, do you?

How to Take the Practice Exams

Each practice exam in this book consists of 170 questions and an essay section, and you should complete it within 3 hours and 45 minutes. This is the same as the number of questions and the amount of time on the real SAT. Just like the SAT, the practice exam is divided into timed sections. You should carefully time yourself on each section so that you do not go over the allotted time.

Please turn to the back of the book to find the answer sheets for the practice exams.

Once you have prepared using the material presented in the earlier chapters of this book, you should take Practice Exam #1 to check how well you are prepared. After the self test is complete, evaluate yourself using the answer key in Chapter 11, "Answer Key for Practice Exam #1." When you evaluate yourself, note the questions you answered incorrectly, identify their corresponding chapters in the book, and then read and understand that material before taking Practice Exam #2. After taking Practice Exam #2, evaluate yourself again and reread the material corresponding to any incorrect answers. Finally, repeat both the self tests until you correctly answer all the questions. Information in the following section helps you in taking the self test and then evaluating yourself.

Exam-Taking Tips

You take these sample exams under your own circumstances, but we strongly suggest that when you take this self test, you treat it just as you would treat the actual exam at the test center. Use the following tips to get the maximum benefit from the self test:

➤ Before you start, create a quiet, secluded environment where you are not disturbed for the duration of the exam.

➤ Allow yourself only the things that you can bring to the real SAT: pencils, a timepiece, and a calculator. Refer to Chapter 9, "Strategies for Raising Your Score," for more information on the actual test-taking conditions.

➤ Don't use any reference material during the exam.

➤ In general, try to take the practice exam just as you will be taking the actual SAT. Pay close attention to the time limits because one of the most important skills you can gain from the practice tests is to learn how to pace yourself.

Self Test

Essay

SECTION 1

Time—**25 minutes**

Turn to your answer sheet to write your ESSAY.

The essay gives you an opportunity to show how effectively you can develop and express ideas. You should, therefore, take care to develop your point of view, present your ideas logically and clearly, and use language precisely.

Your essay must be written on the lines provided on your answer sheet—you will receive no other paper on which to write. You will have enough space if you write on every line, avoid wide margins, and keep your handwriting to a reasonable size. Remember that people who are not familiar with your handwriting will read what you write. Try to write or print so that what you are writing is legible to those readers.

You have twenty-five minutes to write an essay on the topic assigned below. DO NOT WRITE ON ANOTHER TOPIC. AN OFF-TOPIC ESSAY WILL RECEIVE A SCORE OF ZERO.

Think carefully about the issue presented in the following excerpt and the assignment below.

> In 1920, women across the United States won the right to vote. Back then, it was a controversial issue and many opposed it. Certainly, few seriously thought that the citizens of the United States would ever elect a woman to be the president of the United States. Now that we've entered the twenty-first century, electing a woman to be president of the United States seems inevitable.

Assignment: Do you think the United States is ready for a woman president? Write an essay that develops your point of view on this issue. Support your position with reasoning and examples taken from reading, studies, personal experience, or observation.

DO NOT WRITE YOUR ESSAY IN YOUR TEST BOOK. You will receive credit only for what you write on your answer sheet.

BEGIN WRITING YOUR ESSAY ON PAGE 2 OF THE ANSWER SHEET.

If you finish before time is called, you may check your work on this section only. Do not turn to any other section in the test.

SECTION 2

Time—25 minutes

24 Questions

Turn to Section 2 of your answer sheet to answer the questions in this section.

Directions: For each question in this section, select the best answer from among the choices given and fill in the corresponding circle on the answer sheet.

Each sentence below has one or two blanks, each blank indicating that something has been omitted. Beneath the sentence are five words or sets of words labeled A through E. Choose the word or set of words that, when inserted in the sentence, <u>best</u> fits the meaning of the sentence as a whole.

EXAMPLE:

The Internet is _____ now, being available in 78% of all American households.

(A) unimportant
(B) transitory
(C) migrating
(D) negligible
(E) ubiquitous

Answer: (E)

1. The _____ countryside offered little opportunity for an aspiring engineer.

(A) pristine
(B) barren
(C) rolling
(D) agrarian
(E) pastoral

2. Despite their _____ size, the girls were quite healthy and _____.

(A) enormous . . petite
(B) petite . . fragile
(C) unusual . . charming
(D) small . . frail
(E) diminutive . . robust

3. Alfred Nobel was _____ in many languages and wrote his own business letters because he did not trust anyone to _____ for him.

(A) accomplished . . speak
(B) fluent . . translate
(C) knowledgeable . . compose
(D) lacking . . write
(E) illiterate . . perform

4. Jet and rocket technologies developed during World War II were later _____ to create new crafts that _____ the edge of space.

(A) combined . . probed
(B) abandoned . . reached
(C) utilized . . explored
(D) refurbished . . investigated
(E) pooled . . studied

5. Many _____ of the first American colleges had themselves never _____ college but had faith in education.

(A) educators . . completed
(B) professors . . appreciated
(C) founders . . attended
(D) students . . finished
(E) employees . . considered

The passages below are followed by questions based on their content; questions following a pair of related passages may also be based on the relationship between the paired passages. Answer the questions on the basis of what is <u>stated</u> or <u>implied</u> in the passages and in any introductory material that may be provided.

Questions 6–9 are based on the following passages.

Passage 1:

The biggest mistake with the current legal status of computer software is the attempt to apply outdated legal systems, developed for an age of printed books, to computer programs. Software can vastly benefit the public
Line only if it is freely available to all: free to use, free to copy, free to improve.
5 Software is unique in that it is not a limited good. If I give you a copy of a program, that doesn't keep my copy of the program from running. By freely sharing software and its source code, and encouraging everyone who can do so to modify and improve the software, developers can help to improve the human condition. In the long run, attempts to restrict
10 access to software through inappropriate concepts such as copyrights, patents, and property rights are doomed to failure.

Passage 2:

Modern history has shown again and again the immense benefits to be gained by giving inventors the exclusive use of their inventions. This "intellectual property" is typically granted for a period of years through
15   mechanisms such as patents and trademarks, and it encourages invention by providing a reward for inventors. Although software may not seem to resemble plows and lightbulbs, the same drives sustain inventors in the programming field as in more traditional engineering fields. If a software developer is unable to make a reasonable living by selling his or her cre-
20   ations, he or she will have to find another line of work. In the long run, attempts to remove copyright and patent protection from software are foolish and dangerous. If they succeed, there will be less software innovation and the promise of computers will be stillborn.

6. Both of these passages are designed to
  (A) explain the history of intellectual property protection
  (B) demonstrate the importance of computer software in the modern world
  (C) teach the reader how to program a computer
  (D) persuade the reader of the author's point of view
  (E) convince the reader to support changes in the law

7. The author of Passage 2 would most likely consider the second sentence of Passage 1
  (A) shortsighted and unrealistic
  (B) illegally dangerous
  (C) reasonable but incomplete
  (D) novel and possibly true
  (E) true with qualifications

8. Compared to Passage 2, Passage 1 is
  (A) anchored more firmly in real experience
  (B) a better piece of advocacy for software patents
  (C) more concerned with the rights of society than the rights of individuals
  (D) about a wider range of computer software
  (E) less likely to have been written by a software author

9. If software were no longer subject to patent or copyright protection, which of these words would more aptly describe the author of passage 2 than the author of Passage 1?
  (A) relieved
  (B) ecstatic
  (C) confused
  (D) tired
  (E) crestfallen

Questions 10–14 are based on the following passage.

The earliest Indian civilization is cloaked in mystery. It emerged in the Indus River valley, in present-day Pakistan, about 2500 B.C. This civilization flourished for about 1,000 years, then vanished without a trace. Only
Line in this century have its once prosperous cities emerged beneath the
5 archaeologists' picks and shovels.

Archaeologists have not fully uncovered many Indus Valley sites. We have no names of kings or queens, no tax records, no literature, no accounts of famous victories. Still, we do know that the Indus Valley civilization covered the largest area of any civilization until the rise of Persia more than
10 1,000 years later. We know, too, that its cities rivaled those of Sumer.

The two main cities, Harappa and Mohenjo-Daro, may have been twin capitals. Both were large, some three miles in circumference. Each was dominated by a massive hilltop structure, probably a fortress or temple. Both cities had huge warehouses to store grain brought in from outlying
15 villages.

The most striking feature of Harappa and Mohenjo-Daro is that they were so carefully planned. Each city was laid out in a grid pattern, with rectangular blocks larger than modern city blocks. All houses were built of uniform oven-fired clay bricks. Houses had surprisingly modern
20 plumbing systems, with baths, drains, and water chutes that led into sewers beneath the streets. Merchants used a uniform system of weights and measures.

From such evidence, archaeologists have concluded that the Indus Valley cities had a well-organized government. Powerful leaders, perhaps priest-
25 kings, made sure that the tens of thousands of city-dwellers had a steady supply of grain from the villages. The rigid pattern of building and the uniform brick sizes suggest government planners. These experts must also have developed skills in mathematics and surveying to lay out the cities so precisely.

30 As in other early civilizations, most Indus Valley people were farmers. They grew a wide variety of crops, including wheat, barley, melons, and dates. They were also the first people to cultivate cotton and weave its fibers into cloth.

Some people were merchants and traders. Their ships carried cargoes of
35 cotton cloth, grain, copper, pearls, and ivory combs to distant lands. By hugging the Arabian Sea coast and sailing up the Persian Gulf, Indian vessels reached the cities of Sumer. Contact with Sumer may have stimulated Indus Valley people to develop their own system of writing.

From clues such as statues, archaeologists have speculated about the reli-
40 gious beliefs of the Indus Valley people. Like other ancient people, they were polytheistic. A mother goddess, the source of creation, seems to have been widely honored. Indus people also apparently worshipped sacred animals, including the bull. Some scholars think these early practices influenced later Indian beliefs, especially the veneration of, or special
45 regard for, cattle.

By 1750 B.C, the quality of life in Indus Valley cities was declining. The once orderly cities no longer kept up the old standards. Crude pottery replaced the finer works of earlier days.

We do not know for sure what happened, but scholars have offered sever-
50 al explanations. Damage to the local environment may have contributed to the decline. Possibly too many trees were cut down to fuel the ovens of brick makers. Tons of river mud found in the streets of Mohenjo-Daro suggest that a volcanic eruption blocked the Indus, which flooded the city. Other evidence points to a devastating earthquake.

55 Scholars think the deathblow fell about 1500 B.C., when nomadic people arrived in ever larger numbers from the north. The newcomers were the Aryans, whose ancestors had slowly migrated with their herds of cattle, sheep, and goats from what is now southern Russia. With their horse-drawn chariots and superior weapons, the Aryans overran the Indus
60 region. The cities were soon abandoned and eventually forgotten.

10. In the context of the passage, the phrase "vanished without a trace" (line 3) means that

    (A) no physical traces have ever been found of the Indus River civilization

    (B) we don't know why the Indus River civilization collapsed

    (C) there is no written record of the Indus River civilization

    (D) the Indus River civilization no longer exists

    (E) the Indus River civilization was destroyed by the Aryans

11. The sentence "Merchants used a uniform system of weights and measures" (line 21) is used to indicate that

    (A) fraud has always been a problem wherever commerce was present

    (B) weights and measures are important to maintaining a military class

    (C) the Indus River cities included craftsmen who were responsible for shaping weights

    (D) the Indus River civilization was advanced and organized

    (E) a merchant class can only exist after accurate measurement is perfected

12. Words such as "perhaps" (line 24) and "suggest" (line 27) in the passage indicate that

(A) the authors of the passage have not had time to read the most recent research on the subject

(B) readers should draw their own conclusions

(C) there are alternative explanations for the evidence that has been discovered

(D) the authors haven't made up their mind which set of experts to believe

(E) Archaeology is an inherently speculative science

13. In line 41, the word "polytheistic" most nearly means

(A) aggressively religious

(B) feminist

(C) worshipping many gods

(D) retiring

(E) venerators of cattle

14. The author of this passage would most likely agree that

(A) early civilizations were unable to stand up to nomadic pressures

(B) more research is needed to fully appreciate the scope of the Indus River civilization

(C) modern civilizations offer more freedom than ancient ones

(D) our civilization will be destroyed by environmental damage

(E) the domestication of the horse was more important than the invention of writing

Questions 15–24 are based on the following passage:

The following passage is from a collection of short stories by the nineteenth century American writer Stephen Crane.

Four men once came to a wet place in the roadless forest to fish. They pitched their tent fair upon the brow of a pine-clothed ridge of riven rocks whence a boulder could be made to crash through the brush and whirl past the trees to the lake below. On fragrant hemlock boughs they slept
Line
5 the sleep of unsuccessful fishermen, for upon the lake alternately the sun made them lazy and the rain made them wet. Finally they ate the last bit of bacon and smoked and burned the last fearful and wonderful hoecake.

Immediately a little man volunteered to stay and hold the camp while the remaining three should go the Sullivan county miles to a farmhouse for
10 supplies. They gazed at him dismally. "There's only one of you—the devil make a twin," they said in parting malediction, and disappeared down the hill in the known direction of a distant cabin. When it came night and the hemlocks began to sob they had not returned. The little man sat close to

his companion, the campfire, and encouraged it with logs. He puffed
fiercely at a heavy built brier, and regarded a thousand shadows which
were about to assault him. Suddenly he heard the approach of the
unknown, crackling the twigs and rustling the dead leaves. The little man
arose slowly to his feet, his clothes refused to fit his back, his pipe dropped
from his mouth, his knees smote each other.

"Hah!" he bellowed hoarsely in menace. A growl replied and a bear paced
into the light of the fire. The little man supported himself upon a sapling
and regarded his visitor.

The bear was evidently a veteran and a fighter, for the black of his coat
had become tawny with age. There was confidence in his gait and arrogance in his small, twinkling eye. He rolled back his lips and disclosed his
white teeth. The fire magnified the red of his mouth. The little man had
never before confronted the terrible and he could not wrest it from his
breast. "Hah!" he roared. The bear interpreted this as the challenge of a
gladiator. He approached warily. As he came near, the boots of fear were
suddenly upon the little man's feet. He cried out and then darted around
the campfire. "Ho!" said the bear to himself, "this thing won't fight—it
runs. Well, suppose I catch it." So upon his features there fixed the animal
look of going—somewhere. He started intensely around the campfire.
The little man shrieked and ran furiously. Twice around they went.

The hand of heaven sometimes falls heavily upon the righteous. The bear
gained.

In desperation the little man flew into the tent. The bear stopped and
sniffed at the entrance. He scented the scent of many men. Finally he ven-
tured in.

The little man crouched in a distant corner. The bear advanced, creeping,
his blood burning, his hair erect, his jowls dripping. The little man yelled
and rustled clumsily under the flap at the end of the tent. The bear snarled
awfully and made a jump and a grab at his disappearing game. The little
man, now without the tent, felt a tremendous paw grab his coat tails. He
squirmed and wriggled out of his coat like a schoolboy in the hands of an
avenger. The bear bowled triumphantly and jerked the coat into the tent
and took two bites, a punch and a hug before he discovered his man was
not in it. Then he grew not very angry, for a bear on a spree is not a black-
haired pirate.

He is merely a hoodlum. He lay down on his back, took the coat on his
four paws and began to play uproariously with it. The most appalling,
blood-curdling whoops and yells came to where the little man was crying
in a treetop and froze his blood. He moaned a little speech meant for a
prayer and clung convulsively to the bending branches. He gazed with

55 tearful wistfulness at where his comrade, the campfire, was giving dying
flickers and crackles. Finally, there was a roar from the tent which eclipsed
all roars; a snarl which it seemed would shake the stolid silence of the
mountain and cause it to shrug its granite shoulders. The little man
quaked and shriveled to a grip and a pair of eyes. In the glow of the embers
60 he saw the white tent quiver and fall with a crash. The bear's merry play
had disturbed the center pole and brought a chaos of canvas upon his
head.

Now the little man became the witness of a mighty scene. The tent began
to flounder. It took flopping strides in the direction of the lake. Marvelous
65 sounds came from within—rips and tears, and great groans and pants. The
little man went into giggling hysterics. The entangled monster failed to
extricate himself before he had walloped the tent frenziedly to the edge of
the mountain. So it came to pass that three men, clambering up the hill
with bundles and baskets, saw their tent approaching. It seemed to them
70 like a white-robed phantom pursued by hornets. Its moans riffled the
hemlock twigs.

The three men dropped their bundles and scurried to one side, their eyes
gleaming with fear. The canvas avalanche swept past them. They leaned,
faint and dumb, against trees and listened, their blood stagnant. Below
75 them it struck the base of a great pine tree, where it writhed and strug-
gled. The three watched its convolutions a moment and then started ter-
rifically for the top of the hill. As they disappeared, the bear cut loose with
a mighty effort. He cast one disheveled and agonized look at the white
thing, and then started wildly for the inner recesses of the forest.

80 The three fear-stricken individuals ran to the rebuilt fire. The little man
reposed by it calmly smoking. They sprang at him and overwhelmed him
with interrogations. He contemplated darkness and took a long, pompous
puff. "There's only one of me—and the devil made a twin," he said.

15. In the context of the passage, "the devil make a twin" (line 10) most
nearly means
(A) twins are considered devilish
(B) the only company you'll have is the devil
(C) the devil will bring you someone to talk to
(D) we're angry at you for staying behind
(E) the devil comes out at night in these woods

16. The phrase "a thousand shadows which were about to assault him"
(line 15) is best read as

(A) literal
(B) irony
(C) hyperbole
(D) figurative
(E) sly

17. In line 26, the word "magnified" most nearly means

(A) emphasized
(B) enlarged
(C) glorified
(D) increased
(E) overstated

18. In writing of "the boots of fear" (line 29), the author implies that

(A) fear can paralyze the man who is afraid
(B) you can't feel your feet when you're afraid
(C) fear can be conquered by wearing boots
(D) being afraid can make you run faster
(E) the man in the story had magical boots

19. Crane uses the expression "The hand of heaven sometimes falls heavily
upon the righteous" (line 35) to mean that

(A) God punishes those who blaspheme
(B) all creatures are treated equally by heaven
(C) we can't know why something happens
(D) bears do not attack righteous men
(E) the good guys don't always win

20. In line 43 the word "awfully" most nearly means

(A) unpleasantly
(B) poorly
(C) awe-inspiringly
(D) formidably
(E) badly

21. From lines 51 through 60 you can conclude that

(A) the little man thought he was about to die
(B) bears are basically playful animals
(C) everything is scarier in the dark
(D) splitting a party in the woods is a bad idea
(E) nature is harsh and unyielding

22. The phrase "shrug its granite shoulders" (line 58) is used as

(A) a measure of the strength of the little man's quaking

(B) a metaphor for the ferocity of the bear

(C) a way to indicate how loud the bear's roar was

(D) an expression of excitement

(E) a transition between paragraphs

23. The author uses "overwhelmed him with interrogations" (line 81) to mean

(A) attacked him for scaring them

(B) demanded immediate answers

(C) needed his reassurance

(D) argued with him needlessly

(E) asked him many questions

24. Which of these proverbs most aptly summarizes the story in the passage?

(A) The cat in gloves catches no mice.

(B) A stitch in time saves nine.

(C) He that lives on hope will die fasting.

(D) He who laughs last, laughs best.

(E) Beware of little expenses; a small leak will sink a great ship.

STOP

If you finish before time is called, you may check your work on this section only. Do not turn to any other section in the test.

SECTION 3

Time—25 minutes

18 Questions

Turn to Section 3 of your answer sheet to answer the questions in this section.

Directions: This section contains two types of questions. You have 25 minutes to complete both types. For questions 1–8, solve each problem and decide which is the best of the choices given. Fill in the corresponding circle on the answer sheet. You can use any available space for scratchwork.

Notes:

1. The use of a calculator is permitted.

2. All numbers used are real numbers.

3. Figures that accompany problems in the test are intended to provide information that is useful in solving the problems. They are drawn as accurately as possible EXCEPT when it is stated in a specific problem that the figure is not drawn to scale. All figures lie in a plane unless otherwise indicated.

4. Unless otherwise specified, the domain of any function f is assumed to be the set of real numbers x for which $f(x)$ is a real number.

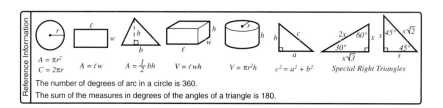

Reference Information

$A = \pi r^2$
$C = 2\pi r$
$A = \ell w$
$A = \frac{1}{2} bh$
$V = \ell wh$
$V = \pi r^2 h$
$c^2 = a^2 + b^2$
Special Right Triangles

The number of degrees of arc in a circle is 360.
The sum of the measures in degrees of the angles of a triangle is 180.

1. m is 250% of n, and 15% of n is 45. What is 12% of m?

   (A) 12
   (B) 30
   (C) 90
   (D) 120
   (E) 450

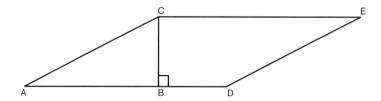

Note: Figure not drawn to scale.

2. In the figure above, $\overline{AC} \parallel \overline{DE}$ and $\overline{AD} \parallel \overline{CE}$ and $\angle ACB = 60°$. What is $\angle CED$?

   (A) 15°
   (B) 30°
   (C) 45°
   (D) 60°
   (E) 90°

3. A jar contains a mix of black beans and white beans. There are 16 white beans in the jar. When you reach into the jar and draw out a bean at random, the probability of drawing a black bean is 75%. How many total beans are in the jar?

(A) 8
(B) 12
(C) 16
(D) 32
(E) 64

4. The greatest common factor of the integers a and b is 7, and the least common multiple of a and b is 210. The value of a is 14. What is the value of b?

(A) 7
(B) 14
(C) 35
(D) 105
(E) 210

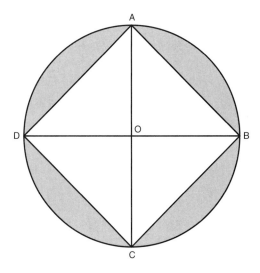

5. The figure above shows a circle with its center at O with four identical isosceles triangles inscribed in the circle. The distance AB is $2\sqrt{2}$ units. What is the area of the shaded region?

(A) 8
(B) $\frac{4}{\pi}$
(C) $4\sqrt{2}$
(D) $16\pi - 8$
(E) $4\pi - 8$

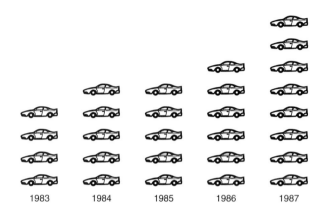

1983   1984   1985   1986   1987

= 50,000 autos

6. Referring to the figure above, what was the average annual sales growth between 1985 and 1987?

(A) 75,000

(B) 50,000

(C) 40,000

(D) 25,000

(E) 10,000

7. The union of sets A and B is {1, 3, 7, 11, 14, 17, 22}. The intersection of sets A and B is {7, 11, 22}. Set A is {1, 3, 7, 11, 22}. What is set B?

(A) {7, 11, 22}

(B) {7, 11, 14, 17, 22}

(C) {14, 17, 22}

(D) {14, 17}

(E) {1, 3, 7, 22}

8. Lines ℓ and m are parallel and intersect the y axis two units apart from each other. The equation of line ℓ is $y = -2x + 4$. Which of these could be the equation of line m?

(A) $y = -\frac{1}{2}x + 4$

(B) $y = \frac{1}{2}x + 4$

(C) $y = 2x + 2$

(D) $y = 2x - 2$

(E) $y = x + 4$

For questions 9–28, please turn to the student-produced response grid in section 3 of the answer sheets.

9. If $a^2 + b^2 = 75$ and $a^2 - b^2 = -25$ then what is one possible value of a?

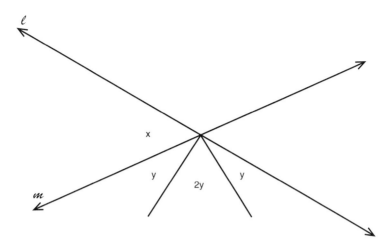

Note: Figure not drawn to scale.

10. In the figure above, ℓ and m are straight lines. Angle y is 17°. What is angle x?

11. Two successive measurements of the number of elk in a game reserve are 52 and 68. What percent change is this?

12. $f(x) = \dfrac{14}{(x-7)}$. What integer is not in the domain of f?

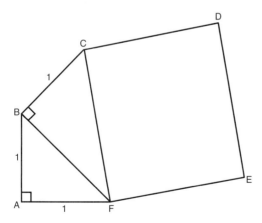

13. What is the area of square CDEF?

14. What is the difference between the median and the mode of the set of numbers 4, 17, 11, 14, 3, 2, 8, 22, 18?

15. Define a><b as 2a + 2b. What is (3><4)><.5?

16. Thirty percent of the students in a school are juniors, and 12% of the students in the same school have red hair. What is the probability that a student selected at random from this school will be a junior with red hair?

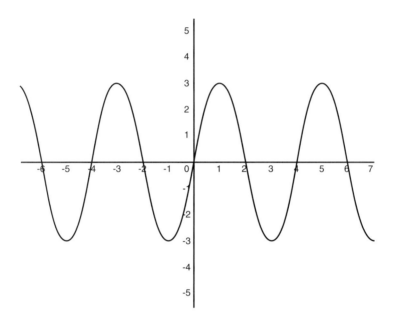

17. The figure above shows a portion of the graph of g(x). What is the first positive zero of the function g(x + 3)?

18. How many axes of reflective symmetry are present in the figure above?

STOP

If you finish before time is called, you may check your work on this section only. Do not turn to any other section in the test.

SECTION 4

Time—25 minutes

35 Questions

Turn to Section 4 of your answer sheet to answer the questions in this section.

> **Directions:** For each question in this section, select the best answer from among the choices given and fill in the corresponding circle on the answer sheet.

> The following sentences test correctness and effectiveness of expression. Part of each sentence or the entire sentence is underlined; beneath each sentence are five ways of phrasing the underlined material. Choice A repeats the original phrasing; the other four choices are different. If you think the original phrasing produces a better sentence than any of the alternatives, select choice A; if not, select one of the other choices.
>
> In making your selection, follow the requirements of standard written English; that is, pay attention to grammar, choice of words, sentence construction, and punctuation. Your selection should result in the most effective sentence—clear and precise, without awkwardness or ambiguity.
>
> EXAMPLE:
>
> The weather that winter was <u>worse than for at least five decades</u>.
>
>   (A) worse than for at least five decades
>   (B) the worse it was for at least five decades
>   (C) worse. Than it had been for at least five decades.
>   (D) the worst that it had been for at least five decades
>   (E) the worst it was for at least five decades.
>
> Answer: (D)

1. Geography, in addition to World History, <u>are offered to</u> the lower classmen.
   - (A) are offered to
   - (B) are not offered to
   - (C) are offered for
   - (D) is offered to
   - (E) is offered for

2. By the time <u>we return to class</u>, the teacher had already handed out the exam papers.
   - (A) we return to class
   - (B) we returned to class
   - (C) he return to class
   - (D) they return to class
   - (E) we got to class

3. She identified the tall man in lineup as <u>the man that</u> stole her purse.
   - (A) the man that
   - (B) the thief that
   - (C) the man who
   - (D) that man that
   - (E) the thief who

4. <u>Vaporization is when</u> a substance changes from a liquid into a gas.
   - (A) Vaporization is when
   - (B) Vaporization is
   - (C) Vaporization is that which occurs when
   - (D) Vaporization occurs when
   - (E) Vaporization is what happens when

5. The pilot turned the gas valve, and the balloon <u>rose up into</u> the sky.
   - (A) rose up into
   - (B) rose into
   - (C) rose up to
   - (D) climbed into
   - (E) climbed up to

6. Unfortunately, Marilyn was <u>more concerned with her</u> social life than her grades.
   - (A) more concerned with her
   - (B) concerned with her
   - (C) less concerned with her
   - (D) less concerned with
   - (E) more concerned about her

7. She <u>feels badly about</u> flunking her midterms.

    (A) feels badly about

    (B) feels bad about

    (C) felt badly about

    (D) feels badly in regards to

    (E) feels bad because she's

8. After listening to last night's forecast, I expected it to <u>be more cold this morning</u>.

    (A) be more cold this morning

    (B) be more colder this morning

    (C) be more cold

    (D) be colder than yesterday this morning

    (E) be colder this morning

9. Though nonsectarian in theory, <u>in reality, many community clubs were havens from</u> social discrimination.

    (A) in reality, many community clubs were havens from

    (B) many community clubs were havens from

    (C) many community clubs were, in reality, havens from

    (D) many community clubs were havens of

    (E) in reality, many community clubs were havens for

10. The desert community seems to offer little diversity at first, offering <u>little but scrub, dry lakebeds, and ugly Joshua trees</u>.

    (A) little but scrub, dry lakebeds, and ugly Joshua trees

    (B) little but low scrub, dry lakebeds, and ugly Joshua trees

    (C) little more than scrub, dry lakebeds, and ugly Joshua trees

    (D) little less than scrub, dry lakebeds, and ugly Joshua trees

    (E) nothing but scrub, dry lakebeds, and ugly Joshua trees

11. Chuck Yeager started life <u>in a small town on the Mud River in Virginia, named Myra</u>.

    (A) in a small town on the Mud River in Virginia, named Myra.

    (B) in Myra, Virginia, a small town on the Mud River

    (C) in Myra, a small town on the Mud River in Virginia

    (D) in a small town on the Mud River in Virginia

    (E) in a small town on the Mud River, named Myra

The following sentences test your ability to recognize grammar and usage errors. Each sentence contains either a single error or no error at all. No sentence contains more than one error. The error, if there is one, is underlined and lettered. If the sentence contains an error, select the one underlined part that must be changed to make the sentence correct. If the sentence is correct, select choice E. In choosing answers, follow the requirements of standard written English.

EXAMPLE:

The modern personal computer is <u>a revolutionary instrument</u>
                                                     A

<u>that can be used</u> for composing a sonnet, planning a bridge,
      B

or <u>to create digital movies</u>, but <u>at the most basic level</u>
          C   D

it is still just a collection of digital impulses. <u>No error</u>
                                                 E

Answer: (C)

12. The park is usually <u>more crowded and noisier</u> <u>on nice days</u>
                             A   B

  <u>when everyone shows up</u> <u>with their kids and dogs</u>. <u>No Error</u>
             C   D   E

13. <u>We thought</u> the birds might <u>reject this new seed</u>,
      A   B

  but <u>they are eating us out of house and home</u> and
                      C

  none of the seed is left. <u>No Error</u>
          D   E

14. Lincoln Steffens was <u>the pioneer investigative reporter</u>, <u>he wrote</u>
                                       A   B

  fearlessly <u>on the abuses</u> <u>of government</u>. <u>No Error</u>
               C   D   E

15. Until Woodrow Wilson was elected President, the United States
       A   B

was in the habit of recognizing de facto governments.
     C   D

No Error
  E

16. The new family home was only one story, not terribly large,
                          A   B

and run down, but had a nice view. No Error
   C   D   E

17. Success in business, any business, no matter how small,
                    A   B

played a more important role in the immigrant's daily life
        C   D

than education. No Error
         E

18. Gems are priceless in her culture, but she kept none
                A   B

of them for herself. No Error
  C   D   E

19. She is to be inducted as an initiate at noon
     A   B   C

on the first Sunday of March. No Error
      D   E

20. In conclusion, Bertha von Suttner profoundly influenced
     A   B

Alfred Nobel, despite the fact that she married
          C

someone else. No Error
   D   E

21. In 1888, Massachusetts became the first state <u>to use ballots</u>
                                                              A

that contained the names <u>of all the candidates</u> <u>on each ballot</u>
                                     B   C

instead of using different colored ballots <u>for each candidate</u>. <u>No Error</u>
                                                        D   E

22. <u>Running madly through the forest,</u> <u>the thunder shook the earth</u>
                        A   B

and <u>the lightning pierced</u> <u>the night sky.</u> <u>No Error</u>
              C   D   E

23. <u>Before you say something you'll regret,</u> <u>take a deep breathe,</u>
                           A   B

<u>calmly clear your mind,</u> <u>and count to 10.</u> <u>No Error</u>
            C   D   E

24. Cinderella <u>looked at the clock</u> <u>but didn't realize</u> it was
                           A   B

midnight <u>until</u> she <u>heard it chime.</u> <u>No Error</u>
               C   D   E

25. Sam and Tom raced to <u>the frozen Mississippi</u>
                                        A

<u>where they scrambled</u> to be the first <u>to don his skates</u> and
            B   C

<u>meet the ice.</u> <u>No Error</u>
        D   E

26. The excitement <u>of the new baby's arrival</u> <u>was challenged by</u>
                                    A   B

the fear <u>that the small and weak child</u> <u>might not</u> survive
                         C   D

the night. <u>No Error</u>
                   E

27. John had <u>a talent</u> for business and <u>subsequently met</u>
     A   B

<u>with great financial success,</u> <u>but he had little patience</u>
    C   D

for family. <u>No Error</u>
     E

28. Samuel Clemens <u>wrote under the pen name</u> Mark Twain,
         A

<u>which was</u> a <u>river-piloting term</u> <u>for deep, safe water.</u>
  B   C   D

<u>No Error</u>
 E

29. The United States Constitution <u>requires the Senate</u>
            A

<u>to confirm</u> any presidential nominations
 B

<u>to the Supreme Court</u> before <u>he can</u> actually be sworn
   C   D

into office. <u>No Error</u>
    E

Directions: The following passage is an early draft of an essay. Some parts of the passage need to be rewritten.

Read the passage and select the best answers for the questions that follow. Some questions are about particular sentences or parts of sentences and ask you to improve sentence structure and word choice. Other questions ask you to consider organization and development. In choosing answers, follow the requirements of standard written English.

Questions 30–35 are based on the following passage.

(1)The saying that we're only as strong as our weakest link may be provincial, but it's remarkably true. (2)Life is such a toe-shoe precision dance that breaking just one cog in the machinery often has unintended consequences.

(**3**)By 1911, the playful and elusive sea otter had been hunted to the brink of extinction for its soft, dense fur. (**4**)Almost too late, the United States, Great Britain, Russia, and Japan established a treaty that banned hunting the sea otter.

(**5**)The sea otter was slow to rebound. (**6**)As their populations plummeted, so did their habitats and primary food source. (**7**)Sea otters rest, nest and feed in floating beds of kelp where sea urchins, their main food source, also live.

(**8**)Sea urchins eat kelp. (**9**)As the sea otters disappeared, the population of sea urchins grew uncontrolled, eating the forests of kelp as their populations exploded. (**10**)In order to sustain their growing colonies, the sea urchins devoured their habitats—the kelp forests.

(**11**)Without the kelp forests, there were no sea urchins. (**12**)Without the sea urchins, the sea otters had no food. (**13**)Ban or no ban, the sea otters were in serious trouble.

30. Sentence 2 doesn't really work. What's the problem with it?
    (A) It's redundant of the first.
    (B) The two subjects don't match: Broken machinery doesn't support or develop the ballerina imagery created in the first phrase.
    (C) It's too wordy.
    (D) It's a bit dire for the opening sentence.
    (E) It would work better as a closing statement.

31. There's a problem between the first and second paragraphs. Can you spot it?
    (A) There should be no paragraph break between sentence 2 and 3.
    (B) It's bad style to start a paragraph with the phrase "By ...,."
    (C) Move sentence 7 to the end of the first paragraph.
    (D) Move sentence 8 to the end of the first paragraph.
    (E) There's no transition from the thesis to the supporting example.

32. Sentence 6 doesn't seem to make sense. It takes four sentences to develop and clarify this statement. What would help?
    (A) Delete the sentence. It isn't needed.
    (B) Replace the first pronoun, their, with a definite noun.
    (C) Move sentences 4 and 5 to a new paragraph following sentence 12.
    (D) Add a transitional sentence between sentences 6 and 7.
    (E) Replace the second phrase with "their habitats and primary food source disappeared."

33. How would you improve sentence 7?

(A) Insert a comma after nest.

(B) It might work better as two sentences: one that discusses habitat and a second that discusses their food source, the sea urchin.

(C) The word "feed" is unnecessary. Remove it and update the "rest, nest" series appropriately by inserting the word "and."

(D) Replace the sea urchin reference with the following phrase: , which they share with their primary food source, the sea urchin.

(E) A combination of (A) and (D).

34. Sentences 8 and 9 are a bit awkward. What would you do to improve the movement?

(A) Change sentence 8 to the following: Kelp is the primary food source for both sea urchins and sea otters, and with the proper balance, there's enough for all.

(B) Combine sentences 8 and 9.

(C) Reposition sentence 8 between sentences 9 and 10.

(D) Change sentence 8 to the following: Both sea others and sea urchins eat kelp.

(E) Delete sentence 8. Sentence 9 makes it clear that sea urchins eat kelp.

35. What would you do to improve the end of the passage?

(A) Nothing, it ends well.

(B) Add a conclusion that tells the fate of the sea otter after the ban.

(C) Add a conclusion that stresses how the ban returned the ecosystem's balance so the sea otters' population can grow while protected by the ban.

(D) Move sentences 4 and 5 between sentences 12 and 13. Then, add a conclusion that stresses how the ban returned the ecosystem's balance so the sea otters' population can grow while protected by the ban.

(E) Move sentences 4 and 5 to the end of the passage and then delete sentence 13.

STOP

If you finish before time is called, you may check your work on this section only. Do not turn to any other section in the test.

SECTION 5

Time—25 minutes

24 Questions

Turn to Section 5 of your answer sheet to answer the questions in this section.

> **Directions:** For each question in this section, select the best answer from among the choices given and fill in the corresponding circle on the answer sheet.

> Each sentence below has one or two blanks, each blank indicating that something has been omitted. Beneath the sentence are five words or sets of words labeled A through E. Choose the word or set of words that, when inserted in the sentence, <u>best</u> fits the meaning of the sentence as a whole.
>
> EXAMPLE:
>
> The Internet is _____ now, being available in 78% of all American households.
>
> (A) unimportant
> (B) transitory
> (C) migrating
> (D) negligible
> (E) ubiquitous
>
> Answer: (E)

1. The teacher makes no _____ for tardiness and sends all late arrivals to the office.
   (A) reception
   (B) exception
   (C) expectations
   (D) exemption
   (E) omission

2. Tax reform is an often-heard _____ that is seldom _____.
   (A) pledge . . honored
   (B) oath . . guaranteed
   (C) quote . . remembered
   (D) vow . . broken
   (E) guarantee . . fulfilled

3. At age 54, Mikhail Gorbachev _____ Chernenko in 1985, becoming the youngest _____ of the USSR since Josef Stalin.
   (A) assassinated . . chairman
   (B) inaugurated . . President
   (C) succeeded . . leader
   (D) preceded . . dictator
   (E) followed . . Prime Minister

4. The 1980s were a(n) _____ of dramatic and stunning change, more so than any other decade in that century.

(A) epoch
(B) bounty
(C) boon
(D) windfall
(E) respite

5. The subject of congressional salaries has been hotly _____ for years, and the _____ isn't likely to end anytime soon.

(A) discussed . . argument
(B) argued . . problem
(C) pondered . . disagreement
(D) deliberated . . hullabaloo
(E) debated . . controversy

6. Tahiti, a tropical paradise under French _____, attracts many vacationers each year.

(A) power
(B) rule
(C) command
(D) dominion
(E) dominance

7. Magellan was the first to _____ the many continents to ----- the globe.

(A) avoid . . orbit
(B) bypass . . circumnavigate
(C) dodge . . encircle
(D) evade . . traverse
(E) circumnavigate . . map

8. The Fourteenth and Fifteenth amendments are said to be the ----- of equal rights, safeguarding the rights of all citizens, not just some citizens.

(A) beginning
(B) defense
(C) bulwark
(D) foundation
(E) objective

> The passages below are followed by questions based on their content;
> questions following a pair of related passages may also be based on the
> relationship between the paired passages. Answer the questions on the
> basis of what is <u>stated</u> or <u>implied</u> in the passages and in any introduc-
> tory material that may be provided.

Questions 9–10 are based on the following passage.

By the time of the Civil War, more than two centuries after the first
colonist arrived in New England, half the nation's land was still nearly
empty. The frontier—a ragged line of settlements from the East—ran
Line through part of Minnesota, along the border of Iowa, Missouri, and
5 Arkansas and then swung westward into Texas. Reaching in from the West
Coast there was also a thin line of settlements in California, Oregon, and
Washington. Between these two frontiers there were only a few islands of
settlers, such as the Mormons in Utah, the miners in Colorado, and the
Mexican Americans in New Mexico. Even in the "settled" areas on the
10 edge of the open land, it was often a long way between neighbors.

9. By 1860, there were two frontiers. List their border states.
   (A) New England and New Mexico
   (B) Minnesota, Iowa, Missouri, and Arkansas; California, Oregon, and
      Washington
   (C) Minnesota, Iowa, Missouri, and Texas; California, Oregon, and
      Washington
   (D) Utah, Colorado, and New Mexico
   (E) Minnesota, Iowa, Missouri, Arkansas and Texas; California, Oregon, and
      Washington

10. This passage would make a good introduction into the discussion of
   what topic?
   (A) settling the great plains between the two 1860 frontiers
   (B) westward expansion
   (C) the hardships faced by pioneers
   (D) how Mormons, miners, and Mexicans settled the great plains
   (E) discovering the western half of the United States

Questions 11–12 are based on the following passage.

AIDS is most often transmitted through physical sexual relations and
through the shared needles of drug users. Those most at risk from the disease were homosexuals and certain drug addicts. Scientists feared that it
Line might spread through the whole population. Suddenly, sexual license, a
5 popular idea in the 1960s was found to be dangerous to the health of all.

Since there was no known cure, education and sexual abstinence became the only ways to slow the spread of AIDS. Dr. C. Everett Koop, Surgeon General under Ronald Reagan, set a wise example by urging that grade school students be taught about the disease. AIDS, the shocking discovery
10 of the early 1980s, threatened to become a worldwide catastrophe. Between 2000 and 2020, it is estimated that 68 million people will die prematurely as a result of AIDS.

11. What does the author mean by the phrase "sexual license?"
   (A) permission to engage in sexual activities
   (B) complete sexual freedom without consideration of consequences
   (C) the freedom to participate in sexual activities without social or religious restrictions
   (D) protected sexual activity
   (E) prostitution

12. Why did Dr. C. Everett Koop, Surgeon General, incorporate AIDS into grade school curriculum?
   (A) to protect the next generation from AIDS.
   (B) to further his sexually repressive agenda.
   (C) It was an excuse to finally introduce sex education into the classroom in communities that still objected.
   (D) to educate the next generation in the hopes of slowing the spread of AIDS.
   (E) to slow the spread of AIDS.

Questions 13–24 are based on the following passages.

These two passages are taken from biographies of George Washington that were published about 25 years apart. Though both authors rely on many of the same sources, they choose to emphasize different aspects of their subject.

Passage 1:

In the House of Burgesses Washington was a taciturn member, yet he seemed to have got a great deal of political knowledge and wisdom so that his colleagues thought of him as the solid man of the House and they
Line referred many matters to him as if for final decision. He followed politi-
5 cal affairs in the newspapers. Above all, at Mount Vernon he heard all sides from the guests who passed his domain and enjoyed his hospitality. From the moment that the irritation between Great Britain and the Colonies became bitter he seems to have made up his mind that the contention of the Colonists was just. After that he never wavered, but he was
10 not a sudden or a shallow clamorer for Independence. He believed that the sober second sense of the British would lead them to perceive that

they had made a mistake. When at length the Colonies had to provide themselves with an army and to undertake a war, he was the only candidate seriously considered for General, although John Hancock, who had
15 made his peacock way so successfully in many walks of life, thought that he alone was worthy of the position. Who shall describe Washington's life as Commander-in-Chief of the Colonial forces during the Revolutionary War? What other commander ever had a task like his? For a few weeks the troops led by Napoleon—the barefooted and ragged heroes of Lodi
20 and Arcola and Marengo—were equally destitute, but victory brought them food and clothes and prosperity. Whereas Washington's men had no comfort before victory and none after it.

Some of the military critics to-day deny Washington's right to be ranked among the great military commanders of the world, but the truth is that
25 he commanded during nearly eight years and won one of the supreme crucial wars of history against far superior forces. The General who did that was no understrapper. The man whose courage diffused itself among the ten thousand starving soldiers at Valley Forge, and enabled them to endure against the starvation and distress of a winter, may very well fail to
30 be classified among the Prince Ruperts and the Marshal Neys of battle, but he ranks first in a higher class. His Fabian[1] policy, which troubled so many of his contemporaries, saved the American Revolution. His title as General is secure. Nor should we forget that it was his scrupulous patriotism which prevented the cropping out of militarism in this country.

35 Finally, a country which owed its existence to him chose him to be for eight years its first President. He saw the planting of the roots of the chief organs of its government. In every act he looked far forward into the future. He shunned making or following evil precedents. He endured the most virulent personal abuse that has ever been poured out on American
40 public men, preferring that to using the power which his position gave him, and denaturing the President into a tyrant. Nor should we fail to honor him for his insistence on dignity and a proper respect for his office. His enemies sneered at him for that, but we see plainly how much it meant to this new Nation to have such qualities exemplified. Had Thomas
45 Jefferson been our first President in his *sans-culotte*[2] days, our Government might not have outlasted the *sans-culottist* enthusiasts in France. A man is known by his friends. The chosen friends of Washington were among the best of his time in America. Hamilton, Henry Knox, Nathanael Greene, John Jay, John Marshall—these were some.

50 Although Washington was less learned than many of the men of his time in political theory and history, he excelled them all in a concrete application of principles. He had the widest acquaintance among men of

different sorts. He heard all opinions, but never sacrificed his own. As I have said earlier, he was the most *actual* statesman of his time; the people
55 in Virginia came very early to regard him as a man apart; this was true of the later days when the Government sat in New York and Philadelphia. If they sought a reason, they usually agreed that Washington excelled by his character, and if you analyze most closely you will never get deeper than that. Reserved he was, and not a loose or glib talker, but he always showed
60 his interest and gave close attention. After Yorktown, when the United States proclaimed to the world that they were an independent Republic, Europe recognized that this was indeed a Republic unlike all those which had preceded it during antiquity and the Middle Age. Foreigners doubted that it could exist. They doubted that Democracy could ever govern a
65 nation. They knew despots, like the Prussian King, Frederic, who walked about the streets of Berlin and used his walking-stick on the cringing persons whom he passed on the sidewalk and did not like the looks of. They remembered the crazy Czar, Peter, and they knew about the insane tendencies of the British sovereign, George. The world argued from these
70 and other examples that monarchy was safe; it could not doubt that the supply of monarchs would never give out; but it had no hope of a Republic governed by a President. It was George Washington more than any other agency who made the world change its mind and conclude that the best President was the best kind of monarch.

75 It is reported that after he died many persons who had been his neighbors and acquaintances confessed that they had always felt a peculiar sense of being with a higher sort of person in his presence: a being not superhuman, but far above common men. That feeling will revive in the heart of any one to-day who reads wisely in the fourteen volumes of
80 "Washington's Correspondence," in which, as in a mine, are buried the passions and emotions from which sprang the American Revolution and the American Constitution. That George Washington lived and achieved is the justification and hope of the United States.

Passage 2:

There must have been something very impressive about a man who, with
85 no pretensions to the art of the orator and with no touch of the charlatan, could so move and affect vast bodies of men by his presence alone. But the people, with the keen eye of affection, looked beyond the mere outward nobility of form. They saw the soldier who had given them victory, the great statesman who had led them out of confusion and faction to order
90 and good government. Party newspapers might rave, but the instinct of the people was never at fault. They loved, trusted and well-nigh

worshiped Washington living, and they have honored and reverenced him with an unchanging fidelity since his death, nearly a century ago.

But little more remains to be said. Washington had his faults, for he was human; but they are not easy to point out, so perfect was his mastery of himself. He was intensely reserved and very silent, and these are the qualities which gave him the reputation in history of being distant and unsympathetic. In truth, he had not only warm affections and a generous heart, but there was a strong vein of sentiment in his composition. At the same time he was in no wise romantic, and the ruling element in his make-up was prose, good solid prose, and not poetry. He did not have the poetical and imaginative quality so strongly developed in Lincoln. Yet he was not devoid of imagination, although it was here that he was lacking, if anywhere. He saw facts, knew them, mastered and used them, and never gave much play to fancy; but as his business in life was with men and facts, this deficiency, if it was one, was of little moment. He was also a man of the strongest passions in every way, but he dominated them; they never ruled him. Vigorous animal passions were inevitable, of course, in a man of such a physical make-up as his. How far he gave way to them in his youth no one knows, but the scandals which many persons now desire to have printed, ostensibly for the sake of truth, are, so far as I have been able to learn, with one or two dubious exceptions, of entirely modern parentage. I have run many of them to earth; nearly all are destitute of contemporary authority, and they may be relegated to the dust-heaps. If he gave way to these propensities in his youth, the only conclusion that I have been able to come to is that he mastered them when he reached man's estate.

He had, too, a fierce temper, and although he gradually subdued it, he would sometimes lose control of himself and burst out into a tempest of rage. When he did so he would use strong and even violent language, as he did at Kip's Landing and at Monmouth. Well-intentioned persons in their desire to make him a faultless being have argued at great length that Washington never swore, and but for their argument the matter would never have attracted much attention. He was anything but a profane man, but the evidence is beyond question that if deeply angered he would use a hearty English oath; and not seldom the action accompanied the word, as when he rode among the fleeing soldiers at Kip's Landing, striking them with his sword, and almost beside himself at their cowardice. Judge Marshall used to tell also of an occasion when Washington sent out an officer to cross a river and bring back some information about the enemy, on which the action of the morrow would depend. The officer was gone some time, came back, and found the general impatiently pacing his tent.

On being asked what he had learned, he replied that the night was dark and stormy, the river full of ice, and that he had not been able to cross. Washington glared at him a moment, seized a large leaden inkstand from 135 the table, hurled it at the offender's head, and said with a fierce oath, "Be off, and send me a *man!*" The officer went, crossed the river, and brought back the information.

But although he would now and then give way to these tremendous bursts of anger, Washington was never unjust. As he said to one officer, "I never 140 judge the propriety of actions by after events;" and in that sound philosophy is found the secret not only of much of his own success, but of the devotion of his officers and men. He might be angry with them, but he was never unfair. In truth, he was too generous to be unjust or even over-severe to any one, and there is not a line in all his writings which even sug-145 gests that he ever envied any man. So long as the work in hand was done, he cared not who had the glory, and he was perfectly magnanimous and perfectly at ease about his own reputation. He never showed the slightest anxiety to write his own memoirs, and he was not in the least alarmed when it was proposed to publish the memoirs of other people, like 150 General Charles Lee, which would probably reflect upon him.

He had the same confidence in the judgment of posterity that he had in the future beyond the grave. He regarded death with entire calmness and even indifference not only when it came to him, but when in previous years it had threatened him. He loved life and tasted of it deeply, but the 155 courage which never forsook him made him ready to face the inevitable at any moment with an unruffled spirit. In this he was helped by his religious faith, which was as simple as it was profound. He had been brought up in the Protestant Episcopal Church, and to that church he always adhered; for its splendid liturgy and stately forms appealed to him and satisfied him. 160 He loved it too as the church of his home and his childhood. Yet he was as far as possible from being sectarian, and there is not a word of his which shows anything but the most entire liberality and toleration. He made no parade of his religion, for in this as in other things he was perfectly sim-ple and sincere. He was tortured by no doubts or questionings, but 165 believed always in an overruling Providence and in a merciful God, to whom he knelt and prayed in the day of darkness or in the hour of tri-umph with a supreme and childlike confidence.

[1] Slow and cautious, after the Roman general Quintus Fabius Maximus Verrucosus who preferred to avoid a decisive contest.

[2] Sans-culotte (literally, "without breeches"): the common people who rose up in the French Revolution, and, by extension, any political movement consisting mainly of artisans, farmers, and workers.

13. In lines 7–12, the author of passage 1 states that

   (A) Washington was in favor of independence as soon as relations with Great Britain turned bitter.

   (B) Washington began to prepare to lead the colonial army after talking to Mount Vernon visitors.

   (C) Washington thought from his earliest days that the colonies should be independent.

   (D) Washington supported the colonists, but hoped that war could be avoided.

   (E) Washington thought that the drive for independence was a mistake.

14. The phrase "it was his scrupulous patriotism which prevented the cropping out of militarism" (lines 33–34) most nearly means

   (A) His vigorous action prevented the loss of the war.

   (B) Winning the war enabled farmers to leave the military ranks and go back to their fields.

   (C) His love of country caused him to decline the chance of military rule.

   (D) His outstanding leadership prevented the colonists from being crushed by a British military.

   (E) His strong character kept local militias from acting precipitously on their own.

15. In mentioning Thomas Jefferson in the third paragraph, the author of passage 1 implies that

   (A) Washington, unlike Jefferson, was careful to keep the nation at a fitting distance from the French government.

   (B) Jefferson would not have used the power of the presidency as wisely as Washington did.

   (C) having a different first president would have had a lasting impression on the way that we perceive the presidency.

   (D) Jefferson was not in the habit of looking far into the future, but preferred to react to circumstances instead.

   (E) The office of the presidency was more important to the new nation than the particular man holding the office.

16. In stating that "the world argued from these and other examples that monarchy was safe" (lines 69–70), the author of passage 1

   (A) suggests that monarchy was a better form of government than a Republic

   (B) is sarcastically attacking advocates of monarchy

   (C) holds up a few monarchs as examples of rulers who were Washington's equal

   (D) shows that Washington was comparable to other heads of state of his day

   (E) dismisses the idea that a Republic is a viable form of government

17. In speaking of "this deficiency" (line 105), the author of passage 2
refers to

(A) a tendency towards silence
(B) a lack of imagination
(C) vigorous animal passions
(D) an inability to write poetry
(E) a lack of success in love

18. Which of these conclusions can be drawn from the sentence beginning
"Well-intentioned persons" in lines 120–123?

(A) Washington never swore.
(B) Washington argued at great length.
(C) Washington never attracted much attention.
(D) Washington was not a faultless person.
(E) Washington desired to be well-intentioned.

19. The sentence "I never judge the propriety of actions by after events"
(line 139) most nearly means

(A) I never decide whether something is right by considering its actual effects.
(B) I never question the politeness of men based on what I read in the papers.
(C) I never evaluate when to act from knowledge of the enemy's actions.
(D) I never fit my own actions to someone else's ideas of right and wrong.
(E) I never hold back when it is better to be generous.

20. The first three sentences of the last paragraph of passage 2 suggest that

(A) regarding death with utter calmness makes it difficult to enjoy life
(B) courage to face death comes from a deep love and appreciation of life
(C) confidence in the judgment of posterity is a source of deep courage
(D) loving life without a faith in the afterlife leaves one with a ruffled spirit
(E) death is a matter that should be regarded with entire calmness and even
indifference

21. Passage 2 as a whole suggests that its author would most likely evaluate
the final paragraph of passage 1 as

(A) truthful
(B) understated
(C) humorous
(D) prescient
(E) overblown

22. Which of the following statements would both authors likely agree on, based on the material in the passages?
    (A) Washington's bursts of bad temper were well-known.
    (B) Washington's courage shored up the soldiers at Valley Forge.
    (C) Washington had a deep religious faith.
    (D) Washington was by nature silent.
    (E) Washington viewed the presidency as an office that ought to be dignified.

23. Compared to passage 1, passage 2
    (A) is more concerned with the personal side of Washington
    (B) tries to judge Washington by acts rather than words
    (C) is skeptical of Washington's military prowess
    (D) credits Washington more plainly with setting the spirit of the presidency
    (E) compares Washington more with other heads of state

24. The author of passage 1 would most likely regard the scandals mentioned at line 110 in passage 2 as
    (A) likely to be true but not important in the grand scheme of things
    (B) impossible to prove or disprove and therefore not to be considered
    (C) incompatible with what we know of Washington from other sources
    (D) slurs dreamed up by Washington's political opponents
    (E) well-documented in Washington's own correspondence

STOP

If you finish before time is called, you may check your work on this section only. Do not turn to any other section in the test.

SECTION 6

Time—25 minutes

20 Questions

Turn to Section 6 of your answer sheet to answer the questions in this section.

> **Directions:** For this section, solve each problem and decide which is the best of the choices given. Fill in the corresponding circle on the answer sheet. You can use any available space for scratchwork.

Notes:

1. The use of a calculator is permitted.

2. All numbers used are real numbers.

3. Figures that accompany problems in the test are intended to provide information that is useful in solving the problems. They are drawn as accurately as possible EXCEPT when it is stated in a specific problem that the figure is not drawn to scale. All figures lie in a plane unless otherwise indicated.

4. Unless otherwise specified, the domain of any function f is assumed to be the set of real numbers x for which $f(x)$ is a real number.

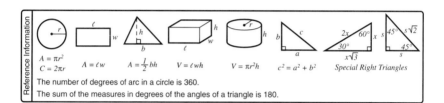

Reference Information

$A = \pi r^2$ $A = \ell w$ $A = \frac{1}{2}bh$ $V = \ell wh$ $V = \pi r^2 h$ $c^2 = a^2 + b^2$ *Special Right Triangles*

$C = 2\pi r$

The number of degrees of arc in a circle is 360.

The sum of the measures in degrees of the angles of a triangle is 180.

1. If $2x + y = 19$ and $x - y = 5$, what is y?
 (A) 3
 (B) 5
 (C) 8
 (D) 13
 (E) 19

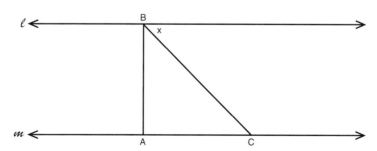

2. In the figure above, $\ell \| m$ and $\triangle ABC$ is an isosceles right triangle. What is $\angle x$?
 (A) 15°
 (B) 30°
 (C) 45°
 (D) 60°
 (E) 90°

3. Which of these expressions gives the largest result?

(A) $3 + 3 + 3$

(B) $3 \times 3 \times 3$

(C) $3^3 + 3^3$

(D) 3^{3^3}

(E) 333

4. Point P is at $(-5, 17)$ and point Q is at $(4\sqrt{3}, 6)$. How many lines can you draw that pass through both point P and point Q?

(A) 0

(B) 1

(C) 2

(D) 3

(E) 4

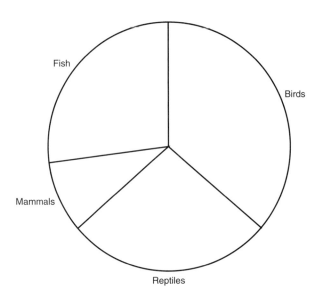

5. The figure above shows the overall holdings of a zoo. The zoo has the same number of reptiles and fish, 20 mammals, and four times as many birds as mammals. If the number of reptiles is $\frac{3}{4}$ the number of birds, how many fish are in the zoo?

(A) 20

(B) 40

(C) 60

(D) 80

(E) 100

6. The sum of four consecutive prime numbers is 72. What is the smallest of these numbers?

(A) 2
(B) 11
(C) 13
(D) 19
(E) 23

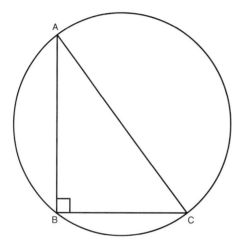

7. In the figure above, AB = 4 and BC = 3. The center of the circle lies on line AC. What is the circumference of the circle?

(A) 3π
(B) $3\pi^2$
(C) 4π
(D) 5π
(E) $5\pi^2$

8. The mean of a set of 10 numbers is 18. When you remove the smallest 3 of these numbers, the mean of the remaining numbers is 22. What is the sum of the smallest 3 numbers?

(A) 9
(B) 10
(C) 18
(D) 22
(E) 26

9. Define $f(x,y) = x^2 - xy$. For which of the below values of x and y is $f(x,y)$ the largest?

(A) $x = 3, y = -3$
(B) $x = 3, y = 3$
(C) $x = -3, y = 0$
(D) $x = -3, y = -3$
(E) $x = 0, y = 3$

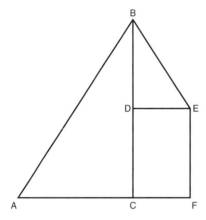

Note: Figure not drawn to scale.

10. In the figure above, $\triangle ABC$ and $\triangle EBD$ are similar triangles. BD = CD = 1 and AC = 1.5. What is the area of rectangle CDEF?

(A) .5
(B) .75
(C) 1
(D) 1.5
(E) 2.25

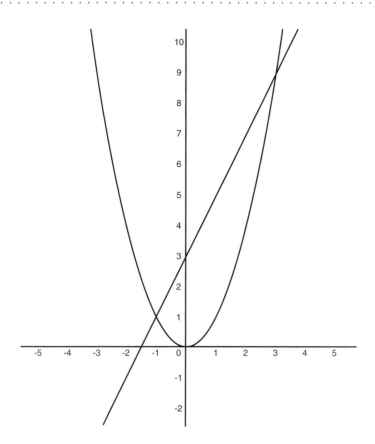

11. The figure above shows the graphs of $y = x^2$ and $y = ax + b$. The two graphs intersect at $x = -1$ and $x = 3$. What is a?

(A) -2
(B) -1.5
(C) 0
(D) 2
(E) 3

12. Define ♥ as follows: $x ♥ y = |x - y|$. If $3 ♥ z = 5$ and $z ♥ w = 2$, which of these is a possible value for w?

(A) -5
(B) -4
(C) -2
(D) 5
(E) 8

13. Let $f(x) = x^2 + ax + b$. If the zeroes of this polynomial are at -4 and -2, what is $f(9)$?
    (A) 35
    (B) 81
    (C) 90
    (D) 143
    (E) 181

14. A fair coin is tossed eight times. What is the probability that only one of the tosses will come up heads?

    (A) $\dfrac{1}{256}$

    (B) $\dfrac{1}{64}$

    (C) $\dfrac{1}{32}$

    (D) $\dfrac{1}{16}$

    (E) $\dfrac{1}{8}$

15. A right circular cone with diameter 2 and height 2 and a cube have the same volume. What is the length of the side of the cube?
    (A) $\sqrt{2\pi}$
    (B) $2\sqrt[3]{2\pi}$
    (C) $2\pi^3$
    (D) $\sqrt[3]{2\pi}$
    (E) 2π

16. Two opposite faces of a cube are colored white, and the other four faces are colored black. Which of the figures below could *not* be produced by cutting along the edges of the cube and flattening the results into the plane?

    (A)

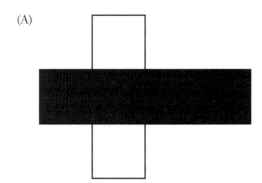

(B)

(C)

(D)

(E)

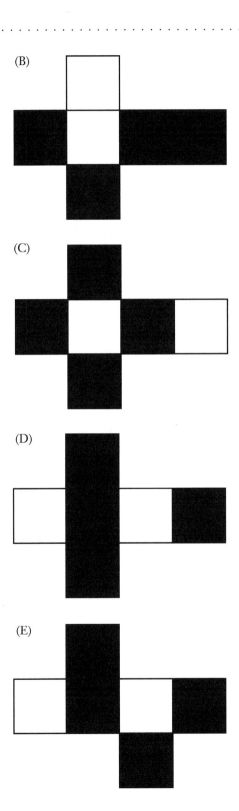

17. If m and n are both even integers, which of these could be an odd integer:

I. m + n

II. m − n

III. $\frac{(m+n)}{2}$

(A) I only
(B) II only
(C) III only
(D) I and II
(E) II and III

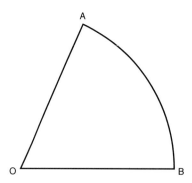

Note: Figure not drawn to scale.

18. In the figure above, OA = 5 and the area of the sector OAB is 5π. What is the length of the arc AB?

(A) 2
(B) 2π
(C) 4
(D) 4π
(E) 5π

19. The summer reading shelf at the library contains 30 books. A student must select three books to read over the summer. How many different sets of three books could the student select?

(A) 6
(B) 812
(C) 4,060
(D) 8,120
(E) 24,360

20. A circle has a diameter that is a positive integer, and an area that is less than 10 units. How many different circles fulfill this condition?

    (A) One
    (B) Two
    (C) Three
    (D) Four
    (E) Five

STOP

If you finish before time is called, you may check your work on this section only. Do not turn to any other section in the test.

SECTION 7

Time—20 minutes

19 Questions

Turn to Section 7 of your answer sheet to answer the questions in this section.

> **Directions:** For each question in this section, select the best answer from among the choices given and fill in the corresponding circle on the answer sheet.

> Each sentence below has one or two blanks, each blank indicating that something has been omitted. Beneath the sentence are five words or sets of words labeled A through E. Choose the word or set of words that, when inserted in the sentence, <u>best</u> fits the meaning of the sentence as a whole.
>
> EXAMPLE:
>
> The Internet is _____ now, being available in 78% of all American households.
>
>   (A) unimportant
>   (B) transitory
>   (C) migrating
>   (D) negligible
>   (E) ubiquitous
>
> Answer: (E)

1. You should always wear a protective apron, gloves, and goggles when
   working with _____ chemicals.
   (A) sarcastic
   (B) corrosive
   (C) caudated
   (D) cauterized
   (E) acrid

2. After the last administration's scandal, the public was _____ of his pre-
   decessor's promises.
   (A) wary
   (B) careless
   (C) trusting
   (D) reticent
   (E) unsuspecting

3. The clerk complained that proofreading the long columns of _____
   symbols was _____ work.
   (A) archaic . . relaxing
   (B) illegible . . dangerous
   (C) impenetrable . . boring
   (D) ancient . . interesting
   (E) unintelligible . . tedious

4. Growing up with a(n) _____ nana was an adventure—we never knew
   what to expect, and she sure did open our young minds to a world of
   possibilities.
   (A) eccentric
   (B) eclectic
   (C) erratic
   (D) temperamental
   (E) menacing

5. Being familiar only with her _____ business persona, we were unpre-
   pared for the _____ personality we met at the office party.
   (A) reclusive . . optimistic
   (B) aloof . . reticent
   (C) malicious . . gregarious
   (D) sanguine . . diffident
   (E) benevolent . . assertive

6. Her _____ mindset was so _____; she was difficult to work with.

(A) notorious . . odious

(B) cantankerous . . amiable

(C) congenial . . amusing

(D) affable . . intolerable

(E) dogmatic . . invidious

The passage below is followed by questions based on its content. Answer the questions on the basis of what is <u>stated</u> or <u>implied</u> in the passages and in any introductory material that may be provided.

The following passage is from a novel set on Santa Catalina island off California in 1920.

It was now something over two years since Harrison Blair, then fresh from Yale, had astonished both those who wished him well and those who, for various envious reasons, did not, with the wholly unreasonable success
Line of his first book. For, to those who did not understand, his sudden fame
5 had seemed all the more surprising in that it rested upon nothing more substantial than a slender volume of Indian verse. So unusual, however, had been his treatment of this well-worn subject as to call forth more than a little comment from even the most conservative of critics. The Brush and Pen had hastened to confer upon him an honorary membership.
10 Cadmon, magic weaver of Indian music, had written a warm letter of appreciation. And, most precious tribute of all, the Atlantic Monthly had become interested in his career.

To be sure, it was nothing more than might have been expected of a man whose undergraduate work in English had aroused the reluctant wonder
15 of more than one instructor. Nevertheless, the fact that he pulled stroke on the varsity crew had somewhat blinded other contemporaries to his more scholarly attainments. Nor had anyone thought it probable, because of his father's wealth, that Blair, in any event, would feel called upon to do much more than make a frolic of life. No one, indeed, had been more
20 taken aback than had his father to find him, a year after graduation, drudging over the assistant editor's desk of a struggling magazine the pay-roll of which, to put it mildly, offered no financial inducements.

"It's good practice for me, though—quickest way to learn," was all he vouchsafed when the older man remonstrated.

25 Yet, had that same father, shrewd capitalist that he was, but taken the trouble to reason back from premises evident enough, he might have been the first to realize that this tall son of his, with the keen gray eyes and a

face the strength of which was but increased by the high cheek bones and squarely molded chin, was scarcely the type of man to sit idly by enjoying
30 the fruits of another's labor.

And now, after two years more of grinding apprenticeship, he had in mind something much bigger than the slender volume of verse—an adventure into authorship more suited to his metal—a story of which an intense personal sympathy would furnish fitting atmosphere, with the final spur to
35 his ambition a letter from the Atlantic even at the moment stowed safely away in his pocket.

Some two hours later, after an unexpectedly excellent dinner in the luxurious dining room, he sauntered over to the hotel desk. There was no more than the faintest probability that a clerk of the St. Catherine would
40 be able to tell him how to reach a secret cavern bower above the Bay of Moons; still, he had to enter an opening wedge somewhere. The one man on duty was for the moment occupied with another guest, and Blair, lighting his after-dinner cigar, prepared with leisurely patience to await his turn.

45 The guest happened to be a young woman, rather pretty, he casually decided, although her greatest claim to beauty lay more, perhaps, in the swift changes in expression of which her face was capable, than in any actual regularity of line. For lack of anything better to do, Blair watched idly her encounter with the clerk. There appeared to be some kind of mis-
50 understanding.

"Awfully sorry it's happened that way, Miss Hastings," the man behind the desk was saying. He lifted with genuine reluctance the key she had just laid down. "We'd be mighty sorry to interfere with your work, but those small rooms always do go first. You know that yourself."

55 "I hadn't heard about it, though. I didn't know they were all gone." Her voice quivered with disappointment.

Blair, whose vocation taught him a certain technical sympathy, shot a swift glance at her. She couldn't be more than twenty-two or thereabouts, he decided less casually, and went on to observe her still further. She wore a
60 shabby, broad-brimmed hat much faded as if from constant exposure to the sun, but the shadows in the coil of hair beneath were warmly golden.

"Couldn't you find a room down in the village somewhere—at Mrs. Merrill's perhaps?" suggested the clerk.

"But Mrs. Merrill isn't here this spring." In spite of its quiver the voice
65 was very sweet.

"No," she started to turn away, "I'll have to put it off again, I suppose. I've looked everywhere."

She took a step or two, hesitated, then returned to the desk.

70 "You're positive there isn't a single one of the small rooms left?" she pleaded. "I wouldn't care how far back it was—anything would do. You can't think how I hate to give up. I had so hoped to finish it this time!"

The man shook his head.

"No, we're absolutely full just now. Later on there might be something, after the season is over."

75 "But that will be after school begins," answered the girl bitterly. "I can't work at all then!" and catching up a bag fully as shabby as the hat, she hurried away.

"Who is she?" asked Blair abruptly, overlooking for the moment his original purpose in seeking the man.

80 "School-teacher from Pasadena," replied the clerk briefly. "Teaches art in some private school over there, I believe." He eyed Blair amusedly. "Think you've met her before somewhere?"

Blair allowed his annoyance to show. "No, never laid eyes on her till just now. But I couldn't help feeling a bit sorry for her," he persisted. "She 85 seemed so sort of cut up. What's the trouble?"

"I'm sorry for her myself," declared the man on the other side as he hung the returned key on its board. "This is the third time that poor little woman's had to leave before she could finish what she came for on account of the expense. But what can we do?" He shrugged his shoulders. "The St. 90 Catherine isn't exactly a Y. W. C. A."

"What is it she's trying to do?"

Amusement deepened in the man's eyes.

"She's supposed to be painting Indians."

"Indians!" To the amazement of the other man Blair suddenly leaned for-95 ward, his eyes agleam with interest.

"But I didn't know there were any around here."

"There aren't."

"Then how—?"

"Makes 'em up out of her head, I guess. I never heard that she had even a 100 model."

7. The first paragraph of the passage portrays Harrison Blair as
   (A) a man with many enemies
   (B) a lover of leisure and women
   (C) a man driven by envy
   (D) someone with little imagination
   (E) a promising young author

8. In line 3, "unreasonable" most nearly means
   (A) immoderate
   (B) excessive
   (C) irrational
   (D) unexpected
   (E) inordinate

9. The phrase "the reluctant wonder of more than one instructor" (lines 14–15) indicates that
   (A) Blair's teachers wondered how he was able to complete his assignments.
   (B) Blair's writing impressed teachers who expected he would do poorly.
   (C) Blair's teachers did not understand how he could be reluctant about writing.
   (D) Blair's teachers wondered whether he was cheating in their courses.
   (E) Blair's instructors were angry at his attitude toward assignments.

10. The phrase "he vouchsafed when the older man remonstrated" (lines 23–24) most nearly means
   (A) He promised when the older man asked.
   (B) He objected when the older man questioned.
   (C) He explained when the older man offered.
   (D) He stated when the older man raged.
   (E) He deigned to reply when the older man objected.

11. The overall impression of Blair that the author of the passage gives is that he is
   (A) extraordinary
   (B) extravagant
   (C) dilatory
   (D) spoiled
   (E) unsympathetic

12. In saying that Blair has "a certain technical sympathy" (line 57), the author implies that

(A) he preferred machines to people.

(B) he was extremely attractive to women.

(C) he spent time worrying about those with less money than himself.

(D) his powers of observation were unusual.

(E) he has developed the power of sharing the feelings of another.

13. The young woman wants one of the small rooms at the hotel because

(A) they have better light for painting.

(B) she can't afford a larger room.

(C) she doesn't need more space for her things.

(D) the intimate surroundings help her concentrate.

(E) she has no companion on this trip.

14. Blair's "annoyance" (line 83) arises from the clerk's

(A) insolence

(B) humor

(C) familiarity

(D) caginess

(E) abruptness

15. Why were Blair's eyes suddenly "agleam with interest" (line 95)?

(A) Because he saw an opportunity to ask the young lady out on a date

(B) Because he was worried that his own room at the hotel would not be available

(C) Because he didn't know it was possible to paint without a model

(D) Because of the coincidence between his own work about Indians and the young lady's paintings of Indians

(E) Because he had found a worthwhile cause on which to spend some of his money

16. The passage suggests that Blair's main strength is

(A) his unusual writing ability

(B) his attractiveness to the fair sex

(C) his ability to spend money wisely

(D) his dogged attention to detail

(E) his athletic ability

17. The major purpose of this passage is to

(A) provide background detail on the locale of the story.

(B) give a purpose for Blair's research into Indians.

(C) introduce some of the characters in the story.

(D) regale the reader with luxurious details of the fine life.

(E) show what life was like on Catalina in the 1920s.

18. The author is apparently most concerned to counteract which of these theories that she considers her audience is likely to have?

(A) School teachers are not paid much money.

(B) Vacation spots are all exotic.

(C) Inherited wealth acts as a bar to hard work.

(D) Hotel clerks are difficult to reason with.

(E) Good looks and intelligence go hand in hand.

19. Blair's father appears in this passage

(A) to show that "like father, like son" holds true in this case.

(B) as a device to introduce important facts about Blair's character.

(C) because he owns the St. Catherine.

(D) as a miser who is in stark contrast with his son.

(E) to indicate that family will play an important role in the story.

STOP

If you finish before time is called, you may check your work on this section only. Do not turn to any other section in the test.

SECTION 8

Time—20 minutes

16 Questions

Turn to Section 8 of your answer sheet to answer the questions in this section.

> **Directions:** For this section, solve each problem and decide which is the best of the choices given. Fill in the corresponding circle on the answer sheet. You can use any available space for scratchwork.

> **Notes:**
>
> **1.** The use of a calculator is permitted.
>
> **2.** All numbers used are real numbers.
>
> **3.** Figures that accompany problems in the test are intended to provide information that is useful in solving the problems. They are drawn as accurately as possible EXCEPT when it is stated in a specific problem that the figure is not drawn to scale. All figures lie in a plane unless otherwise indicated.
>
> **4.** Unless otherwise specified, the domain of any function f is assumed to be the set of real numbers x for which $f(x)$ is a real number.

$A = \pi r^2$
$C = 2\pi r$

$A = \ell w$

$A = \frac{1}{2}bh$

$V = \ell wh$

$V = \pi r^2 h$

$c^2 = a^2 + b^2$

Special Right Triangles

The number of degrees of arc in a circle is 360.
The sum of the measures in degrees of the angles of a triangle is 180.

1. If 40% of x is 10, what is 3x + 7?

   (A) 37
   (B) 47
   (C) 72
   (D) 82
   (E) 407

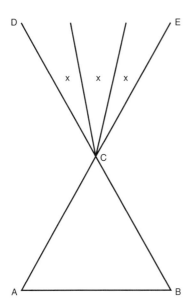

2. In the figure above, ACE and BCD are straight lines, and ∠CAB = ∠CBA = 60°. What is ∠x?

   (A) 15°
   (B) 20°
   (C) 25°
   (D) 30°
   (E) 35°

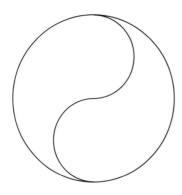

3. What type of symmetry does the figure above possess?

   (A) reflective symmetry across one axis only
   (B) reflective symmetry across two axes only
   (C) rotational symmetry only
   (D) both reflective symmetry and rotational symmetry
   (E) neither reflective symmetry nor rotational symmetry

4. Given that $-4x + 12 < 16$, which of these statements is true?

   (A) $x > 1$
   (B) $x < 1$
   (C) $x < -1$
   (D) $x > -1$
   (E) There is not enough information to solve the problem.

5. A class includes three quizzes and a final exam that counts for as much as two quizzes. A student has an average score of 88 before taking the final exam. What must she score on the final exam to raise her average to 90?

   (A) 90
   (B) 91
   (C) 92
   (D) 93
   (E) 94

6. The price of a widget is originally $90. The manufacturer increases the price by 10% and then decreases the price by 10%. What is the final price of the widget?

   (A) $89.00
   (B) $89.10
   (C) $90.00
   (D) $90.10
   (E) $91.00

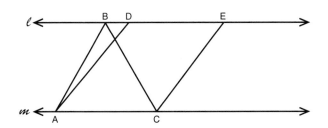

7. In the figure above, $\ell \parallel m$. The area of the equilateral triangle ABC is 6. What is the area of parallelogram ADEC?

(A) $6\sqrt{2}$

(B) $6\sqrt{3}$

(C) 10

(D) 12

(E) 14

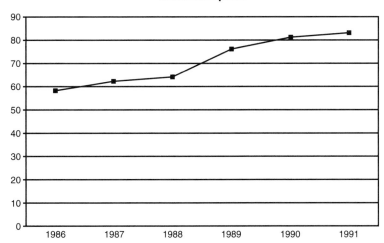

8. According to the graph above, between which two years did the price of transistors increase by the highest percentage?

(A) 1986 and 1987

(B) 1987 and 1988

(C) 1988 and 1989

(D) 1989 and 1990

(E) 1990 and 1991

9. You have an unlimited supply of blocks that are rectangular solids with sides 1 inch, 1 inch, and $\frac{1}{2}$ inch. How many of these blocks will you need to fill a cubical box with each side equal to 12 inches?
   (A) 72
   (B) 144
   (C) 288
   (D) 1,728
   (E) 3,456

10. a, b, c, d, and e are consecutive integers. Which of the following can *not* be the sum of these five integers?
   (A) –8,405
   (B) –100
   (C) 0
   (D) 227
   (E) 9,810

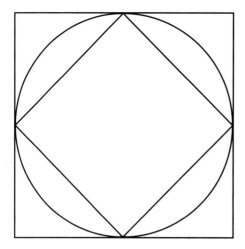

11. The figure shows a circle inscribed in a square, with the circle exactly tangent to the four sides of the square. A second square is inscribed in the circle so that its corners all lie on the circle. If the area of the outer square is 4, what is the area of the inner square?
   (A) $\sqrt{2}$
   (B) 2
   (C) $\frac{5}{2}$
   (D) 2π
   (E) $\frac{3}{2}$

12. The first three terms of an arithmetic sequence are 2, 6, and 10. What is the sum of the 49th and 50th terms of the sequence?

(A) 388

(B) 392

(C) 396

(D) 398

(E) 400

13. One square has an area of 4, and a second square has an area of 16. What is the ratio of the perimeter of the first square to the perimeter of the second square?

(A) 16:1

(B) 16:4

(C) 2:1

(D) 1:1

(E) 1:2

14. One roll of film costs f dollars and can be used to take p pictures. What is the cost per picture in terms of f and p?

(A) fp

(B) $\frac{p}{f}$

(C) $\frac{f}{p}$

(D) f + p

(E) p – f

15. A plane flies a round-trip route that is a total of 2,000 miles each way. The plane itself ordinarily flies at 450 miles per hour, but there is a steady 50 mile per hour wind blowing in one direction. The net effect is that the plane flies at 400 miles per hour in one direction, and 500 miles per hour in the other. What is the average (arithmetical mean) speed of the plane over the entire route?

(A) 425

(B) $444\frac{4}{9}$

(C) 450

(D) $463\frac{2}{9}$

(E) 475

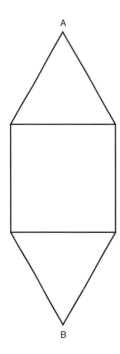

16. All of the line segments in the figure are one unit long, and the central quadrilateral is a square. What is the distance AB?
    (A) $1 + \sqrt{3}$
    (B) $1 + \sqrt{3}/2$
    (C) 2.5
    (D) 3
    (E) $1 + \pi$

STOP

If you finish before time is called, you may check your work on this section only. Do not turn to any other section in the test.

SECTION 9

Time—10 minutes

14 Questions

Turn to Section 9 of your answer sheet to answer the questions in this section.

Directions: For each question in this section, select the best answer from among the choices given and fill in the corresponding circle on the answer sheet.

The following sentences test correctness and effectiveness of expression. Part of each sentence or the entire sentence is underlined; beneath each sentence are five ways of phrasing the underlined material. Choice A repeats the original phrasing; the other four choices are different. If you think the original phrasing produces a better sentence than any of the alternatives, select choice A; if not, select one of the other choices.

In making your selection, follow the requirements of standard written English; that is, pay attention to grammar, choice of words, sentence construction, and punctuation. Your selection should result in the most effective sentence—clear and precise, without awkwardness or ambiguity.

EXAMPLE:

The weather that winter was <u>worse than for at least five decades</u>.

    (A) worse than for at least five decades
    (B) the worse it was for at least five decades
    (C) worse. Than it had been for at least five decades.
    (D) the worst that it had been for at least five decades
    (E) the worst is was for at least five decades.

Answer: (D)

---

1. You may find it difficult to comprehend <u>that which you</u> read if you don't know the underlying grammar rules.

    (A) that which you
    (B) what
    (C) what you
    (D) what is
    (E) that what is

2. First identify the error, and then correct <u>the error</u>.

    (A) the error
    (B) what's wrong
    (C) the mistake
    (D) it
    (E) your mistake

3. The band, in addition to the cheerleaders, <u>is already on their way</u> to the game.

(A) is already on their way
(B) is already on its way
(C) is already gone
(D) has left
(E) is going

4. After two weeks, the children were still unmanageable <u>so the teacher</u> asked for a transfer.

(A) so the teacher
(B) and their teacher
(C) ; the teacher
(D) so she
(E) so their teacher

5. <u>Neither of the girls</u> is going to the prom, although all were invited.

(A) Neither of the girls
(B) Neither girl
(C) None of the girls
(D) None of them
(E) Neither Susan nor Betty

6. <u>Neither the dog nor the cows</u> has been attended to yet.

(A) Neither the dog nor the cows
(B) None of the animals
(C) Neither the cows nor the dog
(D) Either the dog or the cows
(E) Neither the dog nor the cow

7. Cities began <u>to sprout up</u> in the shadow of the virgin forest.

(A) to sprout up
(B) to grow
(C) to take sprout
(D) to sprout
(E) to appear

8. The South is a diverse land of <u>different climates, different soils, and societies</u>.

(A) different climates, different soils, and societies
(B) climates, soils, and societies
(C) different climates, soils and societies
(D) different climates, soils, and societies
(E) different climates, and different soils, and different societies

9. Henry David Thoreau, a transcendentalist, <u>believed that God was an oversoul</u>, whose presence shows us good and evil.

(A) believed that God was an oversoul

(B) believes that God is an oversoul

(C) believed that God is an oversoul

(D) believes that God has an oversoul

(E) believes God was an oversoul

10. By 1929, U.S. businesses <u>had been spending</u> $3 billion a year for advertising through newspapers, magazines, billboards, direct mail, and the new medium of radio.

(A) had been spending

(B) has spent

(C) were spent

(D) were spending

(E) will spent

11. Returning to America a national hero, <u>we were unsure about which political party he belonged to</u>.

(A) we were unsure about which political party he belonged to.

(B) he was unsure about which political party he belonged to

(C) we were unsure about which political party he belonged

(D) we were unsure about which political party we belonged to

(E) he was unsure about which political party we belonged to

12. Foreigners could no longer afford <u>to buy up American goods</u>.

(A) to buy up American goods

(B) to buy up American products

(C) to buy American goods

(D) American goods

(E) American products

13. <u>The sagging economies of post-war Europe</u> contributed to America's Great Depression.

(A) The sagging economies of post-war Europe

(B) Post-war Europe's sagging economies

(C) Europe's post-war sagging economies

(D) The sagging economy of post-war Europe

(E) Europe's sagging post-war economy

14. Because of America's diverse communities, immigrants <u>were likelier to feel</u> at home here than anywhere else except home.

(A) were likelier to feel
(B) was likelier to feel
(C) were more likely to feel
(D) were most likely to feel
(E) was most likely to feel

STOP

If you finish before time is called, you may check your work on this section only. Do not turn to any other section in the test.

Answer Key for Practice Exam #1

Answer Key

Section 1

Grading the essay is subjective, so there's no way we can help you through this process. Our best advice is to ask someone you trust who has the expertise to actually grade your essay to help you. If you have to go it alone, be sure to check for the following:

➤ Is the thesis well developed, insightful, and focused?

➤ Did you use clear and appropriate examples, anecdotes, and reasons to support your position?

➤ Are your thoughts organized logically?

➤ Did you use a variety of writing techniques, such as varied sentence structure and length?

➤ Did you use appropriate words?

➤ Is the essay free of grammatical and spelling errors?

If possible, put a few days between test day and the day you try to grade your own work. Proofing your own work is very difficult—give your mind a chance to forget a bit. A few days later, you'll get a fresher, more objective look at the essay.

Don't try to assign an actual score to your essay. Instead, find your weak points and continue to practice in order to build your skills in that area.

Section 2

1. D	**7.** A	**13.** C	**19.** E
2. E	**8.** C	**14.** B	**20.** D
3. B	**9.** E	**15.** B	**21.** A
4. A	**10.** D	**16.** D	**22.** C
5. C	**11.** D	**17.** A	**23.** E
6. D	**12.** C	**18.** D	**24.** D

Section 3

1. C	**3.** E	**5.** E	**7.** B
2. B	**4.** D	**6.** A	**8.** C

9.   **10.** 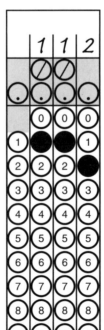   **11.**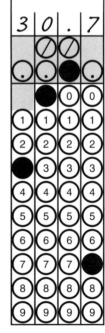

12.

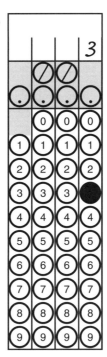

13.

14.

15.

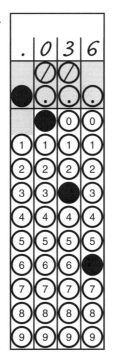

16.

17.

18.

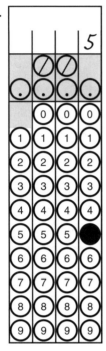

Section 4

1. D	**10.** B	**19.** A	**28.** E
2. B	**11.** B	**20.** A	**29.** D
3. C	**12.** D	**21.** C	**30.** B
4. D	**13.** C	**22.** A	**31.** E
5. B	**14.** B	**23.** C	**32.** D
6. E	**15.** C	**24.** D	**33.** E
7. B	**16.** E	**25.** C	**34.** A
8. E	**17.** D	**26.** B	**35.** D
9. C	**18.** C	**27.** B	

Section 5

1. B	**7.** B	**13.** D	**19.** A
2. A	**8.** C	**14.** C	**20.** D
3. C	**9.** E	**15.** C	**21.** E
4. A	**10.** A	**16.** B	**22.** D
5. E	**11.** C	**17.** B	**23.** A
6. D	**12.** D	**18.** D	**24.** C

Section 6

1. A	**6.** C	**11.** D	**16.** B
2. C	**7.** D	**12.** B	**17.** C
3. D	**8.** E	**13.** D	**18.** B
4. B	**9.** A	**14.** C	**19.** C
5. C	**10.** B	**15.** D	**20.** C

Section 7

1. B	**6.** E	**11.** A	**16.** A
2. A	**7.** E	**12.** E	**17.** C
3. E	**8.** D	**13.** B	**18.** C
4. B	**9.** B	**14.** C	**19.** B
5. D	**10.** E	**15.** D	

Section 8

1. D	**5.** D	**9.** E	**13.** E
2. B	**6.** B	**10.** D	**14.** C
3. C	**7.** D	**11.** B	**15.** B
4. D	**8.** C	**12.** B	**16.** A

Section 9

1. C	**5.** B	**9.** C	**13.** B
2. D	**6.** C	**10.** D	**14.** C
3. B	**7.** D	**11.** B	
4. E	**8.** B	**12.** C	

Detailed Answers

Section 2

Question 1

Answer D is correct. Knowing the definition of all five words certainly helps complete this sentence correctly. All five words could be used, logically, but only one best fulfills the logic of the sentence, and that's agrarian. An agrarian society is an agricultural society and therefore, would have little use for an engineer. The right answer is the best answer. At first glance, "barren" seems good; you might have trouble finding a job in a barren spot. However, "agrarian" contrasts more specifically with "engineer," so that word is better. Always search for the best response, not the first response that seems to work. Answers A, B, C, and E are all incorrect for the same reason—they offer nothing to help explain why an engineer would find it difficult to find employment.

Question 2

Answer E is correct. The word "despite" at the beginning of the sentence is your main clue. You know that despite their size, the girls are otherwise healthy. Answer A is incorrect because it's illogical—"petite" is an antonym for "enormous," not a synonym. In this case, the sentence requires a synonym or logical adjective. Answers B and D are incorrect. Although "petite" and "small" both work, neither "fragile" nor "frail" does. The second word must have a positive connotation to match healthy. Answer C is incorrect, although logically it might work. Remember, you want the best answer, not the first answer that might work. Answer D is incorrect for the same reason as B.

Question 3

Answer B is correct. The clues in this sentence aren't as obvious as the first two, but they're there, even though the two thoughts don't seem to be related. You should be able to glean the following: Alfred Nobel spoke and wrote many languages, and he wrote his own business letters. If you can ascertain that much of the sentence's purpose, answer B is easy to spot. If not, eliminating the other responses should help. Answer A is incorrect. Although "accomplished" might work logically, "speak" doesn't because the statement discusses letters, not public speaking. Admittedly, the word "speak" could fill in, but there's probably a better choice and you should keep looking. Answer C is incorrect. Both words could fit in a pinch, but neither really represents the thoughts. "Knowledgeable" is a bit contrived in this context, and "compose" suggests more original input than would be required for someone writing business letters for someone else. Answers D and E are incorrect because the sentence suggests that the first word is positive—"lacking" and "illiterate" are both illogical in this context.

Question 4

Answer A is correct. You know right from the start that the sentence is discussing more than one technology, so the word "combined" is the most logical choice for the first word, within the context of the entire sentence. In addition, the phrases "new crafts" and "the edge of space" are great clues, and "probe" completes that thought well. Answer B is incorrect. There's no connection between abandoning the technologies and reaching new frontiers. Answer C is incorrect. Both words could be used, but the words in answer A create a stronger, more descriptive sentence. Answer C isn't the best response. Answer D is incorrect because "refurbished" is illogical in this context. You don't refurbish technology—you refurbish machinery. Answer E is incorrect. Like answer C, the words could fit, but within the context of the entire sentence, they're not the best response. Significantly, the word "pooled" means to gather, not necessarily to combine. In addition, you probably wouldn't use rocket and jet technologies to study outer space. You'd use those technologies to visit space, or at least try.

Question 5

Answer C is the correct answer. This sentence is a bit trickier than the others, but you must keep the context of the entire sentence in mind while reading. After reading the sentence, you should be able to ascertain that the first word refers to persons who did not actually attend a college. Answers A and B are incorrect because it's safe to assume that an educator would've completed college. Even the early colleges had standards that required a certain level of academic success for educators. Besides, the word "appreciated" within context is a bit illogical. Why would a person who didn't appreciate college become a professor? Answer D is incorrect—it's easy to determine that the first word probably refers to nonstudents. The words themselves almost fit logically, but even if you miss the nonstudent clue, this response simply isn't the best response. Answer E is incorrect because it's illogical. There's no way to support the idea that employees had faith in education as an ideal.

Question 6

Answer D is correct. Answer A is incorrect because the mention of history in the passages is only passing. Answer B is incorrect; the passages assert that software is important, but they don't demonstrate this point. Answer C is incorrect because there is no material on actual computer programming in the passage. Answer E is incorrect because neither passage calls for any specific changes. Only answer D fits both passages.

Question 7

Answer A is correct. Recognizing that the two passages are directly opposed to one another lets you eliminate the relatively positive statements in answers C, D, and E. On the other hand, answer B is too negative; there's no evidence in the writing here that the author of passage 2 would want to convict the author of passage 1 of a crime. Answer A is a good way to state the disagreements between the two.

Question 8

Answer C is correct. Answer A is incorrect because the passage doesn't mention experience at all. Answer B is incorrect because the author of this passage opposed software patents rather than advocating them. Answer D is incorrect; there's no way to tell which software either passage is talking about specifically. Answer E may be tempting, but it's not justified by the actual content of the passages; be careful not to interject your own prejudices into the exam. Only answer C is taken from the passages themselves.

Question 9

Answer E is correct. The key to answering this one correctly is to sort out the question. The author of the second passage is in favor of patents and copyrights on software, and so would be unhappy if they were discontinued. This eliminates answers A and B, which are not states of unhappiness. The author could be confused or tired (answers C and D), but there's no reason to think so. Answer E fits: "Crestfallen" is a synonym for "dejected."

Question 10

Answer D is correct. Answer A is clearly untrue because the passage goes on to discuss the remains of the civilization that have been found. Answers B and C are true statements, but they're not a good fit for the quoted phrase. Answer E is also supported by the passage, but is not a meaning for the quoted phrase. Only answer D explains what the author meant.

Question 11

Answer D is correct. The paragraph containing this sentence recites a number of facts intended to show how well organized the Indus River civilization was. Answers A and E may be true in the broader context of history, but cannot be inferred from this passage alone. Answer B is there to catch the unwary student who misreads the meaning of the word "uniform." Answer C is implied by the passage, but is not the main point of the sentence.

Question 12

Answer C is correct. There is no evidence in the passage that the author is considering alternative explanations or not summarizing the latest research, which eliminates answers A and D. The tone of the passage indicates that it is meant to teach the reader, so answer B is not correct. Answer E could be correct, but it's too grandiose for what's presented in the passage. You don't know how the authors feel about archaeology as a whole, only how they interpret the evidence in this one particular case.

Question 13

Answer C is correct. Even if you didn't know before the exam that "polytheistic" means "worshipping many gods," you should be able to take a good guess at this one by recognizing that the root word "poly" means "many."

Question 14

Answer B is correct. One of the overarching themes of the passage is how little we actually know about this particular civilization. Answer A is incorrect because the civilization lasted for a thousand years. Answers C and D are not justified by the passage; it doesn't allow one to draw any conclusions about modern civilization. Answer E is incorrect as well; although the group with horses defeated the group with writing, this does not imply that horses are more important than writing.

Question 15

Answer B is correct. In the context of the passage, the departing fishermen are commenting on the fact that the one man will be left at camp alone—that is, with only an imaginary companion. None of the other answers match this meaning.

Question 16

Answer D is correct because the phrase indicates figuratively that the man is scared. Answer A is wrong because the shadows are not about to literally assault the man. Answer B is incorrect because there's nothing ironic about the phrase, and answer C is incorrect because this isn't an exaggeration; the shadows are not about to slightly assault him. Answer E doesn't fit the tone of the paragraph.

Question 17

Answer A is correct. By substituting the proposed answers in place of the word "magnified" in the sentence, you should be able to see that "emphasized" makes the most sense: The red of the fire made the red of the bear's mouth stand out. It did not literally make the mouth larger.

Question 18

Answer D is correct. In the context of the paragraph, it's clear that the boots of fear are meant to show the transition from standing still to "darting around the campfire." Answer A is incorrect because the man was not paralyzed. Answer B is incorrect because there's nothing in the paragraph speaking to lack of feeling. Answer C is incorrect because the man didn't conquer his fear. Answer E is incorrect because, although the story seems unlikely, it does not involve magical elements.

Question 19

Answer E is correct. Here again the easiest way to get the correct answer is to substitute the explanations for the original phrase. The man has been presented as the sympathetic figure and the bear as the villain throughout the piece, but the bear is gaining. Thus, the good guy is not winning.

Question 20

Answer D is correct. The bear is a formidable opponent. This one is a matter of the tone of the passage. The bear didn't do a bad job of snarling, which eliminates answers B and E. Answer A is not strong enough for the sense of a passage that also includes phrases such as "jowls dripping." Answer C is almost true, but the bear inspires fear rather than awe.

Question 21

Answer A is correct. The actions and thoughts portrayed for the little man all indicate that he thinks his life is in danger. Answer B is incorrect; although the bear does something playful in this paragraph, it is not the main point of the paragraph. Answer C is incorrect because we're not given any information to evaluate whether the dark is scarier than the daytime. Answer D is incorrect because the bear's actions don't arise from the party being split. Answer E might be a reasonable conclusion, but the lines indicated are more about the little man than about nature.

Question 22

Answer C is correct. The sentence containing this phrase is about the bear's roar, and it includes flowery language to tell you that the roar was very loud indeed. None of the other answers fits this sentence.

Question 23

Answer E is correct. Although Crane's language is characteristically overblown, the meaning should be clear. Just substitute simpler words for "overwhelmed" and "interrogations," and you'll get the right answer. The other choices are grammatically correct but change the meaning of the sentence if you insert them.

Question 24

Answer D is correct. This sort of question is best answered by outlining the passage as you go along so that you can pick out its main points. If asked to summarize the story, you might come up with something like "a man is left alone by his comrades to face a bear, but he survives and the joke is on them." This is close to "he who laughs last, laughs best," whereas the other choices don't fit the story.

Section 3

Question 1

Answer C is correct. Start by calculating the value of n. If 15% of n is 45, then $n = 45 \div .15 = 300$. Then you know that m is 250% of n, so $m = 2.5n = 750$. Finally, you can use this to calculate 12% of m: $.12m = .12(750) = 90$.

Question 2

Answer B is correct. If $\angle ACB = 60°$ and $\angle CBA = 90°$, then $\angle BAC = 30°$ (because you know that the sum of the angles in any triangle is 180°). Then $\angle CED$ must be 30° as well because the figure ACED is a parallelogram, and the opposite angles of a parallelogram are equal.

Question 3

Answer E is correct. If the black beans represent 75% of the total, the white beans are 25%, or $\frac{1}{4}$, of the total. Thus the total number of beans is $16 \times 4 = 64$.

Question 4

Answer D is correct. First consider the prime factors of 210. $210 = 2 \times 3 \times 5 \times 7$. The value of b must be some combination of these factors. But you know that a is 14 = 2 × 7 and the GCF of a and b is 7. This tells you that 7 must be one of the factors of b, whereas 2 cannot be a factor of b (otherwise the GCF of the two integers would be 14). What about the factors 3 and 5? These *must* be factors of b; otherwise, they would not appear in the factorization of the LCM. Thus the answer is 3 × 5 × 7 = 105.

Question 5

Answer E is correct. To solve this, note that the four triangles make up a square (this must be the case because they are identical) and that each of these triangles is a 45°-45°-90° right triangle. Also note that the area of the shaded region is the area of the circle less the area of the square. Getting the area of the square is easy: If one side of the square (AB) is 2 units, the area of the square is $(2\sqrt{2})^2$ = 8 units. Now consider the circle. To get the area of the circle, you need to know its radius. If AB = $2\sqrt{2}$, AO = 2 units—you can remember the relation for the special triangle or work this out via the Pythagorean Theorem by noting that AO and BO are the same length. So the area of the circle is $\pi2^2$ = 4π, and the area of the shaded region is 4π − 8.

Question 6

Answer A is correct. To answer this question, look at the difference between the stacks of cars for 1985 and 1987. There are three cars different, and the legend tells you that each car stands for 50,000 sales. So the total difference of 2 years is 150,000 sales, for an average of 150,000 ÷ 2 = 75,000.

Question 7

Answer B is correct. Set B must contain all the elements from the intersection, so you know that it must at least contain the elements 7, 11, and 22. This eliminates answers C, D, and E. You also know that every element in the union must come from either A or B or both. But set A does not contain 14 or 17, so these elements must be part of set B.

Question 8

Answer C is correct. By inspecting the equation of line ℓ, you know that its y-intercept is 4, so the y-intercept of line m must be either 2 or 6. If the two lines are parallel, they must have the same slope. Thus, the equation of m is either y = 2x + 2 or y = 2x + 6.

Question 9

Add the two equations to get a third equation, $2a^2 = 50$. Divide by two to get $a^2 = 25$. Thus, $a = \sqrt{25}$. Remember, there are two possible square roots of 25, but the grids do not allow you to enter negative numbers. So grid 5 to receive credit.

Question 10

To answer this question, note that the angles along a line always add up to $180°$ and substitute the given value for angle y:

$x + y + 2y + y = 180$
$x + 4y = 180$
$x + 4(17) = 180$
$x + 68 = 180$
$x = 112$

Grid 112 to receive credit.

Question 11

Use the percent change formula to figure out the answer:

$Change = \frac{(final - starting)}{starting} \times 100\%$

$Change = \frac{(68 - 52)}{52} \times 100\%$

$Change = \frac{16}{52} \times 100\%$

$Change = 30.76\%$

Remember, if there are more digits than will fit on the grid, you can either round or truncate the answer. So grid 30.7 or 30.8 to receive credit.

Question 12

The domain of a function is all points at which the function is defined. $f(x)$ is undefined when the denominator is zero, which happens at x = 7. Grid 7 to receive credit.

Question 13

First consider the right triangle $\triangle ABF$. From the Pythagorean Theorem, BF = $\sqrt{(1 + 1)}$ = $\sqrt{2}$. Now consider the right triangle $\triangle BCF$. Again, you can apply the Pythagorean Theorem:

$$CF = \sqrt{1^2 + \left(\sqrt{2}\right)^2}$$

$$CF = \sqrt{3}$$

CF is one side of the square, so the area of the square is $(\sqrt{3})^2$ = 3. Grid 3 to receive credit.

Question 14

To calculate the median, add the numbers and divide by their count: $(4 + 17 + 11 + 14 + 3 + 2 + 8 + 22 + 18) \div 9 = 11$. To calculate the mode, you must put the numbers in order—2, 3, 4, 8, 11, 14, 17, 18, 22—and then pick the number in the middle, which is 11. In this case, the median and the mode are the same, so the difference between the two is zero. Grid 0 to receive credit.

Question 15

Start with the term inside the parentheses, and don't let the special symbols throw you. From the definition, 3><4 = 2 × 3 + 2 × 4 = 14. Then 14><.5 = 2 × 14 + 2 × .5 = 29. Grid 29 to receive credit.

Question 16

Being a junior and having red hair are independent events, so you can just multiple the probabilities together: $.3 \times .12 = .036$. Grid .036 to receive credit.

Question 17

The graph of $g(x + 3)$ is simply the graph of $g(x)$ shifted three units to the left. The graphs show the positive zeros of $g(x)$ as 2, 4, 6, and so on. If you subtract three from these, you get zeros of –1, 1, 3, and so on. The first positive number in this set is 1, so grid 1 to receive credit.

Question 18

Each line from a point of the star through the center of the star is an axis of reflective symmetry because the figure won't change if it is reflected across that line. Grid 5 to receive credit.

Section 4

Question 1

Answer D is correct. The phrase "in addition to" indicates a singular subject, so the verb must match the noun in number. Answer A is incorrect because the phrase isn't correct as is. Answer B is incorrect because it provides new words that offer nothing to the sentence, and doesn't use the appropriate verb. Answer C is incorrect because it uses the wrong verb and there's no reason to change "to" to "for." Answer E is incorrect because there's no reason to change "to" to "for."

Question 2

Answer B is correct. The verb tense isn't parallel between the two phrases. The first phrase implies something is going to happen, but then the action in the second phrase has already occurred. It doesn't matter which tense you change, but they must match. Answer A is incorrect because the phrase isn't correct as is. Answer C is incorrect because it still uses the wrong verb tense, and there's nothing wrong with the subject's number—it is irrelevant in this sentence. Answers D and E are incorrect. There's no reason to change the verb, just the verb's tense. In addition, there's no reason to change the subject's number.

Question 3

Answer C is correct. A definite noun and its antecedent must agree in number and kind. In this case, you're dealing with kind, a personal or impersonal entity. The pronoun "that" is referring to a definite noun, the man. "That" is used with indefinite pronouns. The correct pronoun is "who." Answer A is incorrect because the phrase isn't correct as is. Answers B and D are incorrect because they repeat the same error as the original sentence. In addition, answer B changes the noun, which is unnecessary. Answer D changes "the" to "that," which is unnecessary. Answer E is incorrect even though it uses the right pronoun. There's no reason to change the noun. Remember, some of the responses may seem correct, but introduce new errors. In this case, both C and E are grammatically correct, but C is the most correct because there's no reason to change the noun as answer E does.

Question 4

Answer D is correct. Interrogative pronouns, such as "when," refer to a definite pronoun. As is, the sentence suggests that vaporization is a time, but it's a noun. The antecedent, vaporization, doesn't answer the question of time. By adding the verb "occurs," you correct the problem. Answer A is incorrect because the phrase isn't correct as is. Answers C and E are incorrect even though they might be considered grammatically correct. They are too wordy and awkward. Answer B is incorrect because the resulting sentence would be grammatically incorrect.

Question 5

Answer B is correct. The preposition "up" isn't necessary. Answer A is incorrect because the phrase isn't correct as is. Answer C is incorrect because it doesn't omit "up." Answers D and E are incorrect because there's no need to change the verb.

Question 6

Answer E is correct. The verb "concerned" requires the preposition "about," not "with." Answer A is incorrect because the phrase isn't correct as is. Answers B and D are incorrect because they don't use the correct preposition. Answer C is incorrect because it changes the sentence's meaning, even though it uses the correct preposition.

Question 7

Answer B is correct. The adverb "badly" modifies "feels," meaning she's not a good feeler. The adjective "bad" modifies the pronoun "she," and that is correct. Remember, as long as you use the word "feel" or "feels" as a linking verb, you can use "good," "well," and "bad" as an adjective. In Chapter 3, "The Critical Reading Section: Sentence Completions," we told you not to worry about the use of bad/badly and good/well because it won't show up on the exam. But, you should still know how to use them correctly. If you use them incorrectly on your essay, it could count against you. Answer A is incorrect because the phrase isn't correct as is. Answer C is incorrect because changing the verb's tense doesn't correct the problem. Answer D is incorrect because it adds more words without correcting the problem. Answer E is incorrect because it's wordy, albeit grammatically correct.

Question 8

Answer E is correct. When using the comparative form of an adjective, add "er." Answer A is incorrect because the phrase isn't correct as is. The sentence's intent is clear—the best response is to correct the comparative form, not remove it. Answers B and C are incorrect because they introduce other grammatical mistakes. Answer D is incorrect even though it's grammatically correct. Introducing the phrase "this morning" is unnecessary in order to correct the sentence.

Question 9

Answer C is correct. The subject of the opening modifying phrase should follow the phrase. Answer A is incorrect because the phrase isn't correct as is. Answers B and D are incorrect because there's no need to omit the phrase "in reality." In fact, doing so weakens the sentence. Answer E is incorrect because changing the preposition changes the sentence's meaning.

Question 10

Answer B is correct. The serial items aren't parallel. Answer A is incorrect because the phrase isn't correct as is. Answers C, D, and E are incorrect. The phrase "little but" isn't the problem. In addition, D actually changes the sentence's meaning. Answer E is incorrect, changing "little" to "nothing" doesn't help the parallelism.

Question 11

Answer B is correct. The verb phrase "named Myra" is misplaced. As is, it seems to modify Virginia. Answer A is incorrect because the phrase isn't correct as is. Although acceptable grammatically, Virginia belongs with Myra, not the Mud River. The Mud River may flow through several states, not just Virginia. Answers C, D, and E are all incorrect because they omit important information.

Question 12

Answer D is correct because the pronoun "their" does not match the indefinite pronoun, "everyone," in number. "Everyone" is singular; "their" is plural.

The park is usually more crowded and noisier on nice days when everyone shows up with <u>his or her</u> kids and dogs.

Question 13

Answer C is correct; you should avoid clichés. The phrase is also an idiom, but in either case, you could completely omit the phrase and not harm the integrity of the sentence.

We thought the birds might reject this new seed, but none of the seed is left.

Question 14

Answer B is correct. The pronoun "he" isn't necessary. Of course, if you omit the pronoun, you must change the tense of the verb "wrote." Or, you could separate the two complete thoughts with a semicolon because in this case, the second thought develops the first.

Lincoln Steffens was the pioneer investigative reporter, writing fearlessly on the abuses of government.

Lincoln Steffens was the pioneer investigative reporter; he wrote fearlessly on the abuses of government.

Question 15

Answer C is correct. The verb tense in phase C is incorrect. The first verb phrase (B) is perfect present; the second (C) is progressive past. Verb tense must be parallel throughout the sentence. As a side note, if you were really using this sentence in an essay, you would want to define de facto.

Until Woodrow Wilson was elected President, the United States had been in the habit of recognizing de facto governments.

Question 16

Answer E is correct. This sentence is a bit wordy, but there are no grammatical mistakes.

The new family home was only one story, not terribly large, and run down, but had a nice view.

Question 17

Answer D is correct. The comparative phrase "than education" should follow its introductory phrase. You might be tempted to delete B, but there's nothing wrong with it. You should avoid repetition generally, but occasionally it works well to emphasize a point.

Success in business, any business, no matter how small, played a more important role than education in the immigrant's daily life.

Question 18

Answer C is correct. Both of the ending prepositional phrases "of them" and "for herself" could be considered unnecessary. However, removing "for herself" changes the tone of the sentence a tad too much.

Gems are priceless in her culture, but she kept none for herself.

Question 19

Answer A is correct. The phrase "is to be" is passive. Use active voice. She isn't performing the action, which is the induction. In this case, the subject, whoever is doing the induction, is implied.

We will induct her as an initiate at noon on the first Sunday of March.

Question 20

Answer A is correct. Although it isn't grammatically incorrect, you should never use the phrase "in conclusion." Your reader knows you're done—if the reader doesn't know you're done, the rest of the essay needs a thorough edit.

Bertha von Suttner profoundly influenced Alfred Nobel, despite the fact that she married someone else.

Question 21

Answer C is correct. You should consider deleting this redundant phrase altogether. It is unnecessary and makes an already wordy sentence worse. This problem may not be readily apparent, but the process of elimination might help. Because none of the other phrases appear to have any grammatical problems, omit each phrase from the sentence, one-by-one. The sentence is strong and stands fine without C.

In 1888, Massachusetts became the first state to use ballots that contained the names of all the candidates instead of using different colored ballots for each candidate.

Question 22

Answer A is correct. The first phrase is a misplaced participial phrase. This is easy to do when the subject is assumed, as it is in this subject. As is, the sentence literally means that the thunder and lightning were running madly through the forest.

She ran madly through the forest as the thunder shook the earth and the lightning pierced the night sky.

Question 23

Answer C is correct. A series of items should be parallel. None of the other verbs are modified by an adverb. To make the sentence parallel, omit "calmly."

Before you say something you'll regret, take a deep breathe, clear your mind, and count to 10.

Question 24

Answer D is correct. The pronoun "it" is too far from its antecedent "clock." Although you know perfectly well what "it" refers to, you should still replace the pronoun with a noun.

Cinderella looked at the clock but didn't realize it was midnight until she heard the clock chime.

Question 25

Answer C is correct. The pronoun "his" doesn't agree in number with "they." This is a tricky one because the phrase "to be the first" tends to make you think in singular terms.

Sam and Tom raced to the frozen Mississippi where they scrambled to be the first to don their skates and meet the ice.

Question 26

Answer B is correct. The verb phrase is passive. This one's a bit harder to find. The real subject of the sentence is "the fear," but the wording might make you think that "the excitement" is the subject.

The fear that the small and weak child might not survive the night challenged the excitement of the new baby's arrival.

Question 27

Answer B is correct. This sentence would benefit from a transition, but "subsequently" is the wrong one. Transitions must match the tone of the sentence. "Subsequently" means in order of, not because of.

John had a talent for business and consequently met with great financial success, but he had little patience for family.

Question 28

Answer E is correct because nothing is grammatically wrong with this sentence.

Samuel Clemens wrote under the pen name Mark Twain, which was a river-piloting term for deep, safe water.

Question 29

Answer D is correct. The problem is the pronoun "they." First, it's unclear which antecedent "he" refers to, although you get the gist of the sentence. Second, "he" is singular. Is the word "any," which is used earlier in the sentence to modify the antecedent, singular or plural? Sometimes a word can be either singular or plural, and when that's the case, you must refer to the noun for more help. In this case, the noun is presidential nominations—plural. Besides, even in these days when political correctness is running amuck, it really is a bit insensitive to use the pronoun "he" in reference to the Supreme Court justices, even when it is grammatically correct. Although you won't run into this last problem on the exam, you might want to steer clear of it on the essay portion of your exam. Even though the readers are trained to look for specific keys, you never know when something that small might trigger a negative response.

The United States Constitution requires the Senate to confirm any presidential nominations to the Supreme Court before they can actually be sworn into office.

Question 30

Answer B is correct. The two thoughts just don't mesh. It's okay to keep the sentence; it helps to develop the main thesis. However, the two phrases must be similar in subject and nature if you're going to use them in a comparative form. Answer A is incorrect; the sentence doesn't repeat the first; it helps develop the first. Answer C is incorrect; the sentence isn't too wordy. A long sentence is acceptable as long as all the words are truly needed. Answer D is incorrect. The mood needs to be set right at the beginning for this essay. Answer E is incorrect, although in the end, you might actually move this statement to the conclusion after you've decided whether you wanted to use "machinery" or "dance" as the subject.

Question 31

Answer E is correct. The passage needs to transition from the thesis—that life is a delicate balance—to the plight of the sea otters and what happened when the balance of their ecosystem was altered. Answer A is incorrect because the paragraph break, as is, is sound. Answer B is incorrect because it isn't true. Answers C and D are incorrect because neither sentence works as a transition. Sentence 7 has promise, but as is, won't do.

Question 32

Answer D is correct. A quick general statement is in order here to let the reader know that the explanation is coming. Answer A is incorrect; the sentence is important. Answer B is incorrect. You might replace the pronoun, but it won't improve the problem discussed in the question. Answer C is incorrect. The suggestion is a good one, but it doesn't resolve the problem in the question. Answer E is incorrect. The sentence is grammatically sound.

Question 33

Answer E is correct. Both would improve the sentence. Answer A is incorrect because it's incomplete. Remember, you're looking for the best answer, not the first one that works. Answer B is incorrect; you don't need two sentences when one will do. Answer C is incorrect; "feed" is vital to the whole discussion. Answer D is incorrect because it's incomplete.

Question 34

Answer A is correct. You need to make the point that they both share the same food source and that tipping the balance didn't favor one or the other, but actually devastated both populations. Answer B is incorrect. Combining the sentences would create a very long sentence, which is fine if it's clear and strong. However, sentence 9 already makes the point that the sea urchins eat kelp. Answer C is incorrect. Moving the sentence doesn't help the problem. Answer D is incorrect. Deleting the sentence won't resolve the problem of making the connection between the primary food source and the loss of balance.

Question 35

Answer D is correct. The passage still needs a lot of work—it needs a final paragraph to pull everything together. Answer A is incorrect because the passage isn't done. Answer B is incorrect. The fate might not be known. If it is, a sentence about it would be good, but it would not be the basis of the entire concluding paragraph. Answer C is incorrect because there's not a good transition into the concluding paragraph. Answer E is incorrect. Moving those sentences does set up a concluding paragraph, but you still need a final paragraph.

Section 5

Question 1

Answer B is correct because that sentence is the most logical. There's really no clue here—you either know the word or you don't. It would be difficult to guess. Process of elimination might help, but chances are, if you don't know the meaning of "exception," you won't know the other words. Answers A, C, D, and E are all incorrect because the thought would be illogical.

Question 2

Answer A is correct because the pair presents the most appropriate sentence. You must understand the nature of the word pledge and how you go about keeping a pledge—you honor a pledge. Answers B, C, and E are all incorrect because the words simply do not go together as well as A's. Answer D is incorrect because broken changes the meaning of the sentence.

Question 3

Answer C is correct because the pair presents the most logical sentence. If you're lucky enough to know Soviet history and politics, you could quickly eliminate answers A, B, D, and E because the equivalent office in the USSR is the General Secretary. If you don't know the Soviet political system, you can still use the process of elimination. Answer A is incorrect because it assumes that the assassin became the leader, and nothing in the sentence supports that. Although the sentence is logical enough, it isn't as strong as C. Answer B is incorrect because it's illogical. If Gorbachev inaugurated Chernenko, the following phrase would be illogical. Answer D is incorrect because "preceded" is actually an antonym for "succeeded" in this context. Answer E is incorrect because it isn't as strong as the verb "succeeded."

Question 4

Answer A is correct. The second phrase lends a clue by referring to the time period, decade. Thus, you should be able to deduce that the missing word has a connotation of measuring time, or at least time. Answers B, C, and D are incorrect. Even though they might all fit logically, none of them create the strongest sentence within the context of the second phrase. Answer E is incorrect because the sentence would be illogical.

Question 5

Answer E is correct because the two words work together to form the strongest possible sentence. The terms support one another. Answers A and B are incorrect. Their logic is sound enough, but the end result isn't as strong as E. Answer C is incorrect; "pondered" doesn't fit the tone of the sentence. Answer D is incorrect because "hullabaloo" has a connotation of chaos.

Question 6

Answer D is correct because it most appropriately expresses the political structure. Answers A and B are incorrect. They are synonyms, but "dominion" is stronger. Answers C and E are incorrect because they change the meaning of the sentence.

Question 7

Answer B is correct because the terms support one another within the context of the sentence, using the most appropriate terms for the subject. Answers A, C, and D are incorrect. The paired words might create a logical sentence, but the words aren't as appropriate to the discussion as B. Answer E is incorrect because it uses the term "circumnavigate" incorrectly.

Question 8

Answer C is correct because it creates the most logical sentence. The second phrase, "safeguarding the rights of all citizens," is your best clue because "safeguarding" is a synonym for "bulwark." Answers A, B, and D are all incorrect. They might create a logical sentence, but the result is not as strong as C, given the context of the second phrase. Answer E is incorrect because it's illogical.

Question 9

Answer E is correct because these two areas encompass the two western frontiers in 1860. Answer A is incorrect because neither were considered frontiers in 1860. Answers B and C are incorrect because they are both incomplete. Answer D is incorrect because these areas were not considered a frontier.

Question 10

Answer A is correct because the crux of the entire paragraph is the emptiness of the area between the two existing frontiers. Answer B is incorrect because it isn't as specific as A. Answers C and D are incorrect—the discussion is of the land, not the people settling it. Answer E is incorrect. The paragraph isn't about discovering; it's a comparison of existing settlements and the empty land in between.

Question 11

Answer C is the most correct interpretation of the term "sexual license" within the context of the passage. Answer A is incorrect. The sexual revolution saw an increase in promiscuity, but it wasn't the essence of the philosophy. Answer B is incorrect because no one can escape the consequences. Answer D is incorrect because some of the behavior was very irresponsible, even by today's standards. Answer E is incorrect because prostitution plays no part in the philosophy.

Question 12

Answer D is the most correct answer. There was no cure for AIDS. The only way to slow the spread was to educate the next generation. Answer A is incorrect because it's incomplete. Answers B and C are incorrect because they're not supported by the passage. Answer E is incomplete because it's vague.

Question 13

Answer D is correct. The author states that Washington became convinced of the colonists' position but that he still hoped that the British would realize they were making a "mistake" and that war only arrived "at length." Answer A is incorrect because that contradicts the assertion that Washington was not a sudden clamorer for independence. Answer B is incorrect because the information in the passage is that Washington was asked to command the army, not that he lobbied for the post. Answer C is incorrect because the author made it clear that his devotion to independence was a gradual process. Answer E is incorrect because the mistake mentioned in the passage is that of the British, not of the colonists.

Question 14

Answer C is correct. The best way to get this one right is to substitute the given answers back into the original sentence and to see which of them does not change the meaning of the paragraph. The word "scrupulous" is also a clue that the correct answer involves making a principled choice, which only fits answer C.

Question 15

Answer C is correct. To get this one right, follow the author's argument: Washington insisted on respect and dignity for the office. His enemies sneered at this. Things might have been different were Jefferson the first president. This makes it clear that the reason for mentioning Jefferson is to note that different men would have left a different stamp on the presidency— and rules out answer E, which directly contradicts that assertion. Answers A, B, and D are potentially true, but they are not directly supported by the passage.

Question 16

Answer B is correct. The three monarchs that the author lists are respectively, vicious, crazy, and insane. The author is writing in glowing terms about Washington, so it is unlikely that he would say anything positive about such a collection of monarchs. Answer B is the only answer that casts these monarchs in a negative light.

Question 17

Answer B is correct. The phrase referring to a deficiency follows directly after a sentence stating that Washington had a lack of imagination. The other answers are incorrect; they all contain words from the paragraph, but none that are referred to from that phrase.

Question 18

Answer D is correct. The author of the passage states that well-intentioned people argued that Washington never swore in order to portray him as a faultless being, and then goes on to give evidence that Washington swore. The logical conclusion from this set of statements is that Washington was not a faultless being. Answer A is incorrect because of the evidence presented that Washington swore. Answers B and E are incorrect because those are statements about the well-intentioned people, not about Washington. Answer C is incorrect because the portion of the sentence about attracting attention refers to arguments, not to Washington.

Question 19

Answer A is correct. A knowledge of the word "propriety" (which means "the quality of being proper") will help you focus in on the right answer immediately; only answers A and D concern what is right. From the construction of the sentence, A is a better choice because the sentence is not solely about the speaker.

Question 20

Answer D is correct. The author of the passage argues that Washington maintained an unruffled spirit despite his love for life because of his faith in an afterlife. The key word "but" tips you off that he feels this faith is necessary for the unruffled spirit. Answer A is contradicted because the passage says Washington enjoyed life even though he regarded death with calmness. Answer B is incorrect because no connection is stated between the love for life and the courage. Answer C is incorrect because the courage referred to in the passage is not tied to the judgment of posterity. Answer E is incorrect because the passage's author doesn't tell readers what they should believe; it only states what Washington did believe.

Question 21

Answer E is correct. The author of passage 2 goes to some effort to portray Washington as a human being with human failings, even though he also mentions superior qualities that Washington had. By contrast, the final paragraph of passage 1 paints Washington as an almost superhuman figure. Thus the author of passage 2 would probably think the author of passage 1 was overstating the case. Answer A is incorrect because the paragraph is a matter of opinion, not fact. Answer B is incorrect because it's exactly the reverse of the truth. Answer C is incorrect because no humor is implied. Answer D is incorrect because "prescient" means "having knowledge of the future," which is inappropriate here.

Question 22

Answer D is correct. Passage 1 speaks of Washington's silence in the first paragraph (where the author calls him taciturn), and passage 2 mentions Washington's silence at the start of its second paragraph. Answers B and E are true of the first passage, but Washington's courage and dignity in office are not mentioned in the second passage. Answers A and C are true of the second passage, but Washington's temper and faith are not mentioned by the first author.

Question 23

Answer A is correct. The author of the first passage is mainly concerned with identifying Washington's place in the broad sweep of history, whereas the second passage provides a more personal evaluation of Washington as a man. Answer B is incorrect because neither passage gives preference to acts over words. Answer C is incorrect because both authors credit Washington as being a victorious military leader. Answers D and E are incorrect because passage 1, not passage 2, concentrates more heavily on those areas.

Question 24

Answer C is correct. The first passage takes a very positive view of Washington and cites his neighbors and acquaintances to support this view. There's no hint of scandal in anything the first author says, nor any indication that he views Washington as imperfect. Answers A, D, and E are incorrect because they assume the truth of the scandals. Answer B is incorrect because there's no indication that the author of the passage would like to hide evidence.

Section 6

Question 1

Answer A is correct. To solve, multiply the second equation by –2 and add it to the first equation. This cancels out the x term, and the remaining equation is 3y = 9. Divide by 3 to confirm y = 3.

Question 2

Answer C is correct. The acute angles of an isosceles right triangle are each 45°. (If you don't remember this, you can determine it by knowing the total angles in the triangle add up to 180°—the right angle itself is 90°, and the other two angles are equal.) Because ∠x and ∠ACB are alternating interior angles of a line through B and C cutting across parallel lines, they must be equal. So x is also 45°.

Question 3

Answer D is correct. Remember, to raise a power to another power, you multiply the exponents together, so answer D is equivalent to 3^9. This is clearly much larger than any of the other choices, though you can confirm that with your calculator if you're unsure of the result (which is 19,683).

Question 4

Answer B is correct. You should be able to answer this one as fast as you can read the question; don't get tricked into performing any calculations or drawing anything. Two points in the plane always define precisely one line.

Question 5

Answer C is correct. You don't actually need the graph to answer this question. Start from what you know and reason to what you need: If there are 20 mammals and 4 times as many birds as mammals, there are 80 birds. If there are $\frac{3}{4}$ as many reptiles as mammals, there are 60 reptiles. If there are the same number of reptiles and fish, there are 60 fish.

Question 6

Answer C is correct. The easiest way to solve this one is probably to just write down a list of prime numbers and inspect to see which set of four sums to about 72. The first few primes are 2, 3, 5, 7, 11, 13, 17, 19, 23, 29, and 31. A little work with your calculator will show that 13 + 17 + 19 + 23 = 72. Then take a look at the question—it asks for the smallest of the four, so the answer is 13.

Question 7

Answer D is correct. By the Pythagorean Theorem, AC is $\sqrt{(3^2 + 4^2)} = 5$. (You may also just recognize the 3-4-5 triangle.) If the center of the circle lies on this line, AC is a diameter of the circle, and the circumference is π times the diameter of the circle.

Question 8

Answer E is correct. If the mean of all 10 numbers is 18, the sum of all 10 numbers is 180 (because the mean is the sum divided by the count). Similarly, the sum of the remaining 7 numbers is $7 \times 22 = 154$. The three removed numbers must account for the difference between 180 and 154, which is 26.

Question 9

Answer A is correct. If the answer isn't immediately evident, you can substitute x and y into the function definition for each answer to simplify. Answer A evaluates to 18, B to 0, C to 9, D to 0, and E to 0. Thus A is largest.

Question 10

Answer B is correct. Because the triangles are similar, their sides have a constant ratio. From the information given, BC = 2. Because BD = 1, this means that the large triangle is twice as large as the small triangle. Thus DE = .5(AC) = .5(1.5) = .75. The area of CDEF is then $.75 \times 1 = .75$.

Question 11

Answer D is correct. You can use the information about the intersections to determine two points on the line by finding the corresponding points on the curve. For x = –1, $x^2 = 1$, and for x = 3, $x^2 = 9$. So (–1, 1) and (3, 9) are two points on the curve. Now recognize from the equation that the desired quantity, *a*, is the slope of the line. You can figure the slope from the expression "rise over run" as follows:

$$a = \frac{(9-1)}{(3--1)}$$

$$a = \frac{(9-1)}{(3+1)}$$

$$a = \frac{8}{4}$$

$$a = 2$$

Question 12

Answer B is correct. Start by considering *z*. 3 🍎 z = 5 means $|3 - z| = 5$. From that, $3 - z = 5$ or $3 - z = -5$, giving two possible values for z (–2 and 8). Now take each of these two possible *z* values and repeat the process for *w*. This leads to four possible equations for *w*:

➤ –2 – w = 2

➤ –2 – w = –2

➤ 8 – w = 2

➤ 8 – w = –2

The four possible values of *w* are then –4, 0, 6, and 10. Only one of these appears in the answer set, so B is the correct answer.

Question 13

Answer D is correct. Knowing the zeroes of the polynomial lets you immediately determine that its factors are x + 4 and x + 2. This means that the actual polynomial $f(x) = (x + 4)(x + 2) = x^2 + 6x + 8$. So $f(9) = 9^2 + 6(9) + 8 = 143$.

Question 14

Answer C is correct. When tossing a coin eight times, there are eight different ways in which you can get a single head: The first toss may come up heads, or the second, and so on. The eight tosses are independent events each with two possible states, so the total number of different possible results is $2^8 = 256$. The probability of a single head is then

$$\frac{8}{256} = \frac{1}{32}$$

Question 15

Answer D is correct. The volume of a right circular cylinder is $\pi r^2 h$. (This is one of the formulas that the SAT gives you at the start of each math section.) The cylinder in the question has a diameter of 2 units, so its radius is 1 unit. With a height of 2, that means its volume is 2π. For a cube to have the same volume, its side must be the cube root of this quantity, which is answer D.

Question 16

Answer B is correct. The two white faces are opposite one another on the cube. This means that they cannot be adjacent to one another when the cube is flattened out to the plane, no matter how the flattening is done.

Question 17

Answer C is correct. If m and n are even integers, their sum and difference must also be even integers. But $(m + n)/2$ can be odd—for example, substitute $m = 4$ and $n = 2$ to get 3, which is an odd number.

Question 18

Answer B is correct. Start by calculating the area of the entire circle. From the formula $A = \pi r^2$, this area is 25π. The sector is thus $\frac{1}{5}$ of the circle, and its arc must be $\frac{1}{5}$ of the total circumference. Calculate the circumference from the formula $c = \pi d = 2\pi r$. The circumference is thus 10π, so the length of the arc must be 2π.

Question 19

Answer C is correct. There are $30 \times 29 \times 28 = 24{,}360$ ways to select three books from the shelf. But in composing sets, the order of books doesn't matter. For each set of three books, there are six different ways to get the set; if you call the books A, B, and C, they are

➤ A B C

➤ A C B

➤ B A C

➤ B C A

➤ C A B

➤ C B A

So the final answer is $\dfrac{24{,}360}{6} = 4{,}060$.

Question 20

Answer C is correct. If the diameter of the circle is an integer, its radius is an exact multiple of .5. Given the formula for the area of a circle, $A = \pi r^2$, you know that $r = \sqrt{(A/\pi)}$. For $A = 10$, this means $r = 1.79$ is the largest radius that would work. So the possible radii that will work here are 1.5, 1.0, and .5.

Section 7

Question 1

Answer B is the most correct answer because corrosive chemicals have the potential to be dangerous if they touch your skin or get in your eyes. Answers A, C, and D are all incorrect because they create illogical statements. Answer E is incorrect because "acrid" doesn't fulfill the sentence's purpose. Chemicals might stink, but smell alone won't hurt you.

Question 2

Answer A is the most appropriate response. You might expect the public to be mistrustful and cautious about any politician's promises, not just those involved in scandal. Answers B, C, and E are incorrect because they aren't believable within the context of the sentence. Answer D is incorrect because it's illogical—being silent is probably the last thing the public would be.

Question 3

Answer E is correct because it creates the strongest most logical sentence of all the sets. Answer A is incorrect because the clerk complained about the work—surely the clerk wouldn't find the work relaxing. Answer B is incorrect because it's a tad illogical. Reading illegible symbols doesn't sound like dangerous work unless you're in the middle of a science fiction meltdown. Sometimes you just have to apply a little common sense. Answer C is incorrect because "impenetrable" is an inappropriate adjective for the noun "symbol." Answer D is incorrect for the same reason as A. It's not likely the clerk would complain about interesting work.

Question 4

Answer B is correct. The sentence suggests a woman of many talents, and that would be "eclectic." Answer A is incorrect. If you were tempted to choose A, read the sentence again and then review the definitions of both "eccentric" and "eclectic." Although the same person might be both, the sentence isn't a good definition of an eccentric person. Answers C, D, and E are incorrect because the sentence would be illogical.

Question 5

Answer D is correct. The sentence is looking for a pair of antonyms, and this pair is the only pair of true antonyms. Answers A and C are incorrect. You can easily eliminate them because they're not good antonym pairs. Answer B is incorrect because "aloof" and "reticent" are synonyms. Answer E is incorrect because neither word fits, nor are they antonyms.

Question 6

Answer E is correct. Although "dogmatic" is not necessarily a bad thing to be, the context of the sentence tells you that in this case, it is. Answer A is incorrect because "notorious" is illogically used in this context. Answer B is incorrect because the two words clash instead of support one another. Answers C and D are incorrect because at least one of the words has a positive connotation.

Question 7

Answer E is correct. The question asks specifically about the first paragraph, so it needs to be answered based only on information in that paragraph. Answer A is incorrect because, although the paragraph mentions that some people do not wish him well, it's not possible to conclude that there are many of those people. Answer B is incorrect because the information on his loving leisure and women is later in the passage. Answer C is incorrect because the envy mentioned is that of other people, not of Harrison Blair. Answer D is incorrect because the information that he wrote a book with an unusual treatment of its subject implies that he is not lacking in imagination. That leaves answer E, which is a reasonable conclusion from the paragraph.

Question 8

Answer D is correct. The passage makes it clear that the book was successful because Blair is talented and that its success was deserved. Thus you need to pick a positive synonym from the list. Only "unexpected" fits. Answers A, B, C, and E are incorrect because they all imply that the book's success was undeserved.

Question 9

Answer B is correct. If you take some notes as you read the passage, you'll discover that Blair was a rich young man who was expected to just coast through college, and he was a "jock" to boot. But his undergraduate work in English was good enough that those who knew about it were not surprised by the success of his book. Thus his teachers were impressed despite themselves. The other answers require you to guess at facts that are not present in the passage or not supported by what is present.

Question 10

Answer E is correct. You can get this one right if you know the meaning of either "vouchsafed" or "remonstrated" (or both, of course). Even if you don't, you should be able to eliminate a couple of the choices to increase your chance of guessing properly. The statement isn't a promise, so answer A is unlikely to be correct even if you know nothing about the words. Similarly, there's no hint of an offer, which eliminates answer C.

Question 11

Answer A is correct. Answer B is incorrect because there's no evidence in the passage of Blair spending excessively. Answer C is incorrect because the passage does not speak of any delaying behavior. Answer D is incorrect because the evidence in the passage is that Blair is not spoiled; rather, he is making his way through the world on his own. Answer E is incorrect because the author paints Blair in a positive light.

Question 12

Answer E is correct. "Sympathy" refers to sharing the feelings of another, and by calling it a technical sympathy, the author implies that it was developed as part of his being a writer. (This is further confirmed by the use of the word "vocation.") Answer A is incorrect based on a poor reading of the word "technical." Answers B and C are based on other possible meanings of "sympathy" that do not fit the passage. Answer D is incorrect; although possibly true, this explanation does not fit the words in question.

Question 13

Answer B is correct. Though any of the answers given might be a plausible explanation for wanting a smaller room, the clerk explains late in the passage that the expense of staying prevents her from finishing her work. The mentions of her shabby hat and bag serve to emphasize her poverty. This implies that a smaller room, being less expensive, is preferable to her.

Question 14

Answer C is correct. In the context of the passage, Blair is annoyed because the clerk has presumed to ask him an insulting question ("familiarity" here means "impropriety"). Answers A, D, and E are incorrect because the passage does not show the clerk with these qualities. Answer B is incorrect; although the clerk is said to be amused, it doesn't mean that he is attempting to be funny.

Question 15

Answer D is correct. The reasonable conclusion from the start of the passage is that Blair has come to the island to pursue his own work on Indians; he was thus interested to find out that someone else was there on a similar pursuit. The other answers are not supported by the text, though you might find any of them reasonable conclusions on their own.

Question 16

Answer A is correct. The author spends much of the passage establishing that Blair is an unusually good author and that he makes writing his vocation. Answers B and C are incorrect; though his looks and money are mentioned in passing, they are not portrayed as his essential qualities. The same applies to his sporting ability (answer E). Answer D is incorrect because there is not enough information in the passage to draw a conclusion about his attention to detail.

Question 17

Answer C is correct. Answers A, D, and E are incorrect because the author does not give much, if any, detail of the setting of the story in this passage. Answer B is incorrect because Blair's motivations are not established in the passage beyond a cryptic reference to a letter from the Atlantic. Answer C fits because most of the passage is concerned with introducing and describing characters in the story.

Question 18

Answer C is correct. Answers A, D, and E are all statements that are supported by the passage—which means that the author is not concerned with counteracting them. There's no evidence one way or the other as to the author's view of vacation spots, which eliminates answer B. The passage directly contradicts answer C by showing how Blair works hard despite inherited wealth, so the author is evidently concerned with counteracting this idea.

Question 19

Answer B is correct. By writing about Blair's father, the author is able to discuss the type of man Blair is and to give Blair's reason for working a menial job. Answer A is incorrect because the father and son are portrayed as distinctly different. Answer C is incorrect because there is no indication of this fact in the passage. Answer D is incorrect because the father, though wealthy, is not described in terms that would brand him a miser. Answer E is incorrect because you can't know from the passage whether family plays a role in the remaining story or not.

Section 8

Question 1

Answer D is correct. The main thing to watch for in this sort of problem is not to go too fast and answer the wrong question. In this case, you know that $.4x = 10$, so $x = 10 .4 = 25$. Then $3x + 7 = 3 \times 25 + 7 = 82$.

Question 2

Answer B is correct. Because the angles of a triangle add up to $180°$, you know that $\angle ACB = 60°$. $\angle DEC$ is then also $60°$ because it is a vertical angle to $\angle ACB$. Then $3x = 60°$, so $x = 20°$.

Question 3

Answer C is correct. No matter how you attempt to draw an axis for reflective symmetry, there is no way to divide the figure into two mirror images. But a rotation of $180°$ leaves the figure unchanged, so it has rotational symmetry.

Question 4

Answer D is correct. Solve the inequality for x:

$-4x + 12 < 16$

$-4x < 4$

$x > -1$

Remember, when you multiply or divide an inequality by a negative number, you must change the direction of the inequality.

Question 5

Answer D is correct. After three quizzes, the total points earned by the student are $88 \times 3 = 264$. For an average of 90, with the exam counting for two quizzes, she must have a total of $90 \times 5 = 450$ points. This means that 186 points must come from the final exam. Divide that by 2 to get the final exam score of 93.

Question 6

Answer B is correct. Increasing the price by 10% sets the new price to $90 + (.1 \times 90) = 99$. But then decreasing by 10% does not return to the original price because the 10% is based on the new price. So the final price is $99 - (.1 \times 99) = 89.1$.

Question 7

Answer D is correct. You don't actually need to do any calculations to solve this one. Remember, the area of a triangle is $\frac{1}{2}$ bh and the area of a parallelogram is bh. The triangle and the parallelogram share the same base and the same height, so the area of the parallelogram is simply twice the area of the triangle.

Question 8

Answer C is correct. The percent increase is measured by the amount of change compared to the base year. Although it's impossible to calculate this precisely for each pair of years on the graph, it's obvious that the 1988 to 1989 change is the largest proportion of its base year.

Question 9

Answer E is correct. Each of the blocks has a volume of $1 \times 1 \times .5 = .5$. The box itself has a volume of $12 \times 12 \times 12 = 1,728$. Thus, you will need $\frac{1,728}{.5} = 3,456$ blocks to fill the box.

Question 10

Answer D is correct. To see this, express each of the integers in terms of a. They then become

➤ a

➤ a + 1

➤ a + 2

➤ a + 3

➤ a + 4

The sum of these integers is then 5a + 10, or 5(a + 2). With a suitable choice of *a*, that can be made to equal any value that is a multiple of 5. The answer is the one choice in the list that is not a multiple of 5.

Question 11

Answer B is correct. Ignore the circle and just concentrate on the two squares. The outer square has an area of 4, so its side is equal to 2, as is its height. This is also the diagonal of the inner square. From the Pythagorean Theorem, you know that the diagonal of a square is $\sqrt{2}$ times the side, so the sides of the small square are $2/\sqrt{2} = \sqrt{2}$. Then the area of the inner square is $\sqrt{2} \times \sqrt{2} = 2$. You can also see this by geometric reasoning: The four triangles surrounding the inner square have a total area exactly equal to that of the inner square, so each of them accounts for half of the total area of the outer square.

Question 12

Answer B is correct. Remember, the formula for the nth term of an arithmetical sequence is a + (n – 1) × b. In this case, the first term is 2, which gives 2 for *a*. Plugging in 6 for the second term then gives

6 = 2 + (2 – 1) × b

4 = b

Now, knowing *a* and *b*, you can calculate the 49th and 50th terms of the series:

2 + (49 – 1) × 4 = 194

2 + (50 – 1) × 4 = 198

The sum of these two numbers, 392, is the desired answer.

Question 13

Answer E is correct. Start by calculating the side of each square by taking the square root of the area. The smaller square then has a side of 2, and the larger square has a side of 4. The perimeters are four times the side, 8 and 16, respectively. Then the ratio of the perimeters is 8:16, which reduces to 1:2.

Question 14

Answer C is correct. Suppose that the roll of film were sufficient to take only a single picture; the cost per picture would then be simply f. If it could take two pictures, each picture would cost half as much, or $\frac{f}{2}$. Similarly, if the roll could take three pictures, they would each take $\frac{1}{3}$ as much, or $\frac{f}{3}$. Note the progression here; the number of pictures is the denominator. So the answer is $\frac{f}{p}$.

Question 15

Answer B is correct. You need to treat this as a weighted average problem rather than simply taking the mean of the two speeds, because the time spent en route is different on the two legs of the trip. On the way out, the plane flies 2,000 miles at 400 miles per hour, which takes 5 hours. On the way back, the plane flies 2,000 miles at 500 miles per hour, which takes 4 hours. The total flight is thus 4000 miles in 9 hours, for an average of $444\frac{4}{9}$ miles per hour.

Question 16

Answer A is correct. Each triangle must be an equilateral triangle because it is composed of three identical sides. Because of the symmetry of the figure, the line segment AB will go through the center of two sides of the square and will include the height of each triangle. Consider the right triangle made up by one side of the equilateral triangle, half of the side of the square, and the height of the triangle. You can now calculate the height using the Pythagorean Theorem:

$$1^2 = h^2 + \left(\frac{1}{2}\right)^2$$

$$h^2 = 1 - \frac{1}{4}$$

$$h = \sqrt{\frac{3}{4}} = \frac{\sqrt{3}}{2}$$

The desired distance is then $2h + 1$, or $1 + \sqrt{3}$.

Section 9

Question 1

Answer C is correct. Although the sentence doesn't break any concrete grammar rules as is, the phrase "that which you" is terribly wordy. Answer A is incorrect because the phrase is incorrect as is. Answer B is incorrect because it omits the pronoun "you." Answer D is incorrect because the use of "is" instead of "you" makes the sentence awkward. Answer E is incorrect because it's just horrible. If you selected E, go directly to jail and do not pass Go.

Question 2

Answer D is correct. Repeating the noun is redundant (although not actually breaking any rules). Answer A is incorrect because the phrase could be better. Answers B, C, and E are all incorrect, although they would all work grammatically. Remember, you're not looking for just any right answer. You're look for the best response.

Question 3

Answer B is correct. The pronoun "their" doesn't match the noun, "band," in number. In this case, "band" is singular, although it's composed of many individuals. Answer A is incorrect because the phrase isn't correct as is. When using the phrase "in addition to," the verb and pronouns must match the first noun in tense and number. "Band" is singular; "are" is plural. Answers C, D, and E are all incorrect because they change the nature of the sentence.

Question 4

Answer E is correct. Although the sentence isn't grammatically incorrect, the use of the possessive pronoun "their" makes the sentence stronger. Answer A is incorrect, because the original phrase isn't as strong as E. Answer B is incorrect, replacing "so" with "and" actually changes the tone of the sentence, although it isn't incorrect. Answer C is incorrect because it doesn't correct the problem. Answer D is incorrect because there's nothing in the sentence to indicate the teacher's sex.

Question 5

Answer B is correct. "Neither of the girls" in itself is an incorrect usage, although it seems perfectly fine. "Neither" is singular; "of the girls" implies plural. Answer A is incorrect because the phrase isn't correct as is. Answer C and D are incorrect because "none" is plural and the verb "is" is singular. You have to correct the underlined portion, so you have to work with the rest of the sentence as is. Answer E is incorrect even though it's grammatically correct. The girls aren't mentioned by name; you can't make stuff up.

Question 6

Answer C is correct. When combining a plural and a singular subject with neither and nor, the verb must match the second subject. In this case, the verb is singular, so transposing "cows" and "dog" does the trick. Answer A is incorrect because the phrase isn't correct as is. Answer B is incorrect because it changes the nature of the sentence. We don't know about the rest of the animals. We only have information about the cows and the dog. Answer D is incorrect as using either/or in this context is wrong. Answer E is incorrect because you can't take liberties with the subject. The sentence says that there's more than one cow—you have to work with that.

Question 7

Answer D is correct. The preposition "up" isn't necessary. Answer A is incorrect because the phrase isn't correct as is. Answers B and E are incorrect because there's no need to change the wording. Answer C is incorrect because it's illogical. Something doesn't "take sprout"—it takes root.

Question 8

Answer B is correct. There are two things going on with this answer. First, the serial items should be parallel. Second, repeating the word "different" with each item is acceptable, but redundant given the prior use of the word "diverse." Answer A is incorrect because the phrase isn't correct as is. Answers C and D are incorrect because they're not parallel. If you are going to use the adjective "different," you'll need to repeat it with each item. Answer E is incorrect because there's no need to include the word "and" before each subsequent item.

Question 9

Answer C is correct. Depending on the context, some verbs are timeless. When this is the case, you should always use present tense. God is timeless. The transcendentalists may no longer be a powerful movement in modern times, but their God is just as timeless as any modern rendition. This is a hard one—don't feel bad if you missed it. Answer A is incorrect because it isn't correct as is. Answer B is incorrect because changing the verb "believe" to present tense isn't necessary. Answer D is incorrect because it changes the meaning of the sentence. Answer E is incorrect as the word "that" is inconsequential in the sentence—its use is preferential, not incorrect.

Question 10

Answer D is correct. This one's a bit tricky. As is, the sentence doesn't really sound wrong. However, the phrase "By 1929" implies an ongoing state. The date clues us in that the ongoing state is in the past. We know the event occurred in the past, but the phrase "by 1929" is inconclusive. It is difficult to discern from the one sentence if the phrase indicates an end or just a stage of this spending phase. The most appropriate tense should be progressive past—which indicates an ongoing state in the past. The verb phrase "had been spending" is perfect past—indicating an event that began and ended in the past. Even if you decide that the proper verb phrase is present past, keep in mind that this tense is rarely necessary and can usually be rewritten in a clearer form without changing the timing. That's what D does. Even if you decide that the verb tense, as is, is acceptable, D is better. Answer A is incorrect because the phrase isn't correct as is. Answer B is incorrect because it's perfect present, indicating that it began in the past but extends to the present. We don't know that to be true. Answers C and E are incorrect because they're grammatically incorrect. Neither represents a valid verb tense within the context of this sentence.

Question 11

Answer B is correct. The first phrase is a participial phrase, and the rule is: When using a participial phrase to begin a sentence, you must follow the phrase with a comma and then the noun it modifies. As is, the subject is unclear. Who is returning to America: we or he? The clue is in the first phrase. A singular subject is returning to America; therefore, he must be the subject. We did take a bit of license with this one, and you probably won't run into a question quite so ambiguous as this one on the real exam. We're just trying to emphasize the grammatical rule. Answer A is incorrect because the phrase isn't correct as is. We wanted to trick you a bit with answer C, which is incorrect. Remember, the exam will *not* use a preposition at the end of a sentence as an error. Answer D is incorrect because it changes the meaning of the sentence, and the subjects don't match in number. Answer E is incorrect, but you might have been tempted by this one. It is grammatically correct, but it does change the meaning of the sentence more than A.

Question 12

Answer C is correct. The preposition "up" is unnecessary. Answer A is incorrect because the phrase isn't correct as is. Answer B is incorrect because it doesn't omit the unnecessary preposition. Answers D and E are incorrect, even though they are grammatically sound, because it is unnecessary to change so much.

Question 13

Answer B is correct. The prepositional phrase "of post-war Europe" is used as an adjective to further define the subject, which is "The sagging economies." When this is the case, the prepositional can almost always be omitted. Answer A is incorrect because the phrase isn't correct as is. Answer C is incorrect because post-war should describe Europe, not their economies. Answers D and E are incorrect because the noun "economies" isn't the problem.

Question 14

Answer C is correct. When using an adjective in comparative form, precede the adjective with more or most; don't add "er" to the adjective. Answer A is incorrect because the phrase isn't correct as is. Answers B and E are incorrect because the verb "was" and the subject "immigrants" don't match in number. Answer D is incorrect because "most" is not comparative; it is absolute.

12

Practice Exam #2

Self Test

Essay

SECTION 1

Time—25 minutes

Turn to the essay page of your answer sheet to write your ESSAY.

The essay gives you an opportunity to show how effectively you can develop and express ideas. You should, therefore, take care to develop your point of view, present your ideas logically and clearly, and use language precisely.

Your essay must be written on the lines provided on your answer sheet—you will receive no other paper on which to write. You will have enough space if you write on every line, avoid wide margins, and keep your handwriting to a reasonable size. Remember that people who are not familiar with your handwriting will read what you write. Try to write or print so that what you are writing is legible to those readers.

You have twenty-five minutes to write an essay on the topic assigned below. DO NOT WRITE ON ANOTHER TOPIC. AN OFF-TOPIC ESSAY WILL RECEIVE A SCORE OF ZERO.

Think carefully about the issue presented in the following excerpt and the assignment below.

> They say the only thing for sure in life is death and taxes, but there's one more thing you can depend on—and that's change. Sometimes change is rewarding, sometimes painful, but almost always challenging.

Assignment: How does change challenge us? Use reasoning and examples taken from personal reading, studies, experience, or observation to support your position.

DO NOT WRITE YOUR ESSAY IN YOUR TEST BOOK. You will receive credit only for what you write on your answer sheet.

BEGIN WRITING YOUR ESSAY ON THE ESSAY PAGE OF THE ANSWER SHEET.

If you finish before time is called, you may check your work on this section only. Do not turn to any other section in the test.

Section 2

Time—25 minutes

18 Questions

Turn to Section 2 of your answer sheet to answer the questions in this section.

> **Directions:** This section contains two types of questions. You have 25 minutes to complete both types. For questions 1–8, solve each problem and decide which is the best of the choices given. Fill in the corresponding circle on the answer sheet. You can use any available space for scratchwork.

> **Notes:**
>
> **1.** The use of a calculator is permitted.
>
> **2.** All numbers used are real numbers.
>
> **3.** Figures that accompany problems in the test are intended to provide information that is useful in solving the problems. They are drawn as accurately as possible EXCEPT when it is stated in a specific problem that the figure is not drawn to scale. All figures lie in a plane unless otherwise indicated.
>
> **4.** Unless otherwise specified, the domain of any function f is assumed to be the set of real numbers x for which $f(x)$ is a real number.

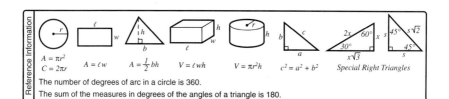

The number of degrees of arc in a circle is 360.
The sum of the measures in degrees of the angles of a triangle is 180.

1. If $2x + y = 15$ and $3x - 4y = -5$, what is y?

(A) −5

(B) 0

(C) 2

(D) 5

(E) 10

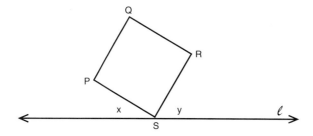

<u>Note</u>: Figure not drawn to scale.

2. In the figure above, ℓ is a line and PQRS is a square. $\angle x$ is 36°. What is $\angle y$?

(A) 16°

(B) 36°

(C) 45°

(D) 54°

(E) 90°

Temperatures

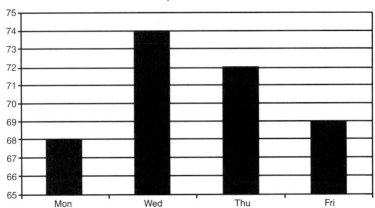

3. The chart above shows a series of temperature readings. What was the temperature on Tuesday?

(A) 68

(B) 70

(C) 71

(D) 74

(E) It cannot be determined from the information given.

4. $r^3 = 27$. What is r^{-3}?

(A) -3

(B) $\dfrac{1}{27}$

(C) $\dfrac{1}{3}$

(D) $\sqrt{3}$

(E) $\dfrac{1}{\sqrt[3]{3}}$

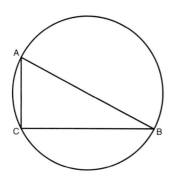

5. In the figure above, ΔABC is a 30°-60°-90° triangle whose vertices lie on the circle. The center of the circle lies on $\overline{AB}$. AC = 1. What is the area of the circle?

(A) $\dfrac{\sqrt{3}\pi}{2}$

(B) π

(C) $\sqrt{3}\pi$

(D) $\dfrac{\sqrt{3}\pi}{2}$

(E) $\dfrac{\sqrt{3}\pi}{4}$

6. Mr. Brown always has either eggs or bacon for breakfast, but not both. He always drinks either tea or coffee with his breakfast, but not both. The probability that he has eggs with coffee is .27. The probability that he has bacon with coffee is .35. The probability that he has eggs with tea is .22. What is the probability that he has bacon with tea?

(A) .10
(B) .11
(C) .16
(D) .22
(E) .27

7. p is a prime number. r = 2 × p; s = 3 × r; t = 6 × r. What is the greatest common factor of s and t?

(A) 2
(B) 2p
(C) 3p
(D) 6
(E) 6p

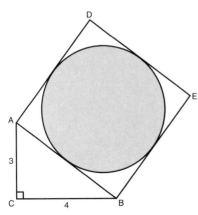

8. What is the circumference of the circle inscribed in the square ABED?

   (A) 3π

   (B) 4π

   (C) $\dfrac{25\pi}{4}$

   (D) 5π

   (E) $\dfrac{6\pi}{2}$

For questions 9–18, turn to the student-produced response grids in section 2 of the answer sheets.

9. A class includes 15 left-handed students and 30 right-handed students. How many different ways can a team be selected from the class, if a team is defined as one right-handed student and one left-handed student?

10. The function $f(x) = -x^2 - 6x + 7$ has its zeroes at –7 and 1. What is the maximum value of the function?

11. Define a line on the coordinate plane with the equation $y = -3x - 5$. What is the slope of a second line that passes through the point (–6, 5) and that is perpendicular to the first line?

12. In the figure above, AB = AC and $\angle$BAC = 36°. What is $\angle$ABC?

13. Define $f(x) = 4x^2 + 5$ and $g(x) = 6x + 4$. What is $f(g(4))$?

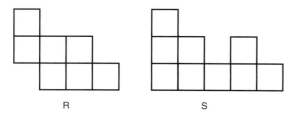

R   S

14. The area of shape R is 11 units. What is the area of shape S?

15. The mean of a set of 6 numbers is 9.5. The mean of a different set of 3 numbers is 3.0. What is the mean of all 9 numbers taken together?

16. The list price of a book is $18.00. One bookstore discounts the book by 5%, whereas a second bookstore marks it up by 15%. What is the difference between the price of the books at the two stores?

17. $\frac{2}{3}$ of $\frac{3}{4}$ of $\frac{5}{6}$ of a number is 8. What is the original number?

18. You flip a coin four times. What is the chance that the final result is three heads and one tail?

STOP

If you finish before time is called, you may check your work on this section only. Do not turn to any other section in the test.

Section 3

Time—25 minutes

35 Questions

Turn to Section 3 of your answer sheet to answer the questions in this section.

Directions: For each question in this section, select the best answer from among the choices given and fill in the corresponding circle on the answer sheet.

The following sentences test correctness and effectiveness of expression. Part of each sentence or the entire sentence is underlined; beneath each sentence are five ways of phrasing the underlined material. Choice A repeats the original phrasing; the other four choices are different. If you think the original phrasing produces a better sentence than any of the alternatives, select choice A; if not, select one of the other choices.

(see next page)

In making your selection, follow the requirements of standard written English; that is, pay attention to grammar, choice of words, sentence construction, and punctuation. Your selection should result in the most effective sentence—clear and precise, without awkwardness or ambiguity.

Example:

The weather that winter was <u>worse than for at least five decades</u>.

    (A) worse than for at least five decades
    (B) the worse it was for at least five decades
    (C) worse. Than it had been for at least five decades.
    (D) the worst that it had been for at least five decades
    (E) the worst it was for at least five decades.

Answer: (D)

1. <u>Born Quakers on a large farm,</u> Herbert Hoover was orphaned at age 10.
    (A) Born Quakers on a large farm
    (B) Born on a large farm
    (C) Born to Quakers on a large farm
    (D) Born to Quakers
    (E) On a large farm, born to Quakers

2. Brian and Bill ordered pizza after realizing <u>he was ravenously hungry</u>.
    (A) he was ravenously hungry
    (B) how ravenously hungry they were
    (C) he was hungry
    (D) they were hungry
    (E) they were ravenously hungry

3. Falling down the steps, <u>Sue's embarrassment, for just a moment, was keen</u>.
    (A) Sue's embarrassment, for just a moment, was keen
    (B) Sue's keen embarrassment was just for a moment
    (C) Sue was keenly embarrassed for just a moment
    (D) for just a moment, Sue was keenly embarrassed
    (E) just a moment, Sue was embarrassed for

4. <u>Jose had just entered the store</u> as the big sale was announced.
   (A) Jose had just entered the store
   (B) Jose entered the store just
   (C) Jose entered the store
   (D) Jose, entering the store, heard
   (E) Entering the store, Jose heard

5. Some students spent more time in gym than <u>science lab</u>.
   (A) science lab
   (B) compared to science lab
   (C) science labs
   (D) in science lab
   (E) their science labs

6. The *Jewish Daily Forward*, <u>a Yiddish newspaper, it encouraged</u> immigrants in the early twentieth century to Americanize themselves, is still active today.
   (A) a Yiddish newspaper, it encouraged
   (B) a Yiddish newspaper, which encouraged
   (C) a Yiddish newspaper, encouraging
   (D) a Yiddish newspaper that encouraged
   (E) a Yiddish newspaper, they encouraged

7. When we made the big move to California, my brother was just half my age, <u>which was twelve</u>.
   (A) which was twelve
   (B) twelve
   (C) which was twelve years old
   (D) ; I was twelve
   (E) of twelve

8. During the Great Depression, <u>many a hungry, homeless, and unemployed men</u> ended up working on a chain gang.
   (A) many a hungry, homeless, and unemployed men
   (B) many a hungry, a homeless, and an unemployed men
   (C) many a hungry, a homeless, and an employed man
   (D) many hungry, homeless, and employed man
   (E) many hungry, homeless, and unemployed men

9. The harmful effects of smoking on the fetus <u>is well documented</u>.
   - (A) is well documented
   - (B) are better documented than a decade ago
   - (C) are well documented
   - (D) has been well documented
   - (E) is being well documented.

10. Working his way through college, Herbert swept floors, cleaned bath-rooms, and <u>many dogs were walked</u>.
   - (A) many dogs were walked
   - (B) dogs were walked
   - (C) walked dogs
   - (D) dogs were walked
   - (E) walked many dogs

11. No one <u>was more sorrier than me</u> to hear that you failed your midterms.
   - (A) was more sorrier than me
   - (B) was sorrier than me
   - (C) was more sorry than I
   - (D) was sorrier than I
   - (E) was as sorry as me

The following sentences test your ability to recognize grammar and usage errors. Each sentence contains either a single error or no error at all. No sentence contains more than one error. The error, if there is one, is underlined and lettered. If the sentence contains an error, select the one underlined part that must be changed to make the sentence correct. If the sentence is correct, select choice E. In choosing answers, follow the requirements of standard written English.

Example:

The modern personal computer is <u>a revolutionary instrument</u>
                                              A

<u>that can be used</u> for composing a sonnet, planning a bridge,
      B

or <u>to create digital movies</u>, but <u>at the most basic level</u>
         C   D

it is still just a collection of digital impulses. <u>No error</u>
                                                      E

Answer: (C)

12. The twins <u>were inspired</u> to become <u>a professional dancer</u>
               A   B

<u>after seeing</u> *The Nutcracker* <u>performed by</u> the celebrated Russian Ballet.
    C   D

<u>No Error</u>
  E

13. My sisters and I <u>all</u> prefer either cake <u>and</u> ice cream
                A   B

<u>for dessert</u>, when we allow <u>ourselves</u> to partake of the calories.
    C   D

<u>No Error</u>
  E

14. A <u>properly secured</u> computer will require <u>that</u> you enter your
        A   B

name and <u>password</u> before you <u>can begin</u> working. <u>No Error</u>
        C   D   E

15. My brother Tim, <u>a talented artist,</u> <u>has been</u> a set designer,
                A   B

<u>and collaborated</u> <u>on a number</u> of television commercials. <u>No Error</u>
    C   D   E

16. This was the <u>only</u> place she'd ever lived <u>that</u> the birds
             A   B

<u>weren't plentiful</u> and <u>didn't flock</u> to her birdfeeders all day long.
    C   D

<u>No Error</u>
  E

17. <u>After</u> several months <u>on the road west</u>, many New England
 A   B

pioneers <u>prematurely ended</u> their move west <u>when reaching</u>
        C   D

the great plains. <u>No Error</u>
           E

18. <u>Mount Rushmore</u>, the <u>only</u> cliff carving of <u>a kind</u>
      A   B   C

    <u>in the United States,</u> is a national monument. <u>No Error</u>
          D   E

19. Many <u>westward bound</u> travelers <u>ended their quest</u> far east
              A   B

    of California, in small towns along the trail <u>in which</u>
                                                      C

    the weary travelers found <u>comfort and community</u>.
                                        D

    <u>No Error</u>
        E

20. Preoccupation <u>on</u> his social life <u>began to affect</u> his grades,
                      A   B

    <u>which</u> made his parents <u>very</u> unhappy. <u>No Error</u>
       C   D   E

21. <u>Joining</u> the expedition <u>at the next stop</u> <u>was</u> a doctor,
        A   B   C

    a paleontologist, and a representative <u>sent by our investors</u>.
                                                    D

    <u>No Error</u>
        E

22. The <u>constant</u> <u>shifting winds</u> made <u>it</u> difficult to navigate the
           A   B   C

    small boat <u>through</u> the narrow cliffs. <u>No Error</u>
                   D   E

23. Jessica <u>was</u> never <u>quite</u> sure if her good looks <u>were</u> a blessing
               A   B   C

    or <u>if they were</u> a curse. <u>No Error</u>
           D   E

24. People <u>which</u> need immediate relief <u>after a natural disaster</u>
            A   B

can often <u>be impatient and unruly</u> <u>with relief workers</u>.
                    C   D

<u>No Error</u>
  E

25. It was <u>never</u> <u>more clearer</u> that Americans expected their
            A   B

government <u>to be</u> their guardian <u>than</u> during the twentieth
                C   D

century. <u>No Error</u>
        E

26. John Muir, an author and naturalist, <u>was</u> a leader in the efforts
                                     A

to make Yosemite a national park, having <u>had to convince</u>
     B   C

Theodore Roosevelt of the importance <u>of conserving the forests</u>.
                                      D

<u>No Error</u>
  E

27. The number <u>of reform mayors</u> elected during the Progressive
               A

period <u>accentuate</u> the belief that <u>more and more</u> Americans
            B   C

wanted <u>to be cared for</u> and not just governed. <u>No Error</u>
        D   E

28. <u>During</u> Governor La Follette's three terms, <u>they</u> managed
    A   B

<u>to enact</u> a number <u>of</u> Progressive measures. <u>No Error</u>
  C   D   E

29. During the first half of the twentieth century, blacks

<u>moved</u> <u>from the south</u> to the north hoping <u>to find better jobs</u>,
  A   B   C

more equality, <u>and more opportunity</u>. <u>No Error</u>
                        D   E

Directions: The following passage is an early draft of an essay. Some parts of the passage need to be rewritten.

Read the passage and select the best answers for the questions that follow. Some questions are about particular sentences or parts of sentences and ask you to improve sentence structure and word choice. Other questions ask you to consider organization and development. In choosing answers, follow the requirements of standard written English.

Questions 30–35 are based on the following passage.

(1)Americans are and have always been a mobile people. (2)The first Americans left their European homes to civilize an untamed land. (3)It didn't take long for Americans, growing crowded in quickly growing coastal cities to once again, get the urge to move. (4)Even in modern times, Americans move from community to community and from coast to coast.

(5)Every year since 1948 one American in five have moved. Most of the time, we're moving from house to house within the same city or county. (6)But by 1970, 25 percent of all Americans were not living in the state in which they were born.

(7)One of the major exodus during this period was from the farms of America's heartland. (8)Young Americans left their farmland homes and headed for the cities in droves. (9)The close proximity of housing and jobs made it easy for some Americans to succeed in business. (10)On the other hand, the city slums began to fill with rural folks unprepared for urban life in a pattern similar to the European immigrants settling the slums of New York, Boston, and Chicago during the first part of the century.

(11)Early Americans had settled a large and mostly untamed land. (12)The twentieth century has brought many of the decendents of those early pioneering Americans full circle. (13)After two centuries of settling American's heartland, more than half of all Americans now live within 50 miles of the oceans, the Gulf of Mexico, or the Great Lakes.

30. Considering the entire passage, which of the following changes is most appropriate for the underlined portion of sentence 4 (reproduced below)?

    Even in modern times, Americans move from community to community and from coast to coast.

    (A) (As it is now)
    (B) After settling the entire country, Americans continue to
    (C) Once they settled the country, modern Americans
    (D) Even with the country settled, contemporary Americans
    (E) Settling the entire country, Americans

31. Which is the best revision for the underlined portion of sentence 5 (reproduced below)?

    Every year since 1948 one American in five have moved.

    (A) Nothing, it's fine just the way it is.
    (B) 1 American in 5 have moved.
    (C) one American in five has moved.
    (D) one American from five have moved.
    (E) one American of five have moved.

32. Which is the best revision for the underlined portion of sentence 6 (reproduced below)?

    But by 1970, 25 percent of all Americans were not living in the state in which they were born.

    (A) in the state where they
    (B) Nothing, it's correct as is.
    (C) in the same state in which they
    (D) in the same state where
    (E) in the state they

33. Which is the best revision for the underlined portion of sentence 7 (reproduced below)?

    One of the major exodus during this period was from the farms of America's heartland.

    (A) One of the major exoduses
    (B) A major exodus
    (C) An exodus
    (D) One of the exoduses
    (E) One of the major flights

34. Sentence 10 (reproduced below) has some problems. What revisions would you make?

    On the other hand, the city slums began to fill with rural folks unprepared for urban life in a pattern similar to the European immigrants settling the slums of New York, Boston, and Chicago during the first part of the century.

    (A) Drop the clause comparing the farm folk to European immigrants.
    (B) Change the verb tense.
    (C) Find a new word for folks.
    (D) A combination of A and B.
    (E) Omit the introductory clause "on the other hand."

35. Which is the best revision for the underlined portion of sentence 11 (reproduced below)?

    Early Americans had settled a large and mostly untamed land.

    (A) had been settling
    (B) have settled
    (C) settled
    (D) have been settling
    (E) had already settled

STOP

If you finish before time is called, you may check your work on this section only. Do not turn to any other section in the test.

Section 4

Time—25 minutes

24 Questions

Turn to Section 4 of your answer sheet to answer the questions in this section.

> **Directions:** For each question in this section, select the best answer from among the choices given and fill in the corresponding circle on the answer sheet.

Each sentence below has one or two blanks, each blank indicating that something has been omitted. Beneath the sentence are five words or sets of words labeled A through E. Choose the word or set of words that, when inserted in the sentence, <u>best</u> fits the meaning of the sentence as a whole.

Example:

The Internet is _____ now, being available in 78% of all American households.

    (A) unimportant
    (B) transitory
    (C) migrating
    (D) negligible
    (E) ubiquitous

Answer: (E)

---

1. We were so used to her _____ nature that her _____ caught us off guard.
    (A) accommodating . . indulgence
    (B) solicitous . . conciliatory
    (C) indulgent . . kindness
    (D) enraging . . hysterics
    (E) convivial . . histrionics

2. Ironically, Abraham Cahan, the long-time editor of the Yiddish newspaper *Jewish Daily Forward*, was as dedicated to the _____ of socialism as he was to Americanization.
    (A) propagation
    (B) broadcast
    (C) circulation
    (D) distribution
    (E) escalation

3. The authorities kept Chuck Yeager's record-breaking flight _____ for several months, warning the crew to tell no one.
    (A) confidence
    (B) classified
    (C) confidential
    (D) unofficial
    (E) clandestine

4. The opposing senator made no attempt to be _____, _____ the opposition like a scolding nanny in front of the entire special assembly.

   (A) coy . . addressing
   (B) restrained . . criticizing
   (C) clever . . managing
   (D) subtle . . haranguing
   (E) devious . . handling

5. The celebrity's entourage was a bevy of self-serving _____.

   (A) autocrats
   (B) minions
   (C) sycophants
   (D) inferiors
   (E) underlings

6. Despite her twisted legs, the doctor gave the kitten such a(n) _____ prognosis that we named her Lucky.

   (A) earnest
   (B) straight
   (C) questionable
   (D) warped
   (E) auspicious

7. Snow White's _____ stepmother was a(n) _____ character—as wicked as she was beautiful.

   (A) nefarious . . enigmatic
   (B) lovely . . perplexing
   (C) callous . . compulsive
   (D) beautiful . . anachronistic
   (E) onerous . . recalcitrant

8. Her _____ response revealed her _____ for the whole affair.

   (A) solicitous . . aversion
   (B) disingenuous . . disdain
   (C) sympathetic . . abhorrence
   (D) peevish . . sympathy
   (E) insolent . . generosity

> The passages below are followed by questions based on their content; questions following a pair of related passages may also be based on the relationship between the paired passages. Answer the questions on the basis of what is <u>stated</u> or <u>implied</u> in the passages and in any introductory material that may be provided.

Questions 9–10 are based on the following passage.

At the outbreak of the Civil War there were only seventeen state universities. Then, in 1862 an energetic Republican congressman, Justin S.
Morrill from rural Vermont, secured the passage of the Morrill Act. This
Line act granted lands to the states from the public domain—30,000 acres for
5 each of the states' senators and representatives in Congress—to support
new state colleges. In these "land-grant" colleges students would be
taught to be better farmers. The land-grant colleges also often offered
solid courses in engineering, science, and literature. So here Newcomers,
too, found an opportunity to learn.

10 After the Civil War, hundreds of other colleges and universities were
founded. In the later years of the 1880s, some of the wealthiest Go-
Getters gave millions of dollars to found and endow still more institutions
of higher learning. In 1876 Johns Hopkins University was established
from the fortune left by a Baltimore merchant. In 1885 a railroad builder,
15 Leland Stanford, in memory of his son, set up Leland Stanford, Jr.,
University. In 1891 John D. Rockefeller, the Go-Getting oil millionaire,
created the University of Chicago. And there were scores of others.

9. What did the Morrill Act of 1862 do?
   (A) Founded state colleges and universities
   (B) Allowed state senators to found colleges and universities in their home
       states
   (C) Paid for new state colleges and universities
   (D) Gave land from the public domain to support new state colleges
   (E) Put the state colleges under Congressional authority

10. How did Johns Hopkins make his millions?
    (A) He was a banker.
    (B) He was a railroad tycoon.
    (C) He was a merchant.
    (D) He discovered oil in Texas.
    (E) He discovered a silver mine in Nevada.

Questions 11–12 are based on the following passage.

Immediately after World War I, there was a large, pent-up demand for
housing and for all peacetime products, such as automobiles and kitchen
appliances, that were hard to get during the war. This demand, backed by
Line wartime savings, gave a big boost to sales. Government spending did not
5 decline and kept the economy booming. American export trade, supported by the billions of dollars the United States government paid out for
foreign aid, flourished.

All sorts of new machines—radios, high fi's, television sets, washing and drying machines, deep freezes, power lawnmowers, and countless
10 others—kept factories busy and customers eager to buy. None was more important than the automobile. Fewer than 1 million new automobiles were produced during World War I. By 1970, 8 million a year were being turned out. These consumed one-fifth of the nation's new steel, half its malleable iron, and two-thirds of its rubber and lead.

15 All these cars needed highways. In 1956, then, the nation began the largest road construction program in its history. Under President Eisenhower, Congress voted $33 billion (later increased) for a ten-year program to build a whole 42,500-mile network of interstate superhighways. By 1975, because of inflation, it would cost $39 billion just to finish
20 the last 5,500 miles of the system. In 1978, President Carter signed a highway bill that provided $9.3 billion a year for three years. Many more billions were spent by states and localities.

11. Economically, what was the most important product demanded, and purchased, after World War I?
   (A) Housing
   (B) Electronics
   (C) Household appliances
   (D) Gardening tools
   (E) Automobiles

12. Eisenhower initiated today's interstate highway system in 1956. It was supposed to be a ten-year project. In 1975, how many miles of highway were wanting to complete the project?
   (A) 42,500
   (B) 5,500
   (C) 37,500
   (D) none
   (E) 48,500

Questions 13–24 are based on the following passage.

This account of African fever comes from one of the books that the celebrated explorer Dr. David Livingstone wrote about his travels in the mid-nineteenth century.

A third visit to Kebrabasa was made for the purpose of ascertaining whether it might be navigable when the Zambesi was in flood, the chief point of interest being of course Morumbwa; it was found that the rapids
Line observed in our first trip had disappeared, and that while they were
5 smoothed over, in a few places the current had increased in strength. As

the river fell rapidly while we were on the journey, the cataract of Morumbwa did not differ materially from what it was when discovered. Some fishermen assured us that it was not visible when the river was at its fullest, and that the current was then not very strong. On this occasion we
10   travelled on the right bank, and found it, with the additional inconvenience of rain, as rough and fatiguing as the left had been. Our progress was impeded by the tall wet grass and dripping boughs, and consequent fever. During the earlier part of the journey we came upon a few deserted hamlets only; but at last in a pleasant valley we met some of the people of the
15   country, who were miserably poor and hungry. The women were gathering wild fruits in the woods. A young man having consented for two yards of cotton cloth to show us a short path to the cataract led us up a steep hill to a village perched on the edge of one of its precipices; a thunderstorm coming on at the time, the headman invited us to take shelter in a hut until
20   it had passed. Our guide having informed him of what he knew and conceived to be our object, was favoured in return with a long reply in well-sounding blank verse; at the end of every line the guide, who listened with deep attention, responded with a grunt, which soon became so ludicrous that our men burst into a loud laugh. Neither the poet nor the responsive
25   guide took the slightest notice of their rudeness, but kept on as energetically as ever to the end. The speech, or more probably our bad manners, made some impression on our guide, for he declined, although offered double pay, to go any further.

A great deal of fever comes in with March and April; in March, if considerable intervals take place between the rainy days, and in April always, for
30   then large surfaces of mud and decaying vegetation are exposed to the hot sun. In general an attack does not continue long, but it pulls one down quickly; though when the fever is checked the strength is as quickly restored. It had long been observed that those who were stationed for any
35   length of time in one spot, and lived sedentary lives, suffered more from fever than others who moved about and had both mind and body occupied; but we could not all go in the small vessel when she made her trips, during which the change of place and scenery proved so conducive to health; and some of us were obliged to remain in charge of the expedi-
40   tion's property, making occasional branch trips to examine objects of interest in the vicinity. Whatever may be the cause of the fever, we observed that all were often affected at the same time, as if from malaria. This was particularly the case during a north wind: it was at first commonly believed that a daily dose of quinine would prevent the attack. For
45   a number of months all our men, except two, took quinine regularly every morning. The fever some times attacked the believers in quinine, while the unbelievers in its prophylactic powers escaped. Whether we took it

daily, or omitted it altogether for months, made no difference; the fever
was impartial, and seized us on the days of quinine as regularly and as
50 severely as when it remained undisturbed in the medicine chest, and we
finally abandoned the use of it as a prophylactic altogether. The best preventive against fever is plenty of interesting work to do, and abundance of
wholesome food to eat. To a man well housed and clothed, who enjoys
these advantages, the fever at Tette will not prove a more formidable
55 enemy than a common cold; but let one of these be wanting—let him be
indolent, or guilty of excesses in eating or drinking, or have poor, scanty
fare,—and the fever will probably become a more serious matter. It is of a
milder type at Tette than at Quillimane or on the low sea-coast; and, as in
this part of Africa one is as liable to fever as to colds in England, it would
60 be advisable for strangers always to hasten from the coast to the high
lands, in order that when the seizure does take place, it may be of the
mildest type. Although quinine was not found to be a preventive, except
possibly in the way of acting as a tonic, and rendering the system more
able to resist the influence of malaria, it was found invaluable in the cure
65 of the complaint, as soon as pains in the back, sore bones, headache, yawn-
ing, quick and sometimes intermittent pulse, noticeable pulsations of the
jugulars, with suffused eyes, hot skin, and foul tongue, began.

Very curious are the effects of African fever on certain minds.
Cheerfulness vanishes, and the whole mental horizon is overcast with
70 black clouds of gloom and sadness. The liveliest joke cannot provoke even
the semblance of a smile. The countenance is grave, the eyes suffused, and
the few utterances are made in the piping voice of a wailing infant. An irri-
table temper is often the first symptom of approaching fever. At such
times a man feels very much like a fool, if he does not act like one.
75 Nothing is right, nothing pleases the fever-stricken victim. He is peevish,
prone to find fault and to contradict, and think himself insulted, and is
exactly what an Irish naval surgeon before a court-martial defined a
drunken man to be: "a man unfit for society."

13. The sentence beginning "On this occasion" (line 9) implies that
   (A) it rains more on the right bank than on the left bank
   (B) the author planned to come back for another trip over the same route
   (C) travel on the left bank would have been less fatiguing
   (D) the author had previously made the same journey on the left bank of the
       river
   (E) travel should have been postponed until the current was less strong

14. In the context of this passage, the word "ludicrous" (line 23) most nearly means

(A) amusing
(B) incongruous
(C) nonsensical
(D) hilarious
(E) conceited

15. By writing of "our bad manners" (line 26), the author refers to

(A) the insensitivity in laughing at the native conversation
(B) the inability to offer the villagers their own hospitality in return
(C) failure to bring gifts for the village headman and his family
(D) flouting local customs to invade a sacred site without permission
(E) wearing English garb instead of native dress

16. The tone of the first paragraph of the passage might best be characterized as

(A) speculative
(B) jocular
(C) cautious
(D) descriptive
(E) outraged

17. The author believes that the fevers he encountered were caused by

(A) rain
(B) sedentary life
(C) quinine
(D) excesses in eating or drinking
(E) mud and decaying vegetation

18. The word "checked" (line 33) is used to mean

(A) halted
(B) inspected
(C) tested
(D) patterned
(E) blocked

19. In the author's opinion, which of these actions would have cut down on the incidence of fever in his expedition?

(A) daily doses of quinine

(B) locating the camp away from the river

(C) more frequent travel for all concerned

(D) a cheerful attitude

(E) staying inside during the rain

20. By "unbelievers in its prophylactic powers" (line 47) the author indicates

(A) those who did not take quinine daily

(B) natives who did not understand medicine

(C) the audience of the missionaries in the party

(D) those who live in the lowlands

(E) men who ate and drank to excess

21. Which of these statements best characterizes the author's attitude toward those who come down with fever?

(A) They are the unlucky victims of random chance.

(B) They should be given the benefits of modern medicine to prevent such problems in the future.

(C) They shouldn't complain about such minor problems.

(D) They are being punished for past misdeeds.

(E) If they took better care of themselves, they wouldn't have such a problem with fever.

22. In line 55, the word "wanting" most nearly means

(A) desiring

(B) needing

(C) overabundant

(D) lacking

(E) requesting

23. According to the author, with respect to African fever, quinine is

(A) a cure and a prophylactic

(B) a treatment but not a preventative

(C) a tonic and a preventative

(D) a complaint and a remedy

(E) a drug but not a tonic

24. Which statement would the author most likely agree with?

(A) I have no patience with those who pretend to suffer severe effects from the fever.

(B) I believe strong drink to be a useful preventative for the fever.

(C) I am not interested in finding a cure for the fever.

(D) I can prevent the fever on my next expedition.

(E) I can tell when a man is about to come down with the fever from his behavior.

STOP

If you finish before time is called, you may check your work on this section only. Do not turn to any other section in the test.

Section 5

Time—25 minutes

20 Questions

Turn to Section 5 of your answer sheet to answer the questions in this section.

Directions: For this section, solve each problem and decide which is the best of the choices given. Fill in the corresponding circle on the answer sheet. You can use any available space for scratchwork.

Notes:

1. The use of a calculator is permitted.

2. All numbers used are real numbers.

3. Figures that accompany problems in the test are intended to provide information that is useful in solving the problems. They are drawn as accurately as possible EXCEPT when it is stated in a specific problem that the figure is not drawn to scale. All figures lie in a plane unless otherwise indicated.

4. Unless otherwise specified, the domain of any function f is assumed to be the set of real numbers x for which $f(x)$ is a real number.

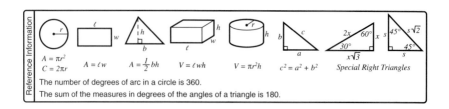

$A = \pi r^2$
$C = 2\pi r$

$A = \ell w$

$A = \frac{1}{2}bh$

$V = \ell w h$

$V = \pi r^2 h$

$c^2 = a^2 + b^2$

Special Right Triangles

The number of degrees of arc in a circle is 360.
The sum of the measures in degrees of the angles of a triangle is 180.

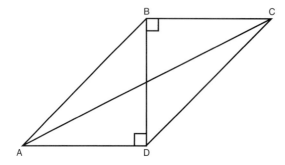

1. In the figure above, AD = BD = BC = 1. What is the ratio of the area of ΔABD to ΔACD?

(A) 1:2

(B) 1:$\sqrt{2}$

(C) 1:1

(D) $\sqrt{2}$:1

(E) 2:1

2. The prime factors of a number include 2 and 3. How many such numbers are there between 1 and 50?

(A) 0

(B) 8

(C) 12

(D) 16

(E) 41

Housing Starts

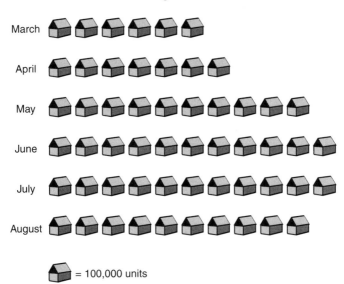

March

April

May

June

July

August

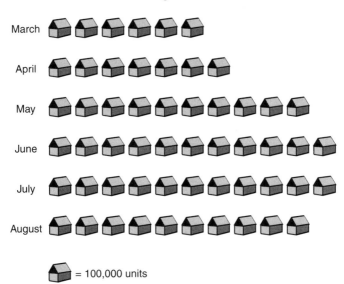 = 100,000 units

3. According to the pictograph above, during which period did housing starts increase by 10%?

(A) March to April
(B) April to May
(C) May to June
(D) June to July
(E) July to August

4. What is the reciprocal of $7\frac{1}{5}$?

(A) $\frac{71}{5}$
(B) $\frac{36}{5}$
(C) $\frac{5}{17}$
(D) $\frac{5}{36}$
(E) $5\frac{1}{7}$

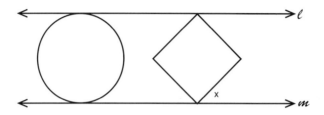

5. In the figure above, $\ell \parallel m$ and x = 45°. If the area of the circle is 9π, what is the area of the square?

(A) 4.5

(B) $6\sqrt{2}$

(C) $\dfrac{6}{\sqrt{2}}$

(D) 18

(E) 36

Table 1	CB Airlines Travel Times	
From	To	Time in Minutes
Dover	Elway	42
Elway	Janestown	15
Jamestown	Smithville	10
Elway	Krebs	27
Elway	Bid City	48

6. CB airlines flies all of its routes at a constant speed. Given the information in the table above, and knowing that Dover, Elway, and Krebs do not lie on a straight line, what can you conclude about the travel time from Dover to Krebs?

(A) It is exactly 69 minutes.

(B) It is at least 69 minutes.

(C) It is no more than 69 minutes.

(D) It is exactly 15 minutes.

(E) No conclusion can be drawn from this data.

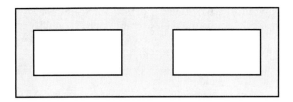

7. The figure above shows a rectangular plate that is used as part of a physics experiment. The plate is 1 inch by 3 inches, and it contains two holes each 1 inch by $\frac{1}{2}$ inch. Particles are shot at random locations on the plate. What is the probability that one of these particles will not pass through one of the holes?

   (A) $\frac{3}{2}$

   (B) $\frac{1}{3}$

   (C) $\frac{1}{6}$

   (D) $\frac{2}{3}$

   (E) $\frac{1}{2}$

8. Rabbits are dropped on a deserted island. The total population of rabbits on the island then increases according to a geometric sequence. After 1 month there are 2 rabbits, after 2 months there are 4 rabbits, after 3 months there are 8 rabbits, and so on. How many rabbits are there at the end of one year, assuming that the sequence continues?

   (A) 2,048
   (B) 4,096
   (C) 8,192
   (D) 16,384
   (E) 32,768

9. A rectangular prism has a top that is 4 inches by 3 inches. If the total surface area of the prism is 45 square inches, what is the height of the prism?

   (A) .75 inches
   (B) 1 inch
   (C) 1.25 inches
   (D) 1.5 inches
   (E) 2 inches

10. The mean annual snowfall in a particular location for four successive five year periods is 12 inches, 14 inches, 22 inches, and 16 inches. What is the mean annual snowfall for the entire 20-year period?

    (A) 13 inches

    (B) $15\frac{3}{4}$ inches

    (C) 16 inches

    (D) $17\frac{1}{4}$ inches

    (E) 18 inches

11. The graph of $f(x)$ is a straight line that intercepts the y axis at y = 3 and has a slope of $\frac{2}{3}$. What is $f(12)$?

    (A) 11

    (B) 21

    (C) $24\frac{1}{3}$

    (D) 27

    (E) $36\frac{2}{3}$

12. A right circular cylinder with a height of 12 units has a volume of 192π. The cylinder's height is changed so that the volume increases by 25% without altering its radius. What is the new height of the cylinder?

    (A) 12.25

    (B) 12.75

    (C) 13

    (D) 14.25

    (E) 15

13. A drawer contains a mix of black socks and white socks. The probability of drawing a black sock from the drawer at random is 0.35. If the drawer contains 13 white socks, how many total socks are in the drawer?

    (A) 7

    (B) 13

    (C) 14

    (D) 20

    (E) 35

14. △ABC is congruent to △DEF. If ∠ABC = 48° and ∠EFD = 71°, what is ∠CAB?
    (A) 48
    (B) 61
    (C) 71
    (D) 109
    (E) 132

15. Which of the following is a prime polynomial?
    (A) $x^2 - 1$
    (B) $x^2 - x - 12$
    (C) $x^2 + 3x + 2$
    (D) $x^2 + 4x - 8$
    (E) $x^2 + 5x + 6$

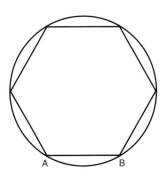

16. The figure above shows a circle with an inscribed regular hexagon. Each side of the hexagon is 2 units long. What is the length of the arc AB?
    (A) 1
    (B) $\frac{\pi}{3}$
    (C) 2
    (D) $\frac{2\pi}{3}$
    (E) 2π

17. Select the largest of these expressions:
    (A) 2^{3^5}
    (B) $2^3 \times 2^5$
    (C) 2
    (D) 2^{-3}
    (E) $2^{\frac{1}{3}}$

18. You roll three ordinary six-sided dice. What is the probability that the total shown on the dice will be 5?

(A) $\frac{1}{72}$

(B) $\frac{1}{36}$

(C) $\frac{5}{216}$

(D) $\frac{1}{54}$

(E) $\frac{1}{27}$

19. Points P, Q, R, and S lie along a line, not necessarily in that order. PQ = 4, QR = 2, and RS = 5. What is one possible value for PS?

(A) 2

(B) 3

(C) 5

(D) 6

(E) 10

20. Define a/b/c to mean a + b × c. Which of these quantities is the smallest?

(A) 1/2/3

(B) 3/1/1

(C) 4/1/1

(D) 1/3/5

(E) 2/1/3

STOP

If you finish before time is called, you may check your work on this section only. Do not turn to any other section in the test.

Section 6

Time—25 minutes

24 Questions

Turn to Section 2 of your answer sheet to answer the questions in this section.

> **Directions:** For each question in this section, select the best answer from among the choices given and fill in the corresponding circle on the answer sheet.

Each sentence below has one or two blanks, each blank indicating that something has been omitted. Beneath the sentence are five words or sets of words labeled A through E. Choose the word or set of words that, when inserted in the sentence, <u>best</u> fits the meaning of the sentence as a whole.

Example:

The Internet is _____ now, being available in 78% of all American households.

    (A) unimportant
    (B) transitory
    (C) migrating
    (D) negligible
    (E) ubiquitous

Answer: (E)

1. A _____ heights might keep one from pursuing a career in aviation.
    (A) fascination for
    (B) passion for
    (C) respect for
    (D) phobia of
    (E) confidence at

2. At three and half hours, you certainly couldn't _____ the show's

_____.
    (A) disparage . . brevity
    (B) commend . . abruptness
    (C) extol . . gaiety
    (D) admire . . intensity
    (E) sustain . . censorship

3. The witness attempted to ----- on his version of the events, but the defense attorney cut him short.
    (A) undermine
    (B) evaluate
    (C) condone
    (D) expound
    (E) ameliorate

4. Despite his _____ salary, Paul was able to _____ a significantly large savings account over the years.

(A) copious . . amass
(B) meager . . accumulate
(C) sporadic . . contribute
(D) extensive . . hoard
(E) miserable . . erect

5. Reading her _____ poetry, he wasn't sure he could help her _____ her inner conflicts.

(A) insightful . . authenticate
(B) intriguing . . supplant
(C) arcane . . resolve
(D) dramatic . . overhaul
(E) formidable . . confront

The passages below are followed by questions based on their content; questions following a pair of related passages may also be based on the relationship between the paired passages. Answer the questions on the basis of what is <u>stated</u> or <u>implied</u> in the passages and in any introductory material that may be provided.

Questions 6–9 are based on the following passages.

Each year, the average American travels about 9,000 miles by car. One-fourth of all the energy consumed in this country is used for transportation. In fact, the use of urban public transit has declined by more than 50 percent since the early 1970s. Tax money pays for both the building and maintenance of roadways and mass transit. However, because this money is limited, governments and citizens must decide if the money should be spent on roadways or on mass transit systems.

Passage 1

The Economy Is Supported by Private-Transportation Use

The use of private transportation supports jobs such as building, selling, and repairing cars. Twenty-two percent of American workers depend on the automobile industry for a living. An increase in the use of mass tran-
Line sit would mean fewer cars, which would cause automobile workers to lose
5 their jobs.

Private transportation is the only way some people can get to their jobs. In addition, many people complain that mass transit is not time efficient. Buses and trains make many stops, which makes taking mass transit slower than driving a car.

Passage 2

The Environment Is Protected by Public-Transportation Use

10 If more people used public transportation, fewer cars would be on the road. This would decrease the amount of automobile exhaust, which is a major source of carbon monoxide and other pollutants. Cars also release large amounts of carbon dioxide. This gas is one of the greenhouse gases that contributes to global warning.

15 Fewer cars on the road would also ease traffic problems. Because it can carry more people than a car, a bus is 1.5 times more fuel efficient. The use of public transportation also saves gasoline. Petroleum must be removed from underground, refined, and shipped to wherever it is needed. Reducing the use of petroleum will reduce the chances of serious envi-
20 ronmental damage.

6. Both passages are primarily concerned with the subject of
   (A) how best to spend tax money on transportation
   (B) protecting the environment by improving public transportation
   (C) protecting the environment by decreasing the amount of automobile exhaust
   (D) conserving fossil fuel
   (E) how public transportation affects the economy and the environment

7. Passage 1 uses the following arguments to support the position that public funds should be used on roadways to make private transportation more accessible:

(A) Mass transit has a negative impact on jobs, mass transit isn't available to everyone, and mass transit is inefficient.

(B) Mass transit puts autoworkers out of work and is slow and unreliable.

(C) Private transportation actually increases industry, therefore increasing the amount of tax dollars available for public transportation.

(D) Private transportation actually increases industry, therefore increasing the amount of tax dollars spent on public transportation; mass transit has a negative impact on jobs, mass transit isn't available to everyone, and mass transit is inefficient.

(E) Mass transit creates more pollution than private cars, mass transit has a negative impact on jobs, mass transit isn't available to everyone, and mass transit is inefficient.

8. Passage 2 suggests that spending more money on mass transit would reduce the number of privately owned cars on the street, resulting in what?

(A) cleaner air and cleaner environment

(B) a decrease in air pollution, a decrease in greenhouse gas, fewer traffic problems, gasoline conservation, and an abatement in the environmental impact of collecting and refining gasoline

(C) a decrease in air pollution, fewer traffic problems, and an abatement in the environmental impact of collecting and refining gasoline

(D) a decrease in air pollution, a reduction in the greenhouse gas carbon dioxide would slow global warming, fewer traffic problems, gasoline conservation, and an abatement in the environmental impact of collecting and refining gasoline

(E) a reduction in the greenhouse gas carbon dioxide would slow global warming, fewer traffic problems

9. Based on passage 1, what might be the consequences of spending more money on mass transit and less on public roadways?

(A) A loss of jobs

(B) A loss of jobs in the auto industry

(C) A loss of jobs and increased inconvenience to workers not using mass transit

(D) A loss of jobs in the auto industry and increased inconvenience to workers who don't have access to mass transit

(E) Increase inconvenience to workers who don't have access to mass transit

Questions 10-14 are based on the following passage.

No one who had visited Theodore Roosevelt as a child could have guessed that he would become a champion of the ordinary American. His father was a well-to-do New York banker who owned country houses and took *Line* his family to Europe for vacations. Among Teddy Roosevelt's early mem-
5 ories were seeing the Pope during a walk in Rome and visiting the tomb of Napoleon in Paris.

Young Teddy had no worries about money. But he had other worries. He suffered from asthma, which made it hard for him to exercise, and his eyesight was poor. He became interested in nature and began collecting spec-
10 imens of plants and animals. When he was 12, his mother told a maid to throw away some dead mice that the boy had stored in a dresser drawer. "The Loss to Science," Teddy cried. "The Loss to Science!"

His father built a gym for the boy at home. There Teddy worked with a punching bag and did pull-ups on the horizontal bars. He also took box-
15 ing lessons. By age 17, he was expert in such track events as running, pole vaulting, and high jumping. On his grandfather's country estate at Oyster Bay on Long Island, he became an enthusiastic horseman and a crack shot. All his life, Teddy Roosevelt felt that he had to make up for the childhood weakness of his body.

20 Roosevelt never lost his boyish excitement. He kept up his boxing. After he was hit in the eye while boxing with a young army officer, his left eye became blind. He managed to keep this a secret, and he devised ways to prevent people from knowing that he could see in only one eye. In spite of it, he became world famous as an explorer and big-game hunter in
25 Africa and South America.

10. What is the primary topic of this passage?

(A) Theodore Roosevelt's childhood
(B) The illnesses Theodore Roosevelt battled during childhood
(C) The young Teddy Roosevelt's enthusiasm for sports and hunting
(D) How the young Teddy Roosevelt met and overcame the challenges of asthma and bad eyesight
(E) Teddy Roosevelt's athletic interests during childhood

11. In lines 8–9, we're told that Theodore Roosevelt suffered from what weaknesses?

(A) asthma
(B) bad eyesight
(C) poverty
(D) a poor education
(E) asthma and bad eyesight

12. Lines 15–16 tell us that in spite of young Roosevelt's asthma, he excelled in several physical activities. What were they?
    (A) running, pole vaulting, and high jumping
    (B) running, pole vaulting, high jumping, and boxing
    (C) running, pole vaulting, high jumping, boxing, and big-game hunting
    (D) running, pole vaulting, high jumping, and big-game hunting.
    (E) running, jumping, and big-game hunting

13. The passage suggests that Roosevelt felt compelled to participate and eventually excelled in sports. Why?
    (A) Teddy Roosevelt felt he had to live up to his father and grandfather's expectations.
    (B) All his life, Teddy Roosevelt felt that he had to make up for the childhood weakness of his body.
    (C) His parents didn't seem to respect his love of nature, and it was his way of winning their approval and praise.
    (D) His father forced him to participate in sports, to the point of building him a gym in their home.
    (E) His older brothers excelled in sports, and he was very competitive with his brothers.

14. Where did Theodore Roosevelt explore and hunt?
    (A) Africa
    (B) South America
    (C) Oyster Bay
    (D) Africa and South America
    (E) Europe and Italy

Questions 15–24 are based on the following passage

The movement of matter and flow of energy are common to all ecosystems on Earth. Yet Earth is a very large and diverse place. Environments range from the ice of Antarctica to the heat and rain of the Amazon.

Line   Differences in temperature and rainfall create a vast array of conditions on
5   the surface of the Earth. Life has adapted to almost all of these environments.

The ecosystems of Earth can be divided into several broad categories. A major type of ecosystem with distinctive temperature, rainfall, and organisms is called a biome (BY-ohm). Biomes are either terrestrial (on land) or
10   aquatic (in water). On land, the type of biome that occurs in a given area depends on the average temperature and amount of precipitation the area receives. The type of aquatic biome is determined by water depth, nutrients, and nearness to land.

The biome is the largest category scientists use to classify ecosystems.
15 Because each biome is a general category, the conditions in a biome may vary from place to place. The many ecosystems within a biome have different habitats with different conditions and organisms. Every habitat on Earth is different, so any attempt to classify these habitats involves generalization. But the concept of the biome is useful as a way to talk about sets
20 of related habitats.

The terrestrial ecosystems of Earth can be divided into nine major biomes. Two of these biomes—the desert and the tundra—receive very little water and support only a small amount of biomass. Recall that biomass is the total mass of organic material in an ecosystem. Desert, for example,
25 covers 25 percent of Earth's land surface but contains only 1 percent of Earth's biomass. The lack of water in the desert and in the tundra makes plant life scarce in these areas.

Forest biomes contain 75 percent of Earth's biomass. There are three forest biomes: the coniferous (ku-NIF-er-us) forest, the deciduous
30 (dih-SIJ-ū-us) forest, and the rain forest. Forests receive abundant precipitation. Rain forest covers only 6 percent of Earth's land surface, but contains more than 50 percent of all Earth's biomass. The rainforest biome is also the most diverse biome. The destruction of the rain forests is a serious environmental problem.

35 Rain forest are found in tropical regions where there is abundant rainfall year-round. In some parts of the tropics, however, a rainy season is followed by a dry season. In these regions, a biome called tropical dry forest occurs. During the dry season, nearly all the trees drop their leaves to conserve water. Tropical dry forests are found in parts of Africa, South and
40 Central America, Mexico, India, Australia, and tropical islands.

Another biome in which precipitation is highly seasonal is temperate woodland and shrubland. Regions in this biome have hot, dry summers and cool, rainy winters. Worldwide, there are only 5 areas of temperate woodland and shrubland: California, central Chile, the region around
45 Cape Town, South Africa, southwestern Australia, and the lands bordering the Mediterranean Sea. What do these regions have in common? All are located along seacoasts. In addition, all except the region around the Mediterranean are on west-facing edges of continents. As a result, their climates are affected by cool ocean currents.

50 The landscapes of the temperate woodland and shrubland biome are made up of a mix of shrub communities and open woodlands. In California, for example, oak woodlands are interspersed with large areas of grasses and wildflowers such as poppies. Another type of community in this biome, called chaparral, is dominated by shrubs. Chaparral is made up of

55 densely growing, low plants that contain flammable oils. Some of these plants are woody evergreen shrubs with small, leathery leaves. Other are fragrant plants, as well as the grasses of the open woodland, catch first easily during the dry season. The plants, however, are adapted to recurrent fires. Some types of plants grow back quickly after the fires, while others
60 have seeds that must be exposed to fire in order to germinate. Thus fire plays an important part in maintaining the ecosystems of this biome.

Some land areas cannot easily be classified as belonging to a particular biome. High mountains, for example, have lower temperatures and receive more precipitation than surrounding areas. For this reason, the
65 plants and animals found in mountain regions can be quite different from those in nearby lowlands. In Earth's polar regions, life is largely absent from the thick icecaps that cover much of Greenland and Antarctica. But where there is exposed land, mosses and lichens can grow, and seabirds and mammals are abundant in coastal areas.

15. The ecosystems of Earth are divided into nine major biomes. What is a biome?

   (A) An ecosystem with distinctive temperature, rainfall, and organisms
   (B) A major type of ecosystem with distinctive temperature, rainfall, and organisms
   (C) Terrestrial or aquatic areas
   (D) The largest category scientists use to classify ecosystems
   (E) An ecosystem determined by average temperature and the amount of precipitation the area receives

16. The kind of land biome that will develop in any given area is determined by temperature and what?

   (A) precipitation
   (B) average wind speed
   (C) barometric pressure
   (D) the types of animals present
   (E) the types of plants present

17. Desert and tundra biomes have different temperatures, but the amount of precipitation each receives is what?

   (A) nearly equal
   (B) very little
   (C) equal
   (D) abundant
   (E) none

18. Which biome contains the most biomass?

    (A) Coniferous forest

    (B) Desert

    (C) Forest

    (D) Temperate woodland and shrubland

    (E) Chaparral

19. The destruction of the rain forest is a serious environmental concern. Why?

    (A) The rain forest covers six percent of the Earth's land surface.

    (B) Rain forests are found only in tropical regions.

    (C) Rain forests have abundant rainfall year-round.

    (D) The rain forest contains more than 50 percent of the Earth's biomass.

    (E) The smoke from the fires used to burn the forest are polluting the air.

20. What's the most significant climatic difference between a rain forest and a tropical dry forest?

    (A) The rain forest gets rain year-round; the tropical dry forest has a dry season.

    (B) Nothing. Both terms are references to the same type of biome.

    (C) The rain forest has a dry season; the tropical dry forest gets rain year-round.

    (D) Rain forests are found in the tropical zones; tropical dry forest aren't restricted to the tropical zones.

    (E) The rain forest has a large percentage of the Earth's biomass; the tropical dry forest has little biomass diversity.

21. There are only five temperate woodland and shrubland areas on the Earth. Where are they?

    (A) The United States, Chile, South Africa, Australia, and the coastlands of the Mediterranean Sea

    (B) California, Chile, Cape Town, Australia, and the coastlands of the Mediterranean Sea

    (C) The United States, Chile, South Africa, Australia, and the Mediterranean Sea

    (D) California, central Chile, Cape Town, South Africa, southwestern Australia, and the coastlands of the Mediterranean Sea

    (E) There are only four, not five temperate woodland and shrubland areas.

22. What do the five temperate woodland and shrubland areas all have in common, besides their biome type attributes?

(A) All are facing west.

(B) All are located along seacoasts and are facing west.

(C) All are located along seacoasts and except for the Mediterranean Sea coastline, all are facing west.

(D) All have hot, dry summers and cool, rainy winters.

(E) All are located along seacoasts.

23. How have the plants of the woodland and shrubland biome adapted to fire?

(A) They haven't, and fire is a serious environmental hazard to these biomes.

(B) Most plants in this biome grow back quickly after fire. Others have seeds that must be exposed to fire before they will germinate.

(C) Some plants contain flammable oils.

(D) Because some seeds must be exposed to fire, the area also produces plants that contain flammable oils.

(E) Some plants grow in winter and die in summer during the fire season.

24. High mountain areas usually belong to this biome type.

(A) Tundra.

(B) Woodland and shrubland.

(C) It is hard to classify areas in the high mountains as belonging to any particular biome.

(D) Mountains and ice caps.

(E) Mountains and ice caps, and woodland and shrubland.

STOP

If you finish before time is called, you may check your work on this section only. Do not turn to any other section in the test.

Section 7

Time—20 minutes

16 Questions

Turn to Section 7 of your answer sheet to answer the questions in this section.

> **Directions:** For this section, solve each problem and decide which is the best of the choices given. Fill in the corresponding circle on the answer sheet. You can use any available space for scratchwork.

Notes:

1. The use of a calculator is permitted.

2. All numbers used are real numbers.

3. Figures that accompany problems in the test are intended to provide information that is useful in solving the problems. They are drawn as accurately as possible EXCEPT when it is stated in a specific problem that the figure is not drawn to scale. All figures lie in a plane unless otherwise indicated.

4. Unless otherwise specified, the domain of any function *f* is assumed to be the set of real numbers *x* for which *f(x)* is a real number.

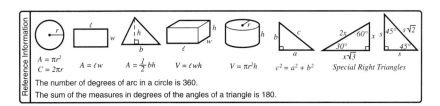

Reference Information

$A = \pi r^2$
$C = 2\pi r$ $A = \ell w$ $A = \frac{1}{2} bh$ $V = \ell wh$ $V = \pi r^2 h$ $c^2 = a^2 + b^2$ *Special Right Triangles*

The number of degrees of arc in a circle is 360.
The sum of the measures in degrees of the angles of a triangle is 180.

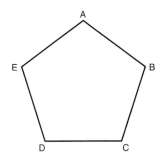

1. The figure above shows a regular pentagon. What is the angle ∠ABC?

   (A) 60°
   (B) 90°
   (C) 108°
   (D) 115°
   (E) 180°

2. c is an even number not divisible by 6. How many such numbers are there between 1 and 100, inclusive?

(A) 16

(B) 34

(C) 38

(D) 49

(E) 50

3. Two numbers A and B have a least common multiple of 72. A is not divisible by 3. Which of these could be B?

(A) 6

(B) 12

(C) 24

(D) 30

(E) 36

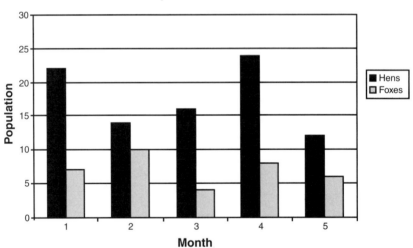

Population levels

4. The graph above shows the total populations of two different kinds of animals across five months. In which month was the difference between the two populations the least?

(A) Month 1

(B) Month 2

(C) Month 3

(D) Month 4

(E) Month 5

5. For a certain function $g(x)$, $g(0) = -3$, $g(1) = 0$, and $g(2) = 5$. Which of these equations defines $g(x)$?

(A) $g(x) = x^2 + 2x - 3$

(B) $g(x) = x^2 - 3x - 3$

(C) $g(x) = 2x^2 - 3$

(D) $g(x) = x^2 + 2x + 3$

(E) $g(x) = 2x^2 + x - 3$

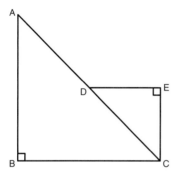

6. In the figure above, $\triangle ABC$ and $\triangle CED$ are similar triangles and $\angle BAC = 45°$. If $AB = 3$ and D is the midpoint of $\overline{AC}$, what is the area of $\triangle CED$?

(A) $9\sqrt{2}$

(B) 9

(C) $\dfrac{9}{4}$

(D) $\dfrac{9}{2}$

(E) $\dfrac{9}{8}$

7. Each book on a shelf is assigned a subject, and no book has more than one subject. The chance of selecting a history book at random from the shelf is $\dfrac{1}{6}$, the chance of selecting a psychology book at random from the shelf is $\dfrac{1}{3}$, and the chance of selecting a mathematics book at random from the shelf is $\dfrac{1}{7}$. Which of these could be the number of books on the shelf?

(A) 21

(B) 84

(C) 18

(D) 98

(E) 36

8. A bird travels due north 18 miles, then due east 6 miles, then due south 14 miles, then due west 3 miles. How far from its starting point is the bird?

(A) 3 miles

(B) 4 miles

(C) 5 miles

(D) 32 miles

(E) 41 miles

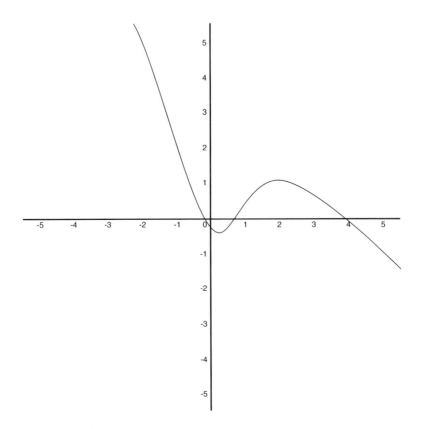

9. The figure above shows part of the graph of $f(x)$. How many zeroes does $f(x)$ have?

(A) 0

(B) 1

(C) 2

(D) 3

(E) At least 3

10. Let a' = (a + 4) ÷ 2. If (x')' = 5, what is x?

(A) 5

(B) 6

(C) 7

(D) 8

(E) 9

11. A bag contains 30 tiles. Three of these tiles are marked with the digit 0, three with the digit 1, and so on. You draw three tiles from the bag to form a three-digit number, starting with the first tile. What is the chance that the number will start with the digit 7?

(A) $\frac{1}{30}$

(B) $\frac{1}{15}$

(C) $\frac{1}{10}$

(D) $\frac{31}{100}$

(E) $\frac{111}{300}$

12. The volume of a cube is K. Each side of the cube is increased by 50%. What is the new volume of the cube?

(A) 1.5K

(B) 2K

(C) 3.375K

(D) 4K

(E) 5.275K

13. If all birds from Leningrad have two layers of feathers, which of the following statements is true?

(A) All birds with two layers of feathers are from Leningrad.

(B) There is at least one bird with three layers of feathers that is from Leningrad.

(C) All birds outside of Leningrad do not have three layers of feathers.

(D) There are no birds from Leningrad with one layer of feathers.

(E) Birds with three layers of feathers are found both in and out of Leningrad.

14. A certain ore consists of iron, tin, and waste in the ratio of 2:1:22. How many tons of iron are contained in 200 tons of ore?

(A) 2

(B) 4

(C) 16

(D) 21

(E) 100

15. Let $M(x)$ be the number of members in the set of all positive integers greater than 1 and less than x by which x is not divisible. Which of these is the same as $M(9)$?

(A) $M(4)$

(B) $M(5)$

(C) $M(7)$

(D) $M(8)$

(E) $M(10)$

16. You have an unlimited supply of black paint, an unlimited supply of white paint, and a cube. Each face of the cube will be painted one solid color, either black or white. How many different ways could you paint the cube? (Two ways of painting the cube are different if a cube painted in one of them cannot be rotated or reflected to match the other way.)

(A) 4

(B) 6

(C) 8

(D) 10

(E) 12

STOP

If you finish before time is called, you may check your work on this section only. Do not turn to any other section in the test.

Section 8

Time—20 minutes

19 Questions

Turn to Section 8 of your answer sheet to answer the questions in this section.

Directions: For each question in this section, select the best answer from among the choices given and fill in the corresponding circle on the answer sheet.

Each sentence below has one or two blanks, each blank indicating that something has been omitted. Beneath the sentence are five words or sets of words labeled A through E. Choose the word or set of words that, when inserted in the sentence, <u>best</u> fits the meaning of the sentence as a whole.

Example:

The Internet is _____ now, being available in 78% of all American households.

    (A) unimportant

    (B) transitory

    (C) migrating

    (D) negligible

    (E) ubiquitous

Answer: (E)

1. The neighbor's _____ bamboo was _____ our outer flower beds, regardless of what we did.

    (A) widespread . . bordering

    (B) hearty . . protecting

    (C) vigilant . . reinforcing

    (D) diminishing . . supporting

    (E) invasive . . encroaching

2. Her childish antics had left her with a/an _____ of self-respect.

    (A) modicum

    (B) degree

    (C) abundance

    (D) plethora

    (E) famine

3. A _____ upbringing can turn someone into a _____ housekeeper—waste not, want not.

(A) miserly . . lavish

(B) deprived . . cheap

(C) generous . . impecunious

(D) penurious . . frugal

(E) indigent . . copious

4. Your lovely flowers can't _____ your despicable actions of last evening.

(A) repudiate

(B) affirm

(C) negate

(D) refuse

(E) eradicate

5. Susie showed her pleasure at being chosen class president with _____—meeting all the challenges immediately.

(A) alacrity

(B) surprise

(C) joy

(D) trepidation

(E) caution

6. He looked past her _____ limbs and saw the once _____ and agile frame of the ballerina he fell in love with years ago.

(A) rickety . . nimble

(B) tremulous . . lithe

(C) waning . . flexible

(D) taunt . . fickle

(E) fragile . . stalwart

The two passages below are followed by questions based on their content and on the relationship between the two passages. Answer the questions on the basis of what is <u>stated</u> or <u>implied</u> in the passages and in any introductory material that may be provided.

> ## Questions 7–19 are based on the following passages.
>
> *These passages present two views of judicial authority in the United States. The first is by Alexander Hamilton, arguing in favor of the ratification of the Constitution. The second is by French observer Alexis de Toqueville writing on the effects of that Constitution about 60 years later.*

Passage 1:

LET US now return to the partition of the judiciary authority between different courts, and their relations to each other, "The judicial power of the United States is" (by the plan of the convention) "to be vested in one
Line Supreme Court, and in such inferior courts as the Congress may, from
5 time to time, ordain and establish."

That there ought to be one court of supreme and final jurisdiction, is a proposition which is not likely to be contested. The reasons for it have been assigned in another place, and are too obvious to need repetition. The only question that seems to have been raised concerning it, is,
10 whether it ought to be a distinct body or a branch of the legislature. The same contradiction is observable in regard to this matter which has been remarked in several other cases. The very men who object to the Senate as a court of impeachments, on the ground of an improper intermixture of powers, advocate, by implication at least, the propriety of vesting the
15 ultimate decision of all causes, in the whole or in a part of the legislative body.

The arguments, or rather suggestions, upon which this charge is founded, are to this effect: "The authority of the proposed Supreme Court of the United States, which is to be a separate and independent body, will be
20 superior to that of the legislature. The power of construing the laws according to the SPIRIT of the Constitution, will enable that court to mould them into whatever shape it may think proper; especially as its decisions will not be in any manner subject to the revision or correction of the legislative body. This is as unprecedented as it is dangerous. In
25 Britain, the judical power, in the last resort, resides in the House of Lords, which is a branch of the legislature; and this part of the British government has been imitated in the State constitutions in general. The Parliament of Great Britain, and the legislatures of the several States, can at any time rectify, by law, the exceptionable decisions of their respective
30 courts. But the errors and usurpations of the Supreme Court of the United States will be uncontrollable and remediless." This, upon examination, will be found to be made up altogether of false reasoning upon misconceived fact.

In the first place, there is not a syllable in the plan under consideration
35 which DIRECTLY empowers the national courts to construe the laws
according to the spirit of the Constitution, or which gives them any
greater latitude in this respect than may be claimed by the courts of every
State. I admit, however, that the Constitution ought to be the standard of
construction for the laws, and that wherever there is an evident opposi-
40 tion, the laws ought to give place to the Constitution. But this doctrine is
not deducible from any circumstance peculiar to the plan of the convention, but from the general theory of a limited Constitution; and as far as
it is true, is equally applicable to most, if not to all the State governments.
There can be no objection, therefore, on this account, to the federal judi-
45 cature which will not lie against the local judicatures in general, and which
will not serve to condemn every constitution that attempts to set bounds
to legislative discretion.

But perhaps the force of the objection may be thought to consist in the
particular organization of the Supreme Court; in its being composed of a
50 distinct body of magistrates, instead of being one of the branches of the
legislature, as in the government of Great Britain and that of the State. To
insist upon this point, the authors of the objection must renounce the
meaning they have labored to annex to the celebrated maxim, requiring a
separation of the departments of power. It shall, nevertheless, be conced-
55 ed to them, agreeably to the interpretation given to that maxim in the
course of these papers, that it is not violated by vesting the ultimate power
of judging in a PART of the legislative body. But though this be not an
absolute violation of that excellent rule, yet it verges so nearly upon it, as
on this account alone to be less eligible than the mode preferred by the
60 convention. From a body which had even a partial agency in passing bad
laws, we could rarely expect a disposition to temper and moderate them
in the application. The same spirit which had operated in making them,
would be too apt in interpreting them; still less could it be expected that
men who had infringed the Constitution in the character of legislators,
65 would be disposed to repair the breach in the character of judges. Nor is
this all. Every reason which recommends the tenure of good behavior for
judicial offices, militates against placing the judiciary power, in the last
resort, in a body composed of men chosen for a limited period. There is
an absurdity in referring the determination of causes, in the first instance,
70 to judges of permanent standing; in the last, to those of a temporary and
mutable constitution. And there is a still greater absurdity in subjecting
the decisions of men, selected for their knowledge of the laws, acquired by
long and laborious study, to the revision and control of men who, for want
of the same advantage, cannot but be deficient in that knowledge. The
75 members of the legislature will rarely be chosen with a view to those

qualifications which fit men for the stations of judges; and as, on this account, there will be great reason to apprehend all the ill consequences of defective information, so, on account of the natural propensity of such bodies to party divisions, there will be no less reason to fear that the pesti-
80 lential breath of faction may poison the fountains of justice. The habit of being continually marshalled on opposite sides will be too apt to stifle the voice both of law and of equity.

Passage 2:

The first characteristic of judicial power in all nations is the duty of arbitration. But rights must be contested in order to warrant the interference
85 of a tribunal; and an action must be brought to obtain the decision of a judge. As long, therefore, as the law is uncontested, the judicial authority is not called upon to discuss it, and it may exist without being perceived. When a judge in a given case attacks a law relating to that case, he extends the circle of his customary duties, without however stepping beyond it;
90 since he is in some measure obliged to decide upon the law in order to decide the case. But if he pronounces upon a law without resting upon a case, he clearly steps beyond his sphere, and invades that of the legislative authority.

The second characteristic of judicial power is that it pronounces on spe-
95 cial cases, and not upon general principles. If a judge in deciding a particular point destroys a general principle, by passing a judgment which tends to reject all the inferences from that principle, and consequently to annul it, he remains within the ordinary limits of his functions. But if he directly attacks a general principle without having a particular case in view, he
100 leaves the circle in which all nations have agreed to confine his authority, he assumes a more important, and perhaps a more useful, influence than that of the magistrate, but he ceases to be a representative of the judicial power.

The third characteristic of the judicial power is its inability to act unless it
105 is appealed to, or until it has taken cognizance of an affair. This characteristic is less general than the other two; but, notwithstanding the exceptions, I think it may be regarded as essential. The judicial power is by its nature devoid of action; it must be put in motion in order to produce a result. When it is called upon to repress a crime, it punishes the criminal;
110 when a wrong is to be redressed, it is ready to redress it; when an act requires interpretation, it is prepared to interpret it; but it does not pursue criminals, hunt out wrongs, or examine into evidence of its own accord. A judicial functionary who should open proceedings, and usurp the censorship of the laws, would in some measure do violence to the
115 passive nature of his authority.

The Americans have retained these three distinguishing characteristics of the judicial power; an American judge can only pronounce a decision when litigation has arisen, he is only conversant with special cases, and he cannot act until the cause has been duly brought before the court. His
120 position is therefore perfectly similar to that of the magistrate of other nations; and he is nevertheless invested with immense political power. If the sphere of his authority and his means of action are the same as those of other judges, it may be asked whence he derives a power which they do not possess. The cause of this difference lies in the simple fact that the
125 Americans have acknowledged the right of the judges to found their decisions on the constitution rather than on the laws. In other words, they have left them at liberty not to apply such laws as may appear to them to be unconstitutional.

I am aware that a similar right has been claimed—but claimed in vain—by
130 courts of justice in other countries; but in America it is recognized by all authorities; and not a party, nor so much as an individual, is found to contest it. This fact can only be explained by the principles of the American constitution.

In France the constitution is (or at least is supposed to be) immutable; and
135 the received theory is that no power has the right of changing any part of it. In England the Parliament has an acknowledged right to modify the constitution; as, therefore, the constitution may undergo perpetual changes, it does not in reality exist; the Parliament is at once a legislative and a constituent assembly. The political theories of America are more
140 simple and more rational. An American constitution is not supposed to be immutable as in France, nor is it susceptible of modification by the ordinary powers of society as in England. It constitutes a detached whole, which, as it represents the determination of the whole people, is no less binding on the legislator than on the private citizen, but which may be
145 altered by the will of the people in predetermined cases, according to established rules. In America the constitution may therefore vary, but as long as it exists it is the origin of all authority, and the sole vehicle of the predominating force.

7. In referring to his opponents' views as "arguments, or rather suggestions" (line 17), the author of passage 1

    (A) agrees that his opponents have a valid point.

    (B) suggests that those views do not form a coherent argument.

    (C) demonstrates that he is unwilling to listen to opposition.

    (D) acquiesces to the desires reflected in those views.

    (E) indicates that he thinks the reader will disagree with him.

8. The word "rectify" (line 29) most nearly means

(A) recognize

(B) ratify

(C) consider

(D) fix

(E) confirm

9. The sentence beginning "There can be no objection" (line 44) in passage 1 can be summarized as

(A) No one can object to the proposed powers of the judiciary.

(B) In general, local courts ought to have more powers than the federal courts.

(C) All legislatures must be able to overrule the courts when necessary.

(D) Any objection to this plan applies to any constitution that restricts the legislature.

(E) Courts can condemn entire constitutions as readily as they can condemn men.

10. The word "militates" (line 67) most nearly means

(A) argues

(B) has influence

(C) prevents

(D) loses

(E) dictates

11. "The pestilential breath of faction" (lines 79–80) might be expressed as

(A) the wrongful interpretation of laws

(B) the evil influence of party divisions

(C) the studious knowledge of judges

(D) the positive effects of debate

(E) the arduous process of legislation

12. The author of passage 2 refers to judicial authority as "passive" (lines 114–115) because

(A) judges are required to apply the law without interpreting it.

(B) judges only decide specific cases rather than general matters.

(C) judges are required to arbitrate between parties who disagree.

(D) judges hold their jobs for life and cannot be forced to work.

(E) judges cannot act on their own without a specific case.

13. The author of passage 2 believes that judges in the United States are "invested with immense political power" (line 121) because

    (A) their sphere of authority is greater than that of judges of other nations.

    (B) they can make decisions based solely on their own personal ideas.

    (C) they can base their decisions on the Constitution rather than laws.

    (D) they can dismiss the legislature in cases of emergency.

    (E) their means of action are more flexible than those of judges of other nations.

14. According to the author of passage 2, judges

    (A) should be guided by the intent of the legislature in all cases.

    (B) must apply all laws equally to the cases before them.

    (C) are to be guided only by the Constitution when making a decision.

    (D) are a fundamental check on the power of the legislature to pass bad laws.

    (E) need not apply unconstitutional laws when deciding cases.

15. In the phrase "it does not in reality exist," (line 138) "it" refers to

    (A) the French constitution

    (B) the English constitution

    (C) the state of England

    (D) Parliament

    (E) the right to modify the constitution

16. Which of these assumptions does the author of passage 2 make that the author of passage 1 would probably question?

    (A) Legislatures are prone to pass unjust laws because of factional interests.

    (B) The judicial power should only be invoked when it is expressly appealed to.

    (C) The ability to review laws is better vested in the judiciary than in the legislature.

    (D) The ability of the courts to review the constitutionality of laws is unquestioned.

    (E) Separation of powers among branches of government is a good thing.

17. In evaluating the arguments of passage 1, the author of passage 2 would most likely

    (A) be glad that those arguments prevailed.

    (B) point out logical inconsistencies.

    (C) hope to find time to write a rebuttal.

    (D) wonder if they were still relevant.

    (E) disagree with them completely.

18. Compared with passage 1, passage 2 is more

(A) argumentative

(B) descriptive

(C) narrative

(D) logical

(E) judicious

19. If he could read passage 2, the author of passage 1 would most likely be

(A) outraged

(B) amused

(C) satisfied

(D) despairing

(E) embarrassed

STOP

If you finish before time is called, you may check your work on this section only. Do not turn to any other section in the test.

Section 9

Time—10 minutes

14 Questions

Turn to Section 9 of your answer sheet to answer the questions in this section.

> **Directions:** For each question in this section, select the best answer from among the choices given and fill in the corresponding circle on the answer sheet.

> The following sentences test correctness and effectiveness of expression. Part of each sentence or the entire sentence is underlined; beneath each sentence are five ways of phrasing the underlined material. Choice A repeats the original phrasing; the other four choices are different. If you think the original phrasing produces a better sentence than any of the alternatives, select choice A; if not, select one of the other choices.

(see next page)

In making your selection, follow the requirements of standard written English; that is, pay attention to grammar, choice of words, sentence construction, and punctuation. Your selection should result in the most effective sentence—clear and precise, without awkwardness or ambiguity.

Example:

The weather that winter was <u>worse than for at least five decades</u>.

    (A) worse than for at least five decades

    (B) the worse it was for at least five decades

    (C) worse. Than it had been for at least five decades.

    (D) the worst that it had been for at least five decades

    (E) the worst it was for at least five decades.

Answer: (D)

1. Many immigrants are actually refugees <u>having need of</u> refuge from political repression.

    (A) having need of

    (B) taking

    (C) having a need for

    (D) taking advantage of

    (E) fleeing

2. Whether serving as tools or toys, computers<u>, they are prevalent in most homes now</u>.

    (A) , they are prevalent in most homes now

    (B) are prevalent

    (C) they are prevalent

    (D) are prevalent in most homes

    (E) are prevalent in most homes now

3. <u>After having played many bit parts</u>, Kate was finally given a leading role in an independent film.

    (A) After having played many bit parts

    (B) Only after taking many bit parts

    (C) After taking many bit parts

    (D) After many bit parts

    (E) Many bit parts later

4. Bill and Susan <u>celebrates their anniversary quietly</u> each year.

    (A) celebrates their anniversary quietly

    (B) celebrate their anniversary quietly

    (C) quietly celebrates their anniversary

    (D) quietly celebrate their anniversary

    (E) celebrate the anniversary quietly

5. <u>Playing in the shade,</u> her parents watched from a table nearby.

    (A) Playing in the shade,

    (B) She played in the shade as

    (C) Playing

    (D) In the shade

    (E) She playing in the shade

6. <u>The presents were met</u> with scant enthusiasm.

    (A) The presents were met

    (B) The presents received

    (C) They met the presents

    (D) Presents were met

    (E) They met the inappropriate presents

7. I was aghast to see <u>on school nights, little children dancing for money late into the night</u>.

    (A) on school nights, little children dancing for money late into the night

    (B) little children on school nights, dancing late into the night for money

    (C) little children dancing for money late into the night on school nights

    (D) dancing for money, little children late into the night

    (E) little children dancing for money late into the night

8. Our entire collection of fine art—<u>all of it—are for sale</u>.

    (A) all of it—are for sale

    (B) all of it—is for sale

    (C) all are for sale

    (D) all of it is for sale

    (E) all of them are for sale

9. Neither those doughnuts <u>nor that hot chocolate entice me to indulge</u> while dieting.

    (A) nor that hot chocolate entice me to indulge

    (B) nor that hot chocolate entices me to indulge

    (C) nor that hot chocolate entice me

    (D) nor that hot chocolate are going to entice me

    (E) nor that hot chocolate entices me

10. <u>She contemplated her diet while smelling the pastries in line.</u>

    (A) She contemplated her diet while smelling the pastries in line.

    (B) She smelled the pastries in line and contemplated her diet.

    (C) She contemplated her diet in line while smelling the pastries.

    (D) Contemplating her diet, she smelled the pastries in line.

    (E) In line, she contemplated her diet while smelling the pastries.

11. <u>Cutting in line, the store manager threw them out.</u>

    (A) Cutting in line, the store manager threw them out.

    (B) The store manager cutting in line, threw them out.

    (C) Throwing them out, the store manager for cutting in line.

    (D) The store manager threw them out for cutting in line.

    (E) Throwing them out for cutting in line, the store manager.

12. Everyone <u>that's going need</u> to be in the lobby by 6:00 A.M. tomorrow morning.

    (A) that's going need

    (B) that's planning to go need

    (C) planning to go needs

    (D) who's going needs

    (E) going needs

13. Bill passed the bags to Mark and <u>he held the door open for the lady in front of them.</u>

    (A) he held the door open for the lady in front of them

    (B) he held the door for the lady in front of them

    (C) he held the door for the lady in front

    (D) and holding the door open for the lady in front of them

    (E) then held the door open for the lady in front of them

14. Someday, <u>we will vacation up on Mars</u> and take short getaway trips to the moon.

(A) we will vacation up on Mars

(B) we will vacation on Mars

(C) we will take vacations on Mars

(D) we will plan vacations on Mars

(E) we will vacation in Mars

STOP

If you finish before time is called, you may check your work on this section only. Do not turn to any other section in the test.

Answer Key for Practice Exam #2

Section 1

Grading the essay is subjective, so there's no way we can help you through this process. Our best advice is to ask someone you trust who has the expertise to actually grade your essay to help you. If you have to go it alone, be sure to check for the following:

➤ Is the thesis well developed, insightful, and focused?

➤ Did you use clear and appropriate examples, anecdotes, and reasons to support your position?

➤ Are your thoughts organized logically?

➤ Did you use a variety of writing techniques, such as varied sentence structure and length?

➤ Did you use appropriate words?

➤ Is the essay free of grammatical and spelling errors?

If possible, put a few days between test day and the day you try to grade your own work. Proofing your own work is very difficult—give your mind a chance to forget a bit. A few days later, you'll get a fresher, more objective look at the essay.

Don't try to assign an actual score to your essay. Instead, find your weak points and continue to practice in order to build your skills in that area.

Section 2

1. D	6. C	11. $\frac{1}{3}$ or .333	16. 3.6
2. D	7. E	12. 72	17. $\frac{96}{5}$ or 19.2
3. E	8. D	13. 3141	18. $\frac{1}{4}$ or .25
4. B	9. 450	14. $\frac{99}{7}$ or 14.1	
5. B	10. 16	15. $\frac{66}{9}$ or 7.33	

Section 3

1. C	10. C	19. C	28. B
2. E	11. D	20. A	29. E
3. C	12. B	21. C	30. D
4. B	13. B	22. A	31. C
5. D	14. E	23. D	32. A
6. B	15. C	24. A	33. B
7. A	16. B	25. B	34. D
8. E	17. D	26. C	35. C
9. C	18. C	27. B	

Section 4

1. E	7. A	13. D	19. C
2. A	8. B	14. D	20. A
3. B	9. D	15. A	21. E
4. D	10. C	16. D	22. D
5. C	11. E	17. E	23. B
6. E	12. B	18. A	24. E

Section 5

1. C	6. C	11. A	16. D
2. B	7. D	12. E	17. A
3. C	8. B	13. D	18. B
4. D	9. D	14. B	19. B
5. D	10. C	15. D	20. B

Section 6

1. D	7. D	13. B	19. D
2. A	8. B	14. D	20. A
3. D	9. D	15. B	21. D
4. B	10. D	16. A	22. E
5. C	11. E	17. B	23. B
6. A	12. A	18. C	24. C

Section 7

1. C	5. A	9. E	13. D
2. B	6. E	10. D	14. C
3. E	7. B	11. C	15. E
4. B	8. C	12. C	16. D

Section 8

1. E	6. B	11. B	16. D
2. A	7. B	12. E	17. A
3. D	8. D	13. C	18. B
4. C	9. D	14. E	19. C
5. A	10. B	15. B	

Section 9

1. B	5. B	9. B	13. E
2. E	6. C	10. E	14. B
3. D	7. C	11. D	
4. B	8. B	12. D	

Detailed Answers

Section 2

Question 1

Answer D is correct. To solve, multiply the first equation by 3 and the second by –2 and then add the two equations together so that the x term drops out:

$$3(2x + y) - 2(3x - 4y) = 3(15) - 2(-5)$$

$$6x + 3y - 6x + 8y = 45 + 10$$

$$11y = 55$$

$$y = 5$$

Question 2

Answer D is correct. The angles along any straight line add up to 180°, and each angle of a square is 90°. So $\angle y = 180° - 90° - 36° = 54°$.

Question 3

Answer E is correct. The chart does not contain a bar for Tuesday, so you don't know what the reading was on Tuesday. You can't assume that the Tuesday reading was the average of the Monday and Wednesday readings.

Question 4

Answer B is correct. You can calculate the answer this way:

$$r^{-3} = \frac{1}{r^3} = \frac{1}{27}$$

Question 5

Answer B is correct. Because the triangle is a 30°-60°-90° triangle, you know that AB = 2. Because the center of the circle is on this line, it must be a diameter of the circle. The radius of the circle is then $\frac{1}{2}$ this amount, or 1. Plug this in to the formula for the area of a circle $A = \pi r^2$ to get the answer.

Question 6

Answer C is correct. When you are considering the probabilities of a set of events that exhaust all the possibilities, they must add up to 1. So the probability of bacon with tea is $1 - (.27 + .35 + .22) = .16$.

Question 7

Answer E is correct. Use the information given to express s and t in terms of p:

$$s = 3 \times r = 3 \times 2 \times p$$
$$t = 6 \times r = 2 \times 3 \times 2 \times p$$

The greatest common factor of these two numbers is determined by multiplying the prime factors that they have in common. You're told that p is prime, so the greatest common factor is $2 \times 3 \times p = 6p$.

Question 8

Answer D is correct. $\triangle ABC$ is a right triangle with legs of length 3 and 4, so its hypotenuse is 5. This is also the side of the square and the diameter of the circle. The circumference is then π times the diameter.

Question 9

There are 15 different ways to pick a left-handed student, and 30 different ways to pick a right-handed student. These are independent events, so just multiply the two together to determine that there are 450 possible teams. Grid 450 to receive credit.

Question 10

You should recognize $f(x) = -x^2 - 6x + 7$ as defining a parabola that opens downward. Because a parabola is symmetric, the maximum will occur at the point halfway between the zeroes of -7 and 1. Thus, the answer is $f(-3) = -(-3)^2 - 6(-3) + 7 = -9 + 18 + 7 = 16$. Grid 16 to receive credit.

Question 11

You don't need to figure out the equation of the second line to solve this problem, although knowing a point on the line lets you do so. Remember, two lines are perpendicular if the product of their slopes is -1. Because the slope of the first line is -3, that means the slope of the second line must be $\frac{1}{3}$. Grid $\frac{1}{3}$ or .333 to receive credit.

Question 12

The angles of a triangle always add up to 180°, so $\angle ABC + \angle ACB = 180 - 36 = 144$. But because AB = AC, this is an isosceles triangle and the two base angles must be equal. So each of them is $\frac{144}{2} = 72°$. Grid 72 to receive credit.

Question 13

To calculate the value of a composition, you must work from the inside out. So first you need to calculate $g(4) = 6 \times 4 + 4 = 28$. Then the answer is $f(28) = 4 \times 28^2 + 5 = 3141$. Grid 3141 for credit.

Question 14

R is made up of 7 squares and has an area of 11 units, so each square has an area of $\frac{11}{7}$. S is made up of 9 squares, so its area is $\frac{9 \times 11}{7} = \frac{99}{7}$. Grid $\frac{99}{7}$ or 14.1 to receive credit.

Question 15

The sum of the first set of numbers is $6 \times 9.5 = 57$. The sum of the second set of numbers is $3 \times 3 = 9$. Thus, the sum of the entire set is $57 + 9 = 66$, and their average is $\frac{66}{9} = 7.33$. Grid $\frac{66}{9}$ or 7.33 for credit.

Question 16

The first bookstore sells the book for $18 - (.05 \times 18) = 17.10$. The second bookstore sells the book for $18 + (.15 \times 18) = 20.70$. The difference between the two is 3.6. Grid 3.6 to receive credit.

Question 17

You can calculate the answer like this:

$$\left(\frac{2}{3} \times \frac{3}{4} \times \frac{5}{6}\right) x = 8$$

$$\frac{2 \times 3 \times 5}{3 \times 4 \times 6} \; x = 8$$

$$30x = 8 \times 72$$

$$x = \frac{576}{30} = \frac{96}{5} = 19.2$$

So grid 19.2 or $\frac{96}{5}$ to receive credit.

Question 18

Start by enumerating the different ways that you can get three heads and one tail in four flips of the coin:

THHH

HTHH

HHTH

HHHT

So, there are four possibilities that give the desired outcome. You can calculate the total number of outcomes by noting that each flip can come up in two different ways, so the total is $2^4 = 16$. The probability of one tail is thus $\frac{4}{16} = \frac{1}{4} = .25$. Grid $\frac{1}{4}$ or .25 to receive credit.

Section 3

Question 1

Answer C is correct. Throughout this book, we've talked a lot about unnecessary prepositions, but this time, the preposition "to" is missing. Otherwise, the plural noun "Quakers" modifies Herbert Hoover, and that just isn't grammatically possible. Answer A is incorrect because the segment is not correct as is. Answers B and D are wrong because there's no reason to drop anything from the sentence. Answer E is incorrect because transposing the phrases introduces new problems.

Question 2

Answer E is correct. The subject is Mike and Bill, and "he" doesn't match in number. When fixing the pronoun's number, you must also fix the verb's number. Answer A is incorrect because the segment is not correct as is. Answer B is incorrect because there's no need to rearrange anything. Answers C and D and both incorrect because there's no need to remove the adverb "ravenously."

Question 3

Answer C is correct. As is, the verb is misplaced—the action isn't "was keen" but "was embarrassed." She was what? She was embarrassed. The word "keen" modifies her embarrassment. Answer A is incorrect because the segment is not correct as is. Answer B is not correct because the verb is still misplaced. Answer D is incorrect because the prepositional phrase "for just a moment" seems to modify the action of falling down the stairs. Answer E is incorrect because it's just plain bad.

Question 4

Answer B is correct. The verb tense between clauses must match. The verb tense in the second clause is simple past, so you must make the first clause simple past. Answer A is incorrect because the segment is incorrect; as is, the segment is perfect past. Answer C is incorrect. It isn't necessary to remove the word "just." In fact, doing so changes the tone of the sentence just a bit. Answers D and E are incorrect as transposing the phrases introduces new problems.

Question 5

Answer D is correct as it makes the two items parallel. Answer A is incorrect because the segment is not correct as is. Answer B is incorrect because the comparison is understood; the additional words aren't necessary. Answer C is incorrect; "lab" should not be plural. Answer E is incorrect because the addition of the pronoun "their" isn't parallel with "in gym."

Question 6

Answer B is correct. The pronoun "it" would be the correct definite pronoun to refer to The *Forward*, but in this context, the pronoun "it" is used incorrectly. Answer A is incorrect because the segment is not correct as is. Answer C is incorrect because you need the pronoun "which." Answer D is incorrect because it gives too much importance to the phrase that follows. Answer E is incorrect because a definite pronoun, regardless of number, is incorrect.

Question 7

Answer A is correct. Even though the sentence sounds a little awkward, the clause is grammatically correct as it is used to describe age. Answers B, C, D and E are incorrect because there's no need to change the sentence.

Question 8

Answer E is correct. The items in the series must be parallel. In addition, the first item doesn't match the noun "men" in number. Answer A is incorrect because the segment is not correct as is. Answer B is incorrect. Although the items are parallel, the items don't match the noun "men" in number. Answer C is incorrect because it's awkward. The use of "a" within the series is colloquial, and should be avoided. Answer D is incorrect because the series items still don't match the noun "man" in number.

Question 9

Answer C is correct. The subject is plural ("effects"); the verb must also be plural. Answer A is incorrect because the segment is not correct as is. Answer B is incorrect. It isn't necessary to change anything but the verb's number. Answers D and E are both incorrect as they change the verb's tense, unnecessarily.

Question 10

Answer C is correct. The items must be parallel. Answer A is incorrect because the segment is not correct as is. Answers B, D, and E are incorrect because they're not parallel. Answer E deserves a little more attention because the correct answer omits the adjective "many." That's because the other two phrases do not contain an adjective.

Question 11

Answer D is correct. Although it isn't apparent, "I/me" is the subject, not no one. Who is sorry? I am sorry. In addition, you don't need "more" when adding "er" to create a comparative adjective or adverb. Answer A is incorrect because the segment is not correct as is. Answer B is incorrect because "me" is the incorrect form of the subject "I." Answer C is incorrect because of "more sorry"—sorrier is the correct comparative form of sorry. Answer E is incorrect because it uses the wrong form of the subject "I."

Question 12

Answer B is correct. The phrase is singular, and the subject, "the twins" is plural. Answers A, C, and D are incorrect because there's nothing wrong with those segments. Answer E is incorrect because there is an error.

The twins were inspired to become professional dancers after seeing The Nutcracker *performed by the celebrated Russian Ballet.*

Question 13

Answer B is correct. Because the items are prefaced with the word "either," you must use "or." Yes, it's a trick question because you're used to seeing ice cream and cake combined as one dish. You could delete "either" and retain "and." But you can't use "either" and "and" together. Answers A, C, and D are incorrect as they are correctly used. Answer E is incorrect because there is a mistake in the sentence.

My sisters and I all prefer either cake or ice cream for dessert, when we allow ourselves to partake of the calories.

Question 14

Answer E is correct. Nothing is grammatically wrong with this sentence.

A properly secured computer will require that you enter your name and password before you can begin working.

Question 15

Answer C is correct. The first verb phrase is present perfect; the second verb phrase is simple past. The verb tense must match. Answers A, B, and D are all correct as these segments are used correctly. Answer E is incorrect because the sentence doesn't contain a mistake.

My brother Tim, a talented artist, has been a set designer, and has collaborated on a number of television commercials.

Question 16

Answer B is correct. "Where" is the correct interrogative pronoun; "where" refers to a place. A is incorrect because "only" is used correctly. Answers C and D are incorrect because the verb phrases are used correctly. Answer E is incorrect because the sentence isn't correct.

This was the only place she'd ever lived where the birds weren't plentiful and didn't flock to her birdfeeders all day long.

Question 17

Answer D is correct. The sentence is in simple past, but the phrase "when reaching" is a progressive tense. The verb phrases must match in tense. Answers A, B, and D are incorrect because those phrases are correct. Answer E is incorrect because there is a problem with the sentence.

After several months on the road west, many New England pioneers prematurely ended their move west when they reached the great plains.

Question 18

Answer C is the correct answer. The phrase "a kind" doesn't use an appropriate pronoun. Answers A, B, and D are incorrect because those segments are correct. Answer E is incorrect because the sentence is not correct as is.

Mount Rushmore, the only cliff carving of its kind in the United States, is a national monument.

Question 19

Answer C is correct. The prepositional phrase "in which" should be replaced by the interrogative pronoun "where." Answers A, B, and D are incorrect because those phrases are correct. Answer E is incorrect because the sentence isn't correct as is.

Many westward bound travelers ended their quest far east of California, in small towns along the trail where the weary travelers found comfort and community.

Question 20

Answer A is correct. The noun "preoccupation" requires the preposition "with," not "on." Answers B, C, and D are incorrect because those components are correct. Answer E is incorrect because there is a problem with the sentence.

Preoccupation with his social life began to affect his grades, which made his parents very unhappy.

Question 21

Answer C is correct. The verb must match the subject in number. In this case, the subject—"a doctor, a paleontologist, and a representative sent by our investors"—is less obvious because of the unusual sentence structure. The truth is, the sentence is still awkward even with the correction. Answers A, B, and D are incorrect because those components are correct. Answer E is incorrect because there is a mistake in the sentence.

Joining the expedition at the next stop were a doctor, a paleontologist, and a representative sent by our investors.

Question 22

Answer A is correct. Used in this context, "constant" is an adverb, not an adjective. Answers B, C, and D are incorrect because those phrases are correct. Answer E is incorrect because the sentence is not correct as is.

The constantly shifting winds made it difficult to navigate the small boat through the narrow cliffs.

Question 23

Answer D is correct. The phrase is completely unnecessary. Answers A, B, and C are incorrect because those components are correct. Answer E is incorrect because the sentence is not correct.

Jessica was never quite sure if her good looks were a blessing or a curse.

Question 24

Answer A is correct. The noun "people" requires the pronoun "who." Answers B, C, and D are incorrect because those phrases are correct. Answer E is incorrect because the sentence is not correct.

People who need immediate relief after a natural disaster can often be impatient and unruly with relief workers.

Question 25

Answer B is correct. When adding "er" to an adjective, don't use "more." Answers A, C, and D are incorrect because those components are correct. Answer E is incorrect because the sentence is not correct.

It was never clearer that Americans expected their government to be their guardian than during the twentieth century.

Question 26

Answer C is correct. The sentence tense is progressive past, but the phrase "having had to convince" is so awkward that it's hard to categorize. At best, it's perfect past. Answers A, B, and D are incorrect because those phrases are correct as is. Answer E is incorrect because the sentence is not correct.

John Muir, an author and naturalist, was a leader in the efforts to make Yosemite a national park, having to convince Theodore Roosevelt of the importance of conserving the forests.

Question 27

Answer B is correct. The verb must match the subject in number. Answers A, C, and D are incorrect because those phrases are correct. Answer E is incorrect because the sentence is not correct.

The number of reform mayors elected during the Progressive period accentuates the belief that more and more Americans wanted to be cared for and not just governed.

Question 28

Answer B is correct. The pronoun "they" doesn't match the subject in number. Answers A, C, and D are incorrect because those phrases are correct. Answer E is incorrect because the sentence does contain an error.

During Governor La Follette's three terms, he managed to enact a number of Progressive measures.

Question 29

Answer E is correct because there are no errors in this sentence. Answers A, B, C, and D are incorrect because those phrases are used correctly.

During the first half of the twentieth century, blacks moved from the south to the north hoping to find better jobs, more equality, and more opportunity.

Question 30

Answer D is correct. The new sentence emphasizes the fact that while settling the country is no longer a reason for moving, Americans continue to move. Answer A is incorrect because the sentence can be improved. Answers B, C, and E are incorrect because the Americans who settled the country are not the same Americans moving today. These changes introduce illogical timing into the passage.

Question 31

Answer C is correct. The singular subject, "one American," doesn't match the plural verb, "have." Answer A is incorrect because the sentence is not fine as is. Answer B is incorrect because it doesn't correct the subject/verb number conflict, and it introduces a new problem. Generally, you should spell out numeric values from one to ten. Answers D and E are incorrect because the propositions "from" and "of" are incorrectly used and neither corrects the subject/verb number conflict.

Question 32

Answer A is correct. The phrase "in which" is wrong as it refers to a place. It should be replaced with the interrogative pronoun "where." Answer B is incorrect because the sentence is not correct. Answers C and D are incorrect because the addition of "same" isn't required. Answer E is incorrect because it omits the interrogative pronoun altogether.

Question 33

Answer B is correct. As is, the number is confusing. Substituting the phrase "one of" with "a" eliminates the confusion. Answer A is incorrect because it's awkward, albeit grammatically correct. Answers C and D are incorrect because they weaken the sentence—"major" is an important part of the sentence. Answer E is incorrect because the word "exodus" is appropriate as used.

Question 34

Answer D is correct. Although technically correct, the immigrant clause makes the sentence wordy, and there's nothing else in the passage about immigrants. It's a bit out of place. In addition, the verb tense doesn't flow well with the rest of the passage. Answer C is incorrect because the term folks is allowable. Answer E is incorrect because there's not enough information to delete the transitional phrase. Within the context of a paragraph or essay, it might be correct.

Question 35

Answer C is correct. Most of the passage is already in simple past tense. The helping verb "had" puts this sentence in perfect past tense. Answers A and E are incorrect because they don't change the tense to simple past. Answers B and D are incorrect because they make the timing illogical.

Section 4
Question 1

Answer E is correct. The sentence is looking for a pair of opposite behaviors. The first is an adjective; the second is a noun. The sentence doesn't offer any clues whether the positive or negative behavior goes first or second—in fact, it doesn't really matter. Answers A, B, C, and D are all incorrect because the pairs aren't opposites. In addition, the second word in answer B is not a noun.

Question 2

Answer A is correct. This is one of those questions in which knowing the general definition of the responses helps. Answers B and C are incorrect because they are illogical. Answers D and E are incorrect because they aren't the best words for the job. Either could be logically correct, but neither is as strong as A.

Question 3

Answer B is correct. You're looking for a synonym to "secret"—the second phrase gives you that clue. Answer A is incorrect because it's illogical. Answer C is incorrect because within the context of this sentence, "confidential" isn't as strong as classified. Also, "confidential" is more of a business or personal secret, not a military secret. Answers D and E are both incorrect because they're illogical.

Question 4

Answer D is correct. You might not be sure if the words are true antonyms, but you can tell from the tone of the sentence that the second word is harsh. Answer A is incorrect because "addressing" isn't strong enough. In addition, "coy" just doesn't work. Answer B is incorrect. It could work if the first word, "restrained," was in another form. Answer C is incorrect because "clever" just doesn't fit and "managing" isn't strong enough. Answer E is incorrect because neither word is strong enough for the sentence.

Question 5

Answer C is correct. You know that you're looking for an unflattering word, and "sycophant" is the only one that has a distasteful connotation. Answer A is incorrect because it's illogical. Answer B is incorrect because it isn't strong enough. Answers D and E are incorrect. The celebrity might think of these people as inferior or underlings, but that wouldn't be the attribute that got them the job.

Question 6

Answer E is correct. The first word, "despite," is a clue that you're looking for a favorable adjective. Answer A is incorrect. We're looking for a favorable prognosis; earnest means truthful and heartfelt, so it just doesn't fit. Answer B is incorrect because it's illogical. Answer C is incorrect because it just doesn't fit—you can tell from the tone of the sentence that the prognosis is good. Answer D is incorrect, because it's illogical.

Question 7

Answer A is correct. Knowing the definition of "nefarious" will help. If you don't know, there's a clue in the phrase "as wicked as she was beautiful." You know these are conflicting qualities. Answer B is incorrect. Although it would work, it isn't as strong as A. Answers C and E are incorrect because they just don't make sense. Answer D is incorrect because "anachronistic" doesn't support the phrase that follows.

Question 8

Answer B is correct. The word "revealed" is your clue. You're looking for a pair of words that support each other as antonyms, without being true antonyms. Answer A is incorrect. A "solicitous" response would reveal just the opposite of disdain. Answer C is incorrect. Similarly to A, a sympathetic response would not reveal hate. Answers D and E are incorrect because the second words in each pair do not support the first words in the appropriate way.

Question 9

Answer D is correct. The Morrill Act was a land grant. Answers A and B are incorrect. Although the Morrill Act resulted in the founding of many new state colleges, doing so was not the act's function. Answer C is incorrect; the Act supplied no public funds for colleges, only land. Answer E is incorrect because the statement is false.

Question 10

Answer C is correct. Johns Hopkins was a Baltimore merchant. Answers A, B, D, and E are all incorrect because he was none of those things.

Question 11

Answer E is correct. Automobiles contributed the most to the booming post-war economy. Answers A, B, C, and D are all incorrect because they did not generate the same levels of trade that the automobile did.

Question 12

Answer B is correct. The system lacked 5,500 miles of being completed in 1975. Answers A, C, D, and E are all incorrect because they're the wrong amounts.

Question 13

Answer D is correct. The words "as the left had been" indicate that the author has previously traveled the alternative route on the left bank of the river. The other suggested answers are not implied by what is written in the passage.

Question 14

Answer D is correct. The spectacle provoked the men to laughter, so it must have been funny. The stronger word "hilarious" is more precise here than the weaker word "amusing" because it more clearly indicates the effect on the men. Answers C and E are incorrect because those are not synonyms for ludicrous, whereas answer B is incorrect because this synonym does not fit the passage.

Question 15

Answer A is correct. The sentence mentioning bad manners comes directly after a description of the men laughing at the native conversation. The other answers require you to assume or invent facts that are not a part of the passage as it is written.

Question 16

Answer D is correct. The first paragraph of this passage is mainly concerned with describing the incidents during a particular portion of the trip. Answers A, C, and E are incorrect because the author doesn't speculate, or indicate caution or outrage, in this paragraph. Answer B is incorrect because the laughter is described, rather than being the point of the paragraph.

Question 17

Answer E is correct. Lines 29 through 32 indicate that the author thinks that the wrong amount of rain leaves mud and decaying vegetation exposed to the hot sun and that this causes the fevers. Answer A is incorrect because rain by itself does not cause the fevers. Answers B and D are incorrect because those factors contribute to making the fevers worse, but do not themselves cause the fevers. Answer C is incorrect because quinine is used to treat the fevers, not to cause them.

Question 18

Answer A is correct. All the choices given are legitimate synonyms for "checked," but only the first fits the meaning of the paragraph.

Question 19

Answer C is correct. The writer makes it clear that he thinks a sedentary lifestyle is a major cause of the fevers and that the members of the party who traveled more often were less susceptible. Answer A is incorrect because he says explicitly that daily quinine doses didn't help. Answer B is incorrect because there's no mention of the fevers being caused by the river. Answer D is incorrect; lacking a cheerful attitude is mentioned as an effect of the fevers, not as a cause. Answer E is incorrect because it is apparently not the rain, but the effects of the rainy season, that are to blame.

Question 20

Answer A is correct. The passage contrasts the believers in quinine with the unbelievers in its prophylactic (that is, preventative) effects, the believers being those who took a daily dose. Answers B and C are incorrect because these answers are not supported at all by the passage. Answers D and E are from the passage, but are not necessarily connected with those who believed quinine would help.

Question 21

Answer E is correct. The author states that the best way to prevent fever is interesting work and a wholesome diet, so he believes that taking care of yourself helps avoid fever. Answers A and D are incorrect because the author doesn't say anything about people being punished by fevers. Answer B is incorrect because even with good medicine, he was unable to prevent fever in his own party. Answer C is incorrect because he doesn't say or imply that people complain too much about fevers in the region.

Question 22

Answer D is correct. Answer C is incorrect because "overabundant" is not a synonym for "wanting." Of the others, only "lacking" fits the original meaning of the sentence.

Question 23

Answer B is correct. The author indicates that quinine is useful in treating the fever, but that it does not prevent the fever. Answers A and C are incorrect because they claim falsely that quinine prevents the fever. Answer D is incorrect because the word "complaint" does not make sense here. Answer E is incorrect because the author does state quinine is a tonic.

Question 24

Answer E is correct. The last paragraph of the passage catalogs the effects of the fever on a man's temper and notes that these effects are often the first sign of the fever. Answer A is incorrect because the author doesn't indicate that he believes anyone is malingering. Answer B is incorrect because he states that drinking to excess increases one's chances of catching the fever. Answer C is incorrect because the author carried out experiments looking for a preventative; this argues that he is interested. Answer D is incorrect because the author suggests things that will lower the incidence of fever but does not say that he can eliminate it.

Section 5

Question 1

Answer C is correct. The two triangles have the same base and the same height; therefore, they have the same area. Thus, the ratio of their areas is 1:1.

Question 2

Answer B is correct. A number includes both 2 and 3 in its factors if it is divisible by 6. Thus, the question comes down to how many multiples of 6 there are between 1 and 50, and the answer is 8.

Question 3

Answer C is correct. The pictograph shows increases from March to April, April to May, and May to June. From March to April, there is an increase of 1 unit in 6, about 18%. From April to May, there is an increase of 3 units in 7, about 42%. From May to June, there is an increase of 1 unit in 10, or 10%.

Question 4

Answer D is correct. To calculate the reciprocal of a mixed number, first convert it to an improper fraction, than invert:

$$7\frac{1}{5} = \frac{(7 \times 5) + 1}{5} = \frac{36}{5}$$

So $7\frac{1}{5} = \frac{36}{5}$ and the reciprocal is $\frac{5}{36}$.

Question 5

Answer D is correct. If the area of the circle is 9π, then from $A = \pi r^2$ you know that $r = 3$. If the radius of the circle is 3, its diameter is 6. This is also the diagonal of the square. (Knowing that x is 45 tells you that the square isn't "tilted" because of the symmetry of the figure.) The diagonal and two sides of the square form a 45-45-90 right triangle, and you know that the ratio of the side to the hypotenuse in such a triangle is $1:\sqrt{2}$. The side of the square is then $\frac{6}{\sqrt{2}}$, and the area is the square of this, $\frac{36}{2} = 18$.

Question 6

Answer C is correct. The cities of Dover, Elway, and Krebs must form a triangle. You know that any side of a triangle can be no longer than the sum of the other two sides of the triangle. This sets an upper limit on the travel time from Dover to Krebs because you're told that the speed is constant.

Question 7

Answer D is correct. This is a simple exercise in geometric probability. The total area is 3 square inches, and the total area of the holes is 1 square inch. Thus, the total area not covered by holes is 2 square inches, and the probability of not hitting a hole is $\frac{2}{3}$.

Question 8

Answer B is correct. In this particular case, it's probably faster to calculate the first 12 terms of the series than it would be to derive a general formula using $a \times (b^{n-1})$ for the nth term:

2, 4, 8, 16, 32, 64, 128, 256, 512, 1,024, 2,048, 4,096

So after 12 months, there are 4,096 rabbits on the island.

Question 9

Answer D is correct. The surface area of a rectangular prism is $2lw + 2lh + 2wh$. Plug in the numbers you know and solve for h:

$A = 2lw + 2lh + 2wh$
$45 = (2 \times 3 \times 4) + (2 \times 3 \times h) + (2 \times 4 \times h)$
$45 = 24 + 6h + 8h$
$21 = 14h$
$1.5 = h$

Question 10

Answer C is correct. You could treat this as a weighted average problem, but there's no need to do so. Because each individual average includes the same number of observations, you can simply average the averages together. So the answer is $(\frac{12 + 14 + 22 + 16}{4})$ = 16 inches. You can check by treating it as a weighted average problem: multiply each average by five, add the results together, and divide by twenty. This gives you $(\frac{60 + 70 + 110 + 80}{20})$ for the same answer of 16 inches.

Question 11

Answer A is correct. Given the slope and y-intercept, you can write the equation that corresponds to $f(x)$: $y = 2/3 x + 3$. From this, you can calculate $f(12)$: $y = 2/3(12) + 3 = 11$.

Question 12

Answer E is correct. The volume of a right circular cylinder is given by the formula $V = \pi r^2 h$. From this, you can see that the volume is directly proportional to the height of the cylinder. If the volume increases by 25% without changing the radius, then the height must also increase by 25%. Thus the new height is $1.25 \times 12 = 15$.

Question 13

Answer D is correct. If the probability of drawing a black sock is .35, then the probability of drawing a white sock is .65 (because the total probability of all possible events always adds up to 1). This is the same as saying that 65% of the socks are white. If 13 socks are 65% of the total, then the total number of socks is $\frac{13}{65} = 20$. You can also think of this as the ratio of desired outcomes to total possible outcomes. The ratio of 13 to B + W is .65. You can easily solve this equation to find the sum.

Question 14

Answer B is correct. Because the two triangles are congruent, you know that the corresponding angles have the same measure. Thus each triangle has a 48° angle and a 71° angle. The angles of a triangle always add up to 180°, so the third angle is $180° - 48° - 71° = 61°$. If you draw the two triangles, you can confirm that $\angle CAB$ does not correspond to either of the two angles given in the question, so it is the 61° angle.

Question 15

Answer D is correct. The polynomial $x^2 + 4x - 8$ is prime because there is no pair of numbers that add up to 4 whose product is –8. The others factor as $(x + 1)(x - 1)$, $(x + 3)(x - 4)$, $(x + 2)(x + 1)$, and $(x + 3)(x + 2)$, respectively.

Question 16

Answer D is correct. A regular hexagon is made up of six equilateral triangles. This means that the radius of the circle is the same as the side of the hexagon, and the diameter of the circle is twice that, or 4 in this case. The total circumference of the circle is $\pi d = 4\pi$. Each arc is $\frac{1}{6}$ of that total, or $\frac{2\pi}{3}$.

Question 17

Answer A is correct. When you raise a power to another power, you multiply the two exponents together, so answer A is equivalent to 2^{15}. Answer B is only 2^8, a smaller number. Remember, a negative power is the reciprocal of the corresponding positive power, whereas a fractional power indicates a root.

Question 18

Answer B is correct. To begin, enumerate the ways in which three dice can add up to 5:

1 2 2

2 1 2

2 2 1

1 1 3

1 3 1

3 1 1

So there are six different ways to get a total of 5. Because the three dice are independent, there are a total of $6 \times 6 \times 6 = 216$ possible outcomes. The probability of getting a 5 is then $\frac{6}{216} = \frac{1}{36}$.

Question 19

Answer B is correct. To see this, place P and Q along a number line with P at 0 and Q at 4. Then R, being 2 units from Q, can be at either 2 or 6. S, being 5 units from R, can be at –3, 1, 7, or 11. That gives distances from P of 3, 1, 7, or 11. Only 3 is in the given set of answers.

Question 20

Answer B is correct. When faced with a question such as this, translate the special symbol back into conventional notation and solve. For this particular problem, remember that in a mixed expression, you perform multiplications before additions. So the five expressions are evaluated as follows:

$1/2/3 = 1 + 2 \times 3 = 7$

$3/1/1 = 3 + 1 \times 1 = 4$

$4/1/1 = 4 + 1 \times 1 = 5$

$1/3/5 = 1 + 3 \times 5 = 16$

$2/1/3 = 2 + 1 \times 3 = 5$

The second of these is the smallest, so B is the correct answer.

Section 6

Question 1

Answer D is correct. You might not want to fly if you're afraid of heights. Answers A, B, C, and E are all incorrect because they create illogical statements.

Question 2

Answer A is correct. The first phrase, "At three and a half hours" is a clue that you're dealing with a time issue. That should help you eliminate all the answers except A. Answers B, C, D, and E are incorrect because none of the second words in these responses expresses time in any way.

Question 3

Answer D is correct. If you don't know the definition of "expound," you should be able to eliminate the others. In addition, the preposition "on" immediately following the missing word will severely limit the possibilities. Answers A, B, C, and E are all incorrect as none of them would grammatically support the following preposition.

Question 4

Answer B is correct. The sentence's first word, "despite," is your biggest clue. The savings account is described as "significantly large," so you know the first word should be an antonym for large. Answer A is incorrect because it's illogical; "copious" would indicate a large salary. Answer C is incorrect. Although the set might be logical, "contribute" doesn't fit grammatically. Answer D is incorrect for the same reason as A. Answer E is incorrect because neither "miserable" nor "erect" are as appropriate as the words in B.

Question 5

Answer C is correct. The clues are subtle, but "her inner conflicts" lets you know that something's not quite right. Answer A is incorrect. Her poetry might be insightful, but you don't authenticate inner conflicts. Answers B and D are incorrect because you don't supplant or overhaul inner conflicts. Answer E is incorrect because the two words don't support one another within the context of the sentence.

Question 6

Answer A is correct, although you might be tempted to choose answer E. Remember, questions are based on the actual passages and any introductory material. The introductory excerpt clearly explains that the purpose of both passages is to support how public money is used to improve public transportation—on roads or by increasing the mass transit systems. Answers B, C, and D are all incorrect, even though all three arguments are used to support the position of one or the other passages. Answer E is incorrect although it appears to be correct if you base your answer solely on the two passages. Yes, it was a bit of a trick question—always read the instructions carefully.

Question 7

Answer D is correct because it is the most complete. Answers A, B, C, and E all contain some right responses, but none is as comprehensive as D. Answer E has a response that isn't even discussed—the passage doesn't discuss pollution.

Question 8

Answer B is correct because it is the most complete, and each item in the answer is fact as stated in the passage, without any assumptions. Be careful about responses that call for a conclusion or assumption unless the question specifically mandates that you draw a conclusion. Answer A in incomplete and assumes too much. You might draw the conclusion that the points made in the passage would result in cleaner air and a clearer environment, but unless asked to draw a conclusion, you should stick to the facts as expressed in the passage. Answer C is incorrect because it's incomplete. Answer D is incorrect because it assumes that a reduction in gas carbon dioxide will slow global warning, and the passage doesn't actually say that. Answer E is incorrect because it's incomplete and it makes the same conclusion about global warming as answer D.

Question 9

Answer D is the most correct. Answers A, B, and E are incorrect because they're incomplete. Answer C is incorrect because it isn't quite specific enough in the mass transit issue—the passage implies that the inconveniences will be borne by those who have no other way to get to work than private cars.

Question 10

Answer D is the most correct because overcoming his childhood weaknesses is the main focus of this passage. Answer A, B, C, and E are incorrect because they are incomplete. All of these items are mentioned in the passage, but they aren't the primary focus of the passage.

Question 11

Answer E is correct. Line 8 tells us specifically that Teddy Roosevelt had asthma and poor eyesight. Answers A and B are incorrect because they're incomplete. Answer C is incorrect. We're told in line 5 that he was not raised in poverty. Answer D is incorrect. There is almost no mention in the passage about his education other than he had an interest in nature.

Question 12

Answer A is correct. Lines 15 and 16 tells us that Teddy Roosevelt was an expert in such track events as running, pole vaulting, and high jumping. Answers B, C, and D are incorrect. Although boxing and big-game hunting are mentioned in the passage, neither is mentioned in lines 15 or 16. Remember, if the question specifies a line, stick to the facts in that line (or lines). Answer E is incorrect because running and jumping aren't as specific as the actual events mentioned in A.

Question 13

Answer B is correct. Line 18 tells us exactly why Teddy felt compelled. Answers A, C, and D are incorrect. Nothing in the passage suggests that Teddy was forced or compelled by anyone other than himself. Answer E is incorrect. No siblings are mentioned in the passage.

Question 14

Answer D is correct. Line 24, the last line in the passage, tells us where he explored and hunted. Answers A and B are incorrect because they're incomplete. Answer C is incorrect. Roosevelt took up horse riding and shooting at Oyster Bay as a child. Answer E is incorrect. Roosevelt visited both Paris and Rome as a child, but did not explore or hunt there.

Question 15

Answer B is correct. Line 8 gives the definition of a biome. Answer A is incorrect because it's incomplete—we omitted the words "major type of." Answer C is incorrect because it's vague. Answer D is incorrect. It's additional information about the biome, but not a definition. Answer E is incorrect. Scientists use these attributes to determine the type of biome, but it isn't a definition of the term.

Question 16

Answer A is correct. Line 11 gives the answer, "precipitation," to this question. Answers B, C, D, and E all affect the type of community present, but they do not determine the major biome type.

Question 17

Answer B is correct. Line 23 tells us that both of these biomes receive "very little" precipitation. Answers A and C are wrong. Either may be true, but they're not the best answer to the question as they're not supported by the passage. Answers D and E are incorrect because they're wrong.

Question 18

Answer C is correct. Line 28 tells us that the forest biomes compose 75 percent of the Earth's biomass. Answer A is incorrect. Coniferous forest is just one type of forest biome. Answers B and D are incorrect as they are not the largest biome. Answer E is incorrect as chaparral is a community, not a biome.

Question 19

Answer D is correct. If the rain forests are destroyed, so is 50 percent of the Earth's biomass. Answers A, B, and C are incorrect because they're not logical responses to the question. Answer E is incorrect. Although it may be a true statement, it isn't supported by the passage.

Question 20

Answer A is correct. The main climatic difference is the amount of rainfall each biome gets. Answers B and C are incorrect because they're wrong. Answer D is incorrect because it's a false statement—tropical dry forest biomes are in the tropical zones. Answer E is incorrect because it doesn't contrast climatic differences. Besides, the second sentence is false.

Question 21

Answer D is correct because it is the most specific answer. Answers A and B are incorrect because naming the countries is not enough—a country can have many different biome types. Answer C is incorrect for the same reason as A and B. In addition, the answer includes the Mediterranean Sea. The Mediterranean Sea is an aquatic biome. You must specify the coastland. Answer E is incorrect because it's a false statement.

Question 22

Answer E is the most correct answer for the question. They all share only one trait—they are all located on coastlines. Answers A and B are incorrect. All but the Mediterranean Sea coastline face west. Answer C is incorrect. Even though it's a true statement, it doesn't answer the question. The question asks what they *all* have in common. Answer D is incorrect even though it too is a true statement. The question asks for something in common besides the biome criteria.

Question 23

Answer B is correct, according to line 59. Answer A is incorrect because it's a false statement. Fires play an important part in maintaining the ecosystems in these biomes. Answer C is incorrect because it simply isn't a logical response to the question. Answers D and E are both incorrect because they make assumptions that may be true but that aren't directly supported by the passage.

Question 24

Answer C is correct as verified in lines 62, 63, and 64. Answers B and C are incorrect because high mountain areas are not tundra or woodland and shrubland. Answer D is incorrect because the passage mentions no such biome. Answer E is incorrect for the reasons cited for answers A, B, and D.

Section 7

Question 1

Answer C is correct. To see this, draw the line segments $\overline{AD}$ and $\overline{AC}$. This divides the figure into three triangles. You know that the sum of angles in a triangle is $180°$, so the sum of angles in the entire pentagon must be $3 \times 180° = 540°$. Because this is a regular pentagon, all the angles are equal, so each angle is $\frac{540°}{5} = 108°$.

Question 2

Answer B is correct. There are 50 even numbers between 1 and 100. Of these, 16 are divisible by 6 because the largest multiple of 6 less than 100 is $6 \times 16 = 96$. Thus the answer is $50 - 16 = 34$.

Question 3

Answer E is correct. All of the factors in the least common multiple must be included in the factors of A or the factors of B or both. $72 = 2 \times 2 \times 2 \times 3 \times 3$. Because A is not divisible by 3, B must include both 3s among its factors, and thus be divisible by 9. 36 is the only choice divisible by 9.

Question 4

Answer B is correct. The difference between the two populations is given by the difference in the height of the bars. This difference is the least in Month 2.

Question 5

Answer A is correct. You could graph the given points on the plane and try to derive the correct equation, but the fastest way to solve this is to just plug 0, 1, and 2 in to the given equations to see which one returns the required results. Answer A works for all three points, so it must be correct.

Question 6

Answer E is correct. The given information shows that both triangles are 45°-45°-90° triangles. The total length AC is then $3\sqrt{2}$, and the distance DC is $\frac{3\sqrt{2}}{2}$ (half the total distance). In turn, this means that both DE and EC are

$\frac{3}{2}$. (Remember, the base and height have to be perpendicular.) The area of the smaller triangle is then

$$A = \frac{1}{2} bh$$

$$A = \frac{1}{2} \times \frac{3}{2} \times \frac{3}{2}$$

$$A = \frac{9}{8}$$

Question 7

Answer B is correct. For the given probabilities to be possible, the number of books on the shelf must be evenly divisible by 6, 3, and 7. The only one of the answers given that fits these requirements is 84.

Question 8

Answer C is correct. Consider first the north and south distances: These have a net effect of going 4 miles north. Similarly, the east and west travels have a net effect of 3 miles east. The directions north and east are perpendicular to each other, so these are two sides of a right triangle. As you know, the hypotenuse of the 3-4-5 right triangle is 5.

Question 9

Answer E is correct. The portion of the graph that you're shown includes three zeroes (places where the graph crosses the x axis), but you have no way of knowing what the graph of $f(x)$ looks like outside of this range. The most precise answer you can give is that there are at least 3 zeroes, and possibly more.

Question 10

Answer D is correct. To solve, first reduce the problem to standard mathematical notation and then find x:

$$(x')' = 5$$

$$\frac{\left(\frac{(x+4)}{2} + 4\right)}{2} = 5$$

$$\frac{(x+4)}{2} + 4 = 10$$

$$\frac{x+4}{2} = 6$$

$$x + 4 = 12$$

$$x = 8$$

Question 11

Answer C is correct. All you care about for this problem is the first digit. There are three ways to draw a 7, out of 30 possible ways to draw a digit, for a total probability of $\frac{3}{30}$ or $\frac{1}{10}$.

Question 12

Answer C is correct. Call the original length of a side s. Then you know that $s^3 = K$. When you increase the length of the sides by 50%, each side becomes 1.5s. The volume of the cube is then $(1.5s)^3 = 3.375s^3 = 3.375K$.

Question 13

Answer D is correct. Although the SAT does not include formal logic on its list of preparatory subjects, you may well encounter a question like this on the exam. To answer it, you can reason through the possible answers. Answer A is incorrect because you're not told that all birds with two layers of feathers are from Leningrad; there may be such birds outside of Leningrad.

Answer B is incorrect because the bird with three layers of feathers can't be from Leningrad. Answer C is incorrect because you don't have enough information to know whether it's true or false. Answer E is incorrect because there can't be any birds with three layers of feathers in Leningrad.

Question 14

Answer C is correct. Another way of stating the ratio 2:1:22 is that there are 2 tons of iron in every 25 tons of ore. Thus in 200 tons of ore, there are $200 \times \frac{2}{25}$ = 16 tons of iron. You can also think of this as a proportion of equal ratios of iron to ore, 2:25 and x:200, then cross-multiply to determine that $25x = 400$ and so $x = 16$.

Question 15

Answer E is correct. To solve this, you can enumerate the members of M() for each number. For 9, the positive integers that are greater than 1, less than 9, and that do not evenly divide 9 are 2, 4, 5, 6, 7, and 8, so $M(9) = 6$. Similarly, you can calculate that $M(4) = 1$, $M(5) = 3$, $M(7) = 5$, $M(8) = 4$, and $M(10) = 6$.

Question 16

Answer D is correct. Consider this problem in stages:

➤ There is one way to paint the cube with all white faces.

➤ There is one way to paint the cube with 5 white faces and 1 black face.

➤ There are two ways to paint the cube with 4 white faces and 2 black faces. Either the 2 black faces can be adjacent to one another, or they can be opposite from each other.

➤ There are two ways to paint the cube with 3 white faces and 3 black faces. Either the 3 black faces can surround a corner of the cube, or they go around the cube.

➤ There are two ways to paint the cube with 2 white faces and 4 black faces.

➤ There is one way to paint the cube with 1 white face and 5 black faces.

➤ There is one way to paint the cube with all black faces.

Adding these choices up, there are $1 + 1 + 2 + 2 + 2 + 1 + 1 = 10$ distinct ways to paint the cube.

Section 8

Question 1

Answer E is correct. A number of words could work in this sentence, but the last phrase lets you know that what's happening isn't acceptable. Answers A, B, and C are all incorrect because they infer that the bamboo is helpful. Answer D is incorrect because it's illogical.

Question 2

Answer A is correct. The phrase "childish antics" is your clue. Answers B and E are incorrect because they're illogical. Answers C and D are incorrect because they're antonyms for the correct word.

Question 3

Answer D is correct. The last phrase is your best clue. Answers A and E are incorrect because "lavish" and "copious" are the opposite of what the sentence means—they don't support the last phrase. Answer B is incorrect, although you might be tempted to choose this response. "Cheap" and "frugal" are not the same thing, and the last phrase, "waste not, want not" describes someone who doesn't waste, not someone who's cheap. Answer C is incorrect because it doesn't support the last phrase.

Question 4

Answer C is correct. Sometimes sentiment, and not rhetoric, is the clue. Answers A and D are incorrect. The cad in question could repudiate or refuse, but the flowers themselves cannot. Answer B is incorrect because the last thing the cad wants is to refresh your memory. Answer E is incorrect. Although you could use the word, it wouldn't be the best word. You eradicate disease, not memories.

Question 5

Answer A is correct. There are two clues: the word "pleasure" and the last phrase. Answers B and C are incorrect. They would support the sentence, but not as strongly as A. Answers D and E are incorrect as they express the opposite of what's needed.

Question 6

Answer B is correct. There are a few clues. The first is "limbs" and the second is "ballerina." Answer A is incorrect. The words might work, but would you describe someone you love as rickety? Fences are rickety, not people. Answer C is incorrect. Again, you might get away with the sentence, but it isn't as strong as B. Answer D is incorrect. "Taunt" would work, but "fickle" certainly would not. Answer E is incorrect. "Fragile" certainly works, but "stalwart" is used to describe construction workers and football players. A ballerina would not appreciate the adjective.

Question 7

Answer B is correct. The author is concerned throughout to demonstrate that his opponents are in the wrong, which rules out answers A, D, and E. But the fact that he recounts the arguments from the other side of the question rules out answer C. Only answer B, which rests on the distinction between "argument" and "suggestion," makes sense.

Question 8

Answer D is correct. Exceptionable decisions are those that are wrong, and to rectify those decisions is to fix them. Answers A, B, and E are incorrect because those answers would not put the legislature in opposition to the exceptionable decisions. Answer C is incorrect because the author clearly expects the legislature to do more than just consider wrong decisions.

Question 9

Answer D is correct. This question tests your ability to follow the argument in the passage. The author is saying that the objections raised would be fatal to any constitution that limited legislative power, which is a nonsensical conclusion. Answer A is incorrect because much of the passage summarizes objections to the proposed plan. Answer B is incorrect because there is nothing about the balance between local and federal courts in this part of the passage. Answer C is incorrect; it's the direct opposite of the argument in the sentence. Answer E is incorrect because the author is arguing that the power is to apply the Constitution, not to overturn it.

Question 10

Answer B is correct. The definition of "militate" is "to have force or influence." The other definitions given are less precise or even (as in answers C and D) simply incorrect.

Question 11

Answer B is correct. The word "pestilential" is a tip-off that you're looking for something negative, which rules out answers C, D, and E. Answer A is incorrect because, if you look back to the previous sentence, you can see that the author is talking about party divisions when referring to factions.

Question 12

Answer E is correct. The phrase occurs in a paragraph devoted to the notion that on their own, judges cannot decide what cases to pursue. Answer A disagrees with one of the points brought out in the passage (that judges can rule a law to be wrong). Answers B and C, although relevant to the passage, do not apply to this particular phrase. Answer D brings in ideas that are not given or implied in the passage.

Question 13

Answer C is correct. The distinction the author assigns to judges in the United States is that they can base decisions on the Constitution. Answers A and E are incorrect because they are directly contradicted by the paragraph in which the phrase in question occurs. Answers B and D are incorrect because there is no basis for them in the passage.

Question 14

Answer E is correct. The author specifically says that judges may disregard unconstitutional laws. Answer A is incorrect because legislative intent does not appear in the passage at all. Answers B and C are incorrect because the author shows how judges are to be guided by both laws and the constitution. Answer D is incorrect because the notion of a judicial check on legislative power is part of passage 1, not of passage 2.

Question 15

Answer B is correct. The author is specifically arguing that the English constitution might as well not exist because the Parliament can modify it at any time with no check on its own authority.

Question 16

Answer D is correct. The author of the second passage states that the ability of the courts to review laws is "recognized by all authorities" in the United States, but the author of passage 1 acknowledges "questioners" when he argues against their viewpoint. The other four potential answers are all things that passage 1 supports rather than questions.

Question 17

Answer A is correct. The second passage supports the argument of the first passage, so you can assume that the author of the second passage would feel positively toward the arguments of the first passage. Only answer A expresses a positive sentiment.

Question 18

Answer B is correct. The first passage argues for a particular point of view, whereas the second passage is content to describe a state of affairs. Neither passage is particularly narrative or judicious, although logic plays a stronger role in the first passage than in the second.

Question 19

Answer C is correct. The second passage shows that the arguments of the first passage were ultimately accepted; most people would be satisfied if their arguments saw wide adoption. The other choices do not fit the situation.

Section 9

Question 1

Answer B is correct. Although the sentence isn't actually incorrect, the phrase "having need of" is wordy. Answer A is incorrect because the sentence isn't correct. Answers C and D are incorrect because they're wordy. Answer E is incorrect because it's illogical.

Question 2

Answer E is correct. There's no need for the pronoun "they." Answer A is incorrect because the sentence isn't correct. Answers B and D are incorrect because they change the meaning of the sentence. Some might argue that "now" is redundant, but it doesn't really hurt anything in this instance. It supports the timing, even though the timing is apparent. Answer C is incorrect because it doesn't eliminate the pronoun "they."

Question 3

Answer D is correct. The verb phrase isn't necessary. Answer A is incorrect because the sentence isn't correct. Answers B and C are incorrect because they still contain an unnecessary verb or verb phrase. Answer E is incorrect because there's no need to change the essence of the phrase.

Question 4

Answer B is correct. The subject and verb don't match in number. Answer A is incorrect because the section has a problem. Answer C is incorrect because it doesn't fix the verb's number. Answer D is incorrect because there's no reason to move the adverb "quietly." Answer E is incorrect. The sentence needs the possessive pronoun "their."

Question 5

Answer B is correct. As is, the sentence says that her parents are playing in the shade because the subject is confused. Answer A is incorrect because the sentence isn't correct. Answers C and D are incorrect because the subject is still confused. Answer E is incorrect because the verb tense is wrong.

Question 6

Answer C is correct. The subject is assumed, and the sentence is in passive voice. Although passive voice isn't grammatically incorrect per se, you should avoid it in your writing. Answer A is incorrect because the sentence isn't correct. Answer B is incorrect because it's illogical. Answer D is incorrect because it's still passive. Answer E is incorrect because you've changed the tone of the sentence. The sentence, as is, gives no clue as to why the presents weren't gladly received. It isn't up to you to guess.

Question 7

Answer C is correct. The prepositional phrase is misplaced. It doesn't modify what the subject sees. Answer A is incorrect because the sentence isn't correct. Answer B is incorrect because it doesn't correctly position the prepositional phrase. Answer D is incorrect because "dancing for money" is misplaced. Answer E is incorrect because omitting the phrase "on school nights" changes the meaning of the sentence.

Question 8

Answer B is correct. The verb and subject must match in number. Although the subject "the entire collection" refers to many individual objects, the subject itself is singular. We tried to trick you by throwing in "all." Some words, such as all, can be singular or plural. When in doubt, always refer to the subject. Answer A is incorrect because the segment isn't correct. Answer C is incorrect because it's grammatically inferior. Answer D is incorrect because you need the em dash. Answer E is incorrect because you need the em dash and because the number is still incorrect.

Question 9

Answer B is correct. When combining a noun phrase using either/or and neither/nor, the verb must agree with the closest item. Answer A is incorrect because the sentence isn't correct. Answers C and E are incorrect because dropping "to indulge" doesn't correct the problem. Answer D is incorrect because you've unnecessarily changed the tense.

Question 10

Answer E is correct. The problem is the dangling participle. These types of mistakes can be hard to correct because you're able to reason the sentence's intent; therefore, you think the sentence is correct. You know the pastries weren't "in line"—and your mind just skips right over the problem. To check a sentence like this, simply rewrite, make sure that all the prepositional phrases are in place next to the appropriate noun. Answer A is incorrect because the sentence isn't correct. Answers B, C, and D are incorrect because the phrase "in line" is still modifying the wrong noun, "diet," "pastries," "diet," and "pastries," respectively. The subject "she" was in line, not the diet nor the pastries.

Question 11

Answer D is correct. As is, the sentence makes the store manager the subject and says the store manager cut in line to throw them out, which although logically possible, isn't the sentence's intent. Answer A is incorrect because the sentence isn't correct. Answer B is incorrect for the same reason as the original sentence. Answers C and E are incorrect because they make no sense.

Question 12

The answer is D. "Everyone" is a singular pronoun, and the verb "need" must match the subject's number. Answer A is incorrect because the verb and subject don't match in number. In addition, the subject "everyone" requires the pronoun "who." Answers B and C are incorrect because they're wordier than necessary. B doesn't correct the number problem and uses "that's" incorrectly. Answer E is incorrect. The sentence may be grammatically correct, but it isn't the best choice.

Question 13

Answer E is correct. The only problem is the unclear antecedent "he." Some might argue that there's nothing wrong here, but the pronoun "he" needs to refer to a clear antecedent. In this case, it doesn't. Someone might mistake "Mark" for the antecedent because it's the closest noun. The truth is, the pronoun "he" isn't even needed, and the sentence is clearer without it. Answer A is incorrect because the sentence isn't as strong as it could be. Answers B and C are incorrect because deleting a few words doesn't correct the problem. Answer D is incorrect because the subject is still unclear.

Question 14

Answer B is correct. The only problem with this sentence is the unnecessary preposition "up." Answer A is incorrect because the sentence isn't correct as is. Answers C and D are incorrect because the additional words don't correct the problem. Answer E is incorrect because the preposition "in" is inappropriate.

For More Information

Our focus in this book has been to give you a refresher course on everything that you need to pass the SAT. But that doesn't mean that you should rely exclusively on our book to get you through. In this appendix, we'll point out a few other resources that you might want to refer to.

➤ Don't ignore your own high school textbooks. For the math section in particular, your texts should pretty well cover the skills that the SAT will test you on. If you don't have your own copies of your old textbooks, your school library probably does. Using your textbooks has a great advantage over trying to find another book to learn from: You should already know how the material is organized in the textbook.

➤ If you feel uncertain about the essay portion of the SAT and want a light, short read to help you along, borrow or purchase a copy of *The Elements of Style*, by William Strunk, Jr. and E.B. White. "Strunk and White," as it's commonly known, has been the darling of composition teachers for decades, and its advice is as timely as ever. It's very likely that whoever grades your essay will have read Strunk and White themselves, and will appreciate your following its rules.

➤ The College Board has its own website at http://www.collegeboard.com, and every SAT taker should visit it at least once. You can register for the SAT online, get the "SAT Practice Question of the Day" to hone your skills, and even download another complete practice test if the ones in this book weren't enough for you. Follow the "For Students" link from the home page to find SAT resources.

➤ Number2.com (http://www.number2.com/) offers free online SAT preparation materials. Its "question of the day" and "word of the day" are good adjuncts to the College Board's daily test question.

➤ If you're worried about the size of your vocabulary, check out the "5000 Free SAT Words" page at http://www.freevocabulary.com/. Don't try to memorize it all at once, though! This is the sort of list that you ought to dip into when you have a few moments, just to expose yourself to more words that you might see on the SAT.

➤ If you have older siblings or friends who took the SAT before you, it's worth buying them lunch to find out what they thought of the whole process and to hear any tips they have to offer. This sort of informal networking is the best way to discover the good test centers in your area. Just be careful if the siblings are *too* much older: They may have taken the old SAT, without the essay and more advanced math questions, and their experience will be less relevant to your own.

Sample Graded Essays

About Scoring

Two people, each giving a score of 0 to 6, grade your SAT essay. The highest score you can receive is 12, the lowest a 0. Fortunately, the SAT readers are on your side. Readers take special training, which more than adequately prepares them for the task. Readers look for reasons to give you a good score. They are not searching for reasons to reduce your score. Now, on the surface, that may not seem important, but reading is so subjective that attitude does matter. But take comfort in knowing that the readers want you to score high.

In order to be fair and objective, a third reader is available. That happens when the two scores differ by more than one point. The third reader doubles his or her score and throws out the first two. Now, for a statistic that should make you feel better about all this: In only eight percent of the tests do essays require a third reader. This fact should reassure you that the essay readers are professionals and well trained. The following reviews a brief synopsis of the criterion they use.

Six—A Perfect Score

The perfect essay will receive a score of 6. A six essay is outstanding and demonstrates that the writer has produced a strong thesis and has mastered skills in supporting that thesis in consistently clear and strong language. A few errors are acceptable. What follows is a specific list of traits or skills an essay must exhibit to land a 6:

➤ The writer develops and supports the thesis (point of view) *consistently* using critical and insightful thinking, clear examples, and reason.

➤ The essay is *well* organized.

➤ The essay is *well* focused.

➤ The essay uses appropriate style and varies sentence structure.

➤ The essay uses accurate language.

➤ The essay is free of most grammatical errors.

A word about that last point: One misspelled word or one grammatical error won't drop your score from a 6 to a 5. However, don't let that go to your head. Even the most critical and focused essay will receive a lower score if you misspell too many words or make too many seemingly insignificant errors. Not only must you be able to think clearly, but you must also be able to follow the accepted rules for communicating your thoughts.

Five

A five essay is effective and demonstrates, for the most part, consistent mastery of the written language. This essay may contain occasional errors. What follows is a specific list of traits or skills an essay must exhibit to score a 5:

➤ The writer develops and supports the thesis (point of view) and *generally* uses critical thinking, clear examples, and reason.

➤ The essay is organized.

➤ The essay is focused.

➤ The essay uses appropriate style and varies sentence structure.

➤ The essay uses accurate language.

➤ The essay is *generally* free of most grammatical errors.

You might be wondering just how different these two scores are. Not much. Both a five and a six essay are great essays. The writer must hit all the same points—the difference being that the six essay consistently uses those points better.

Four

A four essay is competent. This writer will demonstrate an adequate mastery of the language. However, this essay will contain lapses in quality. What follows is a specific list of traits or skills an essay must exhibit to score a 4:

➤ The writer develops the thesis (point of view) and uses *competent* critical thinking, clear examples, and reason.

➤ The essay is *generally* organized.

➤ The essay is *generally* focused, demonstrating some coherence and steady progression of ideas.

➤ The essay displays adequate use of language, albeit applied inconsistently.

➤ The essay *generally* uses accurate language.

➤ The essay will contain some errors in grammar and word usage.

Three

A three essay is inadequate, but does show some signs of development. A three essay will suffer from one or more of the following weaknesses:

➤ The writer shows some skill in developing the thesis (point of view) but does so inconsistently. Or, the essay may use inconsistent or inadequate examples and reason to develop the point.

➤ The essay is somewhat focused, but contains lapses or is somewhat incoherent.

➤ The writer sometimes uses inappropriate words or shows signs of having a limited vocabulary.

➤ The writer fails to vary the sentence structure.

➤ The essay contains a significant number of errors in grammar and word usage.

Two

A two essay is seriously limited and shows very little mastery of the language. A two essay will suffer from one or more of the following weaknesses:

➤ The writer's point of view is weak or seriously limited and shows a weakness in critical thinking, using inappropriate or inadequate examples and reason.

➤ The essay is poorly organized.

➤ The writer uses language inadequately and shows a very limited vocabulary.

➤ The writer uses inadequate sentence structure.

➤ The essay contains enough grammar and word usage errors that the essay is somewhat incoherent.

One

A one essay is fundamentally lacking, and demonstrates nearly no mastery of the language. A one essay will suffer from one or more of the following weaknesses:

➤ The writer fails to make a point and provides little or no examples or reason.

➤ The essay is unorganized or unfocused, resulting in an incoherent essay.

➤ The writer makes fundamental errors in word usage.

➤ The writer makes fundamental and serious errors in sentence structure.

➤ The essay contains persistent and pervasive grammar and word usage errors to the point of interfering with the essay's message.

Zero

This score is left for those students who don't write an essay. Writing something is better than writing nothing. A score of 2 is better than a 0. Also, if the essay is illegible, or is on a topic that has absolutely nothing to do with the assignment, the reader will give it a 0.

Keep in mind that a 0 score is seldom given to a sincere attempt, no matter how bad it is. So write something. Take a chance. Just do it and see what develops. That doesn't mean write gibberish—gibberish will get you a 0.

Understanding the Essay Assignment

Many are familiar with the KISS method—"keep it simple stupid." Unfortunately, the essay assignment questions often seem more than just a bit convoluted and abstract. There's a method behind this method, but that won't help you on exam day.

The exam folks have a major task to fulfill when coming up with essay assignments. The topic must be general enough for a varied audience, yet limited enough to keep you from starting the great American novel. It isn't easy.

The result of meeting such diverse requirements is that the questions themselves aren't always very direct. There's a lot of room for interpretation. Don't let that scare you. Often the assignment will express a specific point of view, and you will be allowed to agree, defend, or challenge that statement. The important thing to remember is that the readers will be looking for specific qualities in your writing—they will *not* grade you on your point of view.

If you have trouble understanding the actual assignment, don't fret—you are probably in good company. Break the assignment down into components. As often as not, you will find the question rather philosophical. Whether that's good or bad is really up to you, but once you understand the nature of the question, you can begin to develop your point of view. For instance, you may be asked to discuss how loss can actually help you grow. Or, you may be required to discuss the qualities of greatness or freedom. These are all very abstract ideas. The key is to use concrete language to communicate your point of view. (We discuss concrete and abstract language in Chapter 2, "The Writing Section: Student-Written Essay.")

Some topics are huge, and these topics present a different kind of problem. There's so much to write about, you may find it difficult to focus. The key here is to find a very tight and direct point of view. For example, suppose the assignment asks you to write about an injustice that hasn't been adequately dealt with by society. Suddenly, your head's full of all kinds of imagery—choosing one might prove more difficult than writing the actual essay. There's no cure for this. Just stay focused and find one specific injustice—you're not going to tackle world peace with this one.

We wish we could wave a magic wand and reduce all the essay questions to the succinct question that's really lying just underneath all the rhetoric. Unfortunately, we can't. What we can do is tell you that you're not alone if you have to spend a few minutes reading the assignment. In addition, we want to stress that the point of view won't make or break your grade. How you develop the point of view will.

The Assignment

What follows is an example of what you can expect to see on exam day, in regards to the essay portion. Be sure to read Chapter 2 thoroughly for good advice on writing your essay. In addition, you might also review Chapters 10 and 12—the two practice tests.

Think carefully about the issue presented in the following excerpt and the assignment below.

> Sometimes a loss leads to victory.

Assignment: **What does the above statement mean to you? Write an essay developing your point of view on this statement. Use reasoning and examples taking from personal experience, historical events, reading, studies, or observations.**

You might be wondering how to use this appendix. First, knowing what the readers are looking for should help you as you practice your essay writings. Second, you can use the example essays as a template of sorts. If you find yourself really suffering with the essays, try to fit your essays into one of the graded categories. Then, using the contents of this appendix, add the elements you're missing, one at a time.

We've written two very different essays to the same question. Each essay is written to all six grading levels, for a total of twelve essays.

The First "Six Essay"

About a year after Microsoft released MS Access, a desktop database application, my managing editor sat down in my office and listed a number of journals that needed a new home. He diplomatically steered me toward the fairly new *Inside Microsoft Access* user journal. I said, "Thanks, but no." Over the next week, we had the same conversation three times. Finally, I said, "You're not really asking me if I will take the journal, are you?" It was his turn to say "No." That gentle coercion transformed my technical focus and my life.

Looking forward, I only saw what I was leaving behind—a reasonably happy career in spreadsheet development, where I was content to be a small fish in a big pond. What I couldn't see then was that I was going nowhere fast. Spreadsheets had found their place in the world and ambitious developers were already moving to bigger and better toys. The desktop database application was just coming into its own. Begrudgingly, I threw the spreadsheet fish back into its pond and took the database bait.

Looking back, I clearly see that my last fifteen years of professional accomplishments would not have been available to me as a spreadsheet developer. The database world has been and still is challenging and full of opportunities—a number of books, hundreds of articles, and even a few interviews during which I was treated with professional respect. Someone actually thought my opinions were important enough to share.

Fifteen years ago, I lost a small battle with my managing editor; I took a job I didn't want. Ultimately, the repercussions of that decision surround me—books written by me sitting on my bookshelves, a full schedule of work that's challenging, notes from publishers asking when I'm available. The pain of that long ago loss was temporary, but I've been living with the victor's spoils ever since.

A Short Analysis

This essay, although certainly not perfect, meets the requirements of a six essay. It demonstrates a mastery of the language and critical thinking. It develops a point of view—that taking on an unwanted job ultimately led to a better career. The essay is focused on the job change and its consequences. It's logically organized, beginning with the unwanted change, what the writer left behind, and then what the writer gained. The essay varies sentence structure and uses appropriate vocabulary.

Notice that nowhere in the essay has the writer repeated the statement used in the assignment. The writer has developed the thesis without actually stating it. Done correctly, this form can be interesting and effective. However, using the statement in your essay is acceptable.

You may have noticed that the essay deviates from a recommendation we made in Chapter 2. In that chapter, we recommend that you avoid using personal pronouns, yet this essay is rife with the pronoun I. Writing in first person isn't wrong and, done correctly, can be creative, effective, and even inspirational. If you're an accomplished writer, by all means, use all the tools at your disposal, and that includes personal pronouns.

 A serious distinction between a six essay and a five essay is *personal insight* or experience. The truth is, most of us can regurgitate content. You can do that on your essay and receive a good score, if you organize the content logically and thoroughly develop your point of view. But regardless of how well you present your thesis, without that spark of originality, you may be looking at a 5 rather than a 6. Don't be afraid to put a bit of yourself into your essay.

The First "Five Essay"

In the early 1990s, Microsoft released MS Access, a desktop database application, and the first of its kind. Soon afterward, my boss tried to steer me toward taking on the fairly new *Inside Microsoft Access* user journal. I didn't want the database journal and told him so. Over the next week, we had the same conversation three times. Finally, I said, "You're not really asking me if I will take the journal, are you?" It was his turn to say "No." Little did I know then this small loss was going to be the beginning of something very big.

Looking forward, I only saw what I thought I was leaving behind. I had a reasonably happy career as a spreadsheet development, where I was content to be a small fish in a big pond. What I didn't see then was that the desktop database application was just coming into its own. Begrudgingly, I threw the spreadsheet fish back into its pond and took the database bait.

Almost fifteen years later, the database world is still challenging and full of opportunities—opportunities that simply don't exist in the spreadsheet world. Opportunities that include a number of books, hundreds of articles and even a few interviews during which I was treated with professional respect. Someone actually thought my opinion was important enough to share.

Looking back, I clearly see that the last fifteen years of professional accomplishments in the database world were not available to me as a spreadsheet developer. I lost a small battle by taking a job I didn't want. Ultimately, the repercussions of that decision surround me—books written by me sitting on my bookshelves, a full schedule of work that's challenging, notes from publishers asking when I'm available. In the end, I won. The pain of that long ago loss was temporary, but I've been living with the victor's spoils ever since.

A Short Analysis

This five essay isn't that much different from the six essay. It clearly develops a point of view using effective and appropriate examples and language. But, it's missing a bit of polish. You'll have to admit, it's a bit chewier than the six essay. The insight's still there, but it isn't as smooth as the six. In addition, it just isn't as cleverly presented as the six.

The introduction is wordier and less creative. Note that the last sentence in that paragraph repeats the assignment. That's alright, but the six essay does a better job in this respect. The language is colorful and positive and sets the mood for the rest of the essay. The five essay doesn't meet this task as well.

The second paragraphs in both essays make the same point, but the five essay's paragraph uses more words than the six. The phrase "I thought" is unnecessary, but not grammatically incorrect. Notice the difference between the words "couldn't" and "didn't"—they change the tone of the sentence. The word "couldn't" in the six essay is more truthful and honest than the word "didn't" in the five essay. It implies a bit of willfulness on the author's part—a willful, albeit perhaps unconscious, inability to pragmatically assess the current situation. The use of the words "bigger and better toys," although bordering a bit on cliché, is more colorful and expressive of the author's perspective. It also implies a tone of ambition that the author seems to be missing at that time.

The transitional phrases for the third and fourth paragraphs are switched. In the six essay, the second and third paragraphs make good use of parallelism to speak of the past and then the future. The five essay loses that movement.

The last paragraph, like the others, is wordier than necessary. Telling the reader "I won" is unnecessary. Use language to let the reader draw that conclusion.

As we mentioned, the essays seem very similar—so similar that you might wonder why the five isn't just as good as the six. As you can see, a few seemingly subtle changes can make a big difference in your essay's tone and overall quality.

You might think the one-point difference between a six and a five is subjective, but the readers are more professional than that. Remember, a five is still a good essay.

The First "Four Essay"

In the early 1990s, Microsoft released MS Access, a desktop database application, and the first of its kind. Soon afterward, my boss tried to make me take on the fairly new *Inside Microsoft Access* user journal. I didn't want that journal. Over the next week, we had the same conversation three times. Finally, I realized he wasn't asking me to take the journal—he was breaking the bad news to me gently. I wasn't happy about the change.

In the midst of a reasonably happy career as a spreadsheet development, I was content to be a small fish in a big pond. What I didn't see then was that the desktop database application was just coming into its own. Disappointed, I threw the spreadsheet fish back into its pond and took the database bait.

Almost fifteen years later, the database world is still challenging and full of opportunities—opportunities that would not have be available to me as a spreadsheet developer. Opportunities that include a number of books, hundreds of articles and even a few interviews during which I was treated with professional respect.

Looking back, I can see that the last fifteen years in the database world wouldn't have been available to me as a spreadsheet developer. Ultimately, the repercussions of that loss are all around me—books written by me sitting on my bookshelves, a full schedule of work, notes from publishers asking if I'm available. A small battle was lost, but in the end, I won.

A Short Analysis

Can you see the steady loss of cohesive thought and appropriate word usage and grammar? The reader is beginning to spend a little time deciphering individual sentences and following the thought from one sentence to another. The basic point of view is still there, but it's a little harder to find. Despite the flaws, the four essay is still competent.

The First "Three Essay"

Several years ago, my boss at the time made me take on a job I didn't want. Happy, I was not. I had been reasonably happy career as a spreadsheet developer. At the time, I fought learning a new skill of database technology.

Years later, I've found that the database world is challenging and full of opportunities—opportunities that would not have be available to me as a spreadsheet developer.

Looking back, I can see how wrong I was to fight the change. Ultimately, the upshot of what I thought was a loss surround me: books I've written and a busy schedule. A small battle was lost, but in the end, I won.

A Short Analysis

Do you really know what the writer's trying to say in this three essay? There's enough to make a guess, but you're not supposed to have to guess. The point of view should be clear. Not only is the point of view not clear, it isn't well developed. The writer doesn't tell us about the opportunities he or she found in the database world. The essay really needs some concrete examples to substantiate the claim of opportunities.

The First "Two Essay"

Several years ago, I had to take a job I didn't want. Before that, I was reasonably happy career as a spreadsheet developer. I fought learning a new skill of database technology.

My boss insisted on the change, although he was a great boss. In retrospect, he was the best boss I ever had.

Years later, I've found that the database world is challenging and full of opportunities. I didn't realize it at the time, but changing careers would be the best that thing could happen to me, at the time.

Looking back, I can see how wrong I was to fight the change. A small battle was lost, but in the end, I won.

A Short Analysis

At this point, we probably don't need to say much. Obviously, the writer doesn't have the necessary skills to share a viewpoint. Notice that the second paragraph has almost nothing to do with the essay's point. The sentence begins on topic but then goes in a totally different direction. This is typical of three and two essays. Don't inject a totally random point into your essay.

The First "One Essay"

Once, I had to take a job I didn't want. Before that, I was reasonably happy. Nowadays, the database world is challenging and full of opportunities.

I was wrong to fight the change. I'm glad I stopped resisting and learned about databases.

A Short Analysis

We probably don't have to say much about this essay and why it scored a one. There are several statements here, but there's no flow, and after reading it, you really don't know what the author was trying to say—you don't even care what the author was trying to say.

The Second "Six Essay"

It's hard to believe that the death of 300 Spartan soldiers in Ancient Greece might have saved democracy and Western Civilization as we know it. But that's what many historians believe. In ancient times, two kings fought a long and costly battle where the losers won the war. The pass at Thermopylae is the famous battle; Darius and Leonidas were the two kings.

Darius, the Persian king, entered Greece with an army of over 250,000 men. His goal was to add Greece and Europe to his huge empire. Leonidas, one of the Spartan kings (Sparta always had two kings) proposed to lead the Spartan army to block the pass at Thermopylae. The plan was to hold the Persians off until the Greeks could form a larger force. The second Spartan king, whom history has mostly forgotten, refused. Such a march would disrupt the religious festival they were all observing. Undaunted, Leonidas marched his personal guard of 300 elite troops day and night until they reached the pass. They were heavily outnumbered by the Persians.

The fighting was horrendous as wave after wave of Persians tried to overrun the Spartan position in the pass, but they were unprepared for the formidable Spartan soldiers. Spartans were raised to return with their shields or carried home dead upon them. A single Spartan soldier was equal to ten Persian warriors. The number of Persians dead or dying on the battlefield was a reflection of the Spartan superiority. Unfortunately, for the Spartans, the Persians found a goat path around the pass and cut off the Spartans, trapping them inside the pass. Leonidas and all of the Spartans died, but at a terrible cost to the Persians. After several days of fierce fighting, so many of the Persian soldiers were dead or wounded that many survivors deserted rather than continue with the campaign. Darius could not afford to continue his campaign with such demoralized men. He withdrew and returned home to Persia.

What might have happened had Leonidas not stopped Darius is purely speculation, but many believe Darius would have marched right through Greece, conquering every city-state in his path to Europe. Eventually, he might have conquered much, if not all, of Europe. A Persian victory at Thermopylae would have meant the death of Greece, and the death of democracy. But that's not what happened. Even though Leonidas and all his men were dead, Darius returned home and he never returned. Because of Theomopoly, democracy is both our history and our future—thanks to Leonidas and 300 brave men.

A Short Analysis

This essay demonstrates a mastery of the language and critical thinking. It develops the point of view that although Thermopylae was a battlefield loss, the battle saved Greece. The essay uses facts about Spartan soldiers and the actual battle to acknowledge the loss, while supporting the victory born of that loss. It's logically organized, beginning with the Persian invasion, followed by Leonidas' response, the subsequent battle, and then the result of the battle. The essay varies sentence structure and uses appropriate vocabulary.

The Second "Five Essay"

It's hard to believe the death of 300 might have saved democracy. In an earlier time, two kings fought a long and costly battle where the losers actually won the war. The pass at Thermopylae is the infamous battle; Darius and Leonidas were the two kings.

Darius, the Persian king, entered Greece with a huge army intent on gaining territory for his empire. Leonidas, a Spartan kings proposed to lead the Spartan army to meet the force at the pass at Thermopylae. The second Spartan king, refused. Undaunted, Leonidas marched his personal guard of 300 elite special forces day and night until they reached the pass.

The fighting was horrendous as the Persians tried to overtake the formidable Spartan soldiers. A single Spartan soldier was equal to ten Persian warriors. Eventually, the Persians found a goat path around the pass and cut off the Spartans, trapping them inside the pass. All 300 of Leonidas special forces died, but at a terrible cost to the Persians. After several days of fierce fighting, so many of the Persian soldiers were dead or wounded that survivors deserted rather than continue to face the Spartans. Darius could not afford to continue his campaign. He withdrew from the pass and returned home.

What might have happened had Leonidas not stopped Darius is purely speculation, but many believe Darius would have marched right through Greece, conquering every city-state in his path to Europe. Eventually, he might have conquered much if not all of Europe. But that's not what happened. Even though Leonidas and all his men were dead, Darius returned home. Because of Theomopoly, democracy is both our history and our future.

A Short Analysis

This essay is shorter than the first, but at the expense of clarity. The introduction doesn't give us enough information. Where is Thermopylae? When did this battle take place? The details left out of the second paragraph don't really hurt the essay, but it certainly isn't as interesting as the six when you omit so much information. Notice the use of the word "overtake" instead of "overrun"—they don't mean the same thing. Remember, word usage is important—use the best word possible to communicate each point. The author does the same thing in the third paragraph. Reading about the Spartan's training and expectations as warriors is interesting and definitely adds to the tone of the piece. Perhaps the concluding paragraph is the weakest though. Dropping the ball by omitting some of the concluding statements that draw the whole essay together weakens the essay more than omitting the details in paragraphs two and three.

The Second "Four Essay"

In an earlier time, two kings fought a long and costly battle where the losers actually won the war. The pass at Themopolis is the infamous battle.

As Darius, a Persian king, entered Greece with a huge army, Leonidas, proposed to lead the Spartan army to meet the force at the pass at Themopolis. The second Spartan king, refused. Undaunted, Leonidas marched his personal guard of 300 day and night until they reached the pass.

Fighting was horrendous. The Persians were unable to overtake the formidable Spartan soldiers in the pass. Eventually, the Persians found a goat path around the pass and cut off the Spartans, trapping them inside the pass. All 300 of Leonidas special forces died, but at a terrible cost to the

Persians. After several days of fierce fighting, so many of the Persian soldiers were dead or wounded that survivors deserted rather than continue
to face the Spartans. Darius withdrew from the pass and returned home.

Many believe Darius would have marched right through Greece, conquering every city-state in his path to Europe had Leonidas not stopped
him. Even though Leonidas and all his men were dead, Darius still
returned home. He was victorious in the battle, but he failed to obtain his
objective of conquering Greece.

A Short Analysis
The point's still made, albeit not as cleverly or as well as the five or six example. The organization is still good. Themopoly is misspelled, but most likely the readers would not take off for that. Word usage is correct, but the
vocabulary is limited.

The Second "Three Essay"
A long time ago, in a place far, far away in the land of Ancient Green
(Before Chirst, B.C.) an event occurred that saved western civilization.

The king of Persia (modern day Iran, Iraq, and Afghanistan and most of
the Middle East and central Asia) decided he wanted to add ancient
Greece (mostly composed of city-states like Athens, Sparta, Ithaca, and a
few others) and the lands beyond (Europe) to his empire. He lead a might
army (estimated at 250,000 troops, plus) accross Asia Minor (what is not
modern day Turkey and into Greece).

Sparta, although not the largest of the Greek city-states, was the most formidable military power. Spartan children began military training almost
as soon as they could walk. When this training was completed (much of
which mothers conducted because most of the fathers were in the army
and away much of the time fighting) the young men would be presented
a shield and told "Either return with it or on it" and the young women
usually married and began the process all over again.

Spartan soldiers were tough, a Spartan was usually the equivalent of ten or
more other warrior's in another army. (Sort of like the U.S. Marine Corp.)

Now, the Persian Army, 250,000 plus has entered Greece and the governments of the Greek city states are trying to decide what action to take, and
they do not have much time nor a history o cooperating with one another even in times of crisis.

A King of Sparta (they always had two) determined that all of Greece
would be conquered unless some quick and decisive action were taken.

King Leonidas proposed to led the Spartan army to the pass of Temopoly to block the Persian army until a larger Greek force could be formed. The other king (whom history has mostly forgotten) needed to concur and because of a religious festival would not agree.

Leonidas realizing the great urgency of the situation ordered his personal body guard (a force of 300 elite special forces) to accompany him on a forced march (day and night) to the narrow pass of Themopoly in hope of stopping the Persian's until the rest of the Spartan army would march to meet them.

A small force, approximately 1000 troops from a neighboring city-state joined the Spartan body guard en route to Themopoly.

Upon arrival at the pass, Leonidas discovered that they were heavily outnumbered and offered to release any warrior that did not want to stay, they all declined.

The battle began, with the Spartans holding the front of the pass and the other Greek warriors behind in reserve. The fighting was horrendous as wave after save of Persians tried to take the Spartan position. Remember that each Spartan was worth ten in other armies and the number of dead Persians reflect this. After several days of fighting, almost no Spartans were lost, the Persian king realized that the morale of his army along with the number of casualties (wounded and dead) might force him to abandon this campaign. He had to find another way. His commanders began to look for a way to flank the Spartan force. They captured a goat herder in the mountains around the pass and forced him to show them a goat trail that lead thru the mountain and around the pass.

Now they could flank the Spartans at the pass. One of the other Greek commanders (from the reserve force) learned that the Persians were flanking them and warned Leonidas what was occurring.

Leonidas realizing that what began as a holding action could become a suicide mission. He ordered the other Greek commander to take his force and retreat and warn Sparta and the Greek states to send troops at once.

Leonidas again offered to release any of his troops who wished to go and they declined.

The stage was now set for the final battle.

Leonidas led his force out of the pass, they were not cut off from escape in the rear. They formed outside the entrance to the pass.

The Persian king upon being informed of this decided to place his personal, elite body guards (some 5,000 strong) at the head of the attacking force and lead in hope of finally crushing the Spartans and ending the battle.

It began, Darius and his elite troops moved forward against Leonidas and his Spartans. The fighting was bloodier than any of the previous encounters. When Leonidas discovered that Darius was with the attacking troops he though that if they could kill him it might end the battle, the war, and the invasion so he ordered the Spartans to attack in the direction where Darius was.

They nearly succeded. Darius fled the field and ordered the rest of his army to attack the Spartans.

The Persian's finally succeded they killed all of the Spartans but at a terrible cost to themselves. After several days of fighting a very large number of the Perisan army was dead or wounded. Large numbers of Persian warriors were deserting.

Darius decided he could not afford to continue this campaign and withdrew with what was left of his army and went home to Persia.

Greece was saved, western civilization was saved and the rest is history.

A Short Analysis

Three guesses as to what's wrong with the essay, and the first two guesses don't count.

We've departed from the norm a bit, just to show you what can happen if you're not focused. The point is made, and the essay is logically organized, but it is way too long. The truth is, you'd probably never get the entire thing written in the allotted time, and an incomplete essay would be worse than the essay that's too long!

Focus! Focus! Focus!

In addition, the essay has several misspelled words and several grammatical errors. If the essay were shorter, the readers would probably forgive you for many of those errors and give this essay a 4. As is, the essay is lucky to get a 3. It could easily receive a two.

The "Second Two Essay"

The battle of Themopoly is a good example of losing the battle but winning the war.

The king of Persia, he lead a mighty army accross Asia Minor and into Greece. A Greek king tried to fight them off a the pass at Themopoly, but there were too many Persian soldiers, and they killed all of the Spartans. Even so, the Persians were tired, because the fighting had been fiercer than they had emancipated. So they went home.

Greece was saved, western civilization was saved, and the rest is history.

A Short Analysis

Did the writer really say emancipated instead of anticipated? The thesis is never stated, nor can the reader glean it from what's written. The grammar is atrocious. There's still a bit of organization, but who could tell? Maybe this is really a 1, but we've given it a 2 because at least the second paragraph seems to be in chronological order.

The Second "One Essay"

The Persian king led an mighty army into Greece, but the Greeks fought hard at a pass named Themopoly. The Persians were tired because the fighting had been fiercer than they had expected. They left and went home.

That's why we live in a democracy today.

A Short Analysis

The author never even says who won the battle or uses the battle to support the point. There is no point. The author failed to focus on the task and made a few statements about a long ago battle.

Glossary

absolute value

The "size" of a number measured by how far it is from zero. The absolute value of 4 and the absolute value of -4 are both 4.

abstract language

Words and phrases that convey an idea or meaning that is subjective.

abstract noun

Nouns that refer to ideas, thoughts, or intangible things.

active or action verb

Places the subject performing the action before the verb.

active voice

When the subject performs the action.

acute angle

An angle of less than 90°.

adjacent angle

When two lines cross, the angles next to one another (which share a common side) are referred to as adjacent angles.

analyses

A type of prose that states facts.

arc

A portion of a circle.

area

The area of a plane figure is the number of unit squares that it would take to exactly cover the figure.

argument

A type of prose used to persuade the reader.

associative law

A law of addition and multiplication that says you can regroup terms as you like. So (a + b) + c = a + (b + c) and (a × b) × c = a × (b × c).

bar graph

A graph consisting of horizontal or vertical bars representing some quantity.

base

The number being raised to a power in an exponential expression. In the expression 2^3, 2 is the base.

chord

A line segment between two points on a circle.

circumference

The distance around a circle, which is π times the diameter.

cliché

An overused phrase.

commutative law

A law of addition and multiplication that says you can rearrange terms as you like. So a + b = b + a and a × b = b × a.

complementary angle

Two angles are complementary angles if they add up to 90°.

composition

Using the output of one function as the input to another function. $f(g(x))$ is a composition of $f(x)$ and $g(x)$.

conclusion

The last paragraph in an essay.

concrete language

Specific nouns and phrases that make the subject and action clear.

cone

A three-dimensional figure constructed by joining every point on a circle to a single vertex with a smooth sheet.

congruent triangles

Two triangles are congruent if they have the same size and shape.

coordinate plane

A two-dimensional plane marked off by an x axis and a y axis at right angles.

cube

A solid figure bounded by six square faces.

cylinder

A solid figure made up of two circles joined by a smooth sheet.

denominator

The number below the line in a fraction.

dependent events

Two events that have some influence on each other are dependent events.

diameter

The diameter of a circle is a line from one point on the circle passing through the center of the circle to the opposite point on the circle.

directly proportional

Two quantities are directly proportional when they vary with each other; that is, they are related by multiplying by some constant, such as a = kb.

distributive law

A law that says when you multiply or divide a grouped sum or difference, you can do the multiplication first (instead of the parenthetical operation first) as long as you do it to each piece of the parenthetical expression.

divisibility

An integer is said to be divisible by another integer if the result of dividing the first integer by the second integer is an integer.

domain

The domain of a function is the set of all input values for which the function is defined.

equilateral triangle

A triangle with all of its sides equal and all of its angles equal.

exponent

The power in an exponential expression. In the expression 2^3, 3 is the exponent.

extended reasoning

Questions that require you to draw a conclusion.

factor

The *factors* of an integer are those integers that can be multiplied together to return the original integer.

function

A mathematical *function* is a rule for associating elements of one set with elements of another set.

future tense

Verb tense indicating that the action takes place in the future.

greatest common factor (GCF)

The greatest common factor of two integers is the largest factor (prime or otherwise) that the two numbers have in common.

hypotenuse

The longest side of a right triangle, which lies opposite the right angle.

imperative

Verb mood that indicates a direct command.

independent events

Two events that have no influence on each other are independent events.

indicative

Verb mood that indicates something real or factual.

inequality

An expression in which the two sides are related by an inequality operator such as >, <, ≥, or ≤.

integer

Integers are sometimes called "counting numbers": They are numbers such as 12, -82, and 0.

intersection

The intersection of two sets is the set consisting of elements that are in both sets.

inversely proportional

Two quantities are inversely proportional when they are related according to an equation such as $A = \frac{k}{B}$ for some constant k.

isosceles triangle

A triangle with two equal sides and two equal angles.

jargon

Slang or colloquial terms that aren't recognizable to the universal reader.

least common multiple (LCM)

The least common multiple of two integers is the smallest number that has both integers as factors.

leg

The sides of a right triangle other than the hypotenuse are referred to as the triangle's legs.

line

An infinite one-dimensional figure defined by two points.

line graph

A graph consisting of a set of points connected by one or more line segments.

line of best fit

The line that best represents the overall data in a scatterplot.

line segment

A portion of a line with a particular beginning and end.

literal comprehension

Questions that require you to identify facts.

mean

The average calculated by adding up a set of numbers and dividing by the count of numbers in the set.

median
The average calculated by finding the middle number in a set of numbers, or the mean of the two middle numbers if there are an even amount of numbers in the set.

midpoint
The point exactly halfway between the endpoints of a line segment.

mode
The most common value in a set of numbers.

narrative
A type of prose that tells a story.

numerator
The number above the line in a fraction.

obtuse angle
An angle of more than 90°.

parallelogram
A quadrilateral with two sets of parallel opposite sides.

passive verb
Places the subject performing the action after the verb.

passive voice
When someone or something other than the subject performs the action.

past tense
Verb tense indicating that an action has been completed in the past.

percent
A percent is a ratio in which the denominator is 100.

perimeter
The distance around the entire outside of a plane figure.

personal nouns
Nouns that specifically identify the subject.

pictograph
A graph made up of small graphics such as cars, trucks, or planes.

pie chart
A chart in which a circle is cut into pie slices representing the proportion of some quantity.

point
A position with no length, width, or thickness.

prepositional phrase
A phrase consisting of a preposition and an object that answers the question when or where.

present tense
Verb tense indicating that the verb is in the present form.

prime
A prime number is an integer that is only divisible by itself and by 1.

prism

A solid figure formed by joining two identical polygons by rectangular faces.

probability

The probability of an event is the chance of that event occurring.

proportion

A proportion is an equation in which two ratios are set equal to one another.

pyramid

A solid figure formed by joining a polygon to a single vertex with a set of triangular faces.

Pythagorean Theorem

The relationship between the sides of a right triangle. The square of the hypotenuse is equal to the sum of the squares of the other two sides.

quadratic formula

A formula for determining the roots of any quadratic equation. The quadratic formula is

$$x = \frac{-b \pm \sqrt{b^2 - 4ac}}{2a}$$

quadrilateral

A polygon with four sides.

radius

A line segment from the center of a circle to any point on the circumference.

range

The range of a function is the set of all values that can be produced by applying the function to values in its domain.

ratio

A ratio is the quotient of two quantities.

rational number

Rational numbers can be expressed as the ratio of two integers.

ray

A portion of a line that starts at a particular point and goes to infinity in one direction.

reciprocal

A number produced by interchanging the numerator and denominator of a fraction.

rectangle

A quadrilateral in which every angle is 90°.

rectangular solid

A prism in which the top and bottom faces are rectangles.

reflection

Creating a copy of a figure by drawing its mirror image on the other side of a specified line.

right angle

An angle of precisely 90°.

right triangle
A triangle containing a right angle.

rotation
Creating a copy of a figure by rotating the figure around a fixed point.

scatterplot
A graph that uses markers such as dots or points to indicate sets of observations of two variables.

scientific notation
A system of expressing numbers as multiples of a power of ten.

sequence
A sequence is an ordered set of numbers.

set
A set is a collection of things that are called the elements or members of the set.

similar triangles
Two triangles are similar if they are the same shape but not necessarily the same size.

sphere
A three-dimensional solid consisting of all points equidistant from a center.

square
A rectangle in which every side is the same length.

subjunctive mode
Verb mood that indicates something hypothetical, conditional, wishful, suggestive, or counter to the fact.

surface area
The total area of the entire surface of a three-dimensional solid.

symmetry
A change (rotation or reflection) that preserves the original figure.

system of equations
A set of equations all of which must be true at the same time.

tangent
A line that touches a curve at precisely one point.

transition
Word or phrase that combines the movement from one thought to another.

translation
Creating a copy of a figure by sliding it within the plane.

union
The union of two sets is another set that contains all the elements from the first two sets, without counting any common elements twice.

verb mood
Indicates the verb's condition.

verb phrase
A phrase that consists of a verb and a modifier.

verb tense
Indicates the action's place and time.

vertical angle
When angles are created by two lines crossing, vertical angles are across from each other.

vocabulary-in-context
Questions that require you to discern the meaning of a word based on the context in which the word is used.

volume
The volume of a solid figure is measured by the number of unit cubes that it would take to completely fill the figure.

weighted average
An average calculated by merging two or more groups according to the number of values in each group or according to the percentage assigned to each group.

zeroes
The points at which the graph of an equation crosses the x axis. These are also called the roots of the equation.

Practice Exam #1
Answer Sheet

Begin your essay on this page. If you need more space, continue on the next page. Do not write outside of the essay box.

_____
_____
_____
_____
_____
_____
_____
_____
_____
_____
_____
_____
_____
_____
_____
_____
_____
_____
_____
_____
_____
_____
_____
_____
_____
_____
_____
_____
_____
_____
_____

Continuation of Essay Section 1 from previous page. Write below only if you need more space.

Section 2

1. Ⓐ Ⓑ Ⓒ Ⓓ Ⓔ   9. Ⓐ Ⓑ Ⓒ Ⓓ Ⓔ   17. Ⓐ Ⓑ Ⓒ Ⓓ Ⓔ
2. Ⓐ Ⓑ Ⓒ Ⓓ Ⓔ   10. Ⓐ Ⓑ Ⓒ Ⓓ Ⓔ   18. Ⓐ Ⓑ Ⓒ Ⓓ Ⓔ
3. Ⓐ Ⓑ Ⓒ Ⓓ Ⓔ   11. Ⓐ Ⓑ Ⓒ Ⓓ Ⓔ   19. Ⓐ Ⓑ Ⓒ Ⓓ Ⓔ
4. Ⓐ Ⓑ Ⓒ Ⓓ Ⓔ   12. Ⓐ Ⓑ Ⓒ Ⓓ Ⓔ   20. Ⓐ Ⓑ Ⓒ Ⓓ Ⓔ
5. Ⓐ Ⓑ Ⓒ Ⓓ Ⓔ   13. Ⓐ Ⓑ Ⓒ Ⓓ Ⓔ   21. Ⓐ Ⓑ Ⓒ Ⓓ Ⓔ
6. Ⓐ Ⓑ Ⓒ Ⓓ Ⓔ   14. Ⓐ Ⓑ Ⓒ Ⓓ Ⓔ   22. Ⓐ Ⓑ Ⓒ Ⓓ Ⓔ
7. Ⓐ Ⓑ Ⓒ Ⓓ Ⓔ   15. Ⓐ Ⓑ Ⓒ Ⓓ Ⓔ   23. Ⓐ Ⓑ Ⓒ Ⓓ Ⓔ
8. Ⓐ Ⓑ Ⓒ Ⓓ Ⓔ   16. Ⓐ Ⓑ Ⓒ Ⓓ Ⓔ   24. Ⓐ Ⓑ Ⓒ Ⓓ Ⓔ

Section 3

1. Ⓐ Ⓑ Ⓒ Ⓓ Ⓔ   4. Ⓐ Ⓑ Ⓒ Ⓓ Ⓔ   7. Ⓐ Ⓑ Ⓒ Ⓓ Ⓔ
2. Ⓐ Ⓑ Ⓒ Ⓓ Ⓔ   5. Ⓐ Ⓑ Ⓒ Ⓓ Ⓔ   8. Ⓐ Ⓑ Ⓒ Ⓓ Ⓔ
3. Ⓐ Ⓑ Ⓒ Ⓓ Ⓔ   6. Ⓐ Ⓑ Ⓒ Ⓓ Ⓔ

Student-Produced Responses

9.

10.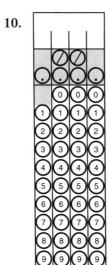

11.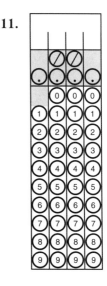

12.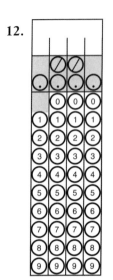

13.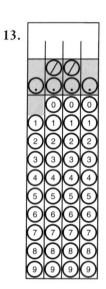

14.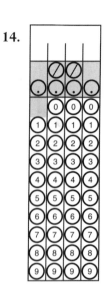

15.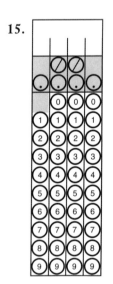

16.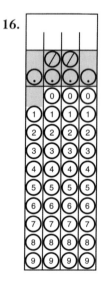

17.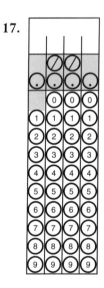

18.

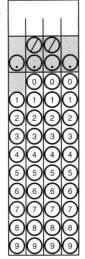

Section 4

1. (A) (B) (C) (D) (E)
2. (A) (B) (C) (D) (E)
3. (A) (B) (C) (D) (E)
4. (A) (B) (C) (D) (E)
5. (A) (B) (C) (D) (E)
6. (A) (B) (C) (D) (E)
7. (A) (B) (C) (D) (E)
8. (A) (B) (C) (D) (E)
9. (A) (B) (C) (D) (E)
10. (A) (B) (C) (D) (E)
11. (A) (B) (C) (D) (E)
12. (A) (B) (C) (D) (E)

13. (A) (B) (C) (D) (E)
14. (A) (B) (C) (D) (E)
15. (A) (B) (C) (D) (E)
16. (A) (B) (C) (D) (E)
17. (A) (B) (C) (D) (E)
18. (A) (B) (C) (D) (E)
19. (A) (B) (C) (D) (E)
20. (A) (B) (C) (D) (E)
21. (A) (B) (C) (D) (E)
22. (A) (B) (C) (D) (E)
23. (A) (B) (C) (D) (E)
24. (A) (B) (C) (D) (E)

25. (A) (B) (C) (D) (E)
26. (A) (B) (C) (D) (E)
27. (A) (B) (C) (D) (E)
28. (A) (B) (C) (D) (E)
29. (A) (B) (C) (D) (E)
30. (A) (B) (C) (D) (E)
31. (A) (B) (C) (D) (E)
32. (A) (B) (C) (D) (E)
33. (A) (B) (C) (D) (E)
34. (A) (B) (C) (D) (E)
35. (A) (B) (C) (D) (E)

Section 5

1. Ⓐ Ⓑ Ⓒ Ⓓ Ⓔ
2. Ⓐ Ⓑ Ⓒ Ⓓ Ⓔ
3. Ⓐ Ⓑ Ⓒ Ⓓ Ⓔ
4. Ⓐ Ⓑ Ⓒ Ⓓ Ⓔ
5. Ⓐ Ⓑ Ⓒ Ⓓ Ⓔ
6. Ⓐ Ⓑ Ⓒ Ⓓ Ⓔ
7. Ⓐ Ⓑ Ⓒ Ⓓ Ⓔ
8. Ⓐ Ⓑ Ⓒ Ⓓ Ⓔ

9. Ⓐ Ⓑ Ⓒ Ⓓ Ⓔ
10. Ⓐ Ⓑ Ⓒ Ⓓ Ⓔ
11. Ⓐ Ⓑ Ⓒ Ⓓ Ⓔ
12. Ⓐ Ⓑ Ⓒ Ⓓ Ⓔ
13. Ⓐ Ⓑ Ⓒ Ⓓ Ⓔ
14. Ⓐ Ⓑ Ⓒ Ⓓ Ⓔ
15. Ⓐ Ⓑ Ⓒ Ⓓ Ⓔ
16. Ⓐ Ⓑ Ⓒ Ⓓ Ⓔ

17. Ⓐ Ⓑ Ⓒ Ⓓ Ⓔ
18. Ⓐ Ⓑ Ⓒ Ⓓ Ⓔ
19. Ⓐ Ⓑ Ⓒ Ⓓ Ⓔ
20. Ⓐ Ⓑ Ⓒ Ⓓ Ⓔ
21. Ⓐ Ⓑ Ⓒ Ⓓ Ⓔ
22. Ⓐ Ⓑ Ⓒ Ⓓ Ⓔ
23. Ⓐ Ⓑ Ⓒ Ⓓ Ⓔ
24. Ⓐ Ⓑ Ⓒ Ⓓ Ⓔ

Section 6

1. Ⓐ Ⓑ Ⓒ Ⓓ Ⓔ
2. Ⓐ Ⓑ Ⓒ Ⓓ Ⓔ
3. Ⓐ Ⓑ Ⓒ Ⓓ Ⓔ
4. Ⓐ Ⓑ Ⓒ Ⓓ Ⓔ
5. Ⓐ Ⓑ Ⓒ Ⓓ Ⓔ
6. Ⓐ Ⓑ Ⓒ Ⓓ Ⓔ
7. Ⓐ Ⓑ Ⓒ Ⓓ Ⓔ

8. Ⓐ Ⓑ Ⓒ Ⓓ Ⓔ
9. Ⓐ Ⓑ Ⓒ Ⓓ Ⓔ
10. Ⓐ Ⓑ Ⓒ Ⓓ Ⓔ
11. Ⓐ Ⓑ Ⓒ Ⓓ Ⓔ
12. Ⓐ Ⓑ Ⓒ Ⓓ Ⓔ
13. Ⓐ Ⓑ Ⓒ Ⓓ Ⓔ
14. Ⓐ Ⓑ Ⓒ Ⓓ Ⓔ

15. Ⓐ Ⓑ Ⓒ Ⓓ Ⓔ
16. Ⓐ Ⓑ Ⓒ Ⓓ Ⓔ
17. Ⓐ Ⓑ Ⓒ Ⓓ Ⓔ
18. Ⓐ Ⓑ Ⓒ Ⓓ Ⓔ
19. Ⓐ Ⓑ Ⓒ Ⓓ Ⓔ
20. Ⓐ Ⓑ Ⓒ Ⓓ Ⓔ

Section 7

1. Ⓐ Ⓑ Ⓒ Ⓓ Ⓔ
2. Ⓐ Ⓑ Ⓒ Ⓓ Ⓔ
3. Ⓐ Ⓑ Ⓒ Ⓓ Ⓔ
4. Ⓐ Ⓑ Ⓒ Ⓓ Ⓔ
5. Ⓐ Ⓑ Ⓒ Ⓓ Ⓔ
6. Ⓐ Ⓑ Ⓒ Ⓓ Ⓔ
7. Ⓐ Ⓑ Ⓒ Ⓓ Ⓔ

8. Ⓐ Ⓑ Ⓒ Ⓓ Ⓔ
9. Ⓐ Ⓑ Ⓒ Ⓓ Ⓔ
10. Ⓐ Ⓑ Ⓒ Ⓓ Ⓔ
11. Ⓐ Ⓑ Ⓒ Ⓓ Ⓔ
12. Ⓐ Ⓑ Ⓒ Ⓓ Ⓔ
13. Ⓐ Ⓑ Ⓒ Ⓓ Ⓔ
14. Ⓐ Ⓑ Ⓒ Ⓓ Ⓔ

15. Ⓐ Ⓑ Ⓒ Ⓓ Ⓔ
16. Ⓐ Ⓑ Ⓒ Ⓓ Ⓔ
17. Ⓐ Ⓑ Ⓒ Ⓓ Ⓔ
18. Ⓐ Ⓑ Ⓒ Ⓓ Ⓔ
19. Ⓐ Ⓑ Ⓒ Ⓓ Ⓔ

Section 8

1. Ⓐ Ⓑ Ⓒ Ⓓ Ⓔ
2. Ⓐ Ⓑ Ⓒ Ⓓ Ⓔ
3. Ⓐ Ⓑ Ⓒ Ⓓ Ⓔ
4. Ⓐ Ⓑ Ⓒ Ⓓ Ⓔ
5. Ⓐ Ⓑ Ⓒ Ⓓ Ⓔ
6. Ⓐ Ⓑ Ⓒ Ⓓ Ⓔ

7. Ⓐ Ⓑ Ⓒ Ⓓ Ⓔ
8. Ⓐ Ⓑ Ⓒ Ⓓ Ⓔ
9. Ⓐ Ⓑ Ⓒ Ⓓ Ⓔ
10. Ⓐ Ⓑ Ⓒ Ⓓ Ⓔ
11. Ⓐ Ⓑ Ⓒ Ⓓ Ⓔ
12. Ⓐ Ⓑ Ⓒ Ⓓ Ⓔ

13. Ⓐ Ⓑ Ⓒ Ⓓ Ⓔ
14. Ⓐ Ⓑ Ⓒ Ⓓ Ⓔ
15. Ⓐ Ⓑ Ⓒ Ⓓ Ⓔ
16. Ⓐ Ⓑ Ⓒ Ⓓ Ⓔ

Section 9

1. Ⓐ Ⓑ Ⓒ Ⓓ Ⓔ
2. Ⓐ Ⓑ Ⓒ Ⓓ Ⓔ
3. Ⓐ Ⓑ Ⓒ Ⓓ Ⓔ
4. Ⓐ Ⓑ Ⓒ Ⓓ Ⓔ
5. Ⓐ Ⓑ Ⓒ Ⓓ Ⓔ
6. Ⓐ Ⓑ Ⓒ Ⓓ Ⓔ

7. Ⓐ Ⓑ Ⓒ Ⓓ Ⓔ
8. Ⓐ Ⓑ Ⓒ Ⓓ Ⓔ
9. Ⓐ Ⓑ Ⓒ Ⓓ Ⓔ
10. Ⓐ Ⓑ Ⓒ Ⓓ Ⓔ
11. Ⓐ Ⓑ Ⓒ Ⓓ Ⓔ
12. Ⓐ Ⓑ Ⓒ Ⓓ Ⓔ

13. Ⓐ Ⓑ Ⓒ Ⓓ Ⓔ
14. Ⓐ Ⓑ Ⓒ Ⓓ Ⓔ

Practice Exam #2
Answer Sheet

Section 1

Begin your essay on this page. If you need more space, continue on the next page. Do not write outside of the essay box.

_____
_____
_____
_____
_____
_____
_____
_____
_____
_____
_____
_____
_____
_____
_____
_____
_____
_____
_____
_____
_____
_____
_____
_____
_____
_____
_____
_____
_____
_____
_____

Continuation of Essay Section 1 from previous page. Write below only if you need more space.

_____

_____

_____

_____

_____

_____

_____

_____

_____

_____

_____

_____

_____

_____

_____

_____

_____

_____

_____

_____

_____

_____

_____

_____

_____

_____

_____

_____

_____

_____

_____

_____

Section 2

1. Ⓐ Ⓑ Ⓒ Ⓓ Ⓔ   7. Ⓐ Ⓑ Ⓒ Ⓓ Ⓔ

2. Ⓐ Ⓑ Ⓒ Ⓓ Ⓔ   8. Ⓐ Ⓑ Ⓒ Ⓓ Ⓔ

3. Ⓐ Ⓑ Ⓒ Ⓓ Ⓔ

4. Ⓐ Ⓑ Ⓒ Ⓓ Ⓔ

5. Ⓐ Ⓑ Ⓒ Ⓓ Ⓔ

6. Ⓐ Ⓑ Ⓒ Ⓓ Ⓔ

Student-Produced Responses

9.

10.

11.

12.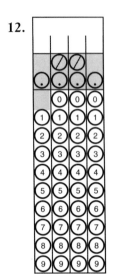

13.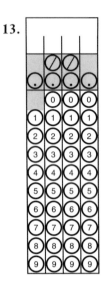

14.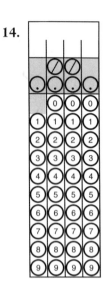

15.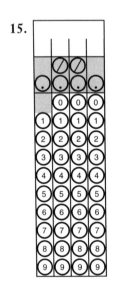

16.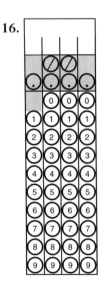

17.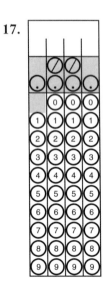

18.

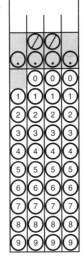

Section 3

1. Ⓐ Ⓑ Ⓒ Ⓓ Ⓔ   13. Ⓐ Ⓑ Ⓒ Ⓓ Ⓔ   25. Ⓐ Ⓑ Ⓒ Ⓓ Ⓔ

2. Ⓐ Ⓑ Ⓒ Ⓓ Ⓔ   14. Ⓐ Ⓑ Ⓒ Ⓓ Ⓔ   26. Ⓐ Ⓑ Ⓒ Ⓓ Ⓔ

3. Ⓐ Ⓑ Ⓒ Ⓓ Ⓔ   15. Ⓐ Ⓑ Ⓒ Ⓓ Ⓔ   27. Ⓐ Ⓑ Ⓒ Ⓓ Ⓔ

4. Ⓐ Ⓑ Ⓒ Ⓓ Ⓔ   16. Ⓐ Ⓑ Ⓒ Ⓓ Ⓔ   28. Ⓐ Ⓑ Ⓒ Ⓓ Ⓔ

5. Ⓐ Ⓑ Ⓒ Ⓓ Ⓔ   17. Ⓐ Ⓑ Ⓒ Ⓓ Ⓔ   29. Ⓐ Ⓑ Ⓒ Ⓓ Ⓔ

6. Ⓐ Ⓑ Ⓒ Ⓓ Ⓔ   18. Ⓐ Ⓑ Ⓒ Ⓓ Ⓔ   30. Ⓐ Ⓑ Ⓒ Ⓓ Ⓔ

7. Ⓐ Ⓑ Ⓒ Ⓓ Ⓔ   19. Ⓐ Ⓑ Ⓒ Ⓓ Ⓔ   31. Ⓐ Ⓑ Ⓒ Ⓓ Ⓔ

8. Ⓐ Ⓑ Ⓒ Ⓓ Ⓔ   20. Ⓐ Ⓑ Ⓒ Ⓓ Ⓔ   32. Ⓐ Ⓑ Ⓒ Ⓓ Ⓔ

9. Ⓐ Ⓑ Ⓒ Ⓓ Ⓔ   21. Ⓐ Ⓑ Ⓒ Ⓓ Ⓔ   33. Ⓐ Ⓑ Ⓒ Ⓓ Ⓔ

10. Ⓐ Ⓑ Ⓒ Ⓓ Ⓔ   22. Ⓐ Ⓑ Ⓒ Ⓓ Ⓔ   34. Ⓐ Ⓑ Ⓒ Ⓓ Ⓔ

11. Ⓐ Ⓑ Ⓒ Ⓓ Ⓔ   23. Ⓐ Ⓑ Ⓒ Ⓓ Ⓔ   35. Ⓐ Ⓑ Ⓒ Ⓓ Ⓔ

12. Ⓐ Ⓑ Ⓒ Ⓓ Ⓔ   24. Ⓐ Ⓑ Ⓒ Ⓓ Ⓔ

Section 4

1. Ⓐ Ⓑ Ⓒ Ⓓ Ⓔ
2. Ⓐ Ⓑ Ⓒ Ⓓ Ⓔ
3. Ⓐ Ⓑ Ⓒ Ⓓ Ⓔ
4. Ⓐ Ⓑ Ⓒ Ⓓ Ⓔ
5. Ⓐ Ⓑ Ⓒ Ⓓ Ⓔ
6. Ⓐ Ⓑ Ⓒ Ⓓ Ⓔ
7. Ⓐ Ⓑ Ⓒ Ⓓ Ⓔ
8. Ⓐ Ⓑ Ⓒ Ⓓ Ⓔ

9. Ⓐ Ⓑ Ⓒ Ⓓ Ⓔ
10. Ⓐ Ⓑ Ⓒ Ⓓ Ⓔ
11. Ⓐ Ⓑ Ⓒ Ⓓ Ⓔ
12. Ⓐ Ⓑ Ⓒ Ⓓ Ⓔ
13. Ⓐ Ⓑ Ⓒ Ⓓ Ⓔ
14. Ⓐ Ⓑ Ⓒ Ⓓ Ⓔ
15. Ⓐ Ⓑ Ⓒ Ⓓ Ⓔ
16. Ⓐ Ⓑ Ⓒ Ⓓ Ⓔ

17. Ⓐ Ⓑ Ⓒ Ⓓ Ⓔ
18. Ⓐ Ⓑ Ⓒ Ⓓ Ⓔ
19. Ⓐ Ⓑ Ⓒ Ⓓ Ⓔ
20. Ⓐ Ⓑ Ⓒ Ⓓ Ⓔ
21. Ⓐ Ⓑ Ⓒ Ⓓ Ⓔ
22. Ⓐ Ⓑ Ⓒ Ⓓ Ⓔ
23. Ⓐ Ⓑ Ⓒ Ⓓ Ⓔ
24. Ⓐ Ⓑ Ⓒ Ⓓ Ⓔ

Section 5

1. Ⓐ Ⓑ Ⓒ Ⓓ Ⓔ
2. Ⓐ Ⓑ Ⓒ Ⓓ Ⓔ
3. Ⓐ Ⓑ Ⓒ Ⓓ Ⓔ
4. Ⓐ Ⓑ Ⓒ Ⓓ Ⓔ
5. Ⓐ Ⓑ Ⓒ Ⓓ Ⓔ
6. Ⓐ Ⓑ Ⓒ Ⓓ Ⓔ
7. Ⓐ Ⓑ Ⓒ Ⓓ Ⓔ

8. Ⓐ Ⓑ Ⓒ Ⓓ Ⓔ
9. Ⓐ Ⓑ Ⓒ Ⓓ Ⓔ
10. Ⓐ Ⓑ Ⓒ Ⓓ Ⓔ
11. Ⓐ Ⓑ Ⓒ Ⓓ Ⓔ
12. Ⓐ Ⓑ Ⓒ Ⓓ Ⓔ
13. Ⓐ Ⓑ Ⓒ Ⓓ Ⓔ
14. Ⓐ Ⓑ Ⓒ Ⓓ Ⓔ

15. Ⓐ Ⓑ Ⓒ Ⓓ Ⓔ
16. Ⓐ Ⓑ Ⓒ Ⓓ Ⓔ
17. Ⓐ Ⓑ Ⓒ Ⓓ Ⓔ
18. Ⓐ Ⓑ Ⓒ Ⓓ Ⓔ
19. Ⓐ Ⓑ Ⓒ Ⓓ Ⓔ
20. Ⓐ Ⓑ Ⓒ Ⓓ Ⓔ

Section 6

1. Ⓐ Ⓑ Ⓒ Ⓓ Ⓔ
2. Ⓐ Ⓑ Ⓒ Ⓓ Ⓔ
3. Ⓐ Ⓑ Ⓒ Ⓓ Ⓔ
4. Ⓐ Ⓑ Ⓒ Ⓓ Ⓔ
5. Ⓐ Ⓑ Ⓒ Ⓓ Ⓔ
6. Ⓐ Ⓑ Ⓒ Ⓓ Ⓔ
7. Ⓐ Ⓑ Ⓒ Ⓓ Ⓔ
8. Ⓐ Ⓑ Ⓒ Ⓓ Ⓔ

9. Ⓐ Ⓑ Ⓒ Ⓓ Ⓔ
10. Ⓐ Ⓑ Ⓒ Ⓓ Ⓔ
11. Ⓐ Ⓑ Ⓒ Ⓓ Ⓔ
12. Ⓐ Ⓑ Ⓒ Ⓓ Ⓔ
13. Ⓐ Ⓑ Ⓒ Ⓓ Ⓔ
14. Ⓐ Ⓑ Ⓒ Ⓓ Ⓔ
15. Ⓐ Ⓑ Ⓒ Ⓓ Ⓔ
16. Ⓐ Ⓑ Ⓒ Ⓓ Ⓔ

17. Ⓐ Ⓑ Ⓒ Ⓓ Ⓔ
18. Ⓐ Ⓑ Ⓒ Ⓓ Ⓔ
19. Ⓐ Ⓑ Ⓒ Ⓓ Ⓔ
20. Ⓐ Ⓑ Ⓒ Ⓓ Ⓔ
21. Ⓐ Ⓑ Ⓒ Ⓓ Ⓔ
22. Ⓐ Ⓑ Ⓒ Ⓓ Ⓔ
23. Ⓐ Ⓑ Ⓒ Ⓓ Ⓔ
24. Ⓐ Ⓑ Ⓒ Ⓓ Ⓔ

Section 7

1. Ⓐ Ⓑ Ⓒ Ⓓ Ⓔ
2. Ⓐ Ⓑ Ⓒ Ⓓ Ⓔ
3. Ⓐ Ⓑ Ⓒ Ⓓ Ⓔ
4. Ⓐ Ⓑ Ⓒ Ⓓ Ⓔ
5. Ⓐ Ⓑ Ⓒ Ⓓ Ⓔ
6. Ⓐ Ⓑ Ⓒ Ⓓ Ⓔ

7. Ⓐ Ⓑ Ⓒ Ⓓ Ⓔ
8. Ⓐ Ⓑ Ⓒ Ⓓ Ⓔ
9. Ⓐ Ⓑ Ⓒ Ⓓ Ⓔ
10. Ⓐ Ⓑ Ⓒ Ⓓ Ⓔ
11. Ⓐ Ⓑ Ⓒ Ⓓ Ⓔ
12. Ⓐ Ⓑ Ⓒ Ⓓ Ⓔ

13. Ⓐ Ⓑ Ⓒ Ⓓ Ⓔ
14. Ⓐ Ⓑ Ⓒ Ⓓ Ⓔ
15. Ⓐ Ⓑ Ⓒ Ⓓ Ⓔ
16. Ⓐ Ⓑ Ⓒ Ⓓ Ⓔ

Section 8

1. Ⓐ Ⓑ Ⓒ Ⓓ Ⓔ
2. Ⓐ Ⓑ Ⓒ Ⓓ Ⓔ
3. Ⓐ Ⓑ Ⓒ Ⓓ Ⓔ
4. Ⓐ Ⓑ Ⓒ Ⓓ Ⓔ
5. Ⓐ Ⓑ Ⓒ Ⓓ Ⓔ
6. Ⓐ Ⓑ Ⓒ Ⓓ Ⓔ
7. Ⓐ Ⓑ Ⓒ Ⓓ Ⓔ

8. Ⓐ Ⓑ Ⓒ Ⓓ Ⓔ
9. Ⓐ Ⓑ Ⓒ Ⓓ Ⓔ
10. Ⓐ Ⓑ Ⓒ Ⓓ Ⓔ
11. Ⓐ Ⓑ Ⓒ Ⓓ Ⓔ
12. Ⓐ Ⓑ Ⓒ Ⓓ Ⓔ
13. Ⓐ Ⓑ Ⓒ Ⓓ Ⓔ
14. Ⓐ Ⓑ Ⓒ Ⓓ Ⓔ

15. Ⓐ Ⓑ Ⓒ Ⓓ Ⓔ
16. Ⓐ Ⓑ Ⓒ Ⓓ Ⓔ
17. Ⓐ Ⓑ Ⓒ Ⓓ Ⓔ
18. Ⓐ Ⓑ Ⓒ Ⓓ Ⓔ
19. Ⓐ Ⓑ Ⓒ Ⓓ Ⓔ

Section 9

1. Ⓐ Ⓑ Ⓒ Ⓓ Ⓔ
2. Ⓐ Ⓑ Ⓒ Ⓓ Ⓔ
3. Ⓐ Ⓑ Ⓒ Ⓓ Ⓔ
4. Ⓐ Ⓑ Ⓒ Ⓓ Ⓔ
5. Ⓐ Ⓑ Ⓒ Ⓓ Ⓔ
6. Ⓐ Ⓑ Ⓒ Ⓓ Ⓔ
7. Ⓐ Ⓑ Ⓒ Ⓓ Ⓔ

8. Ⓐ Ⓑ Ⓒ Ⓓ Ⓔ
9. Ⓐ Ⓑ Ⓒ Ⓓ Ⓔ
10. Ⓐ Ⓑ Ⓒ Ⓓ Ⓔ
11. Ⓐ Ⓑ Ⓒ Ⓓ Ⓔ
12. Ⓐ Ⓑ Ⓒ Ⓓ Ⓔ
13. Ⓐ Ⓑ Ⓒ Ⓓ Ⓔ
14. Ⓐ Ⓑ Ⓒ Ⓓ Ⓔ

Practice Exam #1
Answer Sheet

Begin your essay on this page. If you need more space, continue on the next page. Do not write outside of the essay box.

Continuation of Essay Section 1 from previous page. Write below only if you need more space.

_____

_____

_____

_____

_____

_____

_____

_____

_____

_____

_____

_____

_____

_____

_____

_____

_____

_____

_____

_____

_____

_____

_____

_____

_____

_____

_____

_____

_____

_____

_____

_____

_____

_____

_____

_____

_____

_____

_____

_____

_____

Section 2

1. Ⓐ Ⓑ Ⓒ Ⓓ Ⓔ
2. Ⓐ Ⓑ Ⓒ Ⓓ Ⓔ
3. Ⓐ Ⓑ Ⓒ Ⓓ Ⓔ
4. Ⓐ Ⓑ Ⓒ Ⓓ Ⓔ
5. Ⓐ Ⓑ Ⓒ Ⓓ Ⓔ
6. Ⓐ Ⓑ Ⓒ Ⓓ Ⓔ
7. Ⓐ Ⓑ Ⓒ Ⓓ Ⓔ
8. Ⓐ Ⓑ Ⓒ Ⓓ Ⓔ

9. Ⓐ Ⓑ Ⓒ Ⓓ Ⓔ
10. Ⓐ Ⓑ Ⓒ Ⓓ Ⓔ
11. Ⓐ Ⓑ Ⓒ Ⓓ Ⓔ
12. Ⓐ Ⓑ Ⓒ Ⓓ Ⓔ
13. Ⓐ Ⓑ Ⓒ Ⓓ Ⓔ
14. Ⓐ Ⓑ Ⓒ Ⓓ Ⓔ
15. Ⓐ Ⓑ Ⓒ Ⓓ Ⓔ
16. Ⓐ Ⓑ Ⓒ Ⓓ Ⓔ

17. Ⓐ Ⓑ Ⓒ Ⓓ Ⓔ
18. Ⓐ Ⓑ Ⓒ Ⓓ Ⓔ
19. Ⓐ Ⓑ Ⓒ Ⓓ Ⓔ
20. Ⓐ Ⓑ Ⓒ Ⓓ Ⓔ
21. Ⓐ Ⓑ Ⓒ Ⓓ Ⓔ
22. Ⓐ Ⓑ Ⓒ Ⓓ Ⓔ
23. Ⓐ Ⓑ Ⓒ Ⓓ Ⓔ
24. Ⓐ Ⓑ Ⓒ Ⓓ Ⓔ

Section 3

1. Ⓐ Ⓑ Ⓒ Ⓓ Ⓔ
2. Ⓐ Ⓑ Ⓒ Ⓓ Ⓔ
3. Ⓐ Ⓑ Ⓒ Ⓓ Ⓔ

4. Ⓐ Ⓑ Ⓒ Ⓓ Ⓔ
5. Ⓐ Ⓑ Ⓒ Ⓓ Ⓔ
6. Ⓐ Ⓑ Ⓒ Ⓓ Ⓔ

7. Ⓐ Ⓑ Ⓒ Ⓓ Ⓔ
8. Ⓐ Ⓑ Ⓒ Ⓓ Ⓔ

Student-Produced Responses

9.
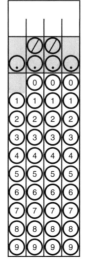

10.
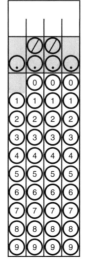

11.
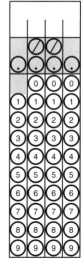

12.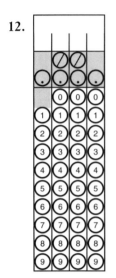

13.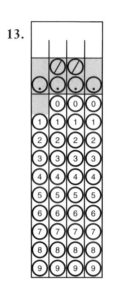

14.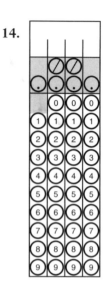

15.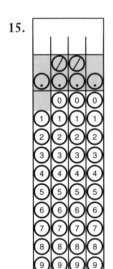

16.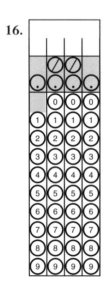

17.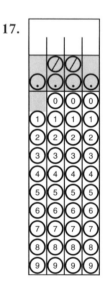

18.

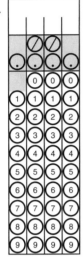

Section 4

1. Ⓐ Ⓑ Ⓒ Ⓓ Ⓔ
2. Ⓐ Ⓑ Ⓒ Ⓓ Ⓔ
3. Ⓐ Ⓑ Ⓒ Ⓓ Ⓔ
4. Ⓐ Ⓑ Ⓒ Ⓓ Ⓔ
5. Ⓐ Ⓑ Ⓒ Ⓓ Ⓔ
6. Ⓐ Ⓑ Ⓒ Ⓓ Ⓔ
7. Ⓐ Ⓑ Ⓒ Ⓓ Ⓔ
8. Ⓐ Ⓑ Ⓒ Ⓓ Ⓔ
9. Ⓐ Ⓑ Ⓒ Ⓓ Ⓔ
10. Ⓐ Ⓑ Ⓒ Ⓓ Ⓔ
11. Ⓐ Ⓑ Ⓒ Ⓓ Ⓔ
12. Ⓐ Ⓑ Ⓒ Ⓓ Ⓔ

13. Ⓐ Ⓑ Ⓒ Ⓓ Ⓔ
14. Ⓐ Ⓑ Ⓒ Ⓓ Ⓔ
15. Ⓐ Ⓑ Ⓒ Ⓓ Ⓔ
16. Ⓐ Ⓑ Ⓒ Ⓓ Ⓔ
17. Ⓐ Ⓑ Ⓒ Ⓓ Ⓔ
18. Ⓐ Ⓑ Ⓒ Ⓓ Ⓔ
19. Ⓐ Ⓑ Ⓒ Ⓓ Ⓔ
20. Ⓐ Ⓑ Ⓒ Ⓓ Ⓔ
21. Ⓐ Ⓑ Ⓒ Ⓓ Ⓔ
22. Ⓐ Ⓑ Ⓒ Ⓓ Ⓔ
23. Ⓐ Ⓑ Ⓒ Ⓓ Ⓔ
24. Ⓐ Ⓑ Ⓒ Ⓓ Ⓔ

25. Ⓐ Ⓑ Ⓒ Ⓓ Ⓔ
26. Ⓐ Ⓑ Ⓒ Ⓓ Ⓔ
27. Ⓐ Ⓑ Ⓒ Ⓓ Ⓔ
28. Ⓐ Ⓑ Ⓒ Ⓓ Ⓔ
29. Ⓐ Ⓑ Ⓒ Ⓓ Ⓔ
30. Ⓐ Ⓑ Ⓒ Ⓓ Ⓔ
31. Ⓐ Ⓑ Ⓒ Ⓓ Ⓔ
32. Ⓐ Ⓑ Ⓒ Ⓓ Ⓔ
33. Ⓐ Ⓑ Ⓒ Ⓓ Ⓔ
34. Ⓐ Ⓑ Ⓒ Ⓓ Ⓔ
35. Ⓐ Ⓑ Ⓒ Ⓓ Ⓔ

Section 5

1. Ⓐ Ⓑ Ⓒ Ⓓ Ⓔ
2. Ⓐ Ⓑ Ⓒ Ⓓ Ⓔ
3. Ⓐ Ⓑ Ⓒ Ⓓ Ⓔ
4. Ⓐ Ⓑ Ⓒ Ⓓ Ⓔ
5. Ⓐ Ⓑ Ⓒ Ⓓ Ⓔ
6. Ⓐ Ⓑ Ⓒ Ⓓ Ⓔ
7. Ⓐ Ⓑ Ⓒ Ⓓ Ⓔ
8. Ⓐ Ⓑ Ⓒ Ⓓ Ⓔ

9. Ⓐ Ⓑ Ⓒ Ⓓ Ⓔ
10. Ⓐ Ⓑ Ⓒ Ⓓ Ⓔ
11. Ⓐ Ⓑ Ⓒ Ⓓ Ⓔ
12. Ⓐ Ⓑ Ⓒ Ⓓ Ⓔ
13. Ⓐ Ⓑ Ⓒ Ⓓ Ⓔ
14. Ⓐ Ⓑ Ⓒ Ⓓ Ⓔ
15. Ⓐ Ⓑ Ⓒ Ⓓ Ⓔ
16. Ⓐ Ⓑ Ⓒ Ⓓ Ⓔ

17. Ⓐ Ⓑ Ⓒ Ⓓ Ⓔ
18. Ⓐ Ⓑ Ⓒ Ⓓ Ⓔ
19. Ⓐ Ⓑ Ⓒ Ⓓ Ⓔ
20. Ⓐ Ⓑ Ⓒ Ⓓ Ⓔ
21. Ⓐ Ⓑ Ⓒ Ⓓ Ⓔ
22. Ⓐ Ⓑ Ⓒ Ⓓ Ⓔ
23. Ⓐ Ⓑ Ⓒ Ⓓ Ⓔ
24. Ⓐ Ⓑ Ⓒ Ⓓ Ⓔ

Section 6

1. Ⓐ Ⓑ Ⓒ Ⓓ Ⓔ
2. Ⓐ Ⓑ Ⓒ Ⓓ Ⓔ
3. Ⓐ Ⓑ Ⓒ Ⓓ Ⓔ
4. Ⓐ Ⓑ Ⓒ Ⓓ Ⓔ
5. Ⓐ Ⓑ Ⓒ Ⓓ Ⓔ
6. Ⓐ Ⓑ Ⓒ Ⓓ Ⓔ
7. Ⓐ Ⓑ Ⓒ Ⓓ Ⓔ

8. Ⓐ Ⓑ Ⓒ Ⓓ Ⓔ
9. Ⓐ Ⓑ Ⓒ Ⓓ Ⓔ
10. Ⓐ Ⓑ Ⓒ Ⓓ Ⓔ
11. Ⓐ Ⓑ Ⓒ Ⓓ Ⓔ
12. Ⓐ Ⓑ Ⓒ Ⓓ Ⓔ
13. Ⓐ Ⓑ Ⓒ Ⓓ Ⓔ
14. Ⓐ Ⓑ Ⓒ Ⓓ Ⓔ

15. Ⓐ Ⓑ Ⓒ Ⓓ Ⓔ
16. Ⓐ Ⓑ Ⓒ Ⓓ Ⓔ
17. Ⓐ Ⓑ Ⓒ Ⓓ Ⓔ
18. Ⓐ Ⓑ Ⓒ Ⓓ Ⓔ
19. Ⓐ Ⓑ Ⓒ Ⓓ Ⓔ
20. Ⓐ Ⓑ Ⓒ Ⓓ Ⓔ

Section 7

1. Ⓐ Ⓑ Ⓒ Ⓓ Ⓔ
2. Ⓐ Ⓑ Ⓒ Ⓓ Ⓔ
3. Ⓐ Ⓑ Ⓒ Ⓓ Ⓔ
4. Ⓐ Ⓑ Ⓒ Ⓓ Ⓔ
5. Ⓐ Ⓑ Ⓒ Ⓓ Ⓔ
6. Ⓐ Ⓑ Ⓒ Ⓓ Ⓔ
7. Ⓐ Ⓑ Ⓒ Ⓓ Ⓔ

8. Ⓐ Ⓑ Ⓒ Ⓓ Ⓔ
9. Ⓐ Ⓑ Ⓒ Ⓓ Ⓔ
10. Ⓐ Ⓑ Ⓒ Ⓓ Ⓔ
11. Ⓐ Ⓑ Ⓒ Ⓓ Ⓔ
12. Ⓐ Ⓑ Ⓒ Ⓓ Ⓔ
13. Ⓐ Ⓑ Ⓒ Ⓓ Ⓔ
14. Ⓐ Ⓑ Ⓒ Ⓓ Ⓔ

15. Ⓐ Ⓑ Ⓒ Ⓓ Ⓔ
16. Ⓐ Ⓑ Ⓒ Ⓓ Ⓔ
17. Ⓐ Ⓑ Ⓒ Ⓓ Ⓔ
18. Ⓐ Ⓑ Ⓒ Ⓓ Ⓔ
19. Ⓐ Ⓑ Ⓒ Ⓓ Ⓔ

Section 8

1. Ⓐ Ⓑ Ⓒ Ⓓ Ⓔ
2. Ⓐ Ⓑ Ⓒ Ⓓ Ⓔ
3. Ⓐ Ⓑ Ⓒ Ⓓ Ⓔ
4. Ⓐ Ⓑ Ⓒ Ⓓ Ⓔ
5. Ⓐ Ⓑ Ⓒ Ⓓ Ⓔ
6. Ⓐ Ⓑ Ⓒ Ⓓ Ⓔ

7. Ⓐ Ⓑ Ⓒ Ⓓ Ⓔ
8. Ⓐ Ⓑ Ⓒ Ⓓ Ⓔ
9. Ⓐ Ⓑ Ⓒ Ⓓ Ⓔ
10. Ⓐ Ⓑ Ⓒ Ⓓ Ⓔ
11. Ⓐ Ⓑ Ⓒ Ⓓ Ⓔ
12. Ⓐ Ⓑ Ⓒ Ⓓ Ⓔ

13. Ⓐ Ⓑ Ⓒ Ⓓ Ⓔ
14. Ⓐ Ⓑ Ⓒ Ⓓ Ⓔ
15. Ⓐ Ⓑ Ⓒ Ⓓ Ⓔ
16. Ⓐ Ⓑ Ⓒ Ⓓ Ⓔ

Section 9

1. Ⓐ Ⓑ Ⓒ Ⓓ Ⓔ
2. Ⓐ Ⓑ Ⓒ Ⓓ Ⓔ
3. Ⓐ Ⓑ Ⓒ Ⓓ Ⓔ
4. Ⓐ Ⓑ Ⓒ Ⓓ Ⓔ
5. Ⓐ Ⓑ Ⓒ Ⓓ Ⓔ
6. Ⓐ Ⓑ Ⓒ Ⓓ Ⓔ

7. Ⓐ Ⓑ Ⓒ Ⓓ Ⓔ
8. Ⓐ Ⓑ Ⓒ Ⓓ Ⓔ
9. Ⓐ Ⓑ Ⓒ Ⓓ Ⓔ
10. Ⓐ Ⓑ Ⓒ Ⓓ Ⓔ
11. Ⓐ Ⓑ Ⓒ Ⓓ Ⓔ
12. Ⓐ Ⓑ Ⓒ Ⓓ Ⓔ

13. Ⓐ Ⓑ Ⓒ Ⓓ Ⓔ
14. Ⓐ Ⓑ Ⓒ Ⓓ Ⓔ

Practice Exam #2
Answer Sheet

Begin your essay on this page. If you need more space, continue on the next page. Do not write outside of the essay box.

_____

_____

_____

_____

_____

_____

_____

_____

_____

_____

_____

_____

_____

_____

_____

_____

_____

_____

_____

_____

_____

_____

_____

_____

_____

_____

_____

_____

_____

Continuation of Essay Section 1 from previous page. Write below only if you need more space.

Section 2

1. Ⓐ Ⓑ Ⓒ Ⓓ Ⓔ   7. Ⓐ Ⓑ Ⓒ Ⓓ Ⓔ

2. Ⓐ Ⓑ Ⓒ Ⓓ Ⓔ   8. Ⓐ Ⓑ Ⓒ Ⓓ Ⓔ

3. Ⓐ Ⓑ Ⓒ Ⓓ Ⓔ

4. Ⓐ Ⓑ Ⓒ Ⓓ Ⓔ

5. Ⓐ Ⓑ Ⓒ Ⓓ Ⓔ

6. Ⓐ Ⓑ Ⓒ Ⓓ Ⓔ

Student-Produced Responses

9.

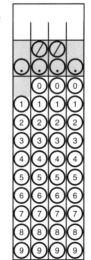

10.

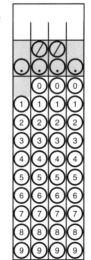

11.

12.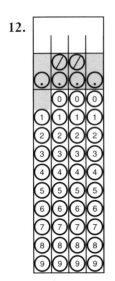

13.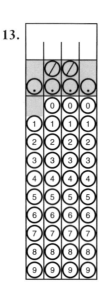

14.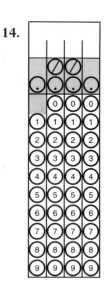

15.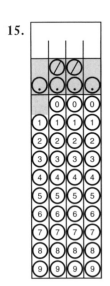

16.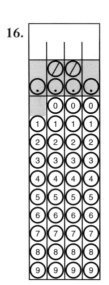

17.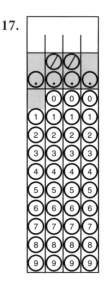

18.

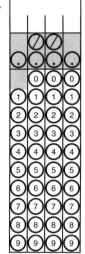

Section 3

1. Ⓐ Ⓑ Ⓒ Ⓓ Ⓔ
2. Ⓐ Ⓑ Ⓒ Ⓓ Ⓔ
3. Ⓐ Ⓑ Ⓒ Ⓓ Ⓔ
4. Ⓐ Ⓑ Ⓒ Ⓓ Ⓔ
5. Ⓐ Ⓑ Ⓒ Ⓓ Ⓔ
6. Ⓐ Ⓑ Ⓒ Ⓓ Ⓔ
7. Ⓐ Ⓑ Ⓒ Ⓓ Ⓔ
8. Ⓐ Ⓑ Ⓒ Ⓓ Ⓔ
9. Ⓐ Ⓑ Ⓒ Ⓓ Ⓔ
10. Ⓐ Ⓑ Ⓒ Ⓓ Ⓔ
11. Ⓐ Ⓑ Ⓒ Ⓓ Ⓔ
12. Ⓐ Ⓑ Ⓒ Ⓓ Ⓔ

13. Ⓐ Ⓑ Ⓒ Ⓓ Ⓔ
14. Ⓐ Ⓑ Ⓒ Ⓓ Ⓔ
15. Ⓐ Ⓑ Ⓒ Ⓓ Ⓔ
16. Ⓐ Ⓑ Ⓒ Ⓓ Ⓔ
17. Ⓐ Ⓑ Ⓒ Ⓓ Ⓔ
18. Ⓐ Ⓑ Ⓒ Ⓓ Ⓔ
19. Ⓐ Ⓑ Ⓒ Ⓓ Ⓔ
20. Ⓐ Ⓑ Ⓒ Ⓓ Ⓔ
21. Ⓐ Ⓑ Ⓒ Ⓓ Ⓔ
22. Ⓐ Ⓑ Ⓒ Ⓓ Ⓔ
23. Ⓐ Ⓑ Ⓒ Ⓓ Ⓔ
24. Ⓐ Ⓑ Ⓒ Ⓓ Ⓔ

25. Ⓐ Ⓑ Ⓒ Ⓓ Ⓔ
26. Ⓐ Ⓑ Ⓒ Ⓓ Ⓔ
27. Ⓐ Ⓑ Ⓒ Ⓓ Ⓔ
28. Ⓐ Ⓑ Ⓒ Ⓓ Ⓔ
29. Ⓐ Ⓑ Ⓒ Ⓓ Ⓔ
30. Ⓐ Ⓑ Ⓒ Ⓓ Ⓔ
31. Ⓐ Ⓑ Ⓒ Ⓓ Ⓔ
32. Ⓐ Ⓑ Ⓒ Ⓓ Ⓔ
33. Ⓐ Ⓑ Ⓒ Ⓓ Ⓔ
34. Ⓐ Ⓑ Ⓒ Ⓓ Ⓔ
35. Ⓐ Ⓑ Ⓒ Ⓓ Ⓔ

Section 4

1. Ⓐ Ⓑ Ⓒ Ⓓ Ⓔ
2. Ⓐ Ⓑ Ⓒ Ⓓ Ⓔ
3. Ⓐ Ⓑ Ⓒ Ⓓ Ⓔ
4. Ⓐ Ⓑ Ⓒ Ⓓ Ⓔ
5. Ⓐ Ⓑ Ⓒ Ⓓ Ⓔ
6. Ⓐ Ⓑ Ⓒ Ⓓ Ⓔ
7. Ⓐ Ⓑ Ⓒ Ⓓ Ⓔ
8. Ⓐ Ⓑ Ⓒ Ⓓ Ⓔ

9. Ⓐ Ⓑ Ⓒ Ⓓ Ⓔ
10. Ⓐ Ⓑ Ⓒ Ⓓ Ⓔ
11. Ⓐ Ⓑ Ⓒ Ⓓ Ⓔ
12. Ⓐ Ⓑ Ⓒ Ⓓ Ⓔ
13. Ⓐ Ⓑ Ⓒ Ⓓ Ⓔ
14. Ⓐ Ⓑ Ⓒ Ⓓ Ⓔ
15. Ⓐ Ⓑ Ⓒ Ⓓ Ⓔ
16. Ⓐ Ⓑ Ⓒ Ⓓ Ⓔ

17. Ⓐ Ⓑ Ⓒ Ⓓ Ⓔ
18. Ⓐ Ⓑ Ⓒ Ⓓ Ⓔ
19. Ⓐ Ⓑ Ⓒ Ⓓ Ⓔ
20. Ⓐ Ⓑ Ⓒ Ⓓ Ⓔ
21. Ⓐ Ⓑ Ⓒ Ⓓ Ⓔ
22. Ⓐ Ⓑ Ⓒ Ⓓ Ⓔ
23. Ⓐ Ⓑ Ⓒ Ⓓ Ⓔ
24. Ⓐ Ⓑ Ⓒ Ⓓ Ⓔ

Section 5

1. Ⓐ Ⓑ Ⓒ Ⓓ Ⓔ
2. Ⓐ Ⓑ Ⓒ Ⓓ Ⓔ
3. Ⓐ Ⓑ Ⓒ Ⓓ Ⓔ
4. Ⓐ Ⓑ Ⓒ Ⓓ Ⓔ
5. Ⓐ Ⓑ Ⓒ Ⓓ Ⓔ
6. Ⓐ Ⓑ Ⓒ Ⓓ Ⓔ
7. Ⓐ Ⓑ Ⓒ Ⓓ Ⓔ

8. Ⓐ Ⓑ Ⓒ Ⓓ Ⓔ
9. Ⓐ Ⓑ Ⓒ Ⓓ Ⓔ
10. Ⓐ Ⓑ Ⓒ Ⓓ Ⓔ
11. Ⓐ Ⓑ Ⓒ Ⓓ Ⓔ
12. Ⓐ Ⓑ Ⓒ Ⓓ Ⓔ
13. Ⓐ Ⓑ Ⓒ Ⓓ Ⓔ
14. Ⓐ Ⓑ Ⓒ Ⓓ Ⓔ

15. Ⓐ Ⓑ Ⓒ Ⓓ Ⓔ
16. Ⓐ Ⓑ Ⓒ Ⓓ Ⓔ
17. Ⓐ Ⓑ Ⓒ Ⓓ Ⓔ
18. Ⓐ Ⓑ Ⓒ Ⓓ Ⓔ
19. Ⓐ Ⓑ Ⓒ Ⓓ Ⓔ
20. Ⓐ Ⓑ Ⓒ Ⓓ Ⓔ

Section 6

1. Ⓐ Ⓑ Ⓒ Ⓓ Ⓔ
2. Ⓐ Ⓑ Ⓒ Ⓓ Ⓔ
3. Ⓐ Ⓑ Ⓒ Ⓓ Ⓔ
4. Ⓐ Ⓑ Ⓒ Ⓓ Ⓔ
5. Ⓐ Ⓑ Ⓒ Ⓓ Ⓔ
6. Ⓐ Ⓑ Ⓒ Ⓓ Ⓔ
7. Ⓐ Ⓑ Ⓒ Ⓓ Ⓔ
8. Ⓐ Ⓑ Ⓒ Ⓓ Ⓔ

9. Ⓐ Ⓑ Ⓒ Ⓓ Ⓔ
10. Ⓐ Ⓑ Ⓒ Ⓓ Ⓔ
11. Ⓐ Ⓑ Ⓒ Ⓓ Ⓔ
12. Ⓐ Ⓑ Ⓒ Ⓓ Ⓔ
13. Ⓐ Ⓑ Ⓒ Ⓓ Ⓔ
14. Ⓐ Ⓑ Ⓒ Ⓓ Ⓔ
15. Ⓐ Ⓑ Ⓒ Ⓓ Ⓔ
16. Ⓐ Ⓑ Ⓒ Ⓓ Ⓔ

17. Ⓐ Ⓑ Ⓒ Ⓓ Ⓔ
18. Ⓐ Ⓑ Ⓒ Ⓓ Ⓔ
19. Ⓐ Ⓑ Ⓒ Ⓓ Ⓔ
20. Ⓐ Ⓑ Ⓒ Ⓓ Ⓔ
21. Ⓐ Ⓑ Ⓒ Ⓓ Ⓔ
22. Ⓐ Ⓑ Ⓒ Ⓓ Ⓔ
23. Ⓐ Ⓑ Ⓒ Ⓓ Ⓔ
24. Ⓐ Ⓑ Ⓒ Ⓓ Ⓔ

Section 7

1. Ⓐ Ⓑ Ⓒ Ⓓ Ⓔ
2. Ⓐ Ⓑ Ⓒ Ⓓ Ⓔ
3. Ⓐ Ⓑ Ⓒ Ⓓ Ⓔ
4. Ⓐ Ⓑ Ⓒ Ⓓ Ⓔ
5. Ⓐ Ⓑ Ⓒ Ⓓ Ⓔ
6. Ⓐ Ⓑ Ⓒ Ⓓ Ⓔ

7. Ⓐ Ⓑ Ⓒ Ⓓ Ⓔ
8. Ⓐ Ⓑ Ⓒ Ⓓ Ⓔ
9. Ⓐ Ⓑ Ⓒ Ⓓ Ⓔ
10. Ⓐ Ⓑ Ⓒ Ⓓ Ⓔ
11. Ⓐ Ⓑ Ⓒ Ⓓ Ⓔ
12. Ⓐ Ⓑ Ⓒ Ⓓ Ⓔ

13. Ⓐ Ⓑ Ⓒ Ⓓ Ⓔ
14. Ⓐ Ⓑ Ⓒ Ⓓ Ⓔ
15. Ⓐ Ⓑ Ⓒ Ⓓ Ⓔ
16. Ⓐ Ⓑ Ⓒ Ⓓ Ⓔ

Section 8

1. Ⓐ Ⓑ Ⓒ Ⓓ Ⓔ
2. Ⓐ Ⓑ Ⓒ Ⓓ Ⓔ
3. Ⓐ Ⓑ Ⓒ Ⓓ Ⓔ
4. Ⓐ Ⓑ Ⓒ Ⓓ Ⓔ
5. Ⓐ Ⓑ Ⓒ Ⓓ Ⓔ
6. Ⓐ Ⓑ Ⓒ Ⓓ Ⓔ
7. Ⓐ Ⓑ Ⓒ Ⓓ Ⓔ

8. Ⓐ Ⓑ Ⓒ Ⓓ Ⓔ
9. Ⓐ Ⓑ Ⓒ Ⓓ Ⓔ
10. Ⓐ Ⓑ Ⓒ Ⓓ Ⓔ
11. Ⓐ Ⓑ Ⓒ Ⓓ Ⓔ
12. Ⓐ Ⓑ Ⓒ Ⓓ Ⓔ
13. Ⓐ Ⓑ Ⓒ Ⓓ Ⓔ
14. Ⓐ Ⓑ Ⓒ Ⓓ Ⓔ

15. Ⓐ Ⓑ Ⓒ Ⓓ Ⓔ
16. Ⓐ Ⓑ Ⓒ Ⓓ Ⓔ
17. Ⓐ Ⓑ Ⓒ Ⓓ Ⓔ
18. Ⓐ Ⓑ Ⓒ Ⓓ Ⓔ
19. Ⓐ Ⓑ Ⓒ Ⓓ Ⓔ

Section 9

1. Ⓐ Ⓑ Ⓒ Ⓓ Ⓔ
2. Ⓐ Ⓑ Ⓒ Ⓓ Ⓔ
3. Ⓐ Ⓑ Ⓒ Ⓓ Ⓔ
4. Ⓐ Ⓑ Ⓒ Ⓓ Ⓔ
5. Ⓐ Ⓑ Ⓒ Ⓓ Ⓔ
6. Ⓐ Ⓑ Ⓒ Ⓓ Ⓔ
7. Ⓐ Ⓑ Ⓒ Ⓓ Ⓔ

8. Ⓐ Ⓑ Ⓒ Ⓓ Ⓔ
9. Ⓐ Ⓑ Ⓒ Ⓓ Ⓔ
10. Ⓐ Ⓑ Ⓒ Ⓓ Ⓔ
11. Ⓐ Ⓑ Ⓒ Ⓓ Ⓔ
12. Ⓐ Ⓑ Ⓒ Ⓓ Ⓔ
13. Ⓐ Ⓑ Ⓒ Ⓓ Ⓔ
14. Ⓐ Ⓑ Ⓒ Ⓓ Ⓔ

Index

B

bad/badly, 12
balancing phrases/clauses with parallelism, 14-15
bar graphs, 228
bases, 196
best fit, lines of, 232-233
bevy, 67
breakfast, eating before exam, 253
but, 53

C

calculators, 136, 253
catalyst, 67
cause and effect keywords, 57
cause and effect relationships, 59
caustic, 67
celestial, 67
center of rotation, 203
centers of circles, 195
charts and graphs, 224
    bar graphs, 228
    line graphs, 226-228
    lines of best fit, 232-233
    pictographs, 229-230
    pie charts, 225-226
    scatterplots, 230-231
    tables, 231-232
checklists
    SAT preparation, 254
    test-taking strategies, 256
chords (circles), 195
chronic, 67
circles, 194-195
circumference of circles, 195
clarity of pronouns, 9
clichés, avoiding in essays, 34
coerce, 67
cognitive, 67
coherent, 67
collaborate, 67
College Board website, 487

combination word problems, solving, 165-166
Communicative Law, 141
comparative adjectives, 12-13
comparative adverbs, 12-13
comparing reading passages, 119-123
    reading questions first, 124-125
    reading strategies, 123-124
compensate, 68
complementary angles, 186
comply, 68
component, 68
composition of functions, 153
conclusions to essays, 40-41
concrete language, 31-32
cones, 197
congruent triangles, 191-192
connotative, 68
consequently, 54
consolidate, 68
contend, 68
context clues, 57-58
context questions (writing section), 17-18
contingent, 68
contrary, 68
contrasting keywords, 57
contrasting relationships, 58
controversy, 69
converting word problems to equations, 166-167
coordinate geometry
    coordinate planes, 197
    distances, 200-202
    midpoints, 200-202
    parallel lines, 200
    slopes and y-intercepts, 198-200
    symmetry, 202-205
    transformations, 202-205
coordinate planes, 197
counterexamples, 97
counterpart, 69
counting problems, solving, 165-166
covert, 69

How can we make this index more useful? Email us at indexes@quepublishing.com

deride, 70
derive, 71
designate, 71
detriment, 71
disparage, 71
disperse, 71
emigrate, 71
empathy, 71
empirical, 71
endanger, 72
endorse, 72
entrench, 72
epidemic, 72
eradicate, 72
excerpt, 72
excursion, 72
exonerate, 72
expertise, 72
exuberant, 73
facilitate, 73
fervent, 73
fratricide, 73
fundamental, 73
genesis, 73
genetics, 73
genocide, 73
hierarchy, 73
hone, 74
hyperbole, 74
hypothesis, 74
impending, 74
incentive, 74
incognito, 74
increment, 74
indict, 74
indigenous, 75
indoctrinate, 75
infanticide, 75
infer, 75
infiltrate, 75
ingest, 75
inherent, 75
insidious, 75
insomnia, 75
integrate, 76
interim, 76
interstate, 76
intramural, 76
intrastate, 76
introspection, 76
introvert, 76

intuition, 76
irrelevant, 76
lateral, 77
laudable, 77
learning cues, 63-64, 83-84
malice, 77
mandatory, 77
maritime, 77
minuscule, 77
narcissism, 77
notorious, 77
nuance, 77
omnipotent, 77
omniscient, 78
opulent, 78
overt, 78
panacea, 78
panorama, 78
paraphrase, 78
passive, 78
pedestal, 78
perceive, 78
perplex, 79
perspective, 79
pervasive, 79
philosophy, 79
podium, 79
precedent, 79
precipitous, 79
predict, 79
prefixes, 60-63
prejudice, 79
preserve, 80
pristine, 80
ratify, 80
rationalize, 80
relinquish, 80
repercussion, 80
repudiate, 80
root words, 60-63
rural, 81
sector, 81
secular, 81
sedentary, 81
suburban, 81
suffixes, 60-63
surpass, 81
temporal, 81
transpire, 81
ubiquitous, 82
urban, 82

How can we make this index more useful? Email us at indexes@quepublishing.com

indict, 74
indigenous, 75
indoctrinate, 75
inequalities, solving, 163-164
infanticide, 75
infer, 75, 98
infiltrate, 75
infinitives, 14-15
informal language, 32
ingest, 75
inherent, 75
insidious, 75
insomnia, 75
installing CramMaster CD-ROM, 508-509
integers, 134
integrate, 76
intercepts (linear equations), 154
interim, 76
interpreting data with graphs/charts, 224
    bar graphs, 228
    line graphs, 226-228
    lines of best fit, 232-233
    pictographs, 229-230
    pie charts, 225-226
    scatterplots, 230-231
    tables, 231-232
interrogative pronouns, 10
intersection of sets, 151
interstate, 76
intramural, 76
intrastate, 76
introductions (student-written essays), 30
introspection, 76
introvert, 76
intuition, 76
inversely proportional, 167
irony, 97
irrational numbers, 134
irregular polygons, 194
irrelevant, 76
isosceles triangles, 188

J-K-L

jargon, avoiding in essays, 33

keywords in sentence completion questions
    cause and effect keywords, 57
    contrasting keywords, 57
    definition keywords, 57
    supporting keywords, 57
    transitional words and phrases, 52-55
lateral, 77
laudable, 77
laws of arithmetic
    Associative Law, 142
    Communicative Law, 141
    Distributive Law, 142-143
LCM (least common multiple), 140
line graphs, 226-228
line segments, 184
linear functions, 154-155
lines, 184
    line segments, 184
    lines of best fit, 232-233
    lines of reflection, 203
    midpoints, 200-202
    parallel lines, 200
    perpendicular lines, 200
lines of best fit, 232-233
lines of reflection, 203
literal comprehension questions (critical
    reading section), 96, 100-101
logic questions, 50

M

malice, 77
mandatory, 77
maritime, 77
mathematics section, 134
    arithmetical operations
        divisibility, 138-141
        factors, 139-141
        fractions, 143-145
        order of operations, 137-138
        percentages and change, 147-149
        power and root operations, 135-137
        prime numbers, 139
        ratios and proportions, 146-147
        sets, 151
    calculators and, 136
    equations, solving
        equations with single variables, 162
        factoring polynomials, 161
        operations on equations, 160-161
        rational equations, 163
    exam prep questions
        numbers and algebra, 169-179
        statistics, probability, and data
        analysis, 241-249

How can we make this index more useful? Email us at indexes@quepublishing.com

Number2.com, 487
numbers
  absolute values, 135
  even numbers, 138
  imaginary numbers, 135
  integers, 134
  irrational numbers, 134
  odd numbers, 138
  prime numbers, 139
  rational numbers, 134
  reciprocals, 145
  scientific notation, 134
numerators, 143

O

obtuse angles, 186
odd numbers, 138
omnipotent, 77
omniscient, 78
one, score of (essays)
  explanation of scoring, 492
  sample graded essays, 499, 505
opulent, 78
organization questions (writing section), 18-19
overt, 78

P

paired passage-based readings
  example, 119-123
  reading questions first, 124-125
  reading strategies, 123-124
panacea, 78
panic, avoiding, 257
panorama, 78
paragraphs, improving
  context, 17-18
  guidelines, 17
  organization, 18-19
parallel lines, 200
parallelism, 14-15
parallelograms, 193
paraphrase, 78
participial phrases, 6-8
participles, 6-8
passage-based readings, 92
  anecdotes, 97
  argument passages, 95

counterexamples, 97
exam prep questions
  longer passages, 126-131
  short passages, 102-108
extended reasoning questions, 96-99
hyperbole, 97
irony, 97
literal comprehension questions, 96, 100-101
longer passage-based readings
  analyzing structure of, 110-112
  budgeting reading time, 117-118
  passage purpose, 112
  reading questions first, 113-117
  themes, 113
  transitions between paragraphs, 112
  types of questions, 118-119
metaphors, 98
narrative passages, 95
paired passages
  example, 119-123
  reading questions first, 124-125
  reading strategies, 123-124
reading skills, 92
  focusing on passage's content, 94
  making notes while reading, 93
  reading efficiently, 93
rephrasing questions, 94
similes, 98
vocabulary-in-context questions, 96, 99-100
passive, 78
past participles, 7
past tense (verbs), 4-5
pedestal, 78
pentagons, 194
perceive, 78
percentages, 147-149
perfect form (verbs), 5-6
perimeters, 205-208
permutation problems, solving, 165-166
perpendicular lines, 200
perplex, 79
personal nouns in essays, 37
personal pronoun *I* in essays, 39-40
perspective, 79
pervasive, 79
philosophy, 79
pictographs, 229-230
pie charts, 225-226
podium, 79

How can we make this index more useful? Email us at indexes@quepublishing.com

How can we make this index more useful? Email us at indexes@quepublishing.com

S

X-Y-Z